Wordsworth's

Second Nature

For who that useth that he knoweth,
Ful selden seknesse on him groweth,
And who that useth metes strange,
Though his nature empeire and change
It is no wonder, lieve Sone,
Whan that he doth agein his wone;
For in Phisique this I finde,
Usage is the seconde kinde.

John Gower, *Confessio Amantis*

You have heard of a Profession to which the luxury of modern times has given birth, that of Landscape-Gardeners, or Improvers of Pleasure-grounds. A competent Practitioner in this elegant art, begins by considering every object, that he finds in the place where he is called to exercise his skill, as having a right to remain till the contrary be proved. If it be a deformity he asks whether a slight alteration may not convert it into a beauty; and he destroys nothing till he has convinced himself by reflection that no alteration, no diminution or addition, can make it ornamental. Modern Reformers reverse this judicious maxim. If a thing is before them, so far from deeming that it has on that account a claim to continue and be deliberately dealt with, its existence to them is sufficient warrant for its destruction. Institutions are to be subverted, Practices radically altered, and Measures to be reversed. All men are to change their places, not because the men are objectionable, or the place is injurious, but because certain Pretenders are eager to be at work, being tired of both.

Wordsworth, *Address to the Freeholders of Westmoreland*

What is often being argued, it seems to me, in the idea of nature is the idea of man; and this not only generally, or in ultimate ways, but the idea of man in society, indeed the idea of kinds of societies.

Raymond Williams, "Ideas of Nature"

Acknowledgments

*O*ne minor premise of this book is that certain circumstances can make it difficult to acknowledge intellectual debts. Such unflattering notions always seem truer of others than of ourselves, but I cannot imagine myself denying what I owe to Jerome McGann and Stuart Tave. It would oversimplify to say that from the former I learned about Romanticism and English poetry, and from the latter about Historicism and English history; they both know both sides. Their teaching always seemed to me mutually complementary, however, and together they did much to shape my subject. They also read and refined a small trunkful of my prose on it over these nine years. Another teacher, John Wallace, and my wife, Becky O'Connor Chandler, helped me to overcome my initial resistance to historical explanation. In their various ways, all of these people warmly encouraged the project in the early going when it most needed it. So did Norman Maclean, who took valuable time out from writing his own stories to talk with me about Wordsworth's. More recently, W. J. T. Mitchell read all ten chapters through in their final form; his extended comments were especially clarifying about the shape of the whole and therefore about what sort of introduction to write for it. At stages along the way, I had the benefit of patient and detailed responses from many quarters. I would especially like to thank three old friends—Rory Holscher, Michael Pownall, and Vincent Sherry—and three present colleagues—Elizabeth Helsinger, Wendy Olmsted, and Robert von Hallberg. Two historians of the French Revolution, D. Carroll Joynes and Keith Baker, provided some much needed guidance in that vast field of research. Another historian, Mark Schwehn, improved my sense of perspective and method in the argument. Richard Cottrell proofread the whole book, thus helping me to finish what he long ago helped me to start.

Parts of chapters 2 and 4 initially appeared in *ELH* (Winter 1980). I lectured from chapter 3 to the Clark Library Seminar in 1982, and from chapter 5 in that same year at the University of Washington, Seattle, and at the California Institute of Technology; all three audiences responded instructively. Jonathan Wordsworth, on behalf of the Dove Cottage Trustees, granted me permission to reprint some manuscript material I consulted at the Cornell Wordsworth Collection in 1979. A summer grant-in-aid from the American Council for Learned Societies enabled me to spend the needed time in Ithaca that year. For help in finding and using rare materials, I wish to thank the staff at the Olin Library at Cornell, as well as the staffs of the Library Company of Philadelphia, the University Library at Berkeley, the Firestone Library at Princeton, the Robarts Library at Toronto, and of course the Regenstein Library at Chicago. Carol Coleman, a student assistant funded through the Federal Work Study Program and the University of Chicago, aided with both research and typing. The bulk of the typing was shared by several secretaries in both the College and the Humanities Division, and my thanks go to them all.

I believe that what I have written down here is peculiarly indebted to unwritten exchanges in the rich intellectual life of colleagues and students at Chicago. They will know what I mean. Finally, I want to thank Becky again, but this time for reasons she and I alone can know.

Abbreviations

BL   Samuel Taylor Coleridge, *Biographia Literaria*, ed. J. Shawcross, 2 vols. (London: Oxford University Press, 1907).

BW   *The Works of the Right Honorable Edmund Burke*, rev. ed., 12 vols. (Boston: Little, Brown & Co., 1865–67).

CWWH   *The Collected Works of William Hazlitt*, ed. P. P. Howe, 21 vols. (London and Toronto: J. M. Dent & Sons, 1931).

EY, MY, LY   *The Letters of William and Dorothy Wordsworth*, arranged and ed. by Ernest de Selincourt, 2d ed. rev. by Chester L. Shaver, vol. 1: *The Early Years*; vol. 2: *The Middle Years*; vol. 3: *The Later Years* (Oxford: Clarendon Press, 1967–78).

Moorman EY   Mary Moorman, *William Wordsworth, A Biography, The Early Years, 1770–1803* (Oxford: Clarendon Press, 1965).

Moorman LY   Mary Moorman, *William Wordsworth, A Biography, The Later Years, 1803–1850* (Oxford: Clarendon Press, 1965).

wrote in 1818 or even 1809. And once we know how to recognize both Burkean views and the means by which they are veiled, we have the means of inquiring further.

Ironically, one of Wordsworth's most effective ways of giving veiled expression to his Burkean views was to use Burke's own topos of veils: second nature, the moral wardrobe of the naked shivering nature. So goes the argument of chapter 4, which provides the first full explication of the notion of second nature and then traces Wordsworth's alignment with Burke all the way back to the seminal period in the early months of 1798 when Wordsworth conceived his ambitious poetic plans. But again, as we move back toward this seminal period and toward the period of Wordsworth's tergiversation, we find the forces of displacement operating more powerfully. At this point Rousseau becomes useful as a second intellectual axis against which to plot Wordsworth's changing position. Chapters 5 and 6 argue that Wordsworth's early knowledge and use of Rousseau are greater than has been assumed. Their second but more important burden is to demonstrate how the five-book *The Prelude*, *The Ruined Cottage*, and, by implication, the literary experiments attempted in *Lyrical Ballads* all translate Burkean politics into (equally Burkean) attacks on Rousseauist systems of (political) education. Like Burke, as I go on to explain more fully in chapter 7, Wordsworth answers these "natural" methods of education with a kind of traditionalism; like Burke, too, he does so in the name of nature. Indeed, with his keener interest in the function of oral culture and more energetic emulation of its practices, Wordsworth proves upon examination to be a more thoroughgoing traditionalist than Burke himself.

Chapter 8 advances the argument into that least explicitly Burkean (because least explicitly political) region of the major poetry, the lyric world of the "spots of time" in which the five-book *Prelude* is itself presumed to have had its origin. The ideological purport of the spots of time resides in the powerful discipline they are supposed to embody. For this discipline is ultimately, like Burke's duty-become-a-part-of-our-nature, both English-nationalist and anti-Gallic in spirit. Chapter 9 attempts at once to confirm and extend these last conclusions by considering the system that had in fact become the official Gallic discipline of the late 1790s, *Idéologie*. The suggestion here is that the foundational epistemology of the French Ideologues provided a crucial negative example for the formation of Wordsworth's characteristic lyric practice in *The Prelude* and elsewhere. This chapter actually completes the book's argument. The tenth and last chapter considers the implications for the history of Wordsworth's celebrated intellectual relationship with Coleridge.

Because of the general scarcity of documentation for Wordsworth's intellectual life in the mid-1790s, some of the suggestions in the penultimate chapter are difficult to establish conclusively. The evidence for Wordsworth's knowledge of the French Ideologues is substantial, however, and I believe that as referents for Wordsworth's camouflaged polemic against system and theory they are in many ways more plausible candidates than, say, William Godwin. We too often forget that, alone among the great English Romantics, Wordsworth had firsthand experience of the French Revolution. Both as proponent and opponent of what Hazlitt called the great French Leviathan, Wordsworth knew the beast whereof he spoke. Contextual studies of Wordsworth have suffered by and large from a kind of provincialism, as the volume of ink spilled over the question of Godwin amply attests. My discussion of the Ideologues in chapter 9, like the discussion of Revolutionary educational schemes in chapter 5, seeks primarily to open up French intellectual history of the 1790s as an area of relevance to Wordsworth's thought and writing. From where Wordsworth stood, English and Continental intellectual history had everything to do with one another. When we lose sight of this point of view, we misconstrue his intellectual commitments both early and late.

This returns us to my initial point about this book's organization, for in describing the argument as being all of a piece I also mean to suggest a kind of coherence in the intellectual context it makes out. What revisions I have to offer in the interpretation of particular poems typically depend upon locating a poem in respect to some figure in the historical background—Burke and "The Old Cumberland Beggar," Rousseau and *Salisbury Plain*, Kant and the "Ode to Duty," Barthold Georg Niebuhr and the late Roman history sonnets. But the argument that joins these readings together into a larger interpretation of Wordsworth also joins Burke, Rousseau, Kant, and Niebuhr together into a larger interpretation of the Wordsworthian context.

Finally, a small word to cover some large omissions. The tasks that this book does not undertake—even the relevant tasks—are too many to be counted here. I must proceed by example. Unlike the latest developmental study of Wordsworth's political views, it ventures neither a Freudian nor a Marxian explanation of Wordsworth's changing ideological outlook.[10] This is not a case of renouncing either such form of explanation, though I regret the omission of the latter far more than the former. The demonstrable power of Marxian categories in these areas can only leave one feeling anxious about discussing "ideology" in the sometimes rarified and idealizing terms of intellectual and literary history. I would hope, nonetheless, to have

provided some of the material upon which further, perhaps more ambi-
tious, ideological study might draw—to have accounted for things within
one ideological horizon, so to speak, in a way that could be useful to those
who may command a longer perspective.[11]

Wordsworth's

Second Nature

One

Beginning with Wordsworth

> I cannot paint
> What then I was.
>
> "Tintern Abbey"

Asked to name the first work of scholarship on Wordsworth, one would probably have to say it was Barron Field's *Critical Memoirs of the Life and Poetry of William Wordsworth*, a book drafted in the late 1830s, available to later scholars in manuscript form, but published only recently. Field's study grew out of a review in which he tried to acquit Wordsworth once and for all of the charges brought against him years earlier by his critical nemesis Francis Jeffrey. It was time, Field thought, to set the record straight: "The poet having now taken his niche for ever in the Temple of Fame . . . , it may afford an useful lesson to both authors and critics, at this distance of time, to look back calmly and dispassionately on the history of this case.[1] Tracing the history of the case with respect to the Jeffrey controversy, however, apparently led to the study of larger Wordsworthian issues. Field broached these issues in the very opening chapter of his "biographical sketch." And when he turned to the vexing topic of Wordsworth's politics, Field posed the problem to which so many of Wordsworth's subsequent students have addressed themselves: "Conservative as Mr Wordsworth is, in his political opinions, there can be no doubt that the poetical reform, for which we are

3

indebted to him and his friends, Mr Coleridge and Mr Southey, was greatly influenced by the French Revolution, which was the leading event of their youth" (p. 25).

The value of Field's formulation of this problem lies in part in the way it reveals the two subproblems at issue. The first involves a potential distinction between Wordsworth's poetry and his politics, the second a distinction between what Wordsworth is ("conservative") and what he was. The first is a question about how the poet's stated political views relate to the implied views of his poems. The second is a question about how these views were formed and about how they lasted or changed over time. Perhaps with any poet, but with Wordsworth especially, these two questions are bound up with one another. His poetry is as ambitious and programmatic as that of any post-Renaissance English writer. Probably no major English poet has been so seriously concerned with his own mental development. Few have developed in ways so interestingly conditioned by the course of social and political events. Not many have lived in such remarkable times.

Field's solution to the problem he poses does, in its way, attempt to respond to both of the component problems at issue:

> Their minds were thus impressed, at the most impressible time, with the worth and rights of the many, as not made for the use of one, or of the few. Mr Wordsworth's poetry is essentially democratic, qualify it as he may by some few political pieces: his best sonnets are dedicated to Liberty: his most touching strains ennoble humble life: and he will always be quoted as the poet of freedom and of the poor:—
> —he did love
> The liberty of Man.
> It has been said of old time, "Once a jacobin, always a jacobin." Mr Coleridge asks, "Oh, why?" But the truth is, as Mr Hazlitt states it of Mr Southey,—"Once a philanthropist and always a philanthropist." [pp. 25–26]

Field contends that we must understand Wordsworth's participation in the Revolution as a sharing of its philanthropy but not its Jacobinism and that we must penetrate to the core feelings for humanity in his poems rather than stopping at his surface opinions. Read in the proper way, in short, Wordsworth is once and always, through and through, a lover of man.

It would be premature to try to say why Field's account is unacceptable.[2] That is, in effect, the task of much of what follows here. Instead, I would redirect attention to Field's way of formulating the problem and to the special difficulty of the task he set himself. One of the fixed premises in Field's understanding of Wordsworth, a matter about which there can be "no doubt," is that the "poetical reform" he instituted was "greatly influenced by the French Revolution." Behind this assumption stands Hazlitt's virtuoso essay on "Mr Wordsworth" in *The Spirit of the Age* (1825), the work from which Field takes his quotation about Southey. Hazlitt's commentary on the political significance of Wordsworth's major poetry is now widely known:

> It is one of the innovations of the time. It partakes of, and is carried along with, the revolutionary movement of our age: the political changes of the day were the model on which he formed and conducted his poetical experiments. His muse (it cannot be denied and without this we cannot explain its character at all) is a levelling one. It proceeds on a principle of equality, and strives to reduce all things to the same standard. [*CWWH* 11:87]

Hazlitt speaks of Wordsworth not only with the authority of a seasoned observer of the age's politics and literature, but also as a man who paid a famous visit to Wordsworth and his literary partner in the *annus mirabilis* of poetical reform, 1798. In fact, Field goes on to quote at length from "My First Acquaintance with Poets," Hazlitt's account of the visit.[3] When such a writer says that what we now call Wordsworth's "program for poetry" is revolutionary in character, the assertion seems unimpeachable. Strangely, however, Hazlitt nowhere in his essay acknowledges Wordsworth's later renunciations of the Revolution.[4]

Field's opening concession, "Conservative as Mr Wordsworth is, in his political opinions . . . ," shows that he was unwilling to suppress his knowledge of Wordsworth's later views. This is to his credit, though such suppression, awkward enough in 1825, had become virtually impossible by 1835. The 1835 *Poems*, for example, included not only the newly appended Tory "Postscript," but also new poems such as the sonnet "Composed After Reading a Newspaper of the Day":

> "People! your chains are severing link by link;
> Soon shall the Rich be levelled down—the Poor
> Meet them half way." Vain boast! for These, the more
> They thus would rise, must low and lower sink
> Till, by repentance stung, they fear to think;
> While all lie prostrate, save the tyrant few
> Bent in quick turns each other to undo,
> And mix the poison, they themselves must drink.

Mistrust thyself, vain Country! cease to cry,
"Knowledge will save me from the threatened woe."
For, if than other rash ones more thou know,
Yet on presumptuous wing as far would fly
Above thy knowledge as they dared to go,
Thou wilt provoke a heavier penalty.

[*PW* 4:128]

Although the poem is written in the manner of some of Milton's topical Petrarchan sonnets of the 1640s and 1650s, its Milton is no revolutionary. Wordsworth alludes to the plot of *Paradise Lost* to suggest that the nation's poor occupy as fixed a place in the social hierarchy as Satan or Adam and Eve occupied in the cosmic hierarchy of Milton's epic. If they attempt to rise above that place they will end up stunned and "prostrate" like Milton's fallen angels.[5] England thinks that "knowledge" will save her from the woe that befell leveling nations like France. But Wordsworth argues that England's superior knowledge will only be held against her if she commits the same Promethean sins of presumption as does a nation with less knowledge (such as France).

In the face of such evidence a commentator in the late 1830s was obliged to acknowledge the "conservative" tilt of Wordsworth's political opinions. Yet this acknowledgment had to be reconciled with Hazlitt's authoritative claim that Wordsworth's muse was a leveling one—"it cannot be denied, and without this we cannot explain its character at all." This was Field's dilemma, and it has been the dilemma of subsequent commentators who have told the story of this poet's relation to the French Revolution. My account here, which stands at odds either wholly or in part with the received versions of the story, rejects Hazlitt's claim about the motive for Wordsworth's poetical experiments. Those who agree with Hazlitt might object that his claim can be supported with testimony from Wordsworth's own pen. To this objection I can only say that in some respects my account stands at odds with Wordsworth's own version of this story. Indeed, I will be arguing that certain views of Wordsworth's changing poetic ideology go wrong precisely because they take his own autobiographical remarks at face value. What Wordsworth says about himself and his attitudes is almost always revealing, but it is seldom directly so.

We might illustrate this last point by looking, not at his first intellectual biography, but at what is perhaps his first intellectual autobiography. In the spring of 1801, he was asked by Anne Taylor, an admirer of *Lyrical Ballads*, for information that might help her to understand the poems she had enjoyed. She wanted "an account of such events in [Words-worth's] life as may have had an influence in forming [his] present opinions" (*EY*:327). Wordsworth responded on 9 April, two days after his thirty-first birthday. He prefaces his narrative with a most puzzling comment—"With this request I should have complied with great pleasure, had the task been more difficult, but the history of my life is very short"—a comment that leaves it unclear whether he is not complying with pleasure or not com-plying at all. The tale itself raises further questions:

> I was born at Cockermouth, about twenty-five miles from the place where I now dwell. Before I was nine years of age I was sent to the Grammar School of Hawkshead, a small market-village near the Lake of Esthwaite: there I continued till the beginning of my eighteenth year, at which time I went to Cambridge, where I remained three years and a half. I did not, as I in some respects greatly regret, devote myself to the studies of the University. This neglect of university studies will be easily comprehended by you, when I inform you, that I employed the last of my summer vacations in a pedestrian tour in the Alps. Since I left Cambridge, my time has been spent in travelling upon the Continent, and in England: and in occasional resi-dences in London, and in different parts of England and Wales. At present I am permanently fixed in my native country. I have taken a house in the Vale of *Grasmere*, (a very beautiful spot of which almost every body has heard,) and I live with my Sister, meaning, if my health will permit me, to devote my life to literature. It may be proper to add that my Father was by profession an Attorney, and that he and my Mother both died when I was a Boy. [*EY*:327]

To read this "history" one would think that Anne Taylor had asked for a *biographia geographia* rather than an account of the events that shaped his opinions. At every turn Wordsworth chooses to mention places rather than occurrences, to dwell on where he was instead of telling what he did there. Several of these precious few lines are given over to long appositional phrases describing Cockermouth, Hawkshead, and Grasmere. Ten differ-ent place names are mentioned in this short passage, many more than once, and only two of the eight sentences do not center on a claim about Wordsworth's relation to some place.

Perhaps readers accustomed to Wordsworth's powerful sense of locale will not be surprised by even so marked an emphasis. But something else is odd about this narrative. Surely the events Anne Taylor wanted to hear about were those of Wordsworth's adult life—those, say, of the last decade. Yet far less than half of Wordsworth's "history" is devoted to these years, and the only "events" he mentions for these years are his travels (abroad and in England) and his residence (at Grasmere). After reading through this curious response, Anne Taylor could hardly have disagreed with Wordsworth's afterthought: "In what I have said I am afraid there will be little which will throw any light on my writings, or gratify the wish which you entertain, to know how I came to adopt the opinions which I have expressed in my preface; and to write in the style in which my poems are written." If she had known more about him, however, she could never have accepted the explanation he goes on to offer: " . . . but in truth my life has been unusually barren of events, and my opinions have grown slowly and, I may say, insensibly" (*EY*:327).

Barren of events? Barren of the kinds of events that might influence his opinions? The idea seems absurd to modern readers familiar with the then-unwritten parts of *The Prelude* and with scholarly reconstruction of Wordsworth's early adult years: his involvement with the French Royalists in Orleans, with Michel Beaupuy, and with revolutionary societies in Paris; his complicated and painful affair with Annette Vallon in Blois and their natural daughter; his probable acquaintance with influential activists in Paris, perhaps even with Jean-Paul Brissot, leader of the powerful Girondist party; his engagement in radical polemics after coming back to London in late 1792; his probable return to Paris in the autumn of 1793 in time to witness the execution of Gorsas at the hands of Robespierre's Montagnards; his plan to form a radical newspaper in London with William Mathews; his friendship with William Godwin, England's most important radical theorist of the mid-1790s; not to mention his friendships with Coleridge, Southey, Lamb, Thelwall, and others equally well known by 1801.[6] By the time he wrote his contributions for *Lyrical Ballads*, Wordsworth had participated intellectually, socially, and politically in what was already recognized as the most momentous of modern revolutions.[7] Yet all he could find to say about the way these years affected his opinions was that, after he left Cambridge, his time had "been spent travelling upon the Continent, and in England: and in occasional residences in London, and in different parts of England and Wales."

Not all the activities listed here could have been included in a short letter, of course, and some would obviously have been inappropriate to the occasion. But such massive distortion is not easily explained away. Besides, one finds a similarly skewed treatment of the revolutionary period in

"Tintern Abbey," the most explicitly autobiographical poem to appear in *Lyrical Ballads*, or perhaps in any volume published during Wordsworth's lifetime. The argument of that poem, to state what every schoolboy used to know, turns on the difference between Wordsworth's experience of a landscape in 1798 and his recollection of a visit to the same place five years earlier. Although 1793 marks the center of his revolutionary phase, the poem makes no mention of political affairs. Instead, it follows the poet's meditation on the difference between his two experiences of the landscape. He concludes that if his earlier experience had been the more ecstatic, the present experience is the more deeply felt because it is the more deeply human. Where in the first instance "Nature . . . was all in all" to him, now his perception of the landscape is attended by "the still sad music of humanity." Further, the poem enacts what it argues in that the movement of the opening stanza, which records the poet's 1798 experience of the place, leads consistently away from the objects perceived and toward a human figure, "the hermit," with which the poet imaginatively associates them.[8]

"Tintern Abbey" asks that we view 1793 as the season of Wordsworth's nature worship and its own time, 1798, as the season of his espousal of the cause of humanity. But for anyone familiar with what Wordsworth did or is likely to have done in these respective years, such an account runs perfectly contrary to intuition. In 1798, Wordsworth was living in rustic isolation and spending much of his time just as he is depicted doing in the poem: wandering the hills with his sister far from all centers of human population, as well as from "evil tongues," "rash judgments," "the sneers of selfish men," "greetings where no kindness is," and indeed from "all / The dreary intercourse of daily life" (129–32). At this time he was contemplating the epic that would preoccupy his thoughts for the next fifteen years. It was to be appropriately entitled *The Recluse*. The republican of 1793, on the other hand, was spending most of his time in London, when not in France, and was soon to consider launching a newspaper dedicated to humanist inquiry and social reform. This project is the proper antecedent to *The Recluse* and it, too, bears the appropriate title, *The Philanthropist*.

The central terms of humanism and naturalism in "Tintern Abbey" thus emerge with connotations roughly the reverse of what we might have guessed. We may always choose to regard this turnabout as Wordsworth's effort to overthrow our expectations. But the more one looks at "Tintern Abbey" as autobiography, the more the poem seems an evasion of what he had actually stood for in 1793, and the more his rhetorical *occupatio*—"I

worth to speak, as it were, for himself, and it allows us to determine for ourselves whether this is the voice of dissolution and dismay, or of something else entirely.

Of all his writings, the Letter to Llandaff is probably the last place to which the mature Wordsworth would have wanted his readers to come first. This consideration may itself be enough to recommend the Letter as a valuable starting point for study of Wordsworth's changing political attitudes. But there are still other considerations. Perhaps the most obvious reason for beginning with the Letter is that it is Wordsworth's first full-fledged exposition of his intellectual, moral, and political views. It would indeed remain his most explicit and thoroughgoing statement about public affairs until *The Convention of Cintra* (1809), a tract not composed until after the great decade of his major poetry. Another reason is that the Letter shows all the marks of a mind just beginning to think of itself as having a public or political dimension. Wordsworth had completed a period of education at Cambridge and a period of initiation in France. Recently returned to London, he was ready to act on what he had learned. His poetry, furthermore, was just appearing in print for the first time, and he was just getting to know what it was like to have his opinions circulated among men and women for whom "W. Wordsworth" would be represented only by what appeared on a printed page. Wordsworth's very first words to Watson show his concern with this question of one's place in the public eye. "My lord," he begins solemnly, "Reputation may not improperly be termed the moral life of a man" (*PrW* 1:31).

Perhaps the most considerable reason for starting with the Letter to Llandaff, however, is that its explicit concern is the very topic that has so exercised students of Wordsworth: the way a writer changes in political outlook. Wordsworth broaches the topic in his initial paragraph by expanding metaphorically the notion of reputation as a man's moral life. "In a sublime allegory well known to your Lordship," he writes, Addison "has represented us as crossing an immense bridge, from whose surface from a variety of causes we disappear one after another, and are seen no more." While Wordsworth concedes that Addison's allegory was originally meant to represent "our natural existence," he wastes no time turning the figure to his own purposes:

> Every one, who enters upon public life, has such a bridge to pass, some slip through at the very commencement of their career from thoughtlessness, others pursue their course a little longer till, misled by the phantoms of avarice and ambition, they fall victims to their delusion. Your Lordship was either

seen, or supposed to be seen, continuing your way for a long time, unseduced and undismayed; but those, who now look for you, will look in vain, and it is feared you have at last fallen, through one of the numberous trap-doors, into the tide of contempt to be swept down to the ocean of oblivion. [p. 31]

Implied in this allegory is Wordsworth's insistence on his own emergence into public life. One sojourner drops off the bridge, and another, through the very act of telling the world, steps up to take his place. The focus of the allegory is clearly on Watson's fall, however, and to see its point one must know enough about Watson to read the topical allusions that Wordsworth only partly spells out.

Through the 1770s and 1780s, Richard Watson had established himself as one of the most outspoken of public apologists for dissenting positions in both religion and politics. He had, in Wordsworth's own words, "stood almost alone as the defender of truth and political charity" (p. 31). In praising Watson's political courage, Wordsworth no doubt had in mind Watson's defense of the American colonies against governmental abuses at home. Watson's university sermon at Cambridge, *Principles of the Revolution Vindicated* (1776), for example, was called treasonable when it appeared in print.[9] It was indeed controversial enough in the 1770s to have cost Watson preferment and celebrated enough in the 1790s to have been invoked (with high praise) by Charles James Fox in his 1795 attack on the Sedition Bill.[10] The Revolution of the sermon's title is not the American but the English. Watson maintained that England's political struggle in the previous century had clarified and confirmed the principle of legislative and executive accountability to the people. In the language of universal human equality and natural rights, Watson defended the validity of this principle and argued its applicability to the turbulence "which hath arisen in the Western continent" over the questions of parliamentary taxation and popular representation.[11] Watson's sermon declares him not only a subscriber to a quite radical version of the English Revolution, but also, because he takes the circumstances to be analogous, a sympathizer with the popular cause in America. In the previous century, he contended, "it was a part of the nation which resisted the King, because he would have taken from them their property, without their consent given by themselves or their representatives; and now it is a part of the empire which resists the Legislature for the very same reason" (p. 21).

The sermon Watson preached at Westminster Abbey in January 1784 shows that he maintained his position on the justice of the colonial cause through the end of the Revolutionary War.[12] His early writings on the

French Revolution show his sympathy with the reforms of 1789.[13] In all these pronouncements, Watson is presumed to be continuing safely across the bridge of reputable public life. What constitutes his "fall," according to Wordsworth, is that after supporting such forbidden causes, Watson should suddenly, "in the extraordinary avowal of his political principles contained in the Appendix to his late sermon" (of late January 1793), turn his back on the cause of the French people. Wordsworth goes on to denounce Watson's degenerate condition in the strongest possible terms and in so doing outlines the virtues that characterize a public man or woman in the "unfallen" state. Standing on the threshold of his own public career, in other words, Wordsworth takes full stock of his position. This is the Letter's powerful claim to priority.

What is true of the Addisonian allegory at the start of the Letter, however, is true of its argument as a whole: to grasp its purport fully we must recapture what it presupposes about its historical circumstances. My discussion in the next chapter begins with the state of the scholarship now available on Wordsworth's radical pamphlet, especially research into its sources. It then extends that research by filling in certain lacunae and by offering an overview of the pamphlet campaign in which Wordsworth in effect enlisted when he wrote the Letter. The reward for attending carefully to this particular context is a fresh understanding of the Letter's complex rhetorical aims. This understanding in turn opens up a new perspective on Wordsworth's changing position in the political life of his times.

Two

Burke Blamed and Praised

> All this moral cement is dissolved, habits and
> prejudices are broken and rooted up.
>
> Wordsworth to Daniel Stuart, 7 April 1817

*B*ecause the arguments of the Letter to Llandaff are largely derivative
from other radical writing, scholarly attention to the Letter tends to focus
on its intellectual sources. Of all such sources, the least mistakable are
probably to be found among the political writings of Rousseau. Words-
worth not only hinges crucial points on Rousseauist ideas such as the
general will (*PrW* 1:39), but he also invokes Rousseau's authority for his
position by quoting (in French) from chapter 2 of *The Social Contract* (p. 36).
Much of the Letter, however, seems to derive from writings more contem-
porary and closer to home, and most of the scholarly disagreement over it
has been occasioned by the effort to identify these sources accurately.

Since E. N. Hooker's persuasive essay of fifty years ago, no one has
seriously challenged the claim that Thomas Paine's *The Rights of Man*
(1791, 1792) is a crucial source for the way Wordsworth formulates and
addresses major issues in the Letter.[1] Doubt remains only about how much
of the credit, if any at all, Paine must share with Godwin's *Enquiry
Concerning Political Justice* (1793). Many of Wordsworth's biographers and
bibliographers have dated the Letter to June 1793.[2] In their recent edition

of the prose works, on the other hand, Owen and Smyser have argued, from topical allusion and other evidence, that the Letter probably dates from February or March of that year. Since Godwin's *Enquiry* was not published until February, Owen and Smyser's date is presumably too early to allow for Wordsworth's procurement of Godwin's exorbitantly priced tract and for his mastery of its abstruse arguments. They conclude, therefore, that Godwin exerted no influence on the Letter and that where "similarities occur . . . it is possible to find a common source, usually Paine" (*PrW* 1:24). Their glosses on the text corroborate this claim and, taken together with Hooker's still valuable scholarship, indicate that Paine was indeed a strong presence in Wordsworth's thinking at this time.

The difference between Paine's influence on the Letter and Rousseau's is that whereas the latter serves Wordsworth as a source of ideas and a canonized authority for his radical views, the former serves him as a kind of rhetorical model. Paine was far and away England's most persuasive and most widely read radical polemicist of the day. It thus makes sense that Wordsworth, like so many other young advocates of political change, should present himself to the world in Paine's image. But influence, as we are now coming to understand more clearly, comes in many forms. Ultimately, an even more imposing English figure than Tom Paine stands behind Wordsworth's statement of position, and indeed behind Paine's own. This mightier one is Edmund Burke.

I

Since Burke is actually mentioned several times in Wordsworth's Letter, his name does tend to come up when the Letter is discussed in its historical relations. The extent of Burke's role, nonetheless, has yet to be fully fathomed. Even Hooker's valuable suggestion that the Letter is a reply to Burke as well as to Watson is made only offhandedly and on the way to a claim about Paine.[3] The failure to see Burke's importance for the Letter, moreover, is part of a larger oversight. Burke's role more generally in the intellectual climate of the 1790s has seldom been adequately registered by modern literary historians of this period, even by those specifically interested in the relation of Romantic literature and politics. Quite apart from the respect Burke earned from both friends and enemies as a literary genius, it would be difficult to overestimate his importance for English political writing in the period of the French Revolution. It goes without saying that he was the acknowledged leader of the antirevolutionary movement in England; that he galvanized Englishmen already hostile to what they saw happening in France; that, by the apparent fulfillment of his dire forecasts for the Revolution, he won over many of its early sympathizers to his side; and that he was largely responsible for the wave of anti-French sentiment which was already gaining momentum by the end of 1792, when Paine was arrested for part 2 of *The Rights of Man*, and which subsequently carried over into war abroad and numerous sedition trials at home. What is more to the point here, however, and seldom recognized outside a relatively small circle of Burke scholars, is Burke's unwitting service to the radical movement itself.[4] Burke contributed much to the formation of an articulate radical ideology in the England of the 1790s.

The *Reflections on the Revolution in France*, we must recall, appeared at the very start of this decade, on 1 November 1790. Burke wrote this long essay quickly in order to provide an immediate criticism of the events of 1789 both in England and in France. Though his intention was to nip the English Jacobin movement in the bud, his book became the occasion of its greatest flowering. The two chief organizations Burke attacked in the book's opening pages—the Revolution Society and the Society for Constitutional Information—were both struggling at the time the *Reflections* appeared. Their revival in 1791 and 1792 owes much to the interest stimulated by hostile reactions to that book. The same is true of the small radical organizations in cities like Sheffield and Manchester. The founding of additional societies at this time can probably be attributed in part to the same cause.[5]

What regenerated these organizations was the powerful resurgence of radical thought and writing—virtually all in response to Burke—which provided a fresh source of arguments, principles, sentiments, and slogans for the "Friends of Liberty." The statistics associated with Burke's *Reflections* suggest both the immediacy and extent of its cultural impact. On 29 November 1790, exactly four weeks after its appearance, Burke remarked that "the demand for this piece has been without example," and then backed up his claim with numbers: "they are now in the sale of the twelfth thousand of their copies."[6] According to James Prior, Burke's early biographer, 30,000 copies in all were sold within the next few years.[7] The radicals among these readers were probably not the most numerous group, but they were clearly the most prolific. Prior counted "no less than 38" answers to the book in the first few months of its publication, and J. T. Boulton has composed a list of more than seventy printed responses through early 1793.[8] All but a few of the items on Boulton's list were vigorously critical of Burke; many opposed him diametrically. Paine's *Rights of Man*, the most popular of these answers to Burke, went through dozens and dozens of editions (legitimate and pirated) that resulted in untold copies of the pamphlet; estimates for part 1 alone range all the way up to a staggering 1,500,000.[9] Richard Altick has even attributed some of the acceleration in literacy rates at this time to widespread interest in reading these two books.[10]

Burke is obviously not the originary source of English radical ideas in the 1790s—nor even, for that matter, of all conservative ones. Rather, his fame and the wide influence of his essay served the radical cause by providing a high occasion for the public declaration of the "Friends of Liberty." It is also fair to say that he enriched and escalated the existing debate. By presenting an ideological position that was fully and, after his fashion, coherently developed, he supplied his opponents with an agenda that made for a new comprehensiveness in their own positions. And by achieving a marriage of form and content, mode and message, in the *Reflections*, he helped his adversaries to see certain ideological relationships that might otherwise have gone unnoticed.[11]

Short of undertaking a thorough analysis of the radical documents in question, the best evidence I could offer to show Burke's role in the radical movement is the testimony of the Friends of Liberty themselves. On 14 July 1791, the Revolution Society and the Society for Constitutional Information, the two organizations that Burke had singled out for attack a year earlier, held a joint dinner meeting in London to commemorate the taking of the Bastille. When the dinner ended, a series of toasts were proposed. Only one of these toasts is germane, but to provide a sense of the context I will include a few items before and after it:

> To the liberty of the press.—To trial by jury, and that the rights of juries to protect the innocent are never attacked.—To the men of letters who have made themselves advocates of the rights of man, and that genius always defend the cause of liberty!—*To Mr. Burke, to thank him for having provoked the great discussion that occupies all thinking beings* (here follows universal applause, which lasts for a full half-hour).—To the patriots of France.—To the precious memory of the citizens who, in France, sacrificed their lives for the freedom of their country.—To friends of the Revolution inside of Parliament and outside.[12]

The thirty-minute ovation after the toast to Burke may indicate that the salute to him was ironic. But if this is irony, it is the kind that enables one to state a truth which is itself ironic: Burke did provoke the "great debate" that led to the very celebration at which these toasts are proposed. In the short run at least, certainly from the perspective of 1791, suffering Burke's polemic was the best thing that could have happened to the radical cause.

To place the Letter to Llandaff against this background, then, is to discover that we must not only understand some of Wordsworth's remarks as being modeled on Paine's, but also conceive of the entire attack on Watson as being modeled on Paine's attack on Burke. And what becomes clear as soon as we conceive of the *Letter* in this way is that the anti-Burke impetus probably accounts in large measure for Wordsworth's very decision to make Watson his target in the first place, as well as to introduce his remarks with those ad hominem arguments about Watson's tergiversation. In the preface to the English edition of *The Rights of Man*, Paine had elaborated his attack on Burke's *Reflections* along lines much the same as we find in Wordsworth's Letter. "I am astonished and disappointed," Paine writes, "as . . . I had other expectations," thus in effect restating what he announced in the book's opening sentence: "From the part Mr Burke took in the American Revolution, it was natural that I should consider him a friend to mankind."[13] Burke had, in his long career in Parliament, criticized Britain's handling of many of the responsibilities of its expanding empire, including its affairs in Ireland and India. It was his speeches on America, however, that earned for him the high esteem of his liberal contemporaries.[14] Nor was Burke's reputation limited to England. We gain some sense of his fame in France from the circumstances that provided the very occasion of his writing the *Reflections*. For when Victor De Pont wrote from France soliciting Burke's views of the 1789 Revolution, he supposed that Burke would write in its favor. And later, like so many others, De Pont recorded his disappointment with what Burke actually had to say.[15]

The point is that the ad hominem attack that serves as Wordsworth's model is important not as an original contribution by Paine but as an epitome of anti-Burkean tactics at the time. Burke's is, so to speak, the crucial influence. Virtually every radical writer of this time saw Burke's position on France as a change of political colors, and at the same time realized that Burke's reputation made him one of the worst English enemies the French Revolution could have made. (This widely shared sense of Burke's special authority surely accounts in part for the extraordinary volume of critical response.) Paine looms so largely over the shoulders of young radicals like Wordsworth because he offers so powerful an example of how to take on this formidable conservative opponent.

If Wordsworth really wanted to respond to Burke in early 1793, why (one may reasonably ask) did he not simply respond to Burke? There are two related reasons why not. If we look over Boulton's useful list of the seventy or so published responses to Burke, we find that nearly four dozen had already appeared by the end of 1792. This means that when Wordsworth had left for France in November 1791 the controversy was already in full swing. Without taking *The Prelude*'s account of Wordsworth's naïveté then at face value—after all, he was curious enough about politics at this time to want to visit Revolutionary France—we may safely guess that his political interests were not sufficiently keen, nor his political ideas sufficiently well formed, to warrant his participation in this already-ongoing debate. By the time he returned, however, anxious to join in what Blake called "Mental Fight," the waves of counterattack against Burke had largely subsided.[16] The issues of the *Reflections* were going stale and becoming exhausted by the repeated challenges of the previous two years. With nothing left to say to Burke, one might simply choose a surrogate like Watson for one's attack.

The second reason is that events of late 1792 and early 1793 had altered the central issues: in August, the Paris revolution; in September, the Massacres and the declaration of the French Republic; in January, the execution of Louis XVI. England registered these events with a change in mood. F. M. Todd has argued that the England to which Wordsworth returned a radical "had largely made up its mind on [i.e., against] the French Revolution."[17] This is surely an exaggeration, but it is undeniable that France was losing allies among the English citizenry by the first months of 1793 and that many of the English were seeing affairs both in France and in England in a new light. Though the principles at stake in the Great Debate had largely remained the same, some of the issues were changing. Since Watson addressed the new issues in his Appendix of late January, his text made an appropriate target for Wordsworth. Wordsworth may have arrived too late for the battle his contemporaries had fought against Burke directly, but the Letter to Llandaff responds to the new issues by raising the same radical banner and by attacking an opponent he makes out to look as much like Burke as he can.

II

Wordsworth did not actually have to work all that hard to make Watson seem a new Burke. For more clearly even than in the case of his pro–American Revolution sermons, many of Watson's anti–French Revolution principles derive from Burke, just as Wordsworth's principles derive from Paine and Rousseau. Wordsworth is quick, moreover, to point out Watson's source. He considers two passages in Watson's Appendix important enough to cite at length and explicitly associates both passages with Burke's *Reflections*.

The immediate occasion of Watson's Appendix is the execution of Louis XVI on 21 January 1793. Both sides on this issue recognized that the monarch was dispatched as a direct consequence of what had happened three months earlier when the constitutional monarchy was abolished in favor of a republic: a living king is a continuing threat to a kingless government. The political principles that Watson extraordinarily avows in the Appendix thus bear chiefly on the relative merits of monarchical and republican forms of government, and Wordsworth is especially interested in what he considers the main argument by which the bishop "pretend[s] to justify [his] anathemas of a republic" (p. 35). The first passage Wordsworth cites from the Appendix is the one he thinks is meant to offer such an argument: "'I dislike a republic for this reason, because of all forms of government, scarcely excepting the most despotic, I think a republic the most oppressive to the bulk of the people: they are deceived in it with a shew of liberty; but they live in it, under the most odious of tyrannies, the tyranny of their equals'" (*PrW* 1:35).

Wordsworth's very first move in the rebuttal of this argument, tellingly, is to identify its position as Burkean:

> Mr Burke, in a philosophic lamentation over the extinction of Chivalry, told us that in those times vice lost half its evil, by losing all its grossness; infatuated moralist! Your Lordship excites compassion as labouring under the same delusion. [pp. 35–36]

This seems to come from nowhere. What does this delusion have to do with Watson's quoted attack on republics? Wordsworth's ingenious argument employs the kind of dialectical reversal identified then with the social criticism of Rousseau and later with that of Shaw. He concedes that a republic may—even that it must—result in an odious tyranny of one's equals, but then goes on to insist that the odiousness of such a tyranny would be its saving grace, the mark that distinguishes it from all current forms of tyranny. "As soon as tyranny becomes odious," he explains, "the principal step is made toward its destruction" (p. 36). The principle at stake here is that grossness is offensive not in itself but only as a sign of vice. To alter the sign is not to mitigate the vice; it is to introduce still further evil into the world. Wordsworth's metaphorical formulation puts the matter clearly: "Slavery is a bitter and poisonous draught; . . . by rendering it more palatable you contribute to its power of destruction" (p. 36).

Wordsworth's response is not quite fair to Watson, since Watson's argument is itself concerned with popular deception. But Wordsworth's way of maneuvering through this rebuttal suggests that his underlying concern it not with Watson at all but rather with Burke, to whom the criticism more aptly pertains. Furthermore, though Wordsworth does not set off his Burkean quotation in inverted commas, it is every bit as accurate as the transcription from Watson, a fact which indicates either that he was writing with a copy of the *Reflections* at hand or else that he had so mastered the text as to know at least its more celebrated passages by heart.

Wordsworth's second long citation from Watson's Appendix is actually two passages strung together to make an extended paean to the status quo in England. The English constitution is singled out for special praise as a code that provides for the greatest freedom, equality, and security possible in civil society. After citing Watson's remarks, Wordsworth chides him with the prediction that his "readers will hardly believe . . . that these passages are copied verbatim" and then, as before, immediately turns to Burke and to another of the already-famous passages from the *Reflections*:

> Mr Burke rouzed the indignation of all ranks of men, when by a refinement in cruelty superiour to that which in the East yokes the living to the dead he strove to persuade us that we and our posterity to the end of time were riveted to a constitution by the indissoluble compact of a dead parchment, and were bound to cherish a corse at the bosom, when reason might call aloud that it should be entombed. Your lordship aims at the same detestable object by means more criminal because more dangerous and insidious. Attempting to lull the people of England into a belief that any enquiries directed towards the nature of liberty and equality can in no other way lead to their happiness than by convincing them that they have already arrived at perfection in the science of government, what is your object but to exclude them forever from the most fruitful field of human knowledge? . . . You have aimed an arrow at liberty and philosophy, the eyes of the human race: why, like the inveterate enemy of Philip, in putting your name to the shaft, did you not declare openly its destination? [p. 48]

Wordsworth's ends-means analysis should be attended to with some care. His claim is that Watson and Burke have, in their recent writings, pursued a common object. This object is to exclude the people from the free field of social inquiry and thus at the same time to preserve (by concealing) "things as they are," as the slogan of the day had it, things that included unjustly acquired power and unequally distributed wealth. In view of this common object, the difference in means between the two writers is minor by comparison. Burke uses an antirational rhetoric—what Wordsworth later in the Letter calls Burke's "intoxicating bowl"—to persuade his readers. Watson uses a soporific rhetoric to stupefy his. But both writers, to shift to the metaphor that describes them equally, aim their arrows at liberty and philosophy, the eyes of the human race.[18]

This discussion of the relation of free intellectual inquiry and social progress lies at the ideological center of the Letter to Llandaff. It is true that Wordsworth's earlier analysis of tyranny and odium addresses what he presents as Watson's fundamental argument. But the later discussion of free inquiry shows not only *what* Wordsworth thinks but also *how* he thinks, and how he thinks the human race must carry on its daily business. These remarks thus account for the manner of the Letter as well as its matter, and this manner is clearly meant to reflect an exemplary commitment to the procedures of enlightened inquiry. Throughout the Letter Wordsworth employs the rationalist diction of "proofs" and "maxims," "causes" and "effects." He is careful to distinguish "argument" from "assertion" (p. 35). He questions more than once whether Watson has established "sufficient reason" for his claims (pp. 34, 46). He uses rhetorical prolepsis: "Perhaps . . . the principle on which I proceed will be questioned . . ." (p. 37). He refutes Watson with a *reductio ad absurdum*—"You are therefore guilty of the most glaring contradiction . . ." (p. 35)—while being sure to show that his own argument steers clear of the same fallacy.[19] Sometimes, in the enlightened manner of a Rousseau, a Voltaire, or a Paine, he simply dismisses Watson's claims with a sneer: "As to your arguments . . . if arguments they may be called . . ." (p. 35).

This self-consciously rationalistic manner, which no doubt owes something to the Letter's anti-Burke context, is accompanied by another characteristic that Burke often provoked in the prose of his critics. As Boulton puts it, Burke's *Reflections* had a way of touching readers personally, leading them to respond as if the issue were "between him and themselves as representative individuals" and to adopt a tone that was therefore "chiefly personal."[20] The same curious combination of rationalist posture and personal tone marks Wordsworth's Letter, and is perhaps nowhere clearer than in its final reference to Burke:

> Upon what principle is your conduct to be explained? In some
> parts of England it is quaintly said, when a drunken man is seen

reeling towards his home, that he has business on both sides of
the road. Observing your lordship's tortuous path, the specta-
tors will be far from insinuating that you have partaken of Mr
Burke's intoxicating bowl; they will content themselves, shak-
ing their heads as you stagger along, with remarking that you
have business on both sides of the road. [p. 49]

Part of the importance of this comment is that it corroborates one's sense of
Wordsworth's logicalistic way of thinking in 1793 and, like the metaphor
of the cup of slavery, tells us much about the way he then used figurative
language. This is the kind of witty conceit that works out to a determinate
and rational point. In the context of the country adage, "business on both
sides of the road" provides a euphemistic mask of sobriety for drunken
behavior. Here, on the other hand, the suggestion is that while Watson,
"labouring under the same delusion" as Burke, may well be only drunk
with Burke's rhetoric, his conduct raises the suspicion that he may soberly
be shifting allegiances to advance his own interests.

As to whether Watson had in fact partaken of Burke's intoxicating
bowl, there can be little doubt that he had. Wordsworth covers the main
points, but he might have cited still further evidence of Watson's debt to
Burke. One item Wordsworth apparently chose not to mention, for exam-
ple, is Watson's assertion that the British constitution, while not so perfect
as to be beyond improvement, is "too far excellent to be amended by
peasants and mechanics."[21] The utility of such men, Watson goes on,
"consists in their discharging well the duties of their respective stations; it
ceases when they affect to become legislators; when they intrude themselves
into concerns, for which their education has not fitted them."[22] Burke had
written in the *Reflections* that the "associations of tailors and carpenters, of
which the republic (of Paris, for instance) is composed, cannot be equal to
the situations into which, by the worst of usurpations, an usurpation on the
prerogatives of Nature, you attempt to force them" (3:295). "Such descrip-
tions of men," he adds, "ought not to suffer oppression from the state; but
the state suffers oppression, if such as they, either individually or collec-
tively, are permitted to rule" (p. 296). Finally, there is Watson's architec-
tural metaphor, which Burke employs repeatedly and to the same effect.[23]

Within the Letter itself, the metaphor of the staggering man returns
Wordsworth to the topic of political turncoatism and prepares for his final,
more general remarks. In yet another of those dialectical reversals that we
associate with Rousseau and Shaw, Wordsworth tells Watson that "the
friends of liberty congratulate themselves upon the odium under which
they are at present labouring; as the causes which produced it have obliged

so many of her false adherents to disclaim with officious earnestness any desire to promote her interest" (p. 49). The final lash of caustic wit is Wordsworth's expression of gratitude to Watson: "Conscious that an enemy lurking in our ranks is ten times more formidable than when drawn out against us, . . . we thank you for your desertion" (p. 49). But Wordsworth's irony is purchased at his own expense in the end, for he would later lay himself open to a similar charge.

III

That the poet who, in 1793, spoke of Burke's delusion and unnatural cruelty eventually changed his mind both about the man and what he stood for can be flatly established if we are willing to look far enough into the years ahead for the evidence. In 1818, Wordsworth, then forty-eight and Distributor of Stamps for Westmoreland and part of Cumberland, published two *Addresses to the Freeholders of Westmoreland* in behalf of Lord Lonsdale's candidacy in the general election. Near the beginning of the First Address, Wordsworth explains that if the Whig party has "dwindled and divided, they must ascribe it to their own errors." Now a politician of sorts himself, Wordsworth blames the Whigs as politicians, though not "as men" (he was not a politician in the 1790s), for having "hoped too ardently of human nature, as they did at the commencement of the French Revolution." "*Politicians*," he emphasizes, "cannot be allowed to plead temptations of fancy, or impulses of feeling, in exculpation of mistakes of judgement." To this general tendency there was, as he now sees it, one exception, Burke:

> Mr. Fox, captivated by the vanities of a system founded upon abstract rights, chaunted his expectations in the House of Parliament; and too many of his Friends partook of the illusion. The most sagacious Politician of his age broke out in an opposite strain. Time has verified his predictions; the books remain in which his principles of foreknowledge were laid down. . . . That warning voice proved vain; the party from whom he separated, proceeded—confiding in splendid oratorical talents and ardent feelings rashly wedded to novel expectations, when common sense, uninquisitive experience, and a modest reliance on old habits of judgement, when either these, or a philosophic penetration, were the only qualities that could have served them. [*PrW* 3:157–58]

Like Mark Twain's father, this father figure to the later Wordsworth seems to get smarter as his son ages. The "infatuated moralist" of 1793 has become "the most sagacious politician of his age" in twenty-five years.

Further, Wordsworth's new position, while accepting the same basic terms of the 1790s controversy, stands thoroughly at odds with the old. Instead of Burke's "delusion" we here find Fox's "illusion." Burke is now praised for just those attributes and values for which he had earlier been vilified: "modest reliance on old habits of judgement" and a faith in "uninquisitive experience." To build a system on the principles of abstract rights, as Wordsworth tries to do in his Letter to Llandaff, is now viewed as an exercise in vanity.[24]

Probably between 1820 and 1828, Wordsworth versified his remarks on Burke in a passage which became part of book 7 of the 1850 version of *The Prelude*:

> Genius of Burke! forgive the pen seduced
> By specious wonders, and too slow to tell
> Of what the ingenuous, what bewildered men,
> Beginning to mistrust their boastful guides,
> And wise men, willing to grow wiser, caught,
> Rapt auditors! from thy most eloquent tongue—
> Now mute, for ever mute in the cold grave.
> I see him,—old but vigorous in age,—
> Stand like an oak whose stag-horn branches start
> Out of its leafy brow, the more to awe
> The younger brethren of the grove. But some—
> While he forewarns, denounces, launches forth,
> Against all systems built on abstract rights,
> Keen ridicule; the majesty proclaims
> Of Institutes and Laws, hallowed by time;
> Declares the vital power of social ties
> Endeared by Custom; and with high disdain,
> Exploding upstart Theory, insists
> Upon the allegiance to which men are born—
> Some—say at once a froward multitude—
> Murmur (for truth is hated, where not loved)
> As the winds fret within the Æolian cave,
> Galled by their monarch's chain. The times were big
> With ominous change, which, night by night, provoked
> Keen struggles, and black clouds of passion raised;
> But memorable moments intervened,
> When Wisdom, like the Goddess from Jove's brain,
> Broke forth in armour of resplendent words,

Startling the Synod. Could a youth, and one
In ancient story versed, whose breast had heaved
Under the weight of classic eloquence,
Sit, see, and hear, unthankful, uninspired?

[512–43]

We have no trouble recognizing in these lines the political and moral opinions of the 1818 Address, though Burke's status seems to have been elevated from predictor to prophet—"he forewarns, denounces, launches forth." He is praised for attacking "systems built on abstract rights" (a clear echo of the 1818 prose) and for exploding "upstart Theory," and he is fully endorsed for placing his faith in the authority of custom and experience. But such a summary of the speaker's views, though not misleading, could never be adequate to a poem of such dramatic complexity. The speaker's request for forgiveness is an event in *The Prelude*'s mental action, and to borrow a metaphor from the poem itself, more is going on here than meets the eye.

The reader of *The Prelude* will recognize the line "Genius of Burke! forgive the pen . . ." as an introduction to one of several passages, scattered through Wordsworth's poem, in which the "eye and progress of the Song" (6:526) is intercepted by forces beyond the conscious control of the poet. Examples of this kind of passage include the address to Coleridge in book 2 (203–37), the long section of book 5 (166–557) that culminates in the address to the "dreamers, . . . / Forgers of lawless tales," the address to the Imagination in book 6 (525–48), and the address to the Maid of Buttermere just prior to the Burke passage in book 7 (346–411). What we are asked to believe in these passages, as their best explicator Hartman explains, is that "something that happened during composition . . . enters the narrative as a new biographical event."[25] In such cases, what "enters the narrative" is the sudden recognition of something that the conscious soul of the composing poet would have left out of its account. The switch to present tense marks these passages off as special. We are to suppose that they have their origin in another realm of being, that they are breakthroughs of unconscious powers or motions into the field of consciousness, the "eye" of the song. In dramatizing these privileged moments in the compositional life of a poet's mind, these passages usually assume the form of a blessing or tribute to the genius or geniuses who would otherwise have gone unsung.

Yet the place of the Burke passage among these others is curious. Biographically, this passage is set off from the others by the two decades or so that have elapsed since the completion of the 1805 poem, which included

them all. There is thus no basis at all in this case for the fiction of
spontaneity which governs such passages. Wordsworth simply inserted the
passage into the compositional flow of the narrative, using the device he had
developed in his creative bursts of 1804–5. This matter concerns the poet's
circumstances, but the Burke passage is equally peculiar when considered
more strictly from the reader's point of view. By book 7, one has come to
expect from these apostrophic passages a confessional outburst from the
poet. "Forgive the pen . . ." seems to signal a sincere admission of personal
failure of the kind that appears in book 5: "While I was travelling back
among those days, / How could I ever play the ingrate's part?" Having
failed to tell of the importance of childhood tales in shaping his develop-
ment, Wordsworth cannot proceed (we are to believe) until he pays tribute
to the romance writers (516–57). In the tortuous syntax of the Burke
passage, one can easily miss the fact that Wordsworth never actually tells us
just what Burke taught him. The forgiveness he seeks, astonishingly, is for
having been too slow to tell of what *other* men learned from Burke—what
the ingenuous, bewildered, and wise men ("willing to grow wiser") caught
from Burke's tongue. Another group is present at the scene Wordsworth
envisions, but he is even further from numbering himself among them, and
even more tortuous in his description of their response: "But some— / . . . /
Some—say at once a froward multitude— / Murmur (for truth is hated
where not loved)." Where is Wordsworth in all this? He is merely an
onlooking "youth," a witness who is unsuspecting, but not "unthankful,"
or "uninspired." Consider what we are left to conclude: Wordsworth asks
forgiveness for not mentioning what other men learned from Burke at a
time when he innocently sat marveling at Burke's eloquence, unaware of
the purport of what was said. Though the elder Wordsworth (returning to
past tense) recalls that "the times were big / With ominous change," the
youthful self he shows us is not supposed to know.

The metaphor in this last phrase echoes a passage from the Letter to
Llandaff that should help break the older poet's trance and toll us back to his
sole self of the early 1790s. "At a period big with the fate of the human
race," young Wordsworth tells Watson, "I am sorry that you attach so
much importance to the personal sufferings of the late royal martyr and that
an anxiety for the issue of the present convulsions should not have prevented
you from joining in the idle cry of modish lamentation which has resounded
from the court to the cottage" (*PrW* 1:32). I do not propose to interpret the
fact that the echo occurs at just the point where Wordsworth ridicules those
who "murmured" at Burke's prophetic revelations. The point is that the
Wordsworth who addresses Watson (alluding to Burke) in 1793 hardly

speaks the tones of naïveté, and that, in his confessional tribute to Burke, Wordsworth sets the scene at a time before he embroils himself in the controversy, thus making it possible to present his youthful self as ignorant of its implications. The elder Wordsworth, who sees the image of Burke before him, unmistakably endorses Burke's views. The younger Wordsworth, ignorant of Burke's views, is thrilled by his eloquence. Wordsworth thus not only refuses to depict himself as one of Burke's opponents but even shies away from identification with those ingenuous and bewildered men who turned to Burke after "beginning to mistrust their boastful guides." We know Wordsworth was once one of Burke's opponents. On the evidence of his endorsement of Burke in this very passage, we must also conclude that he belongs in this second group as well: at some point he, too, turned to Burke.

The strange choreography of Wordsworth's movement through this passage suggests that Burke was a touchy subject for him, one he preferred not to face. Indeed, his reluctance to speak of Burke occasions this "confession" to begin with: "forgive the pen . . . too slow to tell." Leaving aside the point that the confession is not much of a confession, we still face other questions. Why did Wordsworth think he needed Burke's forgiveness in the first place? If it is for having gone on too long without acknowledging the greatness he now saw in a man he once thought deluded, then how long is too long? When did Wordsworth come round to Burke's point of view?

In his late encomium to Burke, Wordsworth's recognition of Burke's "genius" seems to depend on his belief that Burke actually knew, in 1790, what would happen in the years ahead. Looking back on Burke's *Reflections* over the distance of three decades, Wordsworth saw a Burke looking forward, as it were, toward him. In viewing Burke as a kind of prophet, Wordsworth may have had in mind Burke's observation about the National Assembly: "they are surrounded by an army not raised either by the authority of their crown or by their command, and which, if they should order to dissolve itself, would instantly dissolve them" (*BW* 3:320–21). Or he may have come to reflect on the auguries in Burke's description of the day (6 October 1789) on which the king and queen were "led in triumph" into Paris. "A group of regicide and sacrilegious slaughter was indeed boldly sketched" on that day. But it was, Burke emphasizes, "only sketched": "What hardy pencil of a great master, from the school of the rights of man, will finish it, is to be seen hereafter" (pp. 327–28). Whatever the specific predictions he had in mind, Wordsworth's linking of clauses in the First Address to the Westmoreland freeholders—"Time has verified his predictions; the books remain in which his principles of foreknowledge were laid down"—suggests that once he recognized the accuracy of Burke's forecast he would inevitably have turned to Burke's principles. So somewhere between 1793 and 1818 Wordsworth "returned," by way either of memory or of the printed word, to the writings that contained the untheoretical principles of this confirmed genius. But when?

The question has attracted mild interest over the years, somewhat stronger and better informed interest in the early part of this century than in the last few years. Very little of the pertinent evidence has been considered, however, even by those who thought to take the greatest care with the matter, and conclusions therefore tend to be substantially inaccurate.[26] The neglect of this question appears especially unfortunate when we consider that the development of Wordsworth's political ideas has been a central topic in studies of his writing; he is himself reported to have said that, "although he was known to the world as a poet, he had given twelve hours thought to the condition and prospect of society, for one to poetry."[27] Burke is a figure of such seminal importance for the political thought of the period in question, 1790–1835, that one might well believe it heuristically valuable to chart Wordsworth's ideological change against Burke's ideas even if Wordsworth had never mentioned his name. But the fact is that Wordsworth's poetry contains no praise for any political thinker, nor for any political position, that even remotely compares to his tribute to Burke and Burkeanism—a tribute that comes, moreover, after an early attack on the same man's teachings.

Three

A Poet's Reflections on the Revolution in France

Experience is with me.

Burke, *Reflections on the Revolution in France*

*B*ecause Burke is in these years, as Wordsworth's portrait suggests, a symbolic ideological presence and a figure larger than life, more is at stake in this case than the task of studying influence would normally entail.[1] And the dating of the influence is especially important because it involves some crucial issues of periodization within Wordsworth's intellectual career. Most critics and scholars have either argued or taken for granted that the structure of his intellectual biography falls into three parts. At the heart of this career all see what Arnold called the "golden decade" of 1797–1807, the period of his program for poetry and his most accomplished writing. On either side of this, there is the early radical period, when he was not yet a great poet, and the late conservative period, when his imagination stultified and he was no longer one. The strong commitment to Burkeanism is normally found in the later period, sometimes as early as the *Cintra* tract of 1809, sometimes not until 1818 or later.[2]

A careful consideration of the major poetry in the light of Burke's writings must lead one to challenge this understanding of Wordsworth's career. In this chapter I will be arguing that *The Prelude*, the magnum opus

31

of the great decade and Wordsworth's fullest attempt to deal with the French Revolution, is written from an ideological perspective that is thoroughly Burkean. In later chapters I will try to show that if we understand "conservative" to mean ideological proximity to Burke, then the visionary and experimental writing for which Wordsworth is revered, his program for poetry, is from its very inception impelled by powerfully conservative motives.[3]

I

In order to do justice to this task, it will first be necessary to develop a fuller and clearer sense than we have yet established of the sort of ideological position Wordsworth is likely to have associated with Burke's name. Since *The Prelude*'s tribute to the "Genius of Burke" includes a list of basic tenets, the best way to construct a working notion of Burke's doctrine may simply be to gloss these tenets seriatim with statements from Burke's own writings:

1. ". . . *denounces* . . . *all systems built on abstract rights* . . ."

The denunciation of "systems built on abstract rights" is a recurring gesture in Burke's political oratory. The allusion here might be to any one of a number of passages in Burke's published works. In the *Reflections*, for example, we read: "Government is not made in virtue of natural rights, which may and do exist in total independence of it,—and exist in much greater clearness, and in a much greater degree of abstract perfection" (*BW* 3:310). A nearby passage is also apposite: "The science of constructing a commonwealth, or renovating it, or reforming it, is, like every other experimental science, not to be taught *a priori*" (p. 311). In *An Appeal from the New to the Old Whigs* (1791), Burke restated his attack on French radical theorists this way: "These teachers are perfectly systematic. . . . They build their politics, not on convenience, but on truth; and they profess to conduct men to certain happiness by the assertion of their undoubted rights" (4:206). But this tenet, which Wordsworth quite properly lists first, bears on principles so primary in Burke that one may find possible sources for Wordsworth's lines all over Burke's writings. Further, to isolate a single passage is to run the risk of oversimplifying Burke's subtle and shifting argument about the role of abstract thought—or of "system," "theory," or "metaphysics"—in human life.

On the one hand, for example, Burke will say that he is no enemy of abstraction or of theory as such. Quite to the contrary:

> I do not put abstract ideas wholly out of any question; because I
> well know that under that name I should dismiss principles,
> and that without the guide and light of sound, well-understood
> principles, all reasonings in politics, as in everything else,
> would be only a confused jumble of facts and details, without
> the means of drawing out any sort of theoretical or practical
> conclusion. [7:41]

And in the passage quoted earlier from the *Reflections* we see Burke admit-
ting that "natural rights may and do exist" and that they even may have a
degree of "abstract perfection." Yet Burke will also claim, sometimes even
(as in this case) in the next breath, that "their abstract perfection is their
practical defeat" (3:310). And in order that there should be no mistake
about this second part of the claim, Burke will often (as again in this case)
go on to reassert the point even more vehemently: "in proportion as
[abstract rights] are metaphysically true, they are morally and politically
false" (p. 313). Such assertions are indeed commonplace in Burke. In a
speech of 1792 he declared: "No moral questions are ever abstract ques-
tions" (7:55). And in the *Appeal from the New to the Old Whigs* we find the
paradoxically self-exempting proposition: "Nothing universal can ratio-
nally be affirmed on any moral or any political subject" (4:80).

How, then, does abstraction function in human social affairs? The
answer is made difficult by the fact that Burke does not offer an abstract
account of this problem but presents the matter chiefly through pun and
metaphor. Conceptually, the central terms of this account cohere loosely
around the Aristotelian notion of an ethical mean: "extremes," "middle,"
"medium," "means," "end." But what really holds them together is the
multivalent punning on "medium." For Burke, as for Plato, perfectly
abstract ideas occur only as "extremes." Burke speaks of the "extreme
principles" (3:315) and the "perfections of extreme" (4:208) that he finds in
the writings of the French "professors": "The pretended rights of these
theorists are all extremes" (3:313); "Their principles always go to an
extreme" (4:206). Both Burke and Plato agree, furthermore, that human
beings do not live their lives in the world of such ideas. In Burke's terms, we
require a "medium." Where Burke and Plato differ is in their sense of the
demands this medium makes on our moral and political life. Plato insists
they must be resisted in and by the effort to reach the world of the abstract
ideas; Burke believes that these demands must be respected. Only the
pretended rights of man are extremes. The real rights of man, he says, "are
always in a sort of *middle*, incapable of definition, but not impossible to be
discerned" (3:313).[4]

To illustrate how he thinks abstract ideas behave in the human middle, Burke offers an analogy from Newtonian natural philosophy:

> These metaphysic rights entering into common life, like rays of light which pierce into a dense medium, are, by the laws of Nature, refracted from their straight line. Indeed, in the gross and complicated mass of human passions and concerns, the primitive rights of man undergo such a variety of refractions and reflections that it becomes absurd to talk of them as if they continued in the simplicity of their original direction. The nature of man is intricate; the objects of society are of the greatest possible complexity: and therefore no simple disposition or direction of power can be suitable either to man's nature or to the quality of his affairs. [p. 312]

To take the comparison with Plato just a step further, we might say that this is Burke's version of the analogue of the cave: both writers use optical metaphors to show what happens to pure ideas in human circumstances. But for Burke there is never really any stepping out of these circumstances to perceive the ideas as they are, never that moment of purely philosophical vision. On the assumption that human beings cannot escape their murky element, Burke professes the practical science of survival in that element.[5]

It is inconceivable that Plato could ever fault an opponent for building his system "on truth," as Burke does in the *Appeal from the New to the Old Whigs*. Then again, it may seem surprising that *anyone* would imagine laying such a charge at an opponent's doorstep. Burke's ensuing remarks in the *Appeal* explain how he means the criticism to be taken, and, since they offer a third-person summary of his own account in the *Reflections*, they also elaborate those central terms that cohere around the notion of the golden mean:

> The opinions maintained in that book [the *Reflections*] never can lead to an extreme, because their foundation is laid in an opposition to extremes . . . The foundation of government (those who have read the book will recollect) is laid in a provision for our wants and in a conformity to our duties: it is to purvey for the one, it is to enforce the other. These doctrines do of themselves gravitate to a middle point, or to some point near a middle. They suppose, indeed, a certain portion of liberty to be essential to all good government; but they infer that this liberty is to be blended into the government, to harmonize with its forms and its rules, and to be made subordinate to its end.

> Those who are not with that book are with its opposite; for there
> is no medium besides the medium itself. That medium is not
> such because it is found there, but it is found there because it is
> comformable to truth and Nature. [4:206–7]

Burke's way claims to lead us back to truth (and Nature) by not pretending
to start from an unshakably true premise. Such premises are necessarily
abstracted out of a medium with which they are no longer in touch. They
are always formulated as extremes opposed to the middle where life goes on.

2. *"the majesty proclaims / Of Institutes and Laws, hallowed by time"*

The second Burkean tenet in Wordsworth's list, properly enough,
identifies part of what Burke opposes to "abstract rights" in his view of
political legitimacy. Here again it is possible to correlate Wordsworth's
formulation with specific passages in Burke. Burke suggests in the *Reflec-
tions* that, "in the clumsy subtlety of their political metaphysics," the
French theorists have built a Revolution "upon a basis not more solid than
our present formalities." Their politics ought to have been grounded
instead on certain facts of social life that they do not even recognize as facts:

> Whilst they are possessed by these notions, it is vain to talk to
> them of the practice of their ancestors, the fundamental laws of
> their country, the fixed form of a Constitution, whose merits are
> confirmed by the solid test of long experience and an increasing
> public strength and national prosperity. They despise experi-
> ence as the wisdom of unlettered men; and as for the rest, they
> have wrought under ground a mine that will blow up at one
> grand explosion all examples of antiquity, all precedents, char-
> ters, and acts of Parliament. They have the "rights of men."
> [3:307]

The issue here is whether time renders laws and institutions less valid and
less legitimate, as the political metaphysicians in France claim, or more so.
In arguing the latter case, Burke relies on the mutually reinforcing doc-
trines of *prescription* and *presumption*, which he combines to form a political
antecedent to Darwin's biological doctrine of the fitness of survivors.

Prescription is the principle by which a claim to property or title may
be founded upon the fact of long possession, use, or practice; it is "the
establishment of rights by a long exercise of their corresponding powers."[6]
The right or "majesty" that is established by time or custom, however, does
not gain its authority by metaphysical certainty. We have indeed already
seen that human affairs do not in Burke's view admit of such certainty. In

these matters one reaches conclusions only by probable reasoning based on the preponderance of evidence.

In the *Reflections*, the doctrines of prescription and presumption inform virtually all of Burke's arguments concerning laws and institutions, especially those concerning the central law/institution of the land, the English constitution. His most explicit statement on this matter, however, actually comes eight years before the *Reflections*, in his famous *Speech on the Representation of the Commons in Parliament* (1782):

> Our Constitution is a prescriptive constitution; it is a constitu-
> tion whose sole authority is, that it has existed time out of mind
> . . . Prescription is the most solid of all titles, not only to
> property, but, which is to secure that property, to government.
> They harmonize with each other, and give mutual aid to one
> another. It is accompanied with another ground of authority in
> the constitution of the human mind, presumption. It is a
> presumption in favor of any settled scheme of government
> against any untried project, that a nation has long existed and
> flourished under it. [7:94]

Burleigh T. Wilkins, who has successfully reinstated the connection be-tween Burke and Hume made long ago in Sabine's *History of Political Theory*, has also offered some of the most perceptive comments about the doctrine of prescription. What is new about Hume and Burke, Wilkins writes, is "not the concept of prescription but the emphasis upon this concept as crucial to our understanding of political, social, and economic rights and ob-ligations."[7] Wilkins insists that for both thinkers, prescription is "an integral part of their overall deference to that which is, to the customs and conventions of society."[8] Again, for both thinkers, "social conventions such as rules for the acquisition and transmission of property are artificial in the sense of being man-made, but given man's social nature and the mutual dependence of men there is a sense in which they are natural as well" (p. 61). Prescription is one of the important components of the notion of second nature that links Wordsworth not only with Burke, but ultimately with Hume as well.[9]

3. *"Declares the vital power of social ties / Endeared by custom"*

As the previous tenet concerns matters of authority, so this one concerns matters of affection. The syntactical congruence between the two noun-participle phrases—"Institutes hallowed by time," "Social ties en-deared by custom"—betrays the underlying analogy that unites them. In both cases, the effect of long experience is taken to warrant trust rather than suspicion, and in both cases this trust becomes part of the proper basis for sound political organization. Society is for Burke not a machine made and manipulated by human calculation but an organism, and what gives life to the organism are the affective bonds that grow among society's members in the recurring practices of their daily lives.

Here again we have a notion that permeates the *Reflections*. The English, Burke says, "have given to our frame of polity the image of a relation in blood: binding up the Constitution of our country with our dearest domestic ties; adopting our fundamental laws into the bosom of our family affections" (3:275). It is most concisely formulated, however, in another of Burke's works, one which Wordsworth is known to have possessed soon after its publication in 1796, *Letters on a Regicide Peace*.[10] Burke's target again in this passage, as in almost everything he wrote in the 1790s, is the political metaphysics of the Continent:

> The operation of dangerous and delusive first principles obliges us to have recourse to the true ones . . . Men are not tied to one another by papers and seals. They are led to associate by resemblances, by conformities, by sympathies. It is with nations as with individuals. Nothing is so strong a tie of amity between nation and nation as correspondence in laws, customs, manners, and habits of life. They have more than the force of treaties in themselves. They are obligations written in the heart. They approximate men to men without their knowledge, and sometimes against their intentions. The secret, unseen, but irrefragable bond of habitual intercourse holds them together, even when their perverse and litigious nature sets them to equivocate, scuffle, and fight about the terms of their written obligations. [5:317–18]

Common experience creates common customs. Common customs form the basis of social resemblance. Social resemblance engenders sympathies between individuals and between groups. These sympathies amount to a set of "obligations written on the heart" that bond human beings and in some cases bring them together even in spite of conscious intentions or paper contracts to the contrary. Such is the genealogy of society's "vital" connections, the connections by virtue of which all other political links are formed.

4. *"Exploding upstart Theory"*

Burke's attack on theory goes hand in hand, as we have seen, with his attack on abstraction. Theory, for him, is the building of abstract system.

But just as he does not oppose abstraction as such, so he does not rule out theory, but only the elevation of theory to the status of necessity. The principles of prescription and presumption, for example, might well be called part of a political theory. But Burke regards them as principles that are developed in and derived from practice in ways that disallow their becoming grounds for social innovation. They can never become steps in a recipe by which a government is made from scratch. This would be to deny the validity of the practice in which these principles are embedded and from which their authority is derived. Burke was speaking to this same elusive point in his remarks on "the use of history" as a "guide of life." "From this source much political wisdom may be learned," he wrote, but immediately cautioned: "that is, may be learned as habit, not as precept" (4:468). In the *Reflections*, the relation between theory and historical practice is presented this way:

> Old establishments are tried by their effects. If the people are happy, united, wealthy, and powerful, we presume the rest. We conclude that to be good from whence good is derived. In old establishments various correctives have been found for their aberrations from theory. Indeed, they are the results of various necessities and expediences. They are not often constructed after any theory: theories are rather drawn from them. [3:460–61]

There is a place for theory in Burke's social thought. He does not "explode" it from the scene of politics altogether. But that place is just behind practice, not in front of it. Theory is soundest when it most follows political practice, maddest when it tries to lead the way.

5. *"insists / Upon the allegiance to which men are born"*

Recalling Dr. Johnson's famous declaration that "Patriotism is the last refuge of a scoundrel," one might be led to believe that Burke and his friend disagreed vehemently over this topic.[11] But we must not forget Boswell's qualification that Johnson "did not mean a real and generous love of our country, but that pretended patriotism which so many, in all ages and countries, have made a cloak for self-interest" (p. 615). If Boswell's interpolation is valid then Johnson and Burke may not be far apart on the question, for Burke, too, was concerned with the manipulation of patriotic sentiment for self-interested motives.

Burke's most celebrated formulation of his emphasis on "the allegiance to which men are born" occurs in that part of the *Reflections* where he is explaining why the French "speculatists" must not attempt to redescribe the boundaries of the ancient provinces:

> To be attached to the subdivision, to love the little platoon we belong to in society, is the first principle (the germ, as it were) of public affections. It is the first link in the series by which we proceed towards a love to our country and to mankind. The interest of that portion of social arrangement is a trust in the hands of all those who compose it; and as none but bad men would justify it in abuse, none but traitors would barter it away for their own personal advantage. [3:292]

We arrive at last at something that Burke is willing to call a "first principle." It is not for him an abstract first principle, however, and no system is deduced from it. It is simply offered as a fact: the affections radiate outward from the point on which we stand. Elsewhere in the *Reflections* he put it this way: "We begin our public affections in our families. No cold relation is a zealous citizen. We pass on to our neighborhoods, and our habitual provincial connections . . . so many little images of the great country in which the heart found something which it could fill" (p. 494).

After ourselves, we love our place, our family, our town, our nation. These concentric circles form the structure of the phenomenon called "love of kind." Eventually, but only through the mediation of the earlier and narrower affections, this outward movement extends to the human species generally. The reason Johnson and Burke are so concerned about self-interested abuse of the patriotic principle is that it is for them our only way out of selfishness. This principle is of course at the heart of Burke's doctrine of nationalism, which Cobban has elaborated, and Burke's practice tends to suggest that Burke is most concerned with its effect at this level of the nation.[12]

II

I have cited only enough of Burke's writings here to flesh out Wordsworth's summary of the doctrine and to show that Wordsworth's sketch of Burke and his thought finds ample corroboration in Burke's writings. But two aspects of this intellectual portrait deserve separate comment. First, though it is drawn from Wordsworth's middle-aged view of Burke, nothing in it stands at odds with Wordsworth's remarks about Burke in 1793; most of it, indeed, is implied there. Secondly, Wordsworth's account of Burke's thought, both early and late, is little marred by eccentricity and very much in line with what most of Burke's many commentators have taken to be his central ideas.

This second point is easily demonstrated by comparing this fleshed-out version of Wordsworth's sketch with the admirably concise summary recently offered by J. G. A. Pocock:

Burke held—to summarize what may be found in a hundred
text-books on the history of conservatism—that a nation's in-
stitutions were the fruit of its experience, that they had taken
shape slowly as the result, and were in themselves the record, of
a thousand adjustments to the needs of circumstance, each one
of which, if it had been found by trial and error to answer
recurrent needs, had been preserved in the usages and estab-
lished rules of the nation concerned. He also held that political
knowledge was the fruit of experience and that reason in this
field had nothing to operate on except experience; from which it
followed that, since the knowledge of an individual or a genera-
tion of individuals was limited by the amount of experience on
which it was based, there was always a case for the view that the
reason of the living, though it might clearly enough discern the
disadvantages, might not fully perceive the advantages of ex-
isting and ancient institutions, for these might contain the
fruits of more experience than was available to living indi-
viduals as the sum of their personal or reported experience of the
world. It also followed that since the wisdom embodied in
institutions was based on experience and nothing but experi-
ence, it could not be completely rationalized: that is, reduced to
first principles which might be clearly enunciated, shown to be
the cause of the institutions' first being set up, or employed to
criticize their subsequent workings. [13]

To reverse the order of Wordsworth's five tenets, filling in some gaps along
the way, is to discover an account of Burke's thought very close to Pocock's
deliberately neutral synopsis. One recurring term in Pocock's account—it
is used eight times—which does not occur in Wordsworth's tribute to the
genius of Burke is *experience*. And it is hard to quarrel with Pocock's
emphasis. Experience is a term that figures centrally in a number of Burke's
most central passages. When he says, for example, that the science of
constructing or reforming a commonwealth is an "experimental science,"
he means that it is taught by experience. "Nor is it a short experience," he
adds, "that can instruct us in that practical science" (3:311). While the
merits of the British Constitution have been confirmed "by the solid test of
long experience," the falsely enlightened theorists "despise experience as
the wisdom of unlettered men" p. 307.

The doctrine of what Pocock calls "experience and nothing but
experience" may even be said to provide a kind of common denominator for
all the tenets on Wordsworth's list. Experience is for Burke a way of
knowing the world nonabstractly. It conveys that special power on institu-

tions hallowed by time and on affections endeared by custom. It is the mode of practice rather than of theory. It spells the difference between the places to which one owes allegiance and those to which one does not. In the First Address to the Westmoreland freeholders, Wordsworth does speak of the importance of "uninquisitive experience" in connection with Burke, but not in the passage he adds to *The Prelude*. How could he fail to mention so crucial a Burkean notion in the more elaborate commentary added to *The Prelude*?

The answer, I think, is that Burke does not *need* to be depicted praising the virtues of experience, for he is himself the personification of Experience in this passage:

> I see him,—old, but vigorous in age,—
> Stand like an oak whose stag-horn branches start
> Out of its leafy brow, the more to awe
> The younger brethren of the grove.

The idea of experience personified here, moreover, is Burke's own—the idea that Pocock and others have rightly suggested is the basis of his political theory. But lest this idea be mistaken for one of the abstractions Wordsworth knew Burke distrusted, we must also recognize it as the *fact* of experience in Burke's own long career as thinker, writer, speaker, and of course as practicing politician. Following Burke's own notion of experience as simultaneously collective and personal, one is tempted to go further and see the "experience" personified here as the experience of the English people. Burke did, after all, offer himself in the *Reflections* as a kind of *genius loci* for the entire British Isles, and it may well be that he is meant to embody that English spirit in Wordsworth's passage.

Whether or not we choose to see the genius of Burke as the genius of England, it is nonetheless true that his spectral figure appears in book 7 to demand acknowledgment as the presiding genius of Wordsworth's personal and national epic. The poem is, indeed, as I shall argue later, Burkean in spirit from the start. This is not to suggest that Wordsworth could have written his tribute to Burke in 1798, or even in 1805. In acknowledging Burke's genius this passage also acknowledges Wordsworth's inability to write the passage sooner. Wordsworth may have been encouraged to compose it when he finally did because he was then reaching an age when he could himself plausibly aspire to the status of the elder statesman. The principal late portraits of the poet suggest a man concerned to represent himself in the posture of a sage, much as he represents Burke in book 7.[14] But if Wordsworth could not have written the tribute to Burke in the course of his composition of *The Prelude*, it is a fact too often overlooked that when he did write the tribute he thought it ideologically suited to the completed poem.[15]

III

One of the usual forms of evidence brought to bear in a case for intellectual influence is the verbal echo: the term, phrase, or idiom that sounds as if it comes from some earlier writing. Not surprisingly, such evidence is often adduced by those critics who have argued for Burke's influence on certain of Wordsworth's relatively late works, i.e., those written after his great decade. In making his case for the influence of Burke on *The Convention of Cintra*, for example, Cobban observed that Wordsworth's conclusions tend to be drawn "in phrases that wonderfully, and surely not accidentally, echo Burke."[16] Cobban's claim is certainly true, but he cites only a few examples. And though other scholars have cited others, one senses that the surface of the matter has barely been scratched.[17]

How much work remains to be done on the topic of Burke's influence on *Cintra* can be suggested by the example of an extended echo which has completely escaped critical notice.[18] The context for this passage is Wordsworth's suggestion that, since "Spain has nothing to dread from Jacobinism," the Spanish might profit by a reform of their Catholic institutions, such as was attempted in France in 1789, without fearing the consequences that attended the effort in France:

> Nor has the pestilential philosophism of France made any progress in Spain. No flight of infidel harpies has alighted upon their ground. A Spanish understanding is a hold too strong to give way to the meagre tactics of the "Système de la Nature;" or to the pellets of logic which Condillac has cast in the foundry of national vanity, and tosses about at hap-hazard—self-persuaded that he is proceeding according to art. The Spaniards are a people with imagination: and the paradoxical reveries of Rousseau, and the flippancies of Voltaire, are plants which will not naturalise in the country of Calderon and Cervantes. Though bigotry among the Spaniards leaves much to be lamented; I have proved that the religious habits of the nation must, in a contest of this kind, be of inestimable service. [PrW 1:332]

Spain is, in Wordsworth's view, a kind of hybrid of England and France. It has some of the former's virtue and some of the latter's vice. Wordsworth's hope for the Spaniards is that they will rely on their (English) virtue to rid themselves of their (French) vice. Here is the counterpart from the *Reflections*:

> We are not the converts of Rousseau; we are not the disciples of Voltaire; Helvetius has made no progress amongst us. Atheists [a few paragraphs later Burke calls them "Atheists and infidels"—p. 349] are not our preachers; madmen are not our law-givers. . . . In England we have not yet been completely embowelled of our natural entrails: we still feel within us, and we cherish and cultivate, those inbred sentiments which are the faithful guardians, the active monitors of our duty, the true supporters of all liberal and manly morals. [*BW* 3:345]

When Henry Crabb Robinson showed a copy of the *Cintra* pamphlet to his friend Thomas Quayle, the latter responded with a complaint about Wordsworth's long sentences, about their "containing a cluster of Metaphors," and summed up the pamphlet thus: "I don't know who may be the Author's Model:—His Style resembles the worst of Burke's,—But I do not expect that he himself will be a Model to any body else."[19] To compare the two attacks on Rousseau and Voltaire is to appreciate Quayle's hunch about Wordsworth's stylistic "Model," but it is also to understand that the debt extends beyond style. Wordsworth has fully taken over Burke's view of how French "philosophism" must be combated.

   Another such echo occurs in *Cintra* when Wordsworth takes over wholesale Burke's implied figure of the concentric circles of affection that, as we saw above, form the structure of patriotism and ultimately of the love of kind. In the final pages of his tract Wordsworth writes that the "order of life does not require that the sublime and disinterested feelings should have to trust long to their own unassisted power": "The outermost and all-embracing circle of benevolence has inward concentric circles which, like those of the spider's web, are bound together by links, and rest upon each other; making one frame, and capable of one tremor; circles narrower and narrower, closer and closer, as they lie more near to the centre of self from which they proceeded, and which sustains the whole" (*PrW* 1:340). My concern here, however, is not with *Cintra* but with *The Prelude*, where one also finds passages that, to use Cobban's phrase, "wonderfully, and surely not accidentally, echo Burke." These echoes have been even less frequently noticed, for the simple reason that even fewer readers have thought to listen for them there.[20] Cobban's discussion of Wordsworth and Burke is typical of this neglect. In fact, at least one of the passages Cobban hears echoed in *Cintra* is also echoed in *The Prelude*. In discussing the tract, Cobban singles out Wordsworth's assertion that "There is a spiritual community binding together the living and the dead; the good, the brave, and the wise, of all ages" (*PrW* 1:339).[21] Cobban is obviously recalling the famous passage in the *Reflections* in which Burke writes that "Society is, indeed, a contract":

> It is a partnership in all science, a partnership in all art, a partnership in every virtue and in all perfection. As the ends of such a partnership cannot be obtained in many generations, it becomes a partnership not only between those who are living, but between those who are living, those who are dead, and those who are to be born. [*BW* 3:359]

Apart from stating so central a Burkean belief, this passage is especially germane to the subject of Wordsworth's ideological development since it is the same one he ridiculed in the Letter to Llandaff, citing its doctrine as an example of Burke's "unnatural cruelty." The passage in *Cintra*, however, merely elaborates a sentiment recorded in book 10 of *The Prelude*: "There is / One great society alone on earth: / The noble living and the noble dead" (967–69).[22] Furthermore, it elaborates these lines with material also to be found in the poem.[23]

Other telling echoes of Burke in the France books can be found in passages where Wordsworth, in Burkean fashion, turns jacobin language against the jacobin position. Book 9, for example, describes those curious moments when Wordsworth "slipped in thought" from his "earnest dialogues" with Michel Beaupuy to muse upon the legendary chateaux of the Loire Valley. Wordsworth says that at such times the imagination, though indignant at certain wrongs associated with these places, "Did often mitigate the force / Of civic prejudice, the bigotry, / So call it, of a youthful patriot's mind" (499–501). The use of "prejudice" and "bigotry" to describe the mind of the enlightened rationalist is a page taken straight from Burke, who could so readily embrace his own prejudices partly because he believed that France's "atheistical fathers have a bigotry of their own" and that "they have learnt to talk against monks with the spirit of a monk" (*BW* 3:379). And as if to prove that his account of the slip of the mind in book 9 was no slip of the tongue, Wordsworth comes back to this Burkean topos in book 11, where he describes himself in his most rigorously syllogistic phase. He was then, he says, "A bigot to a new idolatry," and, "like a monk who had forsworn the world" did he "Zealously labour to cut off [his] heart / From all the sources of her former strength" (75–78).

The passages I have cited from *The Prelude*, echoing as they do Burke's central statements about a society that binds generations one to another and about the allegedly fatal self-exempting fallacy of jacobin argument, have implications that must run deeper than mere verbal mimicry. By themselves they offer evidence enough to warrant looking more carefully at *The Prelude*'s affinity with Burke's thought and its debt to his writings. In any analysis of this kind, however, one must be prepared to consider evidence other than verbal echo as such, and this is especially true of the present case. There is first of all, as I have tried to suggest, good reason for suspecting that Wordsworth would not at this time have been able to echo Burke in any way that might count as an allusion to Burke's writings. Though his polemical attack on Burke in the Letter to Llandaff had not been published, we must keep in mind the Letter's fervent and unyielding insistence on the ignominy of changing one's political mind. For the young Wordsworth, no political crime was more heinous, not even that of the tyrant himself.[24]

Secondly, at the time of his work on the France books Wordsworth's historical, personal, and rhetorical relation to the experience of the Revolution was very different from Burke's. *The Reflections* are written against what Burke takes to be the French ideology at a time when that ideology posed, in his view, an imminent threat to English security. Wordsworth's reflections on the French Revolution are likewise inimical to French ideology, but he writes as a man who was once, in a time he calls his "youth" and under special circumstances, drawn to accept that ideology. Although Wordsworth may be said to write for much the same audience as Burke did, that audience is now, like Wordsworth himself, a decade older. Their hopes for the Revolution, insofar as they had hopes for it, are now past. There is not the same urgency in denouncing (or, as in some cases renouncing) what the jacobins thought. In the early 1800s, Napoleon's French army poses a more immediate threat to England than Rousseau's French ideology. In such circumstances, the ideology itself can be examined more dispassionately, less xenophobically.

A third consideration that affects what should count as evidence in this matter is related to the first two. Because narrative point of view in *The Prelude* is constantly shifting, especially in the France books, it is very difficult to find anything like straightforward political commentary such as one finds in Burke's *Reflections* or in Wordsworth's Letter to Llandaff or his tract on Cintra. To establish the authorial viewpoint on political and social issues, as on any other issues, one must sort through some difficult changes in perspective. One discerns three distinct ideological points of view in the poem. I have already mentioned one, the authorial point of view, that of the poet who reviews his revolutionary experience from a position that purports to make political as well as psychological and poetic sense of it. Secondly, there is the changing perspective of the young Wordsworth who moves through the celebrated times and places described in the poem. These two perspectives play off one another in the poem in complex ways reminiscent of certain kinds of first-person fiction or perhaps, on a smaller scale, of first-person Romantic lyrics. Another helpful analogue is Hegel's *Phenomenology of Spirit*, a work composed at about the same time by a man just Wordsworth's age (b. 1770) with a strikingly similar history of political sympathies. M. H. Abrams's comments on the parallels between these two texts as Bildungsromans need not be repeated here.[25] What is germane is that in Hegel's autobiography of Spirit, as in Wordsworth's autobiography of Imagination, the narrative argument tends to modulate in and out of the earlier, unformed consciousness. The reader can find himself at a loss to determine the meaning of a given passage in either text for precisely the same reason: a subtle shift in standpoint has occurred unannounced.

One consequence of this kind of subtle modulation in *The Prelude* is that, despite the obvious differences between the early and the later positions, they come to be united by a bond of affinity. That is to say, once the positions are set in this relation to each other, they can be posed over against a third political point of view in the poem, that of the French revolutionists themselves, just as England (both past and present) is made to stand over against France. Besides the relation of the mature Wordsworth to his earlier self, two other relations are therefore possible: that of the young Wordsworth to "France" and that of the older Wordsworth to "France." Wordsworth writes the France books from a doctrinal position toward France very like the one that, both in 1793 and 1818, he recognized as Burke's. Yet he needs at the same time to make plausible his own earlier relationship with French political thought, by showing its continuity with his present views.

Some of these suggestions can be tested by looking at the first lines of the famous passage that is the heart of *The Prelude*'s discussion of the Revolution, the only part of the France books to appear in print during Wordsworth's lifetime:

> O pleasant exercise of hope and joy,
> For great were the auxiliars which then stood
> Upon our side, we who were strong in love.
> Bliss was it in that dawn to be alive,
> But to be young was very heaven! O times,
> In which the meagre, stale, forbidding ways

Of custom, law, and statute took at once
The attraction of a country in romance—
When Reason seemed the most to assert her rights
When most intent on making of herself
A prime enchanter to assist the work
Which then was going forwards in her name.

                                         [10:689–700]

The importance of phenomenological dialectic in this passage is suggested
by the title Wordsworth gave it when he published it in Coleridge's *The
Friend* in 1810: "The French Revolution: As it Appeared to Enthusiasts at
its Commencement." For Wordsworth is dealing with the Revolution,
clearly, not only as it appeared to enthusiasts, but also as that appearance
appears to Wordsworth as the author of *The Prelude*.

Consider, for example, the handling of that important Burkean
slogan about usage: "the ways / Of custom, law, and statute." Although the
author of *The Prelude* writes that these were "meagre, stale, and forbidding"
in the eyes of the enthusiasts, his claim cannot be accepted as it stands. The
enthusiasts would never have attributed such qualities to, or used such
adjectives for, the ways of custom, law, and statute. They would have
said—did say—that the ways of custom to men had been unjustifiable,
unjust, favoritist, outmoded, irrational, unnatural, and so on. But never
"meagre, stale, and forbidding." Just as clearly, the young Wordsworth
could not have accepted the description of the new appearance of custom's
ways as taking on the attraction of a country in romance. The appearance
was for them that of the present world—in a future state, to be sure, but for
them just as real as ever. For most of them the future society was if anything
more real, because more rational, than the delusory world of status quo
slavery and falsehood.

Reason is the topic of the very next clause, which perhaps makes the
point even more plainly: "Reason seemed the most to assert her rights /
When most intent on making of herself / A prime enchanter to assist the
work / Which then was going forward in her name." This formulation
implies a contradiction. The Reason of the enthusiasts wields its greatest
authority in its (or their) most irrational moments. This contradiction is
clearly perceived, and intended for our notice, by the author of *The Prelude*.
Yet it just as clearly is not apparent to the young rationalists for whom
Reason is supposed to "seem" as it does. To reach an accurate sense of the
point of view that controls the poem, then, we must ask ourselves: from

what sort of perspective might the French Revolution be said to appear to its enthusiasts in this particular, contradictory way? So far the signs point to a perspective much like Burke's.

And there are still other signs. R. D. Havens long ago observed of these lines: "it is not generally realized that they refer less to the Revolution as a whole than to the enthusiasm aroused by the Revolution in theories of government."[26] The remark is accurate enough, but I believe it misses the point of the ironic portrayal of the Revolution's dislocation of practice into theory—the portrayal of the Revolution advanced by Burke. One last sign worth mentioning is the language of fantasy Wordsworth uses to discuss the rationalist mind, for Burke can lay a strong claim to such metaphors. Burke's insinuation that the political theorists of the Revolution live in a romantic fairyland is latent in his descriptions of the human rights they advocate as "pretended" and "imaginary." It is more explicit in his criticisms of their "hocus-pocus of abstraction" and of the Jacobins' "sleight of hand" (4:17). Most explicit of all is Burke's initial use of the metaphor in his early *Vindication of Natural Society* (1756), where he speaks of the "abuse of reason" in the "fairy land of philosophy"." (1:5).[27] This is just the sort of metaphor Wordsworth employs to describe the effect of abstract philosophy on his sense of belonging to a transgenerational human community: "as by the simple waving of a wand, / The wizard instantaneously dissolves / Palace or grove, even so did I unsoul / As readily by syllogistic words / . . . / Those mysteries of passion which have made / . . . / One brotherhood of all the human race / Through all the habitations of past years" (*Prel* 11:79–89).

None of this is meant to suggest that Burke could himself have written a passage resembling Wordsworth's. The empathic identification with the young English jacobins would have been impossible for Burke both psychologically (he was not one of them) and politically (the allure of this sort of identification was part of the very power he sought to dispel). Adequately interpreted, however, Wordsworth's lines take a stand that resembles Burke's stand very closely. The speculative self-indulgence Wordsworth describes, though apparently born of love and joy and undertaken in behalf of the rights of men, is the exercise of a faculty that has lost its temper. And in the remaining pages of Wordsworth's reflections on the Revolution, we see this self-indulgence turning into self-destruction for English sympathizers—for the French revolutionists it leads to the destruction of fellow citizens as well. The action of books 10 and 11 unfolds to show an ill-tempered Reason put to uses that play havoc with the English poet's mind and the French national welfare.

This leads to a fourth and final reason why one cannot rely too exclusively on verbal reminiscence to establish the extent of Burke's influence on Wordsworth's political reflections. Burkean assumptions tend to sink down into the France books, not to float near the surface. The central catastrophe of the France books—it is also that of the poem as a whole—is recounted under both its social and mental aspects from Burke's point of view. Burkean conceptions seem to underlie the very scheme according to which both social and mental events are narrated. Beginning, middle, and end, the story of this young Englishman's experience with France has, I would argue, all been told before. Though verbal echoes can help to show that Wordsworth's story is such a retelling of Burke's, the real debt runs deeper.[28]

IV

If we wished to single out a starting point for the action of the France books, we might choose Wordsworth's conversations with Michel Beaupuy, since it is from Beaupuy that Wordsworth first began to think and argue abstractly about political matters. Beaupuy gives him his first lessons in the pleasant exercise of political theory, and it is also in the account of these "earnest dialogues" with Beaupuy that the reader of the 1805 *Prelude* (that is, the text without the "Genius of Burke" lines from book 7) first encounters the Burkean code words:

> Oft in solitude
> With him did I discourse about the end
> Of civil government, and its wisest forms,
> Of ancient prejudice and chartered rights,
> Allegiance, faith, and laws by time matured,
> Custom and habit, novelty and change,
> Of self-respect, and virtue in the few
> For patrimonial honour set apart,
> And ignorance in the labouring multitude.
>
> [9:328–36]

Although these topics happen to resemble those listed by Burke in certain parts of the *Reflections*, Wordsworth seems to invite us, probably not unreasonably, to regard them as constituting a predictable litany for the early 1790s. We are also invited to take note of their balanced arrangement, however, which suggests that both sides of these complex questions are being weighed by the young philosophers. The ensuing lines come as an explanation for this intellectual judiciousness. Well-balanced thoughts come from steady minds:

> For he, an upright man and tolerant,
> Balanced these contemplations in his mind,
> And I, who at that time was scarcely dipped
> Into the turmoil, had a sounder judgement
> Than afterwards, carried about me yet
> With less alloy to its integrity
> The experience of past ages, as through help
> Of books and common life it finds its way
> To youthful minds. . . .
>
> [337–45]

"Afterwards" is the foreshadowing word that looks ahead to the unbridled speculation recorded in books 10 and 11. The difference between now and afterwards for Wordsworth, what makes his judgment sound in the first instance but not in the second, is explicitly identified by the Burkean phrase "the experience of past ages."

Though the conversations with Beaupuy may have sent Wordsworth marching down that road of excess to Versailles (for Burke, a palace of folly), these are not the first French conversations Wordsworth records in book 9. There is the prior encounter with the Royalist soldiers in Orleans, who, as he says, did not "disdain / The wish to bring [him] over to their cause" (199–200). And despite the fact that Wordsworth opposes these ignoble aristocrats in the name of liberty and equality, this passage actually provides the necessary background for understanding what is meant about a hundred and fifty lines later by "the experience of past ages." For just as clearly as in the Beaupuy episodes, Wordsworth also represents himself here as a young man guided by an ancient source of "experience."

Part of what it means for Wordsworth to be so guided is that he is supposed to have no specific instruction in political philosophy. He states explicitly that he was at this time "untaught by thinking or by books /To reason well of polity or law, / And nice distinctions—then on every tongue— / Of natural rights and civil" (201–4). He is further supposed to have been "almost indifferent" then "to acts / Of Nations and their passing interests" (204–7). One might suspect Wordsworth of exaggeration here, but the present concern is simply with his representation of himself at this time. In view of such massive ignorance, we are meant to suppose, Wordsworth should have been the easy mark the Royalists took him for. Despite the odds, however, he remains unconvinced by the Royalist arguments. Indeed, "in their weakness strong," as he says, he "triumphed" (266–67).

Recounting here an event that calls out for an explanation, Wordsworth also does his best to provide one. He says he owes his success over the Orleans aristocrats to the personal history he has recorded in books 1 through 8; that is, to his good egalitarian English rearing and his good egalitarian English education at Cambridge. Newly arrived in France, the young Wordsworth still carried this experience with him "unalloyed." The only surprise, as it turns out, would have been his defeat at the Royalists' hands:

> It could not be
> But that one tutored thus, who had been formed
> To thought and moral feeling in the way
> This story hath described, should look with awe
> Upon the faculties of man, receive
> Gladly the highest promises, and hail
> As best the government of equal rights
> And individual worth.
>
> [242–49]

But in what sense were Wordsworth's moral sentiments formed by the experience of *past* ages? The answer is that "England" is the product of ages-old experience and that in tutoring Wordsworth it is conferring on him the benefit of this long experience. This is indicated at the start of Wordsworth's explanation, where he says not only that he was born in England (191–92) but also that he was born in a district "which yet / Retaineth more of ancient homeliness, / Manners erect, and frank simplicity, / Than any other nook of English land" (218–21).

We must not be misled here by Wordsworth's claim to egalitarian sentiment or by the familiar domesticity of this passage. Burke believed, or argued anyway, that no one exceeded him in championing the cause of equality. But his cause was that of the ancient English tradition of equality, handed down from father to son—not the egalitarianism generated out of cosmopolitan discussion of the abstract rights of men. The stronger the chain through which the manners and attitudes of this way of life are passed on, the better the chance they will be retained. The English sense of equality is both an inherent and an inherited characteristic of "ancient homeliness." In his famous *Conciliation* speech on America (1775), Burke defended his plan for reforming colonial affairs from the objection that it was rashly innovative. His proposal, he said,

is the genuine produce of the ancient, rustic, manly, home-bred
sense of this country. I did not dare to rub off a particle of the
venerable rust that rather adorns and preserves than destroys the
metal. It would be profanation to touch with a tool the stones
which construct the sacred altar of peace. I would not violate
with modern polish the ingenuous and noble roughness of these
truly constitutional materials. Above all things, I was resolved
not to be guilty of tampering, the odious vice of restless and
unstable minds. I put my foot in the tracks of our forefathers,
where I can neither wander nor stumble.[29] [*BW* 2:156]

Burke is best known for defending his English sense of tradition from
working-class attacks, and these defenses have created a misleading sense of
where he stood on these matters, even in the works of the 1790s. The
language of the family, so dominant in works like the *Reflections*, is ulti-
mately rooted in the kind of rustic domesticity Burke discusses here.[30] I
make no claim here that Wordsworth knew the celebrated *Conciliation*
speech, though it is certainly one of the books in which Burke's "principles
of foreknowledge" were laid down. What I do claim is that the above
passage is an accurate version of Burke's vision of tradition, what he calls the
"collected reason of the ages" (*BW* 3:357), and of that "long experience"
which he says is necessary to political and moral virtue.

Too much attention to verbal echo can, I suggested, blind us to
deeper lines of congruity between Wordsworth and Burke. An example in
point is Wordsworth's description of how the Royalists' arguments
"seemed" to him at the time:

> Every word
> They uttered was a dart by counter-winds
> Blown back upon themselves; their reason seemed
> Confusion-stricken by a higher power
> Than human understanding, their discourse
> Maimed, spiritless. . . .
>
>   [261–66]

This passage contains no distinguishable echo of Burke. Implicit in it,
however, is a powerful sense of the providential wisdom that resides in the
wealth of experience. Wordsworth uses no arguments to defeat his oppo-
nents because no arguments are needed. Their words are reduced to babble
by the same God who made the young Englishman wise enough to see their
error—the God whose authority is claimed by Burke.

One of the most fundamental principles of Wordsworth's reflections, as of Burke's, is that experience of the past diminishes as a guiding political force in direct proportion to one's indulgence of abstract political theory—in proportion as one begins, that is, "To think with fervour upon management / Of nations—what it is and ought to be" (10:685–86). It is a principle developed by Burke not primarily to remedy the situation of the French radicals themselves, but to warn about what happens to the young Englishmen who enlist in their ranks. In the *Appeal from the New to the Old Whigs*, Burke put the matter concisely. According to the theory of the French politicians, he explained, "doctrines admit no limit, no qualification whatsoever." Thus: "No man can say how far he will go, who joins with those who are avowedly going to the utmost extremities. What security is there for stopping short at all in these wild conceits?" (*BW* 4:205) The principle stated here is pointedly illustrated in the distended book 10 of the 1805 *Prelude*, the "middle" of the France narrative. Indeed, with this and other such Burkean passages in mind it becomes virtually impossible to read book 10 without seeing it as an extended gloss on Burke. Here, for example, is Wordsworth's account of the period following the establishment of the Directory:

> This was the time when, all things tending fast
> To depravation, the philosophy
> That promised to abstract the hopes of man
> Out of his feelings, to be fixed thenceforth
> For ever in a purer element,
> Found ready welcome. Tempting region that
> For zeal to enter and refresh herself,
> Where passions had the privilege to work,
> And never hear the sound of their own names—
> But, speaking more in charity, the dream
> Was flattering to the young ingenuous mind
> Pleased with extremes, and not the least with that
> Which makes the human reason's naked self
> The object of its fervour. What delight!—
> How glorious!—in self-knowledge and self-rule
> To look through all the frailties of the world,
> And, with a resolute mastery shaking off
> The accidents of nature, time, and place,
> That make up the weak being of the past,
> Build social freedom on its only basis:

The freedom of the individual mind,
Which, to the blind restraint of general laws
Superior, magisterially adopts
One guide—the light of circumstances, flashed
Upon an independent intellect.

[10:805–29]

Compared to the earlier passage about political theory ("O pleasant exercise of hope and joy . . ."), Wordsworth seems less concerned here to establish the plausibility of his youthful views and more concerned to show their error. We therefore find more densely and explicitly in these lines the terms and slogans of the position Wordsworth attributed to Burke first in 1793 and then again in 1818 and after.

One does not have to listen hard, I think, to hear in these lines Burke's attacks on the misleadingly "pure" realm of political metaphysics, or on the self-defeating effort to abstract principles entirely from feeling and passion, or on the delusive weakness of the naked, unhabituated reason. Besides hearing such echoes, however, one must recognize a whole constellation of derivative ideas at work. Wordsworth's account of this radical philosophy is that it seeks to chart out a human future based on "the hopes of man" without respect to what Burke repeatedly calls the medium of human life and what Wordsworth here calls "the accidents of nature, time, and place." In such philosophy, as Wordsworth presents it, the "infirmities" of this medium are presumed to belong to a past human condition with which coming times will be discontinuous, just as the pure realm of their abstract philosophy is (as they falsely assume) discontinuous with the quotidian world of human feeling. The usual Burkean puns also operate in this constellation, either explicitly or implicitly. Pure abstraction is the product of human reason in extremity. Reason in extremity stands in opposition to reason in the medium; that is, reason through habits and the accidents of nature, time, and place. It is also reason in the extremes of Platonic absolutes, such as the Ideas of light and darkness. One wonders if reason in extremity is not also reason in the altogether, what Burke called the human reason's naked self.

But Burke's remarks about the degeneration of a mind beset with theory hold still deeper implications for the story of Wordsworth in France. To see these implications we must return to Burke's ominous rhetorical question in the *Appeal from the New to the Old Whigs*: "What security is there for stopping short at all in these wild conceits?" This is his answer:

Why, neither more nor less than this,—that the moral senti-
ments of some few amongst them do put some check on their
savage theories. But let us take care. The moral sentiments, so
nearly connected with early prejudice as to be nearly one and the
same thing, will assuredly not live long under a discipline
which has for its basis the destruction of all prejudices, and the
making the mind proof against all dread of sequences flowing
from the pretended truths that are taught by their philosophy.
[*BW* 4:205]

The moral sentiments can check the power of this philosophy, but only up
to a point. To place them too long under its savage discipline is to risk one's
moral life.

V

Burke's writings on the Revolution offer a scheme that explains the course
not only of Wordsworth's decline in *The Prelude* but also of his crisis and
recovery. France is the land of abstract speculation. Young Wordsworth is
introduced to such speculation early, but his moral sentiments, formed on
the strength of ancient, homebred, English experience, preserved him from
moral harm through even repeated exposure to danger. Although "from the
first, wild theories were afloat," he says that for a long time he "had but lent
a careless ear" to their "subtleties" (10:774–76). In this school, however,
the moral sentiments must grow weaker every day, and eventually Words-
worth falls vulnerable to near despair. As "events brought less encourage-
ment," he was impelled, as he later puts it, to find a new "proof of
principles": "evidence / Safer, of universal application, such / As could not
be impeached, was sought elsewhere" (788–90). "Elsewhere," of course,
turns out to be that "purer element" of abstraction and naked reason.

    The Prelude shows the young Wordsworth pursuing almost to comple-
tion the course of moral self-annihilation Burke described in 1790. He
describes himself at war with himself, laboring to cut off his heart from "all
the sources of her former strength" (11:78) and nearly succeeding. So
vigorous a campaign did he wage against himself that, in what he would
later call "the crisis of that strong disease, / The soul's last and lowest ebb,"
he is finally supposed to have lost all feeling of conviction and to have given
up on moral questions. What makes this moment in *The Prelude* interesting
both in itself and in relation to Burke is that it deliberately heightens the
parallels between the social and the psychological aspects of the Revolution:

          Thus I fared,
Dragging all passions, notions, shapes of faith,
Like culprits to the bar, suspiciously
Calling the mind to establish in plain day
Her titles and her honours, now believing,
Now disbelieving, endlessly perplexed
With impulse, motive, right and wrong, the ground
Of moral obligation—what the rule,
And what the sanction—till, demanding proof,
And seeking it in every thing, I lost
All feeling of conviction, and, in fine,
Sick, wearied out with contrarieties,
Yielded up moral questions in despair. . . .

                                        [10:888–900]

The moral sentiments, according to Burke, "so nearly connected with early prejudice as to be nearly one and the same thing, will assuredly not live long under a discipline which has for its basis the destruction of all prejudices." That the sentiments under attack in Wordsworth's crisis, the sources of his former strength, are all supposed to be intimately connected with his prejudices is clear from the metaphor of the tribunal. (That they are connected with his early prejudices is clear from the whole structure of *The Prelude*.)[31] The crisis passage presents that debilitating process in which emotions that ought to be taken as "already judged," and therefore as the basis for other judgments, are themselves subjected to the most rigorous inquisition. "False" bottoms continue to fall away under the weight of analysis, and Wordsworth is left with no moral ground on which to stand.

    This same figure of the court of reason also heightens the social-psychological parallels in the overall narrative. For Wordsworth's metaphor analogizes the epistemological challenge to the mind's prejudices (its "passions, notions, shapes of faith") with a legal challenge to prescriptive rights. "Titles" (892) is glossed quite properly in the recent Norton edition of the poem as "deeds to prove legal entitlement." The rationalist challenge to titles and honors is thus the Revolution's challenge to those time-honored rights that stem not from deductive proof but simply from long usage. In fact, Wordsworth's metaphor clarifies the analogue between Burke's crucial concepts in a way that even Burke himself never did. Prescriptive rights are like prejudices in that they, too, are already judged, Wordsworth seems to imply, and his readers would have been well aware that courts like those set up to challenge privileges and prescriptive titles in

France later sat in judgment on the very lives of the French men and women in question. What Wordsworth has ultimately offered here, in other words, is an analogue between his psychological crisis and the Reign of Terror itself.

Reading through Wordsworth's France narrative in the light of Burke's writings, especially those of 1790 and 1791, one is tempted to conclude that Burke accurately predicted the fate of young English radicals like Wordsworth in considerable detail, just as he predicted so much about the Reign of Terror. To draw such a conclusion, however, would be to take *The Prelude*'s account of that crisis at face value. On the other hand if my claims about Burke's influence are in any way true, we may face a far more complicated matter than this straightforward notion of prediction would suggest. We can safely presume that *something* eventually befell Wordsworth—some form of disappointment, let us say, with the course of the Revolution—and that this led him to reconsider what he came to call Burke's "principles of foreknowledge." But to the extent that he already accepts these principles at the time the France books were composed, they inevitably influence the retrospective account of the experience as we read it there. To put it another way, Burke's comments may seem to anticipate Wordsworth's crisis so completely simply because Wordsworth used Burke's terms to reconstruct it. While it would be impossible to determine just to what extent we have a matter of Burke's prediction, on the one hand, and of Wordsworth's Burkean reconstruction, on the other, two facts are pertinent. Many scholars have expressed great difficulty in locating in Wordsworth's mid-twenties a crisis of precisely the same description as the one we find in *The Prelude*. Secondly, there is the Letter to Llandaff, which, as my earlier discussion means to suggest, does not finally sound like the work of the mind represented in books 10 and 11.

If Burke's anticipation of the debility and crisis depicted in *The Prelude* is striking, what is more striking and perhaps more important is the way he anticipates its depiction of recovery. For in that same passage from the *Appeal* Burke said that only a person's moral sentiments, if they could somehow survive theory's inquisition, can save the mind from the false dominion of the naked reason. Late in book 10 Wordsworth offers a proleptic account of the regenerative process he more amply describes in the famous "spots of time" passage in book 11:

> Nature's self, by human love
> Assisted, through the weary labyrinth
> Conducted me again to open day,

Revived the feelings of my earlier life,
Gave me that strength and knowledge full of peace,
Enlarged, and never more to be disturbed,
Which through all the steps of our degeneracy,
All degradation of this age, hath still
Upheld me, and upholds me at this day
In the catastrophe (for so they dream
And nothing less), when, finally to close
And rivet up the gains of France, a Pope
Is summoned in to crown an Emperor. . . .

                                                                [10:921–33]

The feelings of Wordsworth's earlier life, whose revival saves him from a
tragic fate in *The Prelude*, resemble in both kind and function those
redemptive sentiments that Burke claimed were so intimately connected
with early prejudice. When the careful reader of *The Prelude* reaches this
passage he or she should already be aware of the Englishness of these revived
feelings because prior passages, such as the Royalists episode in book 9,
have already told where these feelings came from and what they were like
when still strong. That sense is confirmed in the reference to Napoleon and
to the present state of France. The French suffer the degrading spectacle of a
papal coronation, never fulfilling their apparent national promise, because
of their age-old infatuation with papist splendor and arbitrary power.

Such evidence suggests how firmly the France books align themselves
not only with Burke, but with the entire Whig tradition he claimed to be
upholding. This is precisely the political tradition, dating from the first
Whigs of the 1670s, that views France as the seat of Royalist papism and as
a threat to the rights provided for by the English constitution.[32] Even in his
severest strictures against the overthrow of the French government in 1789,
Burke never depicted that government as the equal of England's. In a
speech on French affairs delivered (on 9 February 1790) before the publica-
tion of the *Reflections*, Burke gave a fuller account of his view of the French
monarchy than the rhetorical aims of the *Reflections* itself would allow. The
context here is a discussion of why "France, by the mere circumstance of its
vicinity, had been, and in a degree always must be, an object of our
vigilance, either with regard to her actual power or to her influence and
example," and the example in question is the "perfect despotism" of Louis
XIV:

Though that despotism was proudly arrayed in manners, gal-
lantry, splendor, magnificence, and even covered over with the
imposing robes of science, literature, and arts, it was, in gov-

ernment, nothing better than a painted and gilded tyranny,—
in religion, a hard, stern intolerance, the fit companion and
auxiliary to the despotic tyranny which prevailed in its govern-
ment. The same character of despotism insinuated itself into
every court of Europe,—the same spirit of disproportioned
magnificence,—the same love of standing armies, above the
ability of the people. In particular, our then sovereigns, King
Charles and King James, fell in love with the government of
their neighbor, so flattering to the pride of kings. A similarity
of sentiments brought on connections equally dangerous to the
interests and liberties of their country. It were well that the
infection had gone no farther than the throne. . . . The good
patriots of that day, however, struggled against it. They sought
nothing more anxiously than to break off all communication
with France, and to beget a total alienation from its country and
its example. [*BW* 3: 216–17]

Burke did not consider Louis XVI the despot his grandfather was, but
neither would he have thought any French monarch, or any French Royal-
ist, beyond the influence of France's inveterate penchant for splendor and
magnificence, paint and gilding. Such courtly excesses may have been
preferable to what Burke regarded as the barbarism of the Revolution, but
they could never compare favorably with the "ancient, rustic, manly,
homebred sense" of the English. Burke claims that the solid habits of the
English patriots prevented the French infection from spreading beyond the
throne of Charles and James in the seventeenth century, and *The Prelude*
shows these same native habits saving Wordsworth from the rhetoric of the
Royalists in book 9 and ultimately from the double reign of terror described
in book 10.[33]

As with other issues we have considered, so with this one: what is
implicit in Wordsworth's major poetry becomes explicit in his later prose.
Burke's "good patriots" of the 1670s are the major prototypes of what he
comes to call the "Old Whigs." It would appear that Wordsworth has the
same men in mind when, in addressing the Westmoreland Freeholders, he
laments the recent decay of "that tree of Whiggism, which flourished
proudly under the cultivation of our Ancestors" (*PrW* 3:162). And, like the
Burke of the *Appeal from the New to the Old Whigs*, Wordsworth explains that
the new Whigs go wrong precisely by failing to cultivate in themselves the
traits of their political ancestors: skepticism toward France and a corre-
sponding confidence in native British character and practice. The new
Whigs, according to the forty-eight-year-old poet, had in effect destroyed
the balance of power between the two parties,

by holding, from the beginning of the French Revolution, such
a course as introduced in Parliament, discord among them-
selves; deprived them, in that House and elsewhere, of the
respect which from their Adversaries they had been accustomed
to command; turned indifferent persons into enemies; and
alienated, throughout the Island, the affections of thousands
who had been proud to unite with them. This weakness and
degradation, deplored by all true Friends of the Commonweal,
was sufficiently accounted for, without even adverting to the
fact that—when the disasters of the war had induced the Coun-
try to forgive, and in some degree, to forget, the alarming
attachment of that Party to French theories: and power, height-
ened by the popularity of hope and expectation, was thrown
into their hands—they disgusted even bigotted adherents, by
the rapacious use they made of that power;—stooping to so
many offensive compromises, and committing so many faults in
every department, that, a Government of Talents, if such be the
fruits of talent, was proved to be the most mischievous sort of
government which England had ever been troubled with. . . .
   How could all this happen? For the fundamental reason,
that neither the religion, the laws, the morals, the manners, nor
the literature of the country, especially as contrasted with those
of France, were prized by the Leaders of the Party as they
deserved. . . . Is the distracted remnant of the Party, now
surviving, improved in that respect? . . . we look in vain for
signs that the opinions, habits, and feelings, of the Party, are
tending towards a restoration of that genuine English character,
by which alone the confidence of the sound part of the People
can be recovered. [pp. 162–63]

This is an approximate summary of the views we have seen to inform the
France books. Wordsworth's use of the political labels does, however, alert
us to see what we might otherwise have missed: that his conservatism, like
Burke's, represents itself as the preservation of true Whiggism.[34]
   What Wordsworth says about Napoleon's 1804 coronation should
perhaps also be compared to Southey's later reflection on Napoleon's
bad-faith negotiations for peace in 1802. The Peace of Amiens, recalled
Southey, "restored in me the English feelings which had long been
deadened, and placed me in sympathy with my country."[35] One crucial
difference between these cases, on the other hand, is that Wordsworth's
debilitated English feelings were revived long before the coronation of 1804
or even the treaty of 1802. This much is clear from Wordsworth's tenses:

"hath still / Upheld me, and upholds me at this day." Moreover, the spots of time narrated in book 11 date to what is now, perhaps misleadingly, called the two-part *Prelude* of 1798–99. In chapter 8 below, the famous passages "scatter'd everywhere" in Wordsworth's life will be examined in light of this Burkean nationalism. For now, it is enough to recognize that the redemptive spots of time are, like Burke's moral sentiments, strongly allied with early prejudice, insensibly formed in particular circumstances, and profoundly indebted to the English past.

Four

The Uses of Second Nature

> Custom reconciles us to every thing.
> Burke, *The Sublime and the Beautiful*

*I*f Burkean categories are so pervasive in the France books of *The Prelude*, and if we regard these books as only spelling out ideological premises already implicit in the poem's design from its beginnings, then we may have cause to look for Wordsworth's debt to Burke in the very earliest years of his golden decade. We may indeed want to go back to the period of *Lyrical Ballads*, back to the very inception of Wordsworth's literary program. If such influence does operate in this earlier work, however, it is likely to be even more diffuse and, at least initially, even harder to recognize than what scrutiny discloses in the France books of 1804 and 1805—just as Burke's role in the France books is less conspicuous than in Wordsworth's later writings. This subtler task requires more careful scrutiny of certain aspects of Burke's unsystematic system.

We have reason to believe, for example, that the priority Burke assigns to feeling in moral and political activity may be one of the important links with the early works of Wordsworth's great decade. Yet at the same time this issue of feeling tends to be one of the most elusive in Burke's thought. It is one thing for him to say, as he does in the *Appeal*, that only the moral sentiments can act as a check on savage theories; or, as he does in the *Reflections*, that the English are morally and politically superior to the speculatists of France because "we still feel within us." It is another thing for him to say what it might *mean* to place one's trust in one's feelings. Burke insists that feelings take priority over theory: when "our feelings contradict our theories . . . , the feelings are true, and the theory is false" (*BW* 4:79). In at least one instance, he even asserts with confidence that feeling is superior to knowledge itself: "We know, and, what is better, we feel inwardly, that religion is the basis of civil society, and the source of all good, and of all comfort" (3:350). But this does not tell us just how feelings provide reliable guidance in moral and political life.

In elaborating his notion of feeling, Burke frequently resorts to extended metaphors:

> We have not been drawn and trussed, in order that we may be filled, like stuffed birds in a museum, with chaff and rags, and paltry, blurred shreds of paper about the rights of man. We preserve the whole of our feelings still native and entire, unsophisticated by pedantry and infidelity. We have real hearts of flesh and blood beating in our bosoms. [p. 345]

Insofar as it manifests the effects of the feelings it describes, this passage epitomizes what the young Wordsworth called Burke's "intoxicating" rhetoric. Many of Burke's early adversaries, like Paine and Mary Wollstonecraft, referred to such passages when they analyzed the power of Burke's way of writing. They criticized Burke's obscurantist emotionalism against the standard of a philosophically more enlightened prose and thus inversely adumbrated Wordsworth's own invidious comparison, later popularized by De Quincey, between the literature of knowledge and the literature of power.[1] Burke's eloquence does not, in any case, much help to illuminate the difficult question at issue here. He would presumably be among the first to agree that not all feelings are trustworthy; the French passion for speculation, for example, is surely not in his eyes trustworthy. So what are we to say distinguishes the right feelings from the wrong?

The general purport of such metaphors provides a kind of answer. The Englishman's reliable sentiments are his natural entrails; he has a natural heart of flesh and blood. The feelings that can be trusted must therefore be the natural ones. This is in effect the answer Burke himself gives when he goes on in this same paragraph to explain why Englishmen respond as they do to God, kings, parliaments, magistrates, priests, and nobility: "Why? Because when such ideas are brought before our minds, it is *natural* to be so affected" (pp. 345–46; Burke's italics). Burke's most categorical statement about the relation of "nature" and reliable feelings appears in his *Letters on a Regicide Peace* (1796–97): "Never was there a jar or discord between genuine sentiment and sound policy. Never, no, never, did Nature say one thing and Wisdom say another" (5:407). Genuine sentiment, as the parallelism makes clear, *is* the voice of nature, an unfailingly reliable counselor.

These are by no means isolated examples. Statements linking nature and true feeling can be found all over Burke's writings of the 1790s. The connection tends to vary from instance to instance, but the occasion is almost always an invidious comparison with the political metaphysicians of France. At one point in the *Reflections*, for example, Burke complains that they "are so taken up with their theories about the rights of man, that they have totally forgotten about his nature." And what man's "nature" means here is suggested by his next words: "Without opening one new avenue to the understanding, they have succeeded in stopping up all those that lead to the heart. They have perverted in themselves, and in those that attend to them, all the well-placed sympathies of the human breast" (3:316). The appositional relation of "nature" and valid feeling is drawn even more sharply in an earlier passage. "All your sophisters," Burke tells De Pont, "cannot produce anything better adapted to preserve a rational and manly freedom than the course that we have pursued, who have chosen our nature rather than our speculations, our breasts rather than our inventions, for the great conservatories and magazines of our rights and privileges" (p. 276). Our "nature" evidently lies in our "breast," the problem with the French being that "nothing is left to Nature in their systems" (5:316). The French are guilty, he says elsewhere, of "the worst of usurpations, an usurpation on the prerogatives of Nature" (3:295). Or again, he tells De Pont that, in pursuing metaphysical programs, "you think you are combatting prejudice, but you are at war with Nature" (p. 296).

None of these scattered comments about nature, however, actually contributes much to a solution of the problem at issue. To suggest that reliable feelings are "natural feelings" risks a begging of the main questions: What makes a natural feeling "natural" and how is it possible to tell the natural from the unnatural without resorting, as the French philosophers seem to have done, to the kind of reason that is supposed to endanger that which it seeks to judge?[2]

I

The passage to which Burke's commentators most often turn for clarification of these matters is the one that immediately follows Burke's assertion that the English feel as they do about things because "it is *natural*" for them to do so. It would seem to be well suited for our purposes since it begins with a statement about the feelings of the English, ends with a statement about their "nature," and develops the relation of both terms to "reason" by way of a quasi-technical use of "prejudice" as a mediating term:

> You see, Sir, that in this enlightened age I am bold enough to confess that we are generally men of untaught feelings: that, instead of casting away all our old prejudices, we cherish them to a very considerable degree; and, to take more shame to ourselves, we cherish them because they are prejudices; and the longer they have lasted, and the more generally they have prevailed, the more we cherish them. We are afraid to put men to live and trade each on his own private stock of reason; because we suspect that the stock in each man is small, and that the individuals would do better to avail themselves of the general bank and capital of nations and of ages. Many of our men of speculation, instead of exploding general prejudices, employ their sagacity to discover the latent wisdom which prevails in them. If they find what they seek, (and they seldom fail,) they think it more wise to continue the prejudice, with the reason involved, than to cast away the coat of prejudice, and to leave nothing but the naked reason; because prejudice, with its reason, has a motive to give action to that reason, and an affection which will give it permanence. Prejudice is of ready application in the emergency; it previously engages the mind in a steady course of wisdom and virtue, and does not leave the man hesitating in the moment of decision, skeptical, puzzled, and unresolved. Prejudice renders a man's virtue his habit, and not a series of unconnected acts. Through just prejudice, his duty becomes a part of his nature. {pp. 346–47}

Central as it is, this passage is helpful chiefly as a way of showing what Burke is *not* claiming. First, although he characteristically praises the English for their "untaught feelings," he clearly does not mean that these feelings are unlearned. Like the feelings Wordsworth brings to his early encounters in Revolutionary France, they have been formed in the course of a tutelary English experience. What makes them praiseworthy, as Burke's sarcastic reference to the *lumières* implies, is that they have been formed without the intervention of "enlightenment," a term which means for Burke what it did for Kant in his definition of six years earlier: putting men to live and trade each on his own stock of reason.[3] Not to be enlightened means not only refusing to cast away old prejudices because they are prejudices, but cherishing them—and for the same reason.

Secondly, Burke is not offering prejudice as an absolute standard or starting point for reason. The epistemology of the Burkean middle does not admit of such pure absolutes. The English cherish their prejudices, but only "to a very considerable degree." When English men of speculation examine prejudices for their inherent value, they "seldom fail" to find it. Not all feelings are natural; not all prejudices are just. Finally, Burke is not banishing reason from his system. On the contrary, he thinks one must distinguish the just from the unjust prejudice according to a rational criterion. The problem is that this rational standard is to some extent inseparable from the forms of human usage that engender prejudice itself. Reason is "involved" in prejudices; wisdom is "latent" in them.[4] Feelings and prejudices are the products of a collective human consciousness and therefore cannot be assessed by an individual's private stock of reason or from a position of presumed disinterestedness, uninvolvement.

Though Burke's discussion of feelings and prejudices is useful for ruling out mistaken views of his thought, it is far less satisfactory for suggesting how his most crucial discriminations are to be made—how one knows, for example, which prejudices reason is in fact "involved" in. Burke says that when English philosophers discover the latent wisdom in prejudices, "they think it more wise to continue the prejudice, with the reason involved, than to cast away the coat of prejudice, and to leave nothing but the naked reason." But not all prejudices contain wisdom.[5] Burke's entire discussion here is predicated on the conditional clause, "*if* they find what they seek." Sometimes they fail. How do they know the latent wisdom in prejudice when they see it? What counts as a failure? What happens to the prejudices that fail the test? Instead of answering such questions, Burke simply goes on to use the word "prejudice" as if it were interchangeable with "just prejudice." Only just prejudice has its reason; only just prejudice engages the mind in a steady course of wisdom and virtue. Burke's closest approximation to answers for these questions is what amounts to a caveat about the dangers of formulating solutions in the abstract. To pursue matters further is again to run up against metaphor, in which for Burke all language use begins and ends since it best displays the refractory quality of the linguistic medium.[6]

Equally troublesome here is Burke's use of "nature," especially in relation to its metaphorical context. This instance should be compared with one from earlier in the *Reflections*, where the word is attended by the same metaphors. There Burke is lamenting what is likely to occur under "the conquering empire of light and reason": "All the superadded ideas, furnished from the wardrobe of a moral imagination, which the heart owns and the understanding ratifies, as necessary to cover the defects of our naked, shivering nature, and to raise it to dignity in our own estimation, are to be exploded, as a ridiculous, absurd, and antiquated fashion" (p. 333). The "coat of prejudice" from the later passage would seem to be an item from the moral imagination's wardrobe. But the garments in the earlier passage clothe "our naked . . . nature" whereas the coat of prejudice clothes the "naked . . . reason." Further, in the second passage, Burke uses "our nature" to refer to something which evidently includes both our reason and our clothes or prejudices—that is, to make Burke's pun explicit, both reason and "habit." To put it another way, "nature" in that second instance includes both our (naked, shivering) "nature" and our "second nature." Burke does not spell out the difference between nature and second nature for the same reason he does not spell out the difference between prejudice and just prejudice. In each case he would debilitate the power of the pure, simple noun and thereby undercut the rhetorical force of his argument. Burke wants to fly in the face of the French by claiming prejudice, *tout simplement*, as an intellectual ally. But he can do so only if he can claim all of "nature" for his side as well.

That a writer should use "nature" inconsistently is hardly to be considered unusual. It is, as Raymond Williams observes in his cultural lexicon, "perhaps the most complex word in the language."[7] Just the same, it comes as no surprise that Williams's first illustration of this word's complexity should be a quotation from Burke (pp. 184–85). The use of "nature" in Burke's writings is notoriously equivocal, and I believe it owes largely to this equivocation that the most recurrent topic in modern Burke studies has been the still unresolved question of whether he is or is not a natural-law theorist.[8] Burke's use of "nature" is peculiarly problematic because he employs the word differently according to the needs of two very different kinds of claims. These are claims on the one hand about the timeless and universal condition of things (including human beings) and on the other about what human beings acquire as a result of their particular times and places; claims about matters often represented, in other words, by such oppositions as "nature" and "nurture." Nor is this duplicity merely grammatical, as becomes clear if we recall Burke's metaphor of the rays of light piercing into a dense medium. The metaphor gains its force from its analogy with Newtonian "laws of nature." In this respect, there is one nature and one set of laws. But the "dense medium" is made to correspond to "man's nature" in this account, as if it were a nature within nature. The metaphor ultimately insists on having it both ways: there is Nature and there is a second nature which is at once within Nature yet parallel to it. Second nature is at once metaphorical and metonymous with Nature.

It goes without saying that "nature" is as central to Wordsworth's vocabulary as it is to Burke's, and that it has as crucial a link to "feeling" in Wordsworth as in Burke. Countless critics, furthermore, have noted equivocation in the way Wordsworth employs the word. One of the best efforts to sort out the inconsistencies is Laurence Lerner's recent essay "What did Wordsworth mean by 'Nature'?" After surveying a number of representative passages, Lerner concludes that "there is a profound—and unresolved—ambiguity in Wordsworth's idea of Nature, and though this ambiguity is not in itself a poetic virtue, it does point very revealingly to what is going on when the poetry is at its most powerful."[9] This, surely, has oft been thought by Wordsworth's readers, but Lerner goes on to express his notion better than most have done:

> To describe the ambiguity I invoke the aid of Shakespeare. The famous conversation between Polixenes and Perdita raises exactly the ambiguity we are dealing with. Perdita has announced that she has no time for carnations and streaked gillivors:
>
>> For I have heard it said
>> There is an art, which in their piedness vies
>> With great creating Nature
>
> Polixenes replies:
>
>> Say there be;
>> Yet Nature is made better by no mean
>> But Nature makes that mean; so over that art
>> Which you say adds to Nature is an art
>> That Nature makes . . .
>> . . . This is an art
>> Which does not mend Nature—change it, rather—but
>> The art itself is Nature.
>
> There is an obvious sense in which Polixenes is right—how can any event or process not be part of Nature, if it happens? But . . . [t]he Perditas never are convinced: since the concept of Nature is no use to us unless we can contrast it with something. If Nature simply means 'all which is', then nothing can be called unnatural, and there is not much point in calling anything natural. Exhortations to follow Nature or to return to the natural life must use Perdita's meaning.
> Was Wordsworth Perdita or Polixenes? [p. 296]

What Lerner has observed in Wordsworth, in effect, is a grammatical structure of "nature" that corresponds very closely with what we find in Burke. Like Burke, Wordsworth insists on both of the mutually exclusive

senses of his crucial term. He is in Lerner's terms both Perdita and
Polixenes. These Shakespearean terms, however, are the weakest part of
Lerner's account. They illuminate the grammar of Wordsworthian "na-
ture" but can claim no historical authority in accounting for this grammar;
nor, to be fair, does Lerner imply that they do. Burke's terms can lay claim
to such authority. [10]

II

To arrive at a proper historical understanding of Burke's double sense of
nature, as well as its analogue in Wordsworth, we must consider Burke's
polemic about the natural feelings of the English in relation to the writer
who is one of its primary targets. This is the writer who heads the list of
adversaries mentioned in the paragraph that precedes the long discussion of
prejudice in the *Reflections*: "We are not," says Burke, "the converts of
Rousseau." Like Burke, Rousseau is interested in developing and applying
the criterion of nature to human feelings and actions. This is why in works
like the *Discourse on the Origin and Foundation of Inequality* (the Second
Discourse) and the *Social Contract*—works on which Wordsworth drew in
his radical writing of the early 1790s—Rousseau insists on beginning with
a proper understanding of human beings in "the state of nature." Like
Burke, too, Rousseau makes a clear distinction between covenanted man in
society and uncovenanted man in the precivil state. Many similarities link
these opposing ideologues of the late-eighteenth century, an irony that has
not been lost on intellectual historians of the period. But more to the point
here is the issue that finally divides them: Rousseau draws his distinction
between the natural and civil states of man in just the sort of absolute terms
that Burke rejects. [11]

   In the Second Discourse, we can see this absolute distinction at work
in Rousseau's discussions of both man as subject and man as object. Under
the subjective aspect, Rousseau's argument holds that the habits of civil life
pose obstacles to the very effort to know the state of nature. Many philos-
ophers, he says, have "felt the necessity of going back to the state of nature,
but none of them has reached it." [12] The reason he assigns to their failure is
that they have all "carried over to the state of nature ideas they had acquired
in society: they spoke about savage man and they described civil man" (p.
102). Previous approaches to the question, in other words, have all resulted
in civil or religious histories of a matter that Rousseau takes to be neither
civil nor religious. Rousseau himself, therefore, sets out to write a natural
history of human beings, much as a geologist would write a natural history
of the land human beings inhabit:

> O man, whatever country you may come from, whatever
> your opinions may be, listen: here is your history as I believe it
> to read, not in the books of your fellowmen, which are liars, but
> in nature, which never lies. Everything that comes from nature
> will be true; there will be nothing false except what I have
> involuntarily put in of my own. The times of which I am going
> to speak are very far off: how you have changed from what you
> were. It is, so to speak, the life of your species that I am going to
> describe to you according to the qualities you received, which
> your education and habits have been able to corrupt but have
> not been able to destroy. [pp. 103–4]

Subjectively speaking, our education and habits, whatever they may be,
inhibit our ability to see "naturally." Only to the extent that we divest
ourselves of these habits can we see the natural man as he really is.

The other side of this argument is that the natural man who is our
object of study will himself be as nude as we can make ourselves in the act of
his reconstruction. To consider man in nature is to imagine him "as he must
have come from the hands of nature," and this in turn means "Stripping
[him] of all the supernatural gifts he could have received and of all the
artificial faculties he could have acquired by long progress" (p. 105).
Rousseau tells us many times that his natural man is "naked." But this
nakedness, like his lack of habitation and his "deprivation of all those
useless things we believe so necessary are not . . . such a great misfortune for
these first men" (p. 111). Indeed, very little about Rousseau's natural man
turns out to be as bad as civilized man would have thought. In the course of
his argument, Rousseau goes on to use his model of nature as the a priori
basis for a critique of virtually all civil codes and civil societies as presently
constituted.

Though not himself always in agreement with the *lumières* Burke
challenged, Rousseau did (in Burke's view) fall prey, just as clearly as a
Voltaire or a Helvétius, to what Burke reviled as their penchant for
absolutes. Rousseau represents the states of nature and civil society as two
such absolutes, and it is clear that Rousseau's distinctions between habit
and nature—or acquired and natural abilities, or the prejudices of civil life
and things as they are—all represent opposing extremes that brook no
compromise. Again, it is not that Burke rejected the possibility of drawing
such distinctions; he defended every one of them at one time or another.
And Burke claims "nature" as vehemently for the foundation of his own
system as Rousseau does for his. But Burke's natural foundation can never
be an extreme. His "opinions can never lead to extremes," "because their

foundation is laid in opposition to extremes." His doctrines "do of themselves gravitate" to that "middle" where life goes on (*BW* 4:206). The function of Burke's doctrine of second nature is to compromise the absolute extremes of a writer like Rousseau by occupying the medium between them.

The idea of second nature is a piece of proverbial wisdom with an ancient pedigree.[13] This is no doubt part of its appeal for Burke. Like most proverbial notions, this one has not been employed with systematic rigor over centuries, and that, too, Burke must have found attractive. Certainly, in his own practice, despite the prevailing aim to mediate metaphysical extremes, its use is unsystematic. From the analogy of the light rays entering the dense medium, for example, one might suppose that the second nature of the medium stood for something like human nature—the "nature of man," as Burke says, as distinct from nature in general. But one of Burke's most explicit expositions of the topic, a 1794 speech at the trial of Hastings, offers a somewhat different picture. "Men are made of two parts," he claimed on this occasion, "the physical and the moral":

> The former he has in common with brute creation. . . . [But]
> Man, in his moral nature, becomes, in his progress through life,
> a creature of prejudice—a creature of opinions—a creature of
> habits, and of sentiments growing out of them. These form our
> second nature, as inhabitants of the country and members of the
> society in which Providence has placed us.[14]

Since all distinctions here are made within the sphere of human nature, human nature is obviously not itself in this case the second nature. But what is? At first it looks as if man's two parts, the physical and the moral, are two natures, the "moral nature" being the second nature. But another, equally plausible way to read the passage is to determine that these two components together form man's nature and that "second nature" is what a person acquires or becomes *in* his moral nature, i.e., in the moral part of his "nature." A similar ambiguity marks one of Burke's earlier comments on the relation of the several natures. This remark also seems simple and straightforward at first glance: "This is the true touchstone of all theories which regard man and the affairs of men,—Does it suit his nature in general?—does it suit his nature as modified by his habits?" (7:97) The "first nature" would seem here to be "nature in general." But is the second nature the nature modified by habits or is it the habits themselves? And in what sense can we say that this is a nature at all if it is not "general"?

Some semantic clarification comes forth in the *Reflections*, where Burke discusses the question of theory as it applies particularly to political lawmaking:

> The legislators who framed the ancient republics knew that their business was too arduous to be accomplished with no better apparatus than the metaphysics of an undergraduate, and the mathematics and arithmetic of an exciseman. They had to do with men, and they were obliged to study human nature. They had to do with citizens, and they were obliged to study the effects of those habits which are communicated by the circumstances of civil life. They were sensible that the operations of this second nature on the first produced a new combination. [3:476–77]

In this case Burke explicitly identifies the "second nature" as the habits generated by social circumstance. The duplicity inherent in the concept of second nature is not so easily contained, however, for the "new combination" that is said to be produced by the operation of the second nature on the first is also, in respect to the first nature, a second nature. Which of *these* are we to suppose is the real second nature?[15]

Since second nature is one of the key concepts in Burke's attack on metaphysical politics, he must be very careful not to let the term be handled as if it belonged to the opposition. A concept developed in practice, it cannot in his view be extractible from practice. One must be prudent rather than systematic in using it: "Metaphysics cannot live without definition; but Prudence is cautious how she defines" (*BW* 4:80–81).[16] Burke takes such abstract oppositions as "nature/culture," or "nature/habit," and gravitating toward the middle, develops his crucial notion of second nature. But rather than allowing the "original" nature and the new "second nature" to become abstract extremes in the place of those they supplant, he develops still another middle ground. A second "second nature" is now supposed to be the *real* basis for political theory—until, of course, it too is opposed to the nature Burke always wants to claim for his side.

What emerges from this analysis, then, is that second nature is for Burke not so much an identifiable fact in the world as a way of thinking that conveniently collapses certain troublesome oppositions. It allows him, for example, to absorb Rousseau's protoanthropological problem of the raw and the cooked without actually addressing it. With his notion of second nature Burke can bake his cake and claim at the same time that nature made it for him. This imaginary cake is not to be confused with the imaginary cake Marie Antoinette recommended to the Parisians as a substitute for bread. But second nature is at least ostensibly what prompts Burke's famous apostrophe to Marie Antoinette in the passage that has accurately been called the "centrepiece" of the *Reflections*.[17] We must recall that Burke launches into his praise of the queen just at the moment when he seemed to have finished with the topic of the 5 October "invasion" of her quarters at Versailles. He wants his reader to believe that the praise of the queen is drawn out of him despite his immediate intentions. "But I cannot stop here," says Burke. "Influenced by the inborn feelings of [his] nature, and not being illuminated by a single ray of this new-sprung modern light," Burke must pay the queen the tribute their mutual humanity requires (3:329–30). For "inborn feelings" read "untaught" and thus "prejudicial" and thus "habitual" feelings, as in the explication of these terms in that central passage (discussed above), which follows several pages after the tribute to the queen.

What makes Burke's tribute to Marie Antoinette the appropriate place to conclude a discussion of his sense of second nature is that it highlights the way in which we must regard the *Reflections* itself as a work of second nature. At the very start of his discussion he provides a prefatory description of his procedure:

> Solicitous chiefly for the peace of my own country, but by no means unconcerned for yours, I wish to communicate more largely what was at first intended only for your private satisfaction. I shall still keep your affairs in my eye, and continue to address myself to you. Indulging myself in the freedom of epistolary intercourse, I beg leave to throw out my thoughts and express my feelings just as they arise in my mind, with very little attention to formal method. [p. 243]

In not adopting a "formal method" for his research and exposition, Burke implies that he is doing what the English do in the conduct of their state, "preserving the method of Nature." Like the English policies he praises, Burke's *Reflections* is itself to be regarded as "the happy effect of following Nature, which is wisdom without reflection [paradoxically], and above it" (pp. 274–75). His informal, epistolary mode shows him practicing as he preaches. It allows him to proceed unsystematically through his discourse, enacting at every point the habitual traits of the native character he describes: tact, courage, common sense, manly honor, devotion to duty, and so on. Paine was thus keenly accurate in his ironic labeling of the book as a "dramatic performance," and nowhere is the English character meant to be more vividly dramatized than in Burke's tribute to Marie Antoinette.[18]

I have pitched my discussion of this passage, as is probably obvious, in such a way as to suggest the striking parallels between Burke's tribute to Marie Antoinette in the *Reflections* and Wordsworth's tribute to Burke in *The Prelude*. This is not to suggest that Burke's famous apostrophe was in any immediate way the model for Wordsworth's, either in the book 7 passage or in any of the poem's other passages where, as Hartman says, an event that occurs during composition enters the narrative as a biographical event. *The Prelude* is arguably a "dramatic performance," however, in something very like the way that the *Reflections* is—and for some of the same reasons. We have already seen how Wordsworth's notion of the way his feelings preserve him in wisdom and sanity is deeply indebted to Burke's idea of habit-based moral sentiment. What still needs to be demonstrated is that Wordsworthian "nature" typically operates according to Burke's dialectic of second nature and not according to the Rousseauist model of nature to which, either implicitly or explicitly, it is most often likened.

III

That for Wordsworth as well as for Burke the most reliable feelings are the most natural is a claim not hard to document. We need only think back to those lines quoted above from book 10 where Wordsworth writes that "Nature's self" revived the feelings that saved him. The real question with Wordsworth (again, as with Burke) has to do with how we are to understand these natural feelings. What is it that makes them natural? There is a long tradition in Wordsworth criticism that would have us believe that Wordsworth's natural feelings are, like Rousseau's, moments when he divests himself of all habits, prejudices, and customs. M. H. Abrams sums up this line of criticism, as he does so many, when he says of Wordsworth's poetic enterprise that its "prime opponent-power is 'custom,'—what Wordsworth in *The Prelude* repeatedly condemns as 'habit,' 'use and custom,' 'the regular action of the world'—which works insidiously and relentlessly to assimilate the unique existent to general perceptual categories."[19] Abrams traces an impressive genealogy for the notion of custom-as-nature's-adversary from Rousseau back to Christ. His mention of Thomas Traherne is typical: "As later in Coleridge and Wordsworth, so in Traherne, custom rather than depravity is the tyrant that holds our innocent senses in bondage: 'Our Misery proceedeth tenthousand times more from the outward Bondage of Opinion and Custom then from any inward corruption or Depravation of Nature: And . . . it is not our Parents Loyns, so much as our Parents lives, that Enthrals and Blinds us' " (pp. 382–83).

The mistaken link in Abrams's genealogy is Coleridge, whose remarks about Wordsworth's project in *Lyrical Ballads* Abrams cites as a primary authority for his view. According to Coleridge, Wordsworth set out "to give the charm of novelty to things of every day, and to excite a feeling analogous to the supernatural, by awakening the mind's attention from the lethargy of custom, and directing it to the loveliness and the wonders of the world before us."[20] This famous claim in the *Biographia Literaria* is partly responsible, I believe, for many of the prevailing assumptions about Wordsworth and custom, assumptions that better suit the work of Emerson and Thoreau, and to some extent that of Coleridge himself. But Coleridge's account merits little of the authority it has been given. Its authenticity has been all but discredited by Mark Reed's reconstruction of the probable "plan" for the *Lyrical Ballads*, and there is the further consideration that, for reasons I will take up in the final chapter, Coleridge may have deliberately misrepresented Wordsworth's intentions.[21]

But what about those passages in *The Prelude* that Abrams suggests are condemnations of habit and custom? One of those which Abrams has in mind is no doubt Wordsworth's introductory comment for the "spots of time" section in the latter part of book 9. This is where Wordsworth explains more fully what he means by the assertion that "Nature's self" revived the feelings of his earlier life. Referring one last time to his practice of bringing all his passions and beliefs before the seat of judgment, Wordsworth recounts:

> I shook the habit off
> Entirely and for ever, and again
> In Nature's presence stood, as I stand now,
> A sensitive and a *creative* soul.
>
> [11:253–56]

Before we rush to claim these lines as corroboration for the notion that Wordsworth simply needed to free his natural, native feelings from the tyranny of custom and habit, we should look to the similar passage that brackets the "spots of time" section on the other side: "Behold me then / Once more in Nature's presence, thus restored, / Or otherwise, and strengthened once again / . . . To habits of devoutest sympathy" (392–96). Being in Nature's presence does not mean being in an original, naked, or habitless condition, or even in an approximation of such a condition. It means being in the condition of one's authentic habits and of their attendant feelings. And this is not a Rousseauist state of nature but a Burkean state of second nature.

Another passage to which Abrams alludes is Wordsworth's defensive denial in book 13 that he ever willfully yielded to mean cares or low pursuits. Rather, he insists, he

> did with jealousy shrink back
> From every combination that might aid
> The tendency, too potent in itself,
> Of habit to enslave the mind—I mean
> Oppress it by the laws of vulgar sense,
> And substitute a universe of death,
> The falsest of all worlds, in place of that
> Which is divine and true.
>
>   [136–43]

To avoid misinterpreting this passage, several points must be borne in mind. The first is that its tenor is strengthened in the 1850 version, where line 139 becomes: " . . . Of use and custom to bow down the soul . . . " (14:158). And in that version it would have appeared with the tribute to Burke in book 7. The second point is that Wordsworth's very apologia acknowledges the need for some explanation on the score of second nature. This explanation, furthermore, lays its emphasis on the phrase "too potent in itself," which is reprinted verbatim in the 1850 text. When we come this far, we are prepared to see that Wordsworth can print this passage with his praise of Burke for the simple reason that the two hold compatible positions. Burke spoke directly to this sort of issue in his *Philosophical Enquiry into the Origin of Our Ideas of the Sublime and the Beautiful* (1757), where the dialectic of nature and second nature is traced, as in the *Reflections*, to a certain kind of constitution. "We are so wonderfully formed," he explains, "that whilst we are creatures vehemently desirous of novelty, we are as strongly attached to habit and custom."[22] The rules of good taste, for Burke, derive from both of these basic qualities, with custom and habit working to moderate extreme emotions of either the sublime or beautiful kind. This moderating tendency is salutary and indeed vital in the course of human experience. *In itself*, however, this tendency is in Burke's account much what it is in Wordsworth's:

> Indeed so far are use and habit from being causes of pleasure, merely as such; that the effect of constant use is to make all things of whatever kind entirely unaffecting. For as use at last takes off the painful effect of many things, it reduces the pleasurable effect of others in the same manner, and brings both

to a sort of mediocrity and indifference. Very justly is use called
a second nature; and our natural and common state is one of
absolute indifference, equally prepared for pain or pleasure. But
when we are thrown out of this state, or deprived of anything
requisite to maintain us in it . . . , we are always hurt. It is so
with the second nature, custom, in all things which relate to it.
[p. 104]

Was the *Enquiry* one of the books in which Burke's "principles of fore-
knowledge" were laid down? Burleigh Wilkins argues as much in his
discussion of the strong connections between the early aesthetics and the
later politics.[23] That Wordsworth learned some of his Burke through the
Enquiry is clear; only the questions how much and how early have not been
settled. The obvious use of the *Enquiry* in the "Sublime and Beautiful"
section written in 1811–12 for the *Guide to the Lakes* sets a latest possible
date (*PrW* 2:349–60). Without pursuing the question here, I would only
suggest that a much earlier date seems probable in light of how Words-
worth recounts the origin of his own passions in the earliest manuscripts of
The Prelude: the twofold categorization of Nature's discipline into moments
of "beauty" and "fear" is the one Burke made famous.[24]

  Wordsworth takes a further step with Burke in the argument from
second nature when he implies that it is precisely the *quest* to reach the state
of pure or original nature, whether through feeling or through reason, that
forms the habits that keep one out of nature's presence—that is, out of
touch with one's true second nature. The France books show not only that
Wordsworth attributes the failure of French moral and political thought in
large measure to such a quest but also that he thinks such a quest depends on
a false distinction between nature on the one hand and habit (or its
cognates, "custom," "institute," "law") on the other, and finally that such
a distinction goes hand in hand with the effort to specify the domain of
nature too narrowly or to define it too precisely.

  At the time of his encounter with the Royalists, for example, the
young Wordsworth, still subservient to "Nature's single sovereignty," is
said to have taken the events of the Revolution as "nothing out of nature's
certain course" (9:238, 253). The young Wordsworth's view here is not
exactly mistaken, but its implicit assumptions become problematic as
"nature" acquires a meaning that is more univocal and less dialectical. In
the course of the France books "nature" itself, paradoxically, becomes a
term of art. Its first appearance as a technical term (in the adjectival form)
occurs a few lines earlier in the Royalists episode where Wordsworth says
that he had not then learned to make "nice distinctions—then on every

tongue— / Of natural rights and civil" (203–4). It is not until book 10, however, that we find the technical sense of "natural" employed as if it were endorsed by the young Wordsworth. Describing a time when his outlook has already begun to change, Wordsworth records himself thinking "That nothing hath a natural right to last / But equity and reason" (10:172–73). In their meanings, these two claims—that the Revolution is nothing out of nature's certain course and that nothing has a natural right to last but equity and reason—are not far apart. Yet the second proposition, implying the technical antithesis to *civil* rights, proves to be symptomatic of the young Wordsworth's changing attitude toward nature itself.

Eventually, of course, the young Wordsworth comes to see the demands of nature in an increasingly rigorous opposition to those of the civil order. The sense of their mutual incompatibility strikes him most forcefully at the time of the declaration of the Republic and the execution of Louis XVI:

> Youth maintains, I knew,
> In all conditions of society
> Communion more direct and intimate
> With Nature, and the inner strength she has—
> And hence, oft times, no less with reason too—
> Than age, or manhood even. To Nature, then,
> Power had reverted: habit, custom, law,
> Had left an interregnum's open space
> For her to stir about in, uncontrolled.
> The warmest judgments, and the most untaught,
> Found in events which every day brought forth
> Enough to sanction them—and far, far more
> To shake the authority of canons drawn
> From ordinary practice.
>
> [10:604–17]

Examining this passage out of context, one can easily mistake its point of view. In normal usage, the presence of "I knew" in a narrative would identify an opinion still considered true by the speaker; an expression like "I thought" would normally identify an opinion now considered false or questionable. But in this case, Wordsworth goes on to make it clear that "juvenile errors are [his] theme" (637), and we must therefore take the use of "I knew" as a measure of how fully he is able to pass over to the earlier point of view in his narrative argument. Neither this point of view nor the mature Wordsworth's attitude toward it is hard to see. Wordsworth's sense of habit, custom, and law as "canons drawn / From ordinary practice" is remarkably close to Burke's own. The clear implication here is that Nature is now seen as alien to the authority of such canons, a view not implied by the young Wordsworth's earlier, healthier notion that the events of 1789 were nothing out of nature's certain course. The alternative to such authority, the only *natural* alternative, is now seen to be "reason." And the young are presumed to have more certain access to the authority of reason precisely because they are unencumbered by those products of experience that bind and blind the "gravest heads" (622).

Although the potential destructiveness of this false opposition between nature and custom is not fully revealed until the accounts of his crisis, Wordsworth prepares us to recognize that the opposition is in fact mistaken as early as the autobiographical tale of Vaudracoeur and Julia in book 9. For when Vaudracoeur, or "Heartsworth" as David Erdman calls him, ignores all prohibitions and decides to lie with Julia out of wedlock, the Wordsworthian narrator speculates that in "some delirious hour" the youth "Was inwardly prepared to turn aside / From law and custom and entrust himself / To Nature for a happy end of all" (9:602–4). The result is a fatal lapse in Vaudracoeur's natural discipline: he "thus abated of that pure reserve / Congenial to his loyal heart" (605–6).[25] Like the young Wordsworth, Vaudracoeur is clearly furthest from nature when he thinks himself closest. And it is equally true of them both that they follow "reasonings false / From the beginning, inasmuch as drawn / Out of a heart which had been turned aside / From Nature" (10:883–86).

In the light of such evidence, we must reject any suggestion that custom and habit are in themselves the villains of *The Prelude*. But during the same months when Wordsworth was pressing onward toward the France books of *The Prelude* (early 1804), he was completing a poem that has also been cited by critics like Abrams who see Wordsworth campaigning against the "lethargy of custom." This poem, the "Intimations Ode," also contains some famous lines about "custom" that look at first like good evidence for such a view. Abrams quotes these lines in his brief characterization of the poem: "that 'celestial light' perceived by the child . . . is darkened, then obliterated, by 'custom . . . with a weight, / Heavy as frost.' "[26] While this is a common enough interpretation of the "Ode," it tells only half the story.

The full story becomes clear only if we regard the poem as a kind of small-scale model for *The Prelude* itself. At one point in the "Ode," its speaker is indeed represented as believing something very close to what Abrams suggests. But this position is the equivalent of the mistaken views of *The Prelude*, book 10, where Wordsworth thinks that custom and habit are the natural enemies, rather than the natural conditions, of life and truth. Indeed, the lines about the deadly weight of custom mark an apparent dead end in the progress of the "Ode," much like the impasse created by young Wordsworth's moral crisis in *The Prelude*. The ensuing stanza of the "Ode" provides a way out of the impasse, accordingly, much like the recovery narrated in *The Prelude*, book 11:

> O joy! that in our embers
> Is something that doth live,
> That nature yet remembers
> What was so fugitive!
>
> [130–33]

Further, what accounts for this abrupt solution in the "Ode" is the same sort of habit-based early sentiment that saves the poet of *The Prelude*. "Nature" is able to remember fleeting emotions through the force of habit. This is the point of the exclamation that opens the final stanza of the "Ode":

> And O, ye Fountains, Meadows, Hills, and Groves,
> Forbode not any severing of our loves!
> Yet in my heart of hearts I feel your might;
> I only have relinquished one delight
> To live beneath your more habitual sway.

The "more habitual sway" is the power of second nature, the strength in what remains behind when the particular repetitions of life's seasons have passed.

To read the "Ode" as a condemnation of custom and habit is thus to miss the reversal of attitude that constitutes its peripeteia. One cannot properly understand the "Ode's" conclusion, I think, without reading it against that "crisis" passage at the end of stanza 8. Here first is the speaker's perplexed and despairing address to the child:

> Full soon thy Soul shall have her earthly freight,
> And custom lie upon thee with a weight,
> Heavy as frost, and deep almost as life!
>
> [127–29]

Though the speaker has not yet realized it, the *weight* of custom is precisely what fits it to be what Wordsworth calls in "Tintern Abbey" the anchor of his purest thoughts. And the depth to which the weight of custom sinks is what insures that some part of ourselves remains out of our own reach, beyond our intellectual tampering. This is the same depth out of which the poet's response to the pansy is generated, the response which triggers the poem's meditation. This is also the depth he glimpses gratefully in the final lines of the poem when he comes to understand that to him "the meanest flower that blows can give / Thoughts that do often lie too deep for tears" (203–4). Here, the world in which he moves about *is* "realized."

IV

But how deep in Wordsworth's overall program for poetry lie Burke's thoughts about second nature? During his residence at Goslar (i.e., perhaps as early as the latter part of 1798), Wordsworth wrote the unfinished prose piece that Owen and Smyser have incorporated into their recent edition of the *Prose Works*.[27] They call it the *Essay on Morals*, but its subject is not so much morality as moral writing—specifically, the relation between moral writing and its rhetorical effect. In 1794, as we saw, Wordsworth had written to Mathews that "a knowledge of [the] rules of political justice . . . cannot but lead to good." The *Essay* opens with a very different opinion: "I think publications in which we formally & systematically lay down rules for the actions of Men cannot be too long delayed."[28] In 1793–94, like most adversaries of Burke, Wordsworth had made "reason" the standard of good conduct and "reasons" the proof of good discourse. The *Essay* calls both of these assumptions into question. The errors of recent moral systems have, indeed, only one cause for the author of this fragment; they are the "consequence of an undue value set upon that faculty which we call reason." What *should* value be set upon? "Our attention," he suggests, "ought principally to be fixed upon that part of our conduct & actions which is the result of our habits."

Such a shift in "value" or "attention" has practical implications for the enterprise of moral writing, for it will lead us to see that "bald & naked reasonings are impotent over our habits, they cannot form them." What is needed, in other words, is a kind of moral writing "with sufficient power to melt into our affection [?s], to incorporate itself with the blood & vital juices of our minds, & thence to have any influence worth our notice in forming those habits of which I am speaking." Such views, I would argue, belong to a man who has come to believe that what Burke called "prejudice" is an inevitable condition of human conduct. They suggest that between 1793 and 1798–99 a profound reversal has already taken place in Wordsworth's politicized epistemology, i.e., in his understanding of the mind and its alterability. Even Wordsworth's figures of speech in the *Essay* are Burkean. When he says, for example, that the rationalists "strip the mind of its old clothing," he is punning on "habit" just as Burke did when he called habits the "moral wardrobe of the imagination." Burke's related figure of reason's "nakedness," which looms so prominently in the France books of *The Prelude*, also appears in the *Essay* where Wordsworth speaks of our "bald & naked reasonings." Burke did not himself invent these figures, of course, but they are properly called Burkean because in the 1790s he invested them with an ideological power distinctively his own.

Unfortunately, the *Essay* remained an unfinished manifesto. We can never be certain of the direction it might have taken. We have a good indication of that direction, however, in the manifesto Wordsworth did complete, the 1800 Preface to *Lyrical Ballads*. That the argument of the Preface is continuous with that of the *Essay* becomes clear at the very beginning of the piece, where Wordsworth tells his reader that he has no "hope of *reasoning* him into an approbation of these poems" (*PrW* 1:120). The Preface is specifically *not* a formal and systematic laying down of rules. It seeks only to win attention for and patience with the poems it introduces. These poems must do their own moral work and embody their own moral purposes.

This question of purposiveness is perhaps the most crucial of all questions raised in the Preface. On the one hand Wordsworth claims that the distinguishing moral feature of these poems is "that each of them has a worthy purpose"; on the other, he insists that he does not always begin to write "with a distinct purpose formally conceived" (pp. 124–26). By emphasizing both the importance and the paradox of his notion of moral purpose, he requires that we attend carefully to his explanation of the origin of the purposes that guide his own work. They derive, he says, from "habits of meditation" that "have so formed my feelings, as that my descriptions of such objects as strongly excite those feelings, will be found to carry along with them a *purpose*" (p. 126). One eventually develops "such habits of mind . . . that by obeying blindly and mechanically the impulses of those habits we shall describe objects and utter sentiments of such a nature and in such connection with each other, that the understanding of the being to whom we address ourselves, if he be in a healthful state of association, must necessarily be in some degree enlightened, his taste exalted, and his affections ameliorated" (p. 126). On this account, clearly, moral authority depends on the predisposition of the writer, not on the inherent reasonableness of what he has written—on the formation of his taste, not on the cogency of his argument. The assumptions at work here, in other words, are very much the same as those which operate in Burke's *Reflections*, and hence point up the importance of self-dramatization for both writers.

We must not be misled by Wordsworth's use of the term "enlightened" to describe the state of mind of a reader so influenced, for the kind of "enlightenment" described here is quite at odds with what Wordsworth had advocated in the Letter to Llandaff and what he spelled out to Mathews, thus, in 1794:

> When I observe that people should be enlightened upon the subject of politics, I severely condemn all inflammatory addresses to the passions of men, even when it is intended to direct those passions to a good purpose. I know that the multitude walk in darkness. I would put into each man's hand a lantern to guide him and not have him to set out upon his journey depending for illumination on abortive flashes of lightning, or the corruscations of transitory meteors. [*EY*:125]

For the republican, enlightened discourse addresses the reason and in so doing restores vision to "liberty and philosophy, the eyes of the human race." To address the passions, as Watson does, is to aim an arrow at these eyes, to blind them. For the author of the Preface, however, enlightenment paradoxically has its genesis in such blindness. It proceeds from "blind and mechanical obedience" to habits of mind, or to use the words of the forty-eight-year-old Distributor of Stamps, from "modest reliance on old habits of judgment."

Wordsworth's work on this new poetry had of course begun long before it was so described in the 1800 Preface, before even the Goslar period when he is presumed to have written the *Essay on Morals*. Indeed, the manuscripts for the first volume of *Lyrical Ballads* (except that for "Tintern Abbey") were probably in the printer's hands more than three months before Wordsworth and Coleridge left for Germany in the autumn of 1798. Although the question of whether Wordsworth and Coleridge ever arrived at an explicit "plan" for this volume remains a matter of debate, we do know that Wordsworth wrote most of his "experimental" poems for this volume in the spring of 1798, the earliest dating from early March.[29] Moreover, the great literary plan to which all others (including that for *Lyrical Ballads*) were ultimately subsidiary, the plan for *The Recluse*, was first announced by Wordsworth in a letter of 6 March. One has to believe, I think, that what Abrams calls Wordsworth's "program for poetry" was born in the weeks immediately preceding early March 1798.[30] Thus the fundamental question is whether the attitudes of the 1800 Preface and the *Essay on Morals* are traceable to this earlier and seminal period.

One of the poems that most occupied Wordsworth's attention during the two months prior to early March 1798 is "The Old Cumberland Beggar."[31] Though not itself an experimental poem in the manner of "The Thorn" or "Simon Lee"—both probably composed between early March and mid-May (Reed *EY*:32)—"The Old Cumberland Beggar" nonetheless anticipates these developments with both its elevation of feeling over incident and its close attention to a character from common life. Further, the poem offers specific recommendations to the "Statesmen" it addresses and thus stands as the most explicitly political verse that Wordsworth produced in the decade between the Salisbury Plain poems of 1794–95 and the France books of *The Prelude*. The poem is germane in another way as well. I suggested above that Wordsworth's more recent critics have neglected to draw the connection between Wordsworth and Burke; one reason is that many have been too intent on seeing him as a prophetic visionary to recognize certain earthly facts about his political and intellectual allegiances. In *The Visionary Company*, a book that both issued from and contributed to this view of Wordsworth, Harold Bloom offers a reading of "The Old Cumberland Beggar" that provides an excellent case in point. Abrams thought enough of this interpretation to include it in a recent collection of essays on Wordsworth, in the introduction to which he praised Bloom's reading of the poem for showing Wordsworth's "reverence for essential human life."[32] According to the rubric under which this discussion appears in *The Visionary Company*, the poem shows us the "Natural Man," and Bloom opens his discussion by calling the poem "Wordsworth's finest vision of the irreducible natural man, the human stripped to the nakedness of primordial condition and exposed as still powerful in dignity, still infinite in value."[33] Bloom's account of the poem thus also epitomizes what I described above as the critical assumption that Wordsworth's idea of the natural is essentially Rousseauist.[34]

In his 1843 notes for Isabella Fenwick, Wordsworth described the political issue that occasioned the poem:

> ["The Old Cumberland Beggar":] Observed, and with great benefit to my own heart, when I was a child: written at Racedown and Alfoxden in my 28th year. The political economists were about that time beginning their war upon mendicity in all its forms, and by implication, if not directly, on Almsgiving also. This heartless process has been carried as far as it can go by the AMENDED poor-law bill, though the inhumanity that prevails in this measure is somewhat disguised by the profession that one of its objects is to throw the poor upon the voluntary donations of their neighbours; that is, if rightly interpreted, to

force them into a condition between relief in the Union poor-
house, and Alms robbed of their Christian grace and spirit, as
being *forced* rather from the benevolent than given by them;
while the avaricious and selfish, and all in fact but the humane
and charitable, are at liberty to keep all they possess from their
distressed brethren. [*PW* 4:445–46]

The "Statesmen" to whom the poem is addressed are evidently those
political economists whose campaign against "mendicity" would later
result in the Poor Law of 1834. The older Wordsworth opposed that law
just as he opposed the Reform Bill of 1832, and we might well expect such
opposition from the man who in 1831 called Burke "the wisest of the
Moderns." We would not expect, however, that the seventy-three-year-old
author of the Fenwick notes should be able to accommodate the politics of
his 1798 poem with such apparent ease. Nor can we dismiss the note as an
interpretation imposed by the elderly poet, for the poem fully supports such
a reading.

One striking feature of the note, for example, is the way Wordsworth
represents the problems of the poor from the point of view of those who are
not poor, beginning with himself: "Observed, and with great benefit to my
own heart, when I was a child." The benefit in question is the "Christian
grace and spirit" which, the poet fears, will no longer accrue to the
Alms*giver* if new legislation is passed. This perspective on the problem is
faithful to that of the poem, where the speaker's central appeal on behalf of
the Beggar is that the old man should not be deemed "useless" (67). " 'Tis
Nature's law," he explains, "That none, the meanest of created things, / Of
forms created the most vile and brute, / The dullest or most noxious, should
exist / Divorced from good" (73–77). The Beggar's "use" or "good" lies in
the benefit that the villagers derive from his presence among them, and
while this benefit may not be described in the explicitly Christian terms of
the Fenwick note, it falls unmistakably on the villagers themselves. Specifi-
cally, the Beggar's use, while he remains a beggar, is threefold. First, he is
an occasion of uncalculating acts of charity:

> Among the farms and solitary huts
> Hamlets, and thinly-scattered villages,
> Where'er the aged Beggar takes his rounds,
> The mild necessity of use compels
> To acts of love; and habit does the work
> Of reason, and yet prepares that after joy
> Which reason cherishes. And thus the soul,

By that sweet taste of pleasure unpursu'd
Doth find itself insensibly dispos'd
To virtue and true goodness.

[88–97]

This endorsement of the force of habit has, in the poem's political context, a number of implications which we will take up below. Here we can simply note that these lines already suggest that the moral epistemology of the *Essay on Morals* and the 1800 Preface was anticipated in those crucial weeks in early 1798. The second aspect of the Beggar's use to the villagers, closely tied to the first, is that he reminds the villagers of their kind offices toward him: "all behold in him / A silent monitor, which on their minds / Must needs impress a transitory thought / Of self-congratulation, to the heart / Of each recalling his peculiar boons, / His charters and exemptions" (114–19). In other words, the Beggar continually augments the benefit that falls to the benefactors—"And 'tis no vulgar service"—by making his blessing felt (124). The poem offers, in effect, an associationist account of the operation of "Christian grace and spirit."

Such a "defense" of the Beggar is unlikely to rest easy with the critic who wishes to see the author of *Lyrical Ballads* as a Blakean visionary or as a radical anthropologist like Rousseau. Bloom, in his reading of the poem, is willing to recognize that the most important function Wordsworth ascribes to the Beggar is, as he puts it, "that of a binding agent for the memories of good impulses for all around him." But Bloom seems curiously unwilling to accept the implications of this view. "We need to be careful in our reaction to this," he warns: "Wordsworth is not preaching the vicious and mad doctrine that beggary is good because it makes charity possible."[35] While Bloom obviously sees the need to caution his reader, he makes no concrete attempt to show why these lines do not mean what they seem to mean. Bloom's formulation of what Wordsworth is not preaching, though perhaps not precisely accurate, is much nearer the mark than Bloom wants to believe—closer, perhaps, than many of us would like to believe.

What *is* Wordsworth preaching in the poem? We might begin to answer this question by considering the passages which bracket the central account of the Beggar's usefulness. Wordsworth introduces this account with an ad hominem attack on the statesmen who are the addressees of the poem:

Statesmen! ye
Who are so restless in your wisdom, ye
Who have a broom still ready in your hands
To rid the world of nuisances; ye proud,

Heart-swoln, while in your pride ye contemplate
Your talents, power, and wisdom, deem him not
A burthen of the earth.

[67–73]

The "pride" of these men, we gather, finds its expression in their quickness
to deal with a problem such as poverty by means of state legislation. In the
poem's conclusion, the speaker advises the statesmen to leave such matters
alone. As for the Beggar, they should simply "let him pass, a blessing on his
head": .

And while, in that vast solitude to which
The tide of things has led him, he appears
To breathe and live but for himself alone,
Unblam'd, uninjur'd, let him bear about
The good which the benignant law of heaven
Has hung around him, and, while life is his,
Still let him prompt the unletter'd Villagers
To tender offices and pensive thoughts.

[55–63]

The Beggar's lot is not a pleasant one, but the speaker insists that the tide of
things which led him to it be allowed to run its course. No legislative
contrivance should curtail the Beggar's wanderings; no "House, misnamed
of Industry" should make him "captive" (172-73). This tide is governed by
the benignant law of heaven, and in the face of *this* legislation, human
lawmakers must remember their place.

The speaker's claims for the Beggar's "use" to the villagers has thus to
be seen as serving this larger quietistic argument about the limits of human
wisdom, the vanity of political science, and the justice of the ways of God to
man. So understood, in other words, the purposes of the poem would seem
to bear out the commentary offered in the 1843 Fenwick note. To gain an
even fuller sense of these purposes, however, we might reverse our perspec-
tive and consider the poem from the point of view of the 1790s. We might
return to the Letter to Llandaff, for example, and read there what Words-
worth had to say in 1793 about the government's duty toward the poor.
"Your lordship tells us that the science of civil government has received all
the perfection of which it is capable. For my part, I am more enthusiastic:
the sorrow I feel from the contemplation of this melancholy picture is not
unconsoled by a comfortable hope that the class of wretches called mendi-
cants will not much longer shock the feelings of humanity" (*PrW* 1:45).
Where the poet of "The Old Cumberland Beggar" laments (in the poem's

headnote) that "the class of Beggars to which the old man here described belongs, will probably soon be extinct," the polemicist to the Letter to Llandaff has hopes that the "class of wretches called mendicants" would soon be eliminated. For the doughty young republican, obviously, the sight of a beggar is not a benefit, not a pleasant reminder of one's good deeds or an emblem of divine law. Quite to the contrary, it is the occasion of a "shock" that should prompt government to develop the "science" necessary to alleviate the sufferings of such men.

In the *Letters on a Regicide Peace*, published in 1796–97 and known to be one of the few books in Wordsworth's possession during that year, Burke touched briefly on the question of the government's role in economic matters:

> An untimely shower or an unseasonable drought, a frost too long continued or too suddenly broken up with rain and tempest, the blight of the spring or the smut of the harvest will do more to cause the distress of the belly than all the contrivances of all statesmen can do to relieve it. Let government protect and encourage industry, secure property, repress violence, and discountenance fraud, it is all that they have to do. In other respects, the less they meddle in these affairs, the better; the rest is in the hands of our Master and theirs. [*BW* 5:465–66]

Burke will "push this matter no further" here, he says, because he has spoken upon it before. One such occasion was his "Thoughts and Details on Scarcity" (1795), in which he not only argues that "to provide for us in our necessities is not in the power of government," but also lends to his commentary that kind of moral dimension which characterizes the commentary of "The Old Cumberland Beggar": "it would be a vain presumption in statesmen to think that they can do it" (*BW* 5:133–34). Burke insists that "Statesmen who know themselves" will confine themselves to "what regards the state" and that "whatever remains will, in a manner, provide for itself" (pp. 166–67). Vain and presumptuous legislators who do not know themselves suffer a fall like Satan's, but obey the laws of Newton's apple in their course: "As they descend from the state to a province, from a province to a parish, and from a parish to a private house, they go on accelerated in their fall" (p. 167). Once they fail to distinguish "what belongs to laws, and what manners alone can regulate," they set themselves and their nation on the course of total confusion. After contrasting French and English practice on this question of the role of government, Burke concludes with this summary: "My opinion is against overdoing any sort of administration, and more especially against this most momentous of all meddling on the part of the authority,—the meddling with the subsistence of the people" (p. 169).

The evident agreement of "The Old Cumberland Beggar" with this opinion might well count for less if it were not grounded in the same social and epistemological principles. But when Burke claims that modern statesmen have neglected the province of "manners" he is referring to what in the *Reflections* he calls "civil habitudes or connections," which comprise "that natural discipline which is the soul of a true republic"—not to be confused with the false republic of Platonic perfectionism (3:435). He is referring to "the effect of those habits which are communicated by the circumstances of civil life" and to what he calls the second nature that operates on the first to produce a new combination, the second nature that the legislators of the ancient republics, unlike most legislators of the modern, know better than to ignore (pp. 476–77). "Manners" in this sense is the real topic of "The Old Cumberland Beggar." The poem advocates natural manners, to be sure, but then so does Burke, as we have seen repeatedly. And that the Burkean sense of "nature" operates in Wordsworth's poem is nowhere clearer than in its famous final lines: "As in the eye of Nature he has liv'd, / So in the eye of Nature let him die." The eye of Nature, we understand from the speaker's earlier remarks, is the eye of the villager whose perception is governed by the mild necessity of use. Far from those "eyes of the human race" ("liberty and philosophy") exalted in the Letter to Llandaff, this is a faculty in which habit does the work of reason and, in other descriptions of its function, feeling the work of willing, divine law the work of human law, providence the work of political science.

If we agree to such terms, we must be prepared to face quite a different poet from the one Bloom presents to us in *The Visionary Company*. We must in fact conclude that the poem is not the radically "humanistic" assertion that Bloom would like us (and like himself) to believe and, second, that the poem is less crucially concerned with "the human stripped to the nakedness of primordial condition" than with those habits in which, as Burke puts it, "our naked shivering nature" must be clothed. But most importantly, because of the crucial position of "The Old Cumberland Beggar" in Wordsworth's poetic development, we must also be prepared to accept a view of his career quite different from the one that is most familiar to us.

V

In arguing for Wordsworth's unacknowledged debt to Burke, I would not wish to be understood as suggesting that Wordsworth ever became Burke's literary twin, or that Burke offers a key to all Wordsworthian mysteries.

Burke may have been regarded as a literary genius by his contemporaries, Wordsworth among them, but he was neither a maker of verses nor a teller of tales. And as I tried to suggest earlier, Wordsworth's historical, rhetorical, and personal circumstances were very different from Burke's. He perceived a different national crisis from the one that enraged and frightened Burke, or at least a different phase of the same crisis. His audience in the major period was different from Burke's. He traveled in a circle of friends very different from Johnson, Goldsmith, Reynolds, and the Rockingham Whigs. On certain issues, moreover, Wordsworth and Burke simply had differences of opinion. Such differences must be conceded, though they may not always be as sharp as they seem.

We might consider the question of social rank, for example, where we would expect strong disagreement between the two writers. In that part of the *Reflections* where Burke develops the idea of second nature as a guide for legislators, he goes on to use it to justify a hierarchical social structure. Having understood the importance of "civil habitudes," the ancient lawmakers (he argues) "thought themselves obliged to dispose their citizens into such classes, and to place them in such situations in the state, as their peculiar habits might qualify them to fill, and to allot to them such appropriated privileges as might secure to them what their specific occasions required, and which might furnish to each description such force as might protect it in the conflict caused by the diversity of interests that must exist, and must contend, in all complex society" (3:477). Of course, Wordsworth could never have committed himself to this kind of endorsement of class distinction, and any reader of the poetry could point to evidence of Wordsworth's opposition to such statements. In a well-known passage from *The Prelude*, for example, Wordsworth criticizes books that flatter "our self-conceit" by depicting "The differences, the outside marks by which / Society has parted man from man, / Neglectful of the universal heart" (12:216–19). And when the speaker of "The Old Cumberland Beggar" decides that "we all of us have one human heart" (146), he is advocating this same democracy of the emotions.

We must beware of pushing the contrast too far, however, for *this* brand of "democracy" was in fact advocated by Burke himself. Burke discriminates this kind of democracy from the false (French) version in his effort to explain to De Pont what France lost in not following the English example: "You would have had a protected, satisfied, laborious, and obedient people, taught to seek and to recognize the happiness that is to be found by virtue in all conditions,—in which consists *the true moral equality of mankind*, and not in that monstrous fiction which, by inspiring false ideas and vain expectations into men destined to travel in the obscure walk of laborious life, serves only to aggravate and embitter that real inequality which it never can remove, and which the order of civil life establishes as much for the benefit of those whom it must leave in an humble state as those whom it is able to exalt to a condition more splendid but not more happy" (3:279–80; italics mine). For Burke, material inequality is inevitable but also inconsequential. Moral equality, on the other hand, is crucial and, with "virtue," attainable. We must therefore ask ourselves whether Wordsworth's doctrine of the universal heart does not go hand in hand with an acknowledgment of inevitable (or "natural") social and economic hierarchies.

This connection is, I believe, fairly explicit in much that Wordsworth has written. The Wanderer of *The Excursion*, explaining that the "primal duties shine aloft," spells out the difference between true and false equality much as Burke does in the *Reflections*:

> The smoke ascends
> To heaven as lightly from the cottage-hearth
> As from the haughtiest palace. He, whose soul
> Ponders this true equality, may walk
> The fields of earth with gratitude and hope.
>
> [9:245–49]

Material disparity (the difference between cottage and palace) is taken for granted in this passage but is rendered "immaterial" by the true spiritual equity represented by the rising smoke. We need not look ahead to "The Wanderer," however, to see this relation at work in Wordsworth's poetry. It is implicit, I think, in what we have already noticed about "The Old Cumberland Beggar," especially when that poem is set against the earlier Letter to Llandaff. That a social hierarchy is implicit in the poem can also be seen in a passage we have not yet considered, the opening description of the Beggar:

> The aged man
> Had placed his staff across the broad smooth stone
> That overlays the pile, and from a bag
> All white with flour, the dole of village dames,
> He drew his scraps and fragments, one by one,
> And scann'd them with a fix'd and serious look
> Of idle computation. In the sun,
> Upon the second step of that small pile,

Surrounded by those wild unpeopled hills,
He sate, and eat his food in solitude;
And ever, scatter'd from his palsied hand,
That still attempting to prevent the waste,
Was baffled still, the crumbs in little showers
Fell on the ground, and the small mountain birds,
Not venturing yet to peck their destin'd meal,
Approached within the length of half his staff.

[6–21]

While the poem insists that the Beggar has a human heart, he is made to seem very like an animal in this description, drawing out his scraps and scanning them dumbly. The picture of the Beggar is clearly not a detail from Burke's historical painting of "the swinish multitude." Yet the analogy between the beggar's dependence on the village dames and the mountain birds' dependence on him is inescapable, and we cannot fail to see the Beggar's status as midway between them on the great chain of being. The state of affairs implicit in this description is simply registered in the text without comment. It is a "given." If the poem is not precisely a celebration of this state of affairs, we are nonetheless not asked to consider how it might be changed. *That* it might be changed would rather seem to be the poet's great fear.

Five

Rousseau and the Politics of Education

> All our wisdom consists in servile prejudices. All our practices are only subjection, impediment, and constraint. Civil man is born, lives, and dies in slavery. At his birth he is sewed in swaddling clothes. . . . So long as he keeps his human shape, he is enchained by our institutions.
>
> Rousseau, *Emile*

"The Old Cumberland Beggar," with its admonishment to "Statesmen," is an explicitly political poem. But although Wordsworth made a point of sending a copy of the two-volume edition of *Lyrical Ballads* to Charles James Fox in 1800, the "Beggar" is virtually the only explicitly political poem to appear in the collection. This fact, curious enough in itself, becomes more curious still when we consider that the "Beggar" was one of the very few of Wordsworth's poems in *Lyrical Ballads* to be composed before the poet's announcement of a new project, one that would occupy his utmost attention through the major period and beyond. "My object," he wrote to James Tobin in the often-quoted letter of 6 March 1798, "is to give pictures of Nature, Man, and Society. Indeed I know not anything which will not come within the scope of my plan" (*EY*: 123). Wordsworth probably composed the political passages for the "Beggar" (such as the address to the statesmen) sometime during the six weeks prior to his announcement to Tobin. He would include no similarly explicit political comment in any poem until 1802.

The Prelude, Wordsworth's most important political poem, though not his most explicit, was of course getting well under way in the period

93

from 1798 to 1802. In the full-length version familiar to modern readers, however, *The Prelude* gives the clearest signs of its ideological orientation in the France books. In the years 1798–1802, as modern scholarship on the poem's genesis has shown, the design called for no treatment whatsoever of Wordsworth's experience of the Revolution. If we look to Wordsworth's work in the years prior to 1798, we find an array of overtly radical poetry and prose. If we look beyond *The Prelude* to *The Excursion* and *The Convention of Cintra*, the political dimension becomes as explicit as it had been in the radical writings of the 1790s. The question, then, is simply this: what happened to Wordsworth's political interests, so evident beforehand and afterward, in the seminal years that comprise the first half of his great decade?

The best lead toward a solution of this problem has emerged from the findings of those scholars who have established a sense of what *The Prelude* was meant to be before Wordsworth decided to expand it into the thirteen-book poem he completed in late 1805. The rough chronology is now fairly clear. Wordsworth began work on the poem in late 1798, and in early 1804 he maintained a view of the poem still probably close to his initial conception: "a Poem on my own earlier life," as he put it to Francis Wrangham in late January or early February, "which will take five books or parts to complete" (*EY*:436). Wordsworth told Wrangham he had three of the books nearly finished. By early March he had completed a fourth and was turning to the last (p. 452). By 12 March he seems already decided on extending the poem (p. 456).[1]

Although the evidence therefore shows that Wordsworth nearly completed the five-book poem before deciding to expand it, the labor of reconstruction has been difficult. Even Jonathan Wordsworth, the five-book *Prelude*'s most ambitious editor, admits that some pieces of the puzzle are probably forever lost or scrambled. Nonetheless, building on the work of those who came before him, he does make a convincing case for his view of the poem's general shape, especially with books 1 through 4. Books 1–3 correspond roughly to the first three books of the 1805 *Prelude*—they were in fact copied before Wordsworth's decision to expand. Book 4 evidently fell into two sections, one corresponding to the narrative of the Long Vacation at Hawkshead in book 4 of the 1805 *Prelude* and the other corresponding to the discussion of books and education in book 5 of the full-length poem. The final book was probably going to feature the account of the ascent of Snowdon and the famous passage that begins "There are in our existence spots of time."[2] This general outline, whose contours have become increasingly clear since de Selincourt's work of decades ago, quite reasonably leads the most recent editors of the five-book poem to conclude that it is "about a poet's education, by nature and by books, down to the end of his formal education when he was twenty."[3]

This well-supported hypothesis has implications that we should not be reluctant to consider. What book 5 ("Books") is doing in the full-length *Prelude*, for example, is a question that has long exercised Wordsworthians. Book 5's discussion of good and bad educational practice has been a particularly vexing issue. The current view of the five-book *Prelude* provides at least a genetic account of why this material is where it is: in the version of the five-book poem outlined above, the remarks on education would have served the crucial function of discursively summing up the implications of the earlier narrative material on Wordsworth's childhood. Another, more speculative line of inquiry suggested by the five-book *Prelude* relates to Rousseau, whose ideas about education are invariably discussed in commentary on the book on "Books."[4] His *Emile*, probably the period's most widely influential book on education, must acquire a new relevance to Wordsworth's project when *both* works can be described as quasi-philosophical arguments in five books that cover the stages of a child's natural education from infancy to early manhood.

I set these issues momentarily aside because I would like to consider them in the light of a more general consequence of the hypothesis about the five-book *Prelude*. Our sense of it may be sketchy, but this poem would have been the most substantial work Wordsworth produced in the years immediately following 1798. Understood as the design for a work about education, I will argue, the plan for this poem furnishes a key to the nature of the larger plan of which it formed a part. To see how requires another look at the circumstances of the larger plan's conception.

I

Apart from possible work on the lines that became the Prospectus, most of Wordsworth's time during the six weeks preceding his announcement to James Tobin was probably occupied by just two tasks. One, as I have mentioned, was the expansion of "The Old Cumberland Beggar" to include its explicitly political dimension. The other was the expansion of *The Ruined Cottage* to include a detailed history of its main character's education. In this compact *Bildungsroman*, Wordsworth worked out ideas, images, and phrases on which he drew heavily in subsequent writings. Nothing else he wrote compares with the power of these 250-odd lines to feed Wordsworth's future years.

Nor is it difficult to see why this exercise proved so valuable to him.

He had composed *The Ruined Cottage* in the previous summer, and now he found himself returning to it. Although the central narrative of the poem relates the pathetic story of Margaret, the last human tenant of the cottage, the ideological center of the poem is the character of the Pedlar, who tells Margaret's story to the speaker. He wields the poem's moral authority. The education Wordsworth wrote for the Pedlar therefore had to establish the old man's character on the strongest possible grounds, a requirement that left Wordsworth with the task of constructing for him the best of all possible educations. As it happened, this perfect upbringing turned out to resemble Wordsworth's own. The poet admitted as much decades later when he told Isabella Fenwick that "the character I have represented in his person is chiefly an idea of what I fancied my own character might have become in his circumstances" (*PW* 5:373). But the difference in circumstances was no doubt helpful in allowing Wordsworth to draw on his own experience at this trial stage without risking the charge of self-aggrandizement. It is only one measure of the importance of these lines on the growth of the Pedlar's mind that Wordsworth could later incorporate many of them, sometimes changing only third-person pronouns to first-person, into the poem on the growth of his own.[5]

Since the influence of the Pedlar's educational biography pervades so much of the writing undertaken in the service of Wordsworth's great plan, and since the announcement of the plan itself comes so quickly on the heels of this passage's composition, it would seem that Wordsworth's work on a model education is the immediate context of the invention of the plan. But what would lead Wordsworth to think that a character's moral authority is best established by showing the quality of his education? The answer to this question lies, in turn, in the immediate context of the work on the Pedlar's education. This story, which was first told by David Erdman, has to do with Wordsworth's and Coleridge's involvement with the educational schemes of Thomas Wedgwood in late 1797.[6] "Vistas of considerable reach," Erdman argued, "are opened by the discovery that when Tom Wedgwood visited Coleridge and Wordsworth in September 1797 he had it in mind to sound them out as candidates—'the only persons that I know of as at all likely'—for superintendents of a Nursery of Genius" (p. 487). Erdman does see far-reaching implications in his discovery. He believes that "Wedgwood's ideas about systematic growth" provided a polemical target and a suggestive source for much of Wordsworth's subsequent writing. For although book 5 of the completed *Prelude* "satirize[s] the whole idea of artificial tutelage," Erdman contends that Wedgwood's ideas proved to be "the most fruitful stimulus of [Wordsworth's] career" (p. 497). The proof is in the writing: "before meeting Wedgwood he had not articulated a single thought upon the subject of *the influence of natural objects on the growth of genius*—nor had he made the slightest attempt at a biographical study of his own or anyone else's mental growth" (pp. 497–98). And to document his claim for the immediacy of Wedgwood's impact, Erdman points to Wordsworth's work on the Pedlar's biography later that winter.

Writing in 1956, Erdman did not have the benefit of either Reed's *Chronology* or the recent reconstruction of the design of the five-book *Prelude*. If he had, he might have seen that the vistas opened by his discovery of Wordsworth's involvement with Wedgwood reach even further than he suggested. There is also a problem internal to Erdman's argument, however, for in demonstrating the role of the Wedgwood plan as a crucial moment in Wordsworth's intellectual biography, Erdman tends to slight the role of other, more momentous educational schemes. For example, against the observations by de Selincourt that book 5 alludes to *Emile* in making an "explicit criticism of Rousseau's 'tutor,' with his artificial manipulation of Nature's lessons," Erdman apparently feels he has to argue from manuscript evidence that the original passage about modern educators, which dates to 1798–99, "reads rather like a direct attack on such grand improvements in Education as Wedgwood and Beddoes were advocating" (p. 493). Addressing himself chiefly to Erdman's argument, Joel Morkan, in a discussion of the "unity" of book 5, has argued for the necessity of reading the book "in the light of [Wordsworth's] reaction to current educational ideas" in general and to Rousseau in particular:

> Among the major philosophers, however, Rousseau's educational theory, camouflaging an elaborate set of controls beneath a surface appearance of freedom and spontaneity, would have appeared to Wordsworth the most subtle and insidious of plans. There is an illusion of liberty, but it merely hides the most rigid of limitations. Everything is calculated. . . .[7]

While noting the apparent clash between the points of view of Erdman and de Selincourt, Morkan contends that there is no need to choose between them. "It is more useful," he explains, "to focus on the general intention of the satire in book 5 than on a specific target."[8]

This revision of Erdman is largely salutary, but it fails to see what is finally at stake in this question of educational "freedom." Like Erdman, Morkan locates Wordsworth's writing in the context of educational theory without appreciating the "ideological horizon" circumscribing the educational theory itself. This oversight leads Morkan to represent Wordsworth anachronistically as a Dickensian liberal of the 1840s and 1850s: "He feared that the changes which were taking place in early nineteenth-century educational practice were transforming the world of childhood freedom, symbolized by Hawkshead, into a mental prison with a Gradgrind-like chief warden."[9] But even if the world of *Hard Times* was, in Dickens' pun, "bound to be," it was still several decades away. To understand the purport of Wordsworth's educational program on its own terms, we must look to the world Wordsworth actually knew, to an England influenced by Revolutionary France and a Revolutionary France influenced by decades of philosophical enlightenment. For in this world, educational schemes and political schemes went hand in hand, and the systematic education associated with the name of Rousseau had a well-established political meaning. The five-book *Prelude* could so easily grow into a poem about Enlightenment and Revolution, in other words, because in some sense that is what it had been all along.

II

It may be true, as some suggest, that a political utopia is implicit in every theory of education.[10] It may be equally true that utopian political schemes, when they are taken seriously, necessarily produce fresh thinking about education. But whether or not the relationship between political and educational theory is necessarily reciprocal, it was certainly thought to be reciprocal in the age of Rousseau, and this view was strongly held by the intellectual leadership of the French Revolution. One reason why the Revolution recognized Rousseau as its natural father was almost certainly that it perceived him to have illuminated the connection between the two domains. In France's public rhetoric during the 1790s, Rousseau was routinely referred to as "the author of *Emile* and the *Social Contract*." And Rousseau himself encouraged the conjunction of the two works (and of the kind of theory each work involved) not only by publishing them within months of one another in 1762, but also by taking pains to show that each followed from the same principles of right, principles derived in the analysis of the State of Nature published six years earlier in the Second Discourse. As the *Social Contract* showed how the just society should be governed, so *Emile* showed how the good citizen should be raised.[11]

Both the public regard for Rousseau and the nature of his perceived legacy to the Revolution can be suggested by the Revolution's official acts of homage to him. The first of these acts occurred in December 1790, a month after Burke's *Reflections* had appeared, when the National Assembly voted unanimously in favor of the following proposal: "Il sera élevé à l'auteur d'*Emile* et du *Contrat social* une statue portant cette inscription: LA NATION FRANÇAISE LIBRE A J.-J. ROUSSEAU."[12] Rousseau was the first individual so to be honored by the Revolutionary government, and the action immediately prompted Burke to launch a fresh attack against both the revolution in general and Rousseau in particular. This attack was published under the title *Letter to a Member of the National Assembly* in May 1791, just months after the Assembly's decree. The Letter shows clearly that Burke understood the French to be honoring Rousseau the educator as well as Rousseau the political writer; its discussion of Rousseau's unfitness as a moral teacher provides the occasion for what is perhaps Burke's only detailed comment on the relation of political concerns to the education of the young.[13]

In spite of the unanimity for the Assembly's first decree, there was no public ceremony in Rousseau's honor until a second decree was carried out three years later in the first months of the Thermidorean period, a time when, as we know from *The Prelude*, Wordsworth was paying special attention to affairs in France. On 11 October 1794, Rousseau's remains were solemnly transported from Ermenonville and enshrined in the newly established Pantheon for Revolutionary heroes.[14] The principal speaker at the dedication ceremony, fittingly, was Joseph Lakanal, the educational theorist who had ushered the proposal for Rousseau's Pantheonization through the Convention a month earlier. His dedicatory address, which circulated in pamphlet form as the "Report on J. J. Rousseau," was delivered "in the name of" the Convention's powerful Committee on Public Instruction.[15] Both this document and its sequel will repay far more attention than we can afford to give them here, where discussion is restricted to matters most relevant to Wordsworth's later enterprise.

Lakanal's speech takes for granted the reciprocity of Rousseau's political and educational views. Sensing that the actual influence of Rousseau's ideas about education has not been fully appreciated, however, Lakanal seeks to redress the balance. He concedes the immense *value* of "the Social Contract and other political writings": "It is true that in these immortal works, and chiefly in that first one, [Rousseau] developed the true principles of social theory, and reached back into the primitive essence of human associations" (pp. 3–4). At the same time, Lakanal wants to argue for what he takes to be the greater *impact* of the *Emile*:

> The great maxims developed in the *Social Contract*, self-evident and simple as they seem to us today, actually produced little effect. One did not sufficiently understand them either to have profited from them or to have feared them. . . . It was, in a

sense, the Revolution that explained them to us. Thus another
work had to lead us to the Revolution, elevate us, instruct us,
fashion us for it. This work is *Emile*, the only code of education
sanctioned by nature. [pp. 4–5]

When Lakanal goes on to enumerate some of the beneficial effects of the
book, he makes their political consequences apparent:

The very name of this work immediately recalls great services
rendered to humanity. Childhood delivered from the barbarous
ties that deform it; the method of reason substituted for that of
prejudice and of routine; learning [*enseigner*] rendered easy for
him who could receive it, and the road of virtue [*la route de la
vertu*] smoothed out like that of science. [p. 6]

The many who heeded the command of nature as interpreted by Rousseau in
Emile had already accomplished "an immense revolution in our institutions
and in our manners," so the argument goes, and this revolution is what
made it possible, perhaps inevitable, to carry out the political revolution
promised in the *Social Contract* (p. 6).

The sequel came two weeks after the Pantheonization ceremony when
Lakanal addressed the National Convention on the subject of education,
again "*au nom du comité d'instruction publique.*"[16] Like the earlier speech, too,
it was grounded firmly on the notion of a strong reciprocity between
education and politics. "Education," Lakanal told the Convention, "holds
so essentially to the primary social institutions of a people—the constitu-
tion so needs to be made for education, and education for the constitution—
that both will be lacking if they are not the work of the same mind, the same
genius, if they are not somehow the correlative parts of one and the same
conception" (p. 347). Since Lakanal himself had urged the Convention to
approve Rousseau's Pantheonization a few weeks earlier, and since the
spectacular tribute to Rousseau as philosopher and educator would still
have been fresh in the minds of the Convention's representatives, the single
mind, genius, and conception would probably have been understood as
Rousseauist. *Emile* and *La Nouvelle Héloïse*, furthermore, are the only two
books Lakanal mentions by name.

Lakanal's aim in addressing the Convention was not, however, to
praise Rousseau again but to promote an "organizational plan" for a system
of national education. When Lakanal and the Abbé Sieyes had proposed
roughly the same plan to the Jacobin-dominated Convention in June 1793,
Robespierre's forces had squelched it, but now that Robespierre was gone
the convention showed a clear willingness to listen.[17] In the Pantheoniza-

tion, which was conceivably part of a Lakanalian strategy both to test the political waters and to make the Convention more receptive to his Committee's proposal, Lakanal was seeking primarily to raise the prestige of Rousseau as educator. He therefore claimed on that occasion that *Emile* had already effected the revolution in education, had already supplanted the education of prejudice and routine with that of reasoned method. Before the Convention, on the other hand, Lakanal argued that the real educational revolution had hardly begun. And his address relies on a sense of the reciprocity between politics and education somewhat altered from that offered in the Pantheonization speech.

Lakanal prefaces his remarks with an accusation and an apology, both having to do with what he calls the embarrassing failure of the five-year-old Revolution to approve and implement a system of public education. The accusation is aimed at Robespierre and those who accompanied or followed him to the guillotine: "A few months ago, men who had their own motives for wanting to cover everything in darkness were ready to treat as criminals those who would have spoken to you of education and enlightenment" (p. 347). These were men who, perhaps more than the tyrants they helped to oust, "could truly be said to have feared enlightened men as brigands and assassins fear street lamps." But the Jacobins were only part of a larger problem that had not adequately been perceived by Lakanal and his enlightened colleagues. Those who pressed for educational reform during the Terror, he now admits, "had consulted the impatience of our desires rather than the nature of things, and our wishes rather than our means." They had only recently come to recognize certain principles in "the nature of things":

> To succeed in establishing a plan of public instruction on which the human mind can base its grand and legitimate hopes, several conditions are necessary. It is first necessary that the principles of government be such that, far from having anything to fear from the progress of reason, they gain from reason an ever-renewed force and authority. It is then necessary that experience, be it good or bad, should naturally consolidate this government as good; that it be full of life and movement, but that it be no longer tormented by tempests; that liberty have no further conquests to make; and that the entire people should feel that, to push back forever the criminal attacks of the monarchy and the aristocracy, one must submit democracy to reason; finally it is necessary that the human mind have made sufficient progress to be sure of possessing the methods and the instruments that will enable them to enlighten every mind and to make every possible advance. [p. 347]

When did these conditions first obtain? "Not until the present time," says Lakanal, "perhaps not even until the present moment."

I won't rehearse the argument by which Lakanal shows how each of these conditions had come to be fulfilled both in the long history of enlightenment that he traces back to Bacon and in the immediate history of the Revolution that he follows up to the fall of Robespierre. It is clear, however, that where the Pantheonization speech presented a simple history of an educational change leading to a political change, the address to the Convention traces a complicated dialectic in which enlightenment and the reconstruction of society on just principles are mutually dependent, mutually reinforcing activities. The fundamental law of this dialectic is that monarchy and pure rational instruction cannot coexist: "Either the instruction would topple the throne, or the throne would corrupt the instruction" (p. 348). In France, instruction had not only toppled the throne, but also survived the Terror, and all Europe now "submits to the power of reason." But Lakanal goes on to warn the Convention that unless this reason is fully refined, the accomplishments of the Revolution will come to a halt. "It is the moment," he says, "when we must gather together in a plan of public instruction worthy of you, worthy of France and of human kind, the enlightenment accumulated by the centuries that preceded us, and the seeds of enlightenment that will be purchased by the centuries that follow us" (p. 348).

The essence of the plan Lakanal proposes lies in the notion of applying to social problems the rational method of scientific inquiry. This is the method—Lakanal calls it "analysis"—that "counts all the steps it takes, but that never takes a step backward or to the side" (p. 348). Analysis is able to carry the "same simplicity of language" and "the same clarity" in the development of social and moral ideas as in scientific ones because "in all kinds of ideas the formation of our ideas is the same, only the objects different." The moral leverage of this analysis is as sure as its procedures are valid:

> By this method, which alone can re-create human understanding, the moral sciences so necessary to people who govern themselves by their own virtues, will be surmised as rigorous in their demonstration as the exact and physical sciences; by this method one spreads over the principles of our duties a light so lively that it cannot be obscured even by the cloud of passions. . . . [p. 348]

Just as political and economic liberty destroyed "the monstrous inequality of riches," so "analysis, applied to all kinds of ideas, will destroy the inequality of enlightenment." Analysis is therefore, according to this argument, "an instrument indispensable to a great democracy" (p. 348).

The goal of Lakanal's plan is to put this indispensable tool into the hands not only of every citizen in France but ultimately of every citizen in an evisioned European republic. On the analogy of fluids affected by gravity, Lakanal imagines enlightenment spreading ("trickling down," we would say now) from the top to the lowest possible levels. The most enlightened philosophers in Europe would be assembled in Paris where they would bring in promising students whom they would teach to teach the method:

> As soon as these courses in the art of teaching human knowledge are terminated, the wise and philosophic youths who have received these great lessons will go and repeat them in all parts of the republic from which they were called: they will open normal schools everywhere; in going back over the art they have come to learn, they will fortify themselves in it, and in teaching it to others, the necessity of questioning their own genius will enhance their views and their talents. This source of so pure an enlightenment, so abundant, when it goes out from the first men of the republic in all forms, overflowing reservoir after reservoir, spreads from space to space through all of France, without losing anything of its purity in its course. To the Pyrenees and to the Alps, the art of teaching will be the same as in Paris, and this art will be that of nature and genius. [p. 349]

Lakanal's is a vision of a Continent educated by French philosophes—indeed a Continent composed of French philosophes. It is a Gallic, enlightened version of Blake's biblical wish that all the Lord's people were prophets. This image of Europe's future was sufficiently pleasing to the Convention that, after a friendly debate and minor revision, they adopted the Committee's plan in early 1795, a decision that marked a new era in the history of French education.

This same plan, with its political implications, is also the chief target of Wordsworth's polemic in book 5 of *The Prelude* and the unstated subject of his initial five-book poem about education. Ultimately, it must be recognized as embodying the spirit against which Wordsworth developed his own great plan in 1798. Before suggesting how this anti-Rousseauism bears on the interpretation of the poetry in question, I should say something

about the likelihood of Wordsworth's familiarity with the ambitions of the
Committee on Public Instruction.[18]

III

We know from book 10 of *The Prelude* (568–86) that, although back in
England, Wordsworth watched affairs in France closely during the Ther-
midorean period that included both the Pantheonization of Rousseau and
the Committee's new educational proposal. There is reason to believe that
Wordsworth would have taken special note, however, of these particular
events. In June 1794, a month before the fall of Robespierre and four
months before Lakanal's important speeches, Wordsworth wrote a letter to
his friend William Mathews in reference to their intended collaboration on
a political journal to be called *The Philanthropist*. Because Wordsworth
thinks it appropriate to make a solemn declaration of his political views
before entering into such a collaboration, this letter, though it was obvi-
ously not, like the *Letter to the Bishop of Llandaff* (1793), intended for print,
offers almost as much information as the earlier document about Words-
worth's politics in the first phase of his adult career. And the opening
profession of political faith shows that his views are basically unchanged
from what he held when he attacked Bishop Watson: he says that he
"disapprove[s] of monarchical and aristocratical governments, however
modified"; he thinks "Hereditary distinctions and privileged orders of
every species . . . must necessarily counteract the progress of human
improvement," and "hence it follows" that he is "not amongst the admirers
of the British Constitution"; he conceives that "a more excellent system of
civil policy" might be established in England; and he hails "the changes of
opinion respecting matters of Government which within these few years
have rapidly taken place in the minds of speculative men" (*EY*:123-24).

These announcements make Wordsworth's stand on the major issues
quite clear. In the body of the letter Wordsworth tells Mathews in similarly
certain terms what he thinks the magazine should aim to do and what it
should contain. After stating his notions about the magazine in a general
way, he offers some concrete suggestions:

> It would contribute much to render our work interesting could
> we have any foreign correspondence informing us of the prog-
> ress of knowledge in the different metropolises of Europe, and of
> those new publications which either attract or merit attention.
> These writings our knowledge of languages would enable us to
> peruse and it would be well to extract from them the parts
> distinguished by particular excellence. It would be well also if

you could procure a perusal of the french monitor; for while we expressed our detestation of the execrable measures pursued in France we should belie our title if we did not hold up to the approbation of the world such of their regulations and decrees as are dictated by the spirit of Philosophy. [p. 128]

Because we have so little documentation of Wordsworth's interests in the years after his graduation from Cambridge, we can easily draw the mistaken conclusion that he simply did not read much then, a conclusion that even finds apparent support in some of Wordsworth's own retrospective accounts. *The Prelude* itself does not name a single writer or book that Wordsworth read at this time—not even Rousseau, who is quoted so knowingly in the Letter to Llandaff. The autobiographical letter to Anne Taylor of 1801 would have its reader believe that the poet had lived in virtual isolation from contemporary intellectual influences (*EY*:326–29). But on those rare occasions when we do hear the twenty-three- or twenty-four-year-old Wordsworth speaking for himself, we are left with a very different impression. In the 1794 letter to Mathews the sentence of particular relevance is of course the one about the "french monitor." The *Moniteur* was the official organ of the French National Assembly and printed its proceedings. Both the September 1794 debate on the Pantheonization of Rousseau and the subsequent discussions of the proposal for the reorganization of the schools appeared in its pages. Lakanal's important address before the Convention, furthermore, was printed in full.[19] Wordsworth's remark to Mathews supplies good reason to believe that he would have been reading the *Moniteur* with considerable care in the early Thermidorean period. Nor are we required to imagine that he merely happened upon the address, for his comment indicates that he would have been combing the pages of the *Moniteur* for just this sort of material.

What could better epitomize what he calls "regulations and decrees . . . dictated by the spirit of Philosophy" than Lakanal's enlighted proposal, especially if we take as our guide the spirit of Wordsworth's philosophic magazine? Here is Wordsworth's own radical vision of education, the one the *Philanthropist* project was meant to help realize:

A writer who has the welfare of mankind at heart should call forth his best exertions to convince the people that they can only be preserved from a convulsion by œconomy in the administration of the public purse and a gradual and constant reform of those abuses which, if left to themselves, may grow to such a height as to render, even a revolution desirable. There is a further duty incumbent upon every enlightened friend of man-

kind; he should let slip no opportunity of explaining and
enforcing those general principles of the social order which are
applicable to all times and to all places; he should diffuse by
every method a knowledge of those rules of political justice,
from which the farther any government deviates the more
effectually must it defeat the object for which government was
ordained. A knowledge of these rules cannot but lead to good;
they include an entire preservative from despotism, they will
guide the hand of reform, and if a revolution must afflict us,
they alone can mitigate its horrors and establish freedom with
tranquillity. [p. 124]

There are obvious differences between what Wordsworth says to Mathews
and what Lakanal would say to the Convention four months later. Words-
worth speaks not in the aftermath of a violent revolution in his country but
in the hope of averting one, and he clearly has adult education rather than
primary education in view. Nonetheless, the spirit of these remarks is as
"Rousseauist" as Lakanal's, and if Wordsworth actually carried out his
intention to peruse the *Moniteur*, then Lakanal's systematic application of
what he took to be the principles established in *Emile* could hardly have
failed to catch the poet's eye. If Wordsworth did take notice of the
Committee's project he would surely have greeted it as hopefully as he had
awaited it, especially after the Revolution had managed to make an end of
Robespierre and his "execrable measures."

Taken in sum, the external evidence for Wordsworth's firsthand
knowledge of what Lakanal said about education in the autumn of 1794
would seem considerable. I believe the internal evidence, especially that
associated with the argument of book 5 of the 1805 *Prelude*, also tends to
corroborate this suggestion. But since what Lakanal says about Rousseau,
education, and politics is representative of a widely shared view of these
matters, my use of Lakanal is also, in part, heuristic. Whether or not
Wordsworth knew, say, the October address to the Convention, he prob-
ably knew (and held) the widely shared view. What he wrote to Mathews in
June of 1794, as we have seen, suggests attitudes already close to the
position represented by Lakanal. Prior pronouncements of the Committee
on Public Instruction may well have figured in the early formation of
Wordsworth's radical creed—before the Jacobin period, that is, and there-
fore before the Committee suffered the temporary decline in prestige from
which it was rebounding in the Thermidorean period.[20] The great forerun-
ner of the Sieyes-Lakanal educational plan was that proposed in 1792 by
Condorcet, the celebrated philosophe who was the Committee's first

leader.[21] Condorcet's plan, which resembled Lakanal's in points of both
theory and practice, was debated in Paris and circulated in pamphlet form
in the spring of that year, precisely the time that Wordsworth was living on
the banks of the Loire and trying to catch up with the Revolution.
Although Lakanal's plan was adopted and Condorcet's was not, Condorcet's
Report on the General Organization of Public Instruction is a text that might also
have served the heuristic purposes of contextualizing Wordsworth's
position.[22] It is not far-fetched to think that Wordsworth knew both texts
well. What would be far-fetched is to think that a young radical so involved
in the enlightened Girondist movement of the Revolution could have failed
to know about the Committee on Public Instruction, about its general
educational aims and some of its specific recommendations, and about how,
like Rousseau, it considered its educational and political views mutually
translatable.

IV

The answer I am proposing to the initial question should now be clear: in
the first half of his great decade, Wordsworth's political interests found
expression in the poetry he composed on the topic of education. To
understand his political perspective, in other words, we must look to what
he says about education. Since the most explicit poetic comment on
education comes in the lines composed for what became book 5 of the 1805
Prelude, the best passage to consider first might be the one Wordsworth is
thought to have composed first. It appears in MS. 18a:

> There are who tell us that in recent times
> We have been great discoverers, that by dint
> Of nice experience we have lately given
> To education principles as fixed
> And plain as those of a mechanic trade
> Fair books and pure have been composed that act
> Upon the infant mind as does the Sun
> Upon a flower, in the corrected scheme
> Of modern days all error is block'd out
> So jealously that wisdom thrives apace
> And in our very boyhood we become
> Familiar friends with cause and consequence.
> Great feats have been performed, a smooth high-way
> So they assert has lately overbridged
> The random chaos of futurity.

> Hence all our steps are firm and we are made
> Strong in the power of knowledge. Ample cause
> Why we now living in this happy age
> Should bless ourselves.
>   For briefly 'tis maintained
> We now have rules and theories so precise
> That by the inspection of unwearied eyes
> We can secure infallible results.
> But if the shepherd to his flock should point
> The herb which each should feed on were it not
> Service redundant and ridiculous?[23]

Since this passage dates to 1798–99, it cannot refer to what Morkan calls "early nineteenth-century educational schemes." And while Erdman cites it to support his argument about Wordsworth's debt to Wedgwood, rather than to Rousseau, it stacks up very neatly against the Rousseauist vision of Lakanal and his committee. Certainly the culprits Wordsworth singles out are depicted as making the same kinds of claims the Thermidoreans make under the aegis of Rousseau. Interpreted in light of Lakanal's speech, for example, Wordsworth's "recent times" would refer not to the previous few years but to the Enlightenment, in which we became "discoverers" by virtue of the scientific method that Lakanal says "Bacon, Locke, and their disciples . . . found in sounding the depths of nature." After providing this common orientation in intellectual history, the two texts go on to make some strikingly similar observations that are couched in similar terms and metaphors. Wordsworth speaks of the effort to give to education "principles as fixed / And plain as those of a mechanic trade." Lakanal says that the method enables the moral sciences (such as education) to draw conclusions "as rigorous in their demonstration as the exact and physical sciences" and thus to spread over "the principles of our duties" the brightest of lights. Wordsworth suggests that the aim of the destructive educators is to see that "all our steps are firm" and that "we are made / Strong in the power of knowledge"—all error ("wandering") must be blocked—and Lakanal's metaphor is the same when he insists that the method "counts all the steps it takes," but "never takes a step backward or to the side." Even the road metaphor, which is perhaps only an extension of the idea of unerring steps, is common to both accounts.[24]

Because MS. 18a dates to 1798–99, we must not fail to notice how substantially it anticipates the most directly topical lines from book 5 of the completed *Prelude*, which were not composed until five years later:

> These mighty workmen of our later age
> Who with a broad highway have overbridged
> The froward chaos of futurity,
> Tamed to their bidding—they who have the art
> To manage books, and things, and make them work
> Gently on infant minds as does the sun
> Upon a flower—the tutors of our youth,
> The guides, the wardens of our faculties
> And stewards of our labour, watchful men
> And skilful in the usury of time,
> Sages, who in their prescience would controul
> All accidents, and to the very road
> Which they have fashioned would confine us down
> Like engines—when will they be taught
> That in the unreasoning progress of the world
> A wiser spirit is at work for us,
> A better eye than theirs, most prodigal
> Of blessings, and most studious of our good,
> Even in what seem our most unfruitful hours?
>
> (370–88)

This later passage is somewhat less strident in its irony and perhaps a shade subtler in its implication: here the modern instructor's problem is that he himself needs to be taught by the most studious educator of all, divine providence. Much of the passage, however, is just a recasting of the ur-passage from MS. 18a. Further, in both that early manuscript and in book 5, these passages introduce the famous lines that begin "There was a boy." We can infer, therefore, not only that Wordsworth's polemic against contemporary education runs back to the period of his earliest work toward *The Recluse*, but also that this polemic is associated from the start with the (superficially) nonpolitical poetry that marks Wordsworth's most characteristic accomplishment in this early major period. It was a pair of lines from "There was a boy," we must recall, about which Coleridge said: "had I met these lines running wild in the deserts of Arabia, I should have instantly screamed out 'Wordsworth!' "[25]

In what would become book 5 of the completed *Prelude*, the Boy of Winander serves as a natural foil to set off the deformities of the child raised according to the new system; and there, the portrait of system's child (no child at all, according to Wordsworth, "But a dwarf man") comprises the central section of Wordsworth's polemic against modern education.

Although the lines from MS. 18a show no evidence of Wordsworth's early
work on this portrait, its main features conform with his early criticisms of
those who propound "the corrected scheme / Of modern days." If Rousseau
is in some refracted way the target of Wordsworth's remarks, therefore, we
should expect to find a resemblance between this monster child of the
mighty workmen and Rousseau's own ideal pupil Emile—sufficient re-
semblance, anyway, for the purposes of parody.

In certain respects, the monster child does bear a striking and
straightforward resemblance to Emile. Consider for example the first half of
Wordsworth's description of the child. He is said to be

> Not quarrelsome, for that were far beneath
> His dignity; with gifts he bubbles o'er
> As generous as a fountain; selfishness
> May not come near him, gluttony or pride;
> The wandering beggars propagate his name,
> Dumb creatures find him tender as a nun.
>
> . . . .
>
> Arch are his notices, and nice his sense
> Of the ridiculous; deceit and guile,
> Meanness and falsehood, he detects, can treat
> With apt and graceful laughter; nor is blind
> To the broad follies of the licensed world;
> Though shrewd, yet innocent himself withal,
> And can read lectures upon innocence.
> He is fenced round, nay armed, for ought we know,
> In panoply complete; and fear itself,
> Natural or supernatural alike,
> Unless it leap upon him in a dream,
> Touches him not.

> [299–318]

Both in its overall tone and in a number of its particulars, I believe,
Wordsworth's satiric set-piece description alludes to those passages in *Emile*
where Jean-Jacques pauses to sum up the virtues his protégé has acquired at
the various stages of his moral development:[26]

> Emile is laborious, temperate, patient, firm, and full of cour-
> age. His imagination is in no way inflamed and never enlarges
> dangers. He is sensitive to few ills, and he knows constancy in
> endurance because he has not learned to quarrel with destiny.

. . . In a word, of virtue Emile has all that relates to himself. To have the social virtues, too, he lacks only the knowledge of the relations which demand them. . . . [At this stage,] he counts on himself, for he is all that one can be at his age. [p. 208]

Opinion, whose action he sees, has not acquired its empire over him. The passions, whose effect he feels, have not yet agitated his heart. He is a man; he is interested in his brothers; he is equitable; he judges his peers. Surely, if he judges them well, he will not want to be in the place of any of them; for since the goal of all the torments they give themselves is founded on prejudices he does not have, it appears to him to be pie in the sky. . . . He pities these miserable kings, slaves of all that obey them. He pities these false wise men, chained to their vain reputations. He pities these rich fools, martyrs to their display. He pities these conspicuous voluptuaries, who devote their entire lives to boredom in order to appear to have pleasure. [p. 244]

Emile dislikes both turmoil and quarrels, not only among men but even among animals. Never did he incite two dogs to fight with one another, never did he get a dog to chase a cat. [pp. 250–51]

What great views I see settling little by little in his head! What sublime sentiments stifle the germ of the petty passions in his heart! What judicial clarity, what accuracy of reason I see forming in him, as a result of the cultivation of his inclinations, of the experience which concentrates the wishes of a great soul within the narrow limit of the possible and makes a man who is superior to others and, unable to raise them to his level, is capable of lowering himself to theirs! The true principles of the just, the true models of the beautiful, all the moral relations of beings, all the ideas of order are imprinted on his understanding. He sees the place of each thing and the cause which removes it from its place. . . . Without having experienced the human passions, he knows their illusions and their effects. [p. 253]

Granting that the lines about the monster child point to these summaries of Emile's attributes, one must not draw the wrong conclusions. Wordsworth is interested in exposing the general attitude of the teacher, not the specific characteristics of the pupil. Indeed, none of the particular virtues he ascribes to the monster child is under attack. Though the author of *The Prelude* depicts himself invading a raven's nest as a boy, we cannot assume that he is opposed to tenderness toward animals. And we know from "The Old Cumberland Beggar" that he approves of kindness toward wandering mendicants. Wordsworth's particulars are intended to recall the overall impression conveyed by Rousseau's description of Emile, the sense that, in Wordsworth's mocking phrase, "Briefly, the moral part / Is perfect" (318–19). The chief target is a delusive fantasy of moral perfectionism, the notion that virtue can be systematically taught. And we must also be careful not to confuse Wordsworth's objection with the one Rousseau tries to anticipate. "I know," he wrote of (and to) his readers, "that they will take the young man whom I evoke to be an imaginary and fantastic being because he differs from those with whom they compare him. They do not stop to think that he must certainly differ from these young men, since he is raised quite differently, affected by quite contrary sentiments, and in-structed quite otherwise from them" (p. 253). Wordsworth's position is not, however, that one child cannot be made "different" from others by dint of training. He would concede that the peculiarity of the child is real enough; the child's ethical superiority is what he thinks illusory.[27]

In respect to the "moral part," then, the portrait of the monster child tallies quite closely with Rousseau's depiction of Emile. But other problems emerge in the second half of the portrait, where Wordsworth depicts the child's intellectual part. "In learning and in books," the passage continues, the child "is a prodigy." His discourse is "embossed with terms of art." He is supposed to be knowledgeable in astronomy, chemistry, geography, navigation, geology, foreign policy; he can "string you names of districts, cities, towns, / The whole world over." And he must live

> Knowing that he grows wiser every day,
> Or else not live at all, and seeing too
> Each little drop of wisdom as it falls
> Into the dimpling cistern of his heart.

[319–45]

These remarks have probably been a further obstacle to the appreciation of Rousseau's symbolic importance for book 5, for *Emile* might be cited in any number of places in support of the claim that Rousseau was as suspicious as Wordsworth of a child's early acquisition of too much information and "book learning." Jean-Jacques's dictum that his pupil must "Know how to be ignorant" typifies this apparently anti-intellectual strain in *Emile*.

To resolve this difficulty we must first recognize that in dividing his description of the monster child into two components, Wordsworth is heeding a distinction that was commonplace among the mighty workmen in France's Revolutionary legislature: the distinction between *éducation* (moral training) and *instruction* (intellectual training).[28] For those who made a sharp distinction between the thought of Rousseau and that of the *philosophes*, *éducation* was usually associated with the former and *instruction* with the latter. But some leaders of the 1790s saw Rousseau as both moralist and scientist—in effect, as the *philosophe* par excellence—and they saw *Emile* as a book concerned with both *éducation* and *instruction*. Lakanal is a case in point. Certainly his addresses in behalf of the Committee on Public Instruction suggest that in the Thermidorean period Rousseau had come to stand for both kinds of training.

Emile itself, furthermore, offers definite support for this view. Rousseau may have placed Emile's moral education first, but the boy's intellectual training was attended to as soon as he was deemed ready for it. And some of the specific intellectual traits to be cultivated in Emile were characteristic of the Enlightenment mentality attacked by Wordsworth. Another of Rousseau's dicta, for example, "that no authority govern [Emile] beyond that of his own reason" (p. 255) corresponds to the monster child's penchant for putting "All things . . . to question (341). The monster child "shifts, weighs, / Takes nothing upon trust" (337–38), and Rousseau's pupil, similarly, does "nothing on anybody's word" (p. 178). Even some of Rousseau's apparently anti-intellectual statements—"Were he to know nothing it would be of little importance to me . . ."—are qualified by his insistence on rational method—". . . provided he made no mistakes" (p. 171).

Taken in context, then, the portrait of the monster child does appear to be a reasonably coherent satire of the revolution's Rousseauist dream of an ideal pupil. But when Wordsworth goes on to say what lies at the heart of the child he has pictured, his analysis seems to substantiate still another sort of potential objection to the claim that Rousseauism is his target:

> Now this is hollow, 'tis a life of lies
> From the beginning, and in lies must end.
> Forth bring him to the air of common sense
> And, fresh and shewy as it is, the corps
> Slips from us into powder. Vanity,
> That is his soul: there lives he, and there moves—
> It is the soul of everything he seeks—
> That gone, nothing is left which he can love.

Nay, if a thought of purer birth should rise
To carry him towards a better clime,
Some busy helper still is on the watch
To drive him back, and pound him like a stray
Within the pinfold of his own conceit,
Which is his home, his natural dwelling-place.

[350–63]

The objection here is simple. In *Emile* Rousseau clearly states that vanity is for him the worst of human foibles, "the sole folly of which one cannot disabuse a man who is not mad" (p. 245), and Rousseau's method is specifically aimed at making his pupil the least vain of creatures. He describes Emile again and again as unaffected, sincere, and heedless of the superficial judgment of others. If Wordsworth's satire is indeed aimed at *Emile*, his calling this trait the key to Emile's character requires some explanation. Perhaps the first thing to say is that, according to proverbial wisdom, the effort to become, or to produce, the world's humblest person is likely to backfire egregiously. Himself breathing what he calls "the air of common sense," where such wisdom thrives, Wordsworth might simply have concluded that Rousseau's attempt to block all vanity in Emile was itself a colossal act of vanity. Some such commonplace may well be enough to account for the remarks about vanity in book 5. It is worth bearing in mind, however, that the most celebrated discussion of Rousseau to appear in England during the Revolution—Burke's *Letter to a Member of the National Assembly* (May 1791)—was in fact an attack on him as a teacher of vanity.

Burke's *Letter* was his first work to appear after the publication of the *Reflections*, six months earlier, and is best understood as a sequel to it. Speaking of the October march on Versailles in the *Reflections*, Burke had said that "the most important of all revolutions, which may be dated from that day [was] a revolution in sentiments, manners, and moral opinions" (*BW* 3:337). In respect to this revolution, Burke's primary aim in the *Reflections* had been to show the meaning and cost of overturning the "mixed system of opinion and sentiment" that dated back to the age of chivalry. In the *Letter*, on the other hand, Burke turned his attention to France's effort to construct a new system of opinion and sentiment, and thus he addressed himself to such topics as the National Assembly's "scheme of educating the rising generation, the principles which they intend to instil and the sympathies which they wish to form in the mind at the season in which it is the most susceptible" (4:23–24). The "great problem" facing legislators in this position, as Burke sees it, is "to find a substitute for all the principles

which hitherto have been employed to regulate the human will and action."
And what he claims the French have chosen in the place of "plain duty,"
which for him sums up the older, chivalric principles, is "a selfish,
flattering, seductive, ostentatious vice." Their object, he says, is "to merge
all natural and social sentiment in inordinate vanity" (pp. 25–26).

Burke suggests that the members of the Assembly chose vanity as
their guiding principle because of the kind of men they are: "Statesmen like
your present rulers exist by everything which is spurious, fictitious, and
false,—by everything which takes the man from his house, and sets him on
a stage,—which makes him up an artificial creature" (p. 28). But his more
central claim in the *Letter* pertains to the choice he sees following from their
choice of this "principle": the singling out of Rousseau, in the decree of
December 1790, as the patron of their "regeneration of the moral constitu-
tion of man" (p. 28).[29] Burke's argument, indeed, makes the Assembly's act
of homage to Rousseau seem inevitable. "They chose Rousseau," he says,
"because in him that peculiar vice which they wished to erect into ruling
virtue was by far the most conspicuous" (p. 26). Rousseau entertained "no
principle, either to influence his heart or to guide his understanding, but
vanity"; he is the "philosophic instructor in the *ethics of vanity*," nay, the
"great professor and founder of *the philosophy of vanity*" (pp. 26, 28; Burke's
italics).

No one is quicker than Burke to point out that building a system of
opinion and sentiment is a difficult task. But he does offer sarcastic praise to
the "practical philosophers" of the National Assembly for the speed of their
work. The initial choice of vanity was an expeditious one, he points out,
since "[v]anity is too apt to prevail in all of us" even without deliberate
effort. But of course the Assembly's work is nothing if not deliberate.
"Systematic in everything," he says, they "have wisely begun at the
source," the relation of the parent to the child. And with the same *esprit de
système*, the "next relation which they regenerate by their statues to Rous-
seau is that which is next in sanctity to that of a father," that of a teacher.
Given its initial attractiveness, vanity attains its mature form when two
such powerful institutions are pressed into its service. It then becomes a
truly formidable adversary:

> In a small degree, and conversant in little things, vanity is of
> little moment. When full-grown, it is the worst of vices, and
> the occasional mimic of them all. It makes the whole man false.
> It leaves nothing sincere or trustworthy about him. His best
> qualities are poisoned and perverted by it, and operate exactly as
> the worst. [p. 26]

Such an account of vanity helps to explain, I think, why Wordsworth can list a series of genuinely good qualities in his description of the morally deformed child of modern education. No matter how good a quality may be in itself, vanity makes it operate as an evil. For Burke, as for Wordsworth, moral judgment must consider the feeling attached to the quality; vanity, says Burke, "finds its account in reversing the train of our natural feelings" (p. 28).

How closely we should link Wordsworth's analysis of vanity in modern education to Burke's *Letter* is difficult to say. I believe that the author of the Letter to Llandaff would have read Burke's attack, and amid the slim documentation of Wordsworth's reading at this time we find some evidence that he did.[30] It is certainly *possible* that book 5's remarks about vanity come from somewhere other than Burke and that they have nothing to do with Rousseau. But such a view does not seem *probable* to me in view of the circumstances I have described. We must not fall back into the common error of underestimating the extent of Burke's influence on English opinion in these years. The range of this influence has certainly not been lost on those scholars who have traced the history of Rousseau's reputation in England through this time. Each reaches some version of the conclusion that for decades afterward Burke's *Letter* all but determined *"la fortune de Rousseau dans l'opinion anglaise."*[30] When these same scholars discuss Wordsworth's major work, I should add, they tend to see it as Rousseauist rather than anti-Rousseauist. And none suspects that this work bears what I have been describing as the stamp of Burke's writings. Since they regard Wordsworth from the distance of a general survey, their oversight is quite understandable. After all, five years before composing his ideal education for the Pedlar, Wordsworth had engaged Burke in intellectual combat with weapons forged by Rousseau.

V

In the lines that introduce the long discussion of education in book 5, Wordsworth writes that what we are reading "is dedicate to Nature's self / And things that teach as Nature teaches" (230–31). Like much else in *The Prelude*, this comment encourages us to think that Wordsworth opposed Rousseauist education in the name of natural education. We have already seen, however, that when Wordsworth opposes Rousseauist politics with a politics of nature, he is attacking a writer who himself advocated a politics of nature. Careful analysis of the France books of *The Prelude* shows that Wordsworth sought to maintain a different sense of "nature" in his political critique, a sense closer to Burke's sense of (second) nature. A similar distinction must be observed with respect to Wordsworth's advocacy of natural education.

The need for such a distinction becomes clear as soon as we recall that *Emile* was perceived by revolutionaries like Lakanal as offering "the only code of education sanctioned by nature." Furthermore, Rousseau specifically represented his project as a casting out of artificial education in favor of natural. Even Wordsworth himself seems to acknowledge that modern educators held some such view of their work when he says that they "have the art / To manage books, and things, and make them work / Gently upon infant minds as does the sun / Upon a flower" (373–76). What evidently has to be established is how this kind of teaching-as-Nature-teaches differs from the teaching-as-(second)-Nature-teaches that Wordsworth would oppose to it.

The Rousseauist position is concisely articulated in the very first paragraphs of *Emile*, where Jean-Jacques announces his concern about man's contamination of the world providence intended for his natural development. Here are the bold opening sentences:

> Everything is good as it leaves the hands of the Author of things; everything degenerates in the hands of man. He forces one soil to nourish the products of another, one tree to bear the fruit of another. He mixes and confuses the climates, the elements, the seasons. He mutilates his dog, his house, his slave. He turns everything upside down; he disfigures everything; he loves deformity, monsters. He wants nothing as nature made it, not even man; for him, man must be trained like a school horse; man must be fashioned in keeping with his fancy like a tree in his garden. [p. 37]

These are familiar Rousseauist sentiments, and the account to this point offers nothing to which Wordsworth would object, least of all its claim for the vast superiority of divine agency over human. Wordsworth criticized the "mighty workmen," we recall, for disbelieving that "a wiser spirit is at work for us, / A better eye than theirs." With respect to this issue of providence as well as to other related issues, however, Rousseau's argument now takes a turn that marks a crucial parting of ways between the two writers. For Rousseau immediately asserts that if man were not actively to train and fashion man, "everything would go even worse"! "Our species," he explains,

does not admit of being formed halfway. In the present state of
things a man abandoned to himself in the midst of other men
from birth would be the most disfigured of all. Prejudices,
authority, necessity, example, all the social institutions in
which we find ourselves submerged would stifle nature in him
and put nothing in its place. Nature there would be like a shrub
that chance had caused to be borne in the middle of a path and
that the passers-by soon cause to perish by bumping into it from
all sides and bending it in every direction. [p. 37]

A man who lives in the midst of other men from birth necessarily suffers the
influence of human institutions—what Rousseau calls prejudice, authority,
example, and so on. These institutions are not a part of nature and, by a law
that Rousseau claims to "have proved . . . countless times," "everything
that is not nature is against nature" (p. 405).

On Rousseau's account, therefore, these institutions constitute a kind
of antinature, which, if left to operate haphazardly on the individual, tends
to stifle natural growth and eventually to produce a monster. One's only
recourse, so the argument runs, is to regularize these institutions according
to the laws of nature, the rational scheme established by the Author of
things. Rousseau's "plan" or "method" (both his terms) is nothing other
than the set of rules and maxims for which he claims such rational and
natural foundation. This is the essence of what Lakanal calls the substitu-
tion of rational method for the influence of prejudice and routine.

The speaker of "Lines Written in Early Spring" (lines in fact written
soon after Wordsworth's announcement to Tobin on 6 March 1798) may
sound Rousseauist in suggesting that he has "reason to lament / What man
has made of man" (23–24). But Wordsworth's reason proves to be the
reverse of Rousseau's. If the latter's worries about man's corruption of man
stem from his view that human culture, unguided by systematic human
planning, lacks the order of divinely created nature, Wordsworth's worries
stem from his fear of the very effort to systematize culture—an effort he
indeed represents as a failure of confidence in the providential scheme that
the human system claims for its authority. Rousseau says that "the child is
at birth already a disciple, not of the governor, but of nature" and that the
governor himself "only studies under this first master and prevents its care
from being opposed" (p. 61). Wordsworth sees no reason to suspect that
nature's care *would* be opposed, except in those cases where someone like a
Rousseauist governor interferes. At its best, Wordsworth suggests, such
meddling amounts to nothing better than "service redundant and ridicu-
lous." At its worst, it meets the harsher judgment implied in book 5's

Miltonic allusion to the bridge over Chaos, the charge of Satanic usurpation of divine prerogatives.

For Rousseau, we might say, there is nature and derivative rational method on the one side and the antinature of human institutions on the other. For Wordsworth, there is nature and derivative second nature on the one side and rational method on the other. But is it fair to identify Wordsworth's second nature with the human institutions singled out by Rousseau? And how are we to understand the agency of second nature's teaching in Wordsworth's account? What are its normal circumstances, its characteristic forms and procedures? What, in short, serves Wordsworth's natural teaching as the knowledge and application of a method serve Rousseau's?

Six

Natural Lore

Oh, why hath not the mind
Some element to stamp her image on
In nature somewhat nearer to her own?
Why, gifted with such powers to send abroad
Her spirit, must it lodge in shrines so frail?

The Prelude, book 5 ("Books")

*T*oward the conclusion of the verse biography he added to *The Ruined Cottage* in early 1798, Wordsworth summarizes the happy ethical consequences of the Pedlar's natural education. The lines were among those later assimilated into the autobiographical narrative of *The Prelude*:

    . . . though he was untaught,
In the dead lore of schools undisciplined,
Why should he grieve: he was a chosen son
To him was given an ear which deeply felt
The voice of Nature in the obscure wind
The sounding mountain and the running stream.
To every natural form, rock, fruit and flower
Even the loose stones that cover the highway
He gave a moral life, he saw them feel
Or linked them to some feeling. In all shapes
He found a secret and mysterious soul,
A fragrance and a spirit of strange meaning.

[270–81]

I noted earlier that when Burke made so bold as to announce in an age of enlightenment that the English were "men of untaught feelings" he did not mean that these feelings were unlearned. The same must be said of the claim about the untaught feelings of the Pedlar. The feelings that qualify him as the authoritative moral interpreter of "every natural form" were not disciplined in the dead lore of schools. But he would not be able to hear the voice of Nature in the sounds of the landscape if his feelings had not been disciplined in a lore of some (more vital) kind. To use the celebrated vocabulary of "The Tables Turned," written just a few months after these lines, the Pedlar's mind has been nourished not on knowledge gained by the "meddling intellect" that "murders to dissect," but on "the lore which nature brings." Since the very grammar of the phrase tells us that the lore which nature brings is not nature itself, we need to know what this lore is, or at least what it is like. If we determine that it is like nature, we must try to specify *how* it is like nature.

I

As the answer to the question about Wordsworth's disappearing politics required sorting through the genesis of the five-book *Prelude*, so the answer to these questions about natural lore requires some attention to the genesis of *The Ruined Cottage*. Although many details of this case, too, are difficult to establish, one can be clear about a number of pertinent dates. Wordsworth probably began work on the tale of Margaret soon after completing a draft of *The Borderers*, around March 1797. He read a presumably finished poem to Coleridge in early June of that year and to Lamb a month later. Since the pages from which he read on these occasions are now missing, the first complete version of the poem must be extrapolated backward from a fair copy manuscript of early 1798. This text, now called "the original MS. B," is thought by the poem's most recent editor to be "the text closest to what Coleridge and Lamb heard" the summer before, even though other manuscripts of early 1798 show that parts of it "were written later than 1797."[1]

The original MS. B presents a poem of 528 lines and dates to a period after 25 January 1798, but well before 5 March of the same year. Compared with the fragmentary working manuscripts that predate the version read to Coleridge and Lamb, this text offers a quite elaborately developed version of the central tale of Margaret, and most of this narrative material is thought to have appeared in the version Coleridge heard. Other features of the text, however, are probably developments of early 1798. These are features that begin, but only begin, to establish a framework around the telling of the central tale: there is an introductory passage charting the speaker's progress toward the grove where he sees the ruined cottage and meets the old man who will tell him about the "last human tenant of these ruined walls"; there is a brief version (fifty-odd lines long) of the Pedlar's history; and the tale itself, evidently for the first time, is now broken into two parts that are spanned by comments from the Pedlar. The summary passage quoted above (". . . though he was untaught . . .") first appears in this text, where it occupies much of the space devoted to the Pedlar's history.

The next phase of the poem's development, for our purposes the decisive one, was completed by early March, as we know from Dorothy's transcription of the poem in a letter to Mary Hutchinson (*EY*:199–210). The poem at this stage is an expanded version of the original MS. B, and is familiar to users of de Selincourt and Darbishire's edition of the *Poetical Works* simply as "MS. B" (*PW* 5:379–99).[2] The full-length educational history of the Pedlar, the narrative that tries to account for the moral powers already ascribed to the Pedlar in earlier drafts, is now complete. It is in this verse biography, as we might expect, that we encounter the first clear suggestion of how we should understand the nature of natural lore. The passage in question occurs about midway through the account:

> Small need had he of books; for many a tale
> Traditionary round the mountains hung,
> And many a legend peopling the dark woods
> Nourished Imagination in her growth,
> And gave the mind that apprehensive power
> By which she is made quick to recognize
> The moral properties and scope of things.
>
> [167–73]

These are only seven of the scores of lines that elaborate the account of the Pedlar's mental growth. The expanded verse biography describes at some length, for example, the youngster's earlier religious training and his rovings over the local countryside. Nonetheless, because of the crisp straightforwardness of their claim, these seven stand out from the rest. The "apprehensive power" mentioned here is the very capacity that later in the account is said to be responsible for the Pedlar's moral authority in the poem. And what "gave" the Pedlar his perceptive powers, so it is unequivocally asserted in these lines, are traditional tales and rustic legends.

In "Michael," a poem that closes the three-year period of *Lyrical Ballads* much as *The Ruined Cottage* opens it, a similar passage asserts the role of such stories in moral development even more explicitly. The speaker of this blank-verse poem, another of Wordsworth's quasi-autobiographical personae, opens with a direct address to the reader, in which he describes the landscape around a place called Green-head Gill and then singles out an "object which you might pass by, / Might see and notice not" (15–16). The ensuing lines explain:

> Beside the brook
> There is a straggling heap of unhewn stones!
> And to that place a story appertains,
> Which, though it be ungarnish'd with events,
> Is not unfit, I deem, for the fire-side,
> Or for the summer shade. It was the first,
> The earliest of those tales that spake to me
> Of Shepherds, dwellers in the vallies, men
> Whom I already lov'd, not verily
> For their own sakes, but for fields and hills
> Where was their occupation and abode.
> And hence this Tale, while I was yet a boy
> Careless of books, yet having felt the power
> Of Nature, by the gentle agency
> Of natural objects led me on to feel
> For passions that were not my own, and think
> At random and imperfectly indeed
> On man; the heart of man and human life.
>
> [16–33]

Identifying in this landscape an object that others are likely to miss, the Wordsworthian poet here lays claim to the same "apprehensive power" for recognizing moral properties that is claimed for the Pedlar. Further, the speaker of "Michael" makes the claim on the same grounds as those offered in the Pedlar's case—that his imagination has been nourished by local stories. And like the remarks about the Pedlar, these lines are unequivocal about matters of causality. The poet "sees" what others are likely to miss because of a story he has heard. It may employ the "agency of natural objects" and rely on prior experience of the "power / Of nature," but the "Tale" itself (along with others like it) is credited with effecting the decisive change that humanizes the poet, leads him to feel for passions that are not his own.

If we put them together, these two passages add up to a suggestion about how we are to understand that crucial transition about which so much of Wordsworth's poetry is concerned, what in *The Prelude* he calls "Love of

Nature Leading to Love of Mankind." Wordsworth's representation of this transition is often, and not unreasonably, traced back to the association psychology of Hartley.[3] Yet to explain Wordsworth's *interest* in this question, we may do better to return to *Emile*, where Jean-Jacques emphasized that the transition to love of man was the most important stage in his pupil's education:

> So long as his sensibility remains limited to his own individuality, there is nothing moral in his actions. It is only when he begins to extend outside of himself that it takes on, first, the sentiments and, then, the notions of good and evil which truly constitute him as a man and an integral part of his species. [pp. 219–20]

Rousseau argues that observations on this topic, the birth of what he calls pity or the "first relative sentiment," are difficult "because, in order to make them, we must reject the examples which are before our eyes and seek for those in which the successive developments take place according to the order of nature" (p. 220). Indeed, his approach to this crucial problem is an epitome of his systematic procedure in education generally. He reflects on "the order of nature," formulates "three maxims which are precise, clear, and easy to grasp," and then extends his "method" to organize the pupil's experience at this crucial stage accordingly (p. 223).[4]

If we had nothing but the evidence of "Michael" to rely on, the speaker's qualification that the tales he has heard have led him to think on man only "at random and imperfectly" would nonetheless suffice to tell us that Wordsworth is not pursuing Rousseau's approach to the problem. Considering the other evidence, however, and the very fact of the speaker's strange qualification, we may have reason to think that Wordsworth may be pointedly rejecting Rousseau's approach to fostering "love of man." But in either case we still need to consider how Wordsworth's "tales traditionary" are supposed to accomplish without method the transition that Rousseau claims only method can accomplish.

II

My brief genetic account of *The Ruined Cottage* shows plainly that as the poem developed toward the stage it had reached in March 1798 Wordsworth placed more and more emphasis on the dramatic framework for the telling of Margaret's tale. The full purport of this framework only becomes explicit, however, in the so-called Reconciling Addendum he composed, probably in early March, to resolve the action played out between the speaker and the Pedlar, the action of the central narrative having been resolved much earlier in the poem's genesis. What makes the Addendum so important, apart from its being composed so close to the drafting of Wordsworth's letter to Tobin about his "plan," is that it establishes vital connections between the two chief developments that had so changed the poem in the preceding weeks: the expansion of the Pedlar's educational history and the elaboration of the tale's dramatic framework. The Addendum links the moral-educational function of the tales the Pedlar heard as a boy, or child figure, with the tale he now tells as a man, or father figure.

Although it took Wordsworth several drafts to strike the tone he wanted in the Reconciling Addendum, his concern with this connection is evident from his first attempt:

> The old man ceased: he saw that I was moved.
> From that low bench rising instinctively
> I turned away in weakness, and my heart
> Went back into the tale which he had told,
> And when at last returning from my mind
> I looked around, the cottage and the elms,
> The road, the pathway, and the garden wall
> Which old and loose and mossy o'er the road
> Hung bellying, all appeared, I know not how
> But to some eye within me all appeared
> Colours and forms of a strange discipline.
> The trouble which they sent into my thought
> Was sweet, I looked again, and to myself
> I seemed a better and a wiser man.
>
> [*PW* 5:400]

We have no reason to question the speaker's sense that he is, like the Ancient Mariner's Wedding-Guest, indeed better and wiser. Nor can we doubt that, like the Wedding-Guest's, his moral improvement is the consequence of the narrative he has just heard related. This causal relation is even more emphatically stated in the next draft, which concludes: "And for the tale which you have told I think / I am a better and a wiser man" (p. 400). Unlike the Wedding-Guest, however, the speaker's sense of his new virtue is founded specifically on the recognition of an emerging "discipline" in his humanized perceptive faculties. Since this discipline seems to replicate the moral powers acquired by the Pedlar in his exposure to tales and legends, the lines suggest that the Pedlar's present narrative, the tale of Margaret, is an example of the living natural lore that fosters genuine moral sympathy.

The final draft of the Addendum is a passage of nearly 150 lines that were eventually printed without much revision as part of the Wanderer's long address to the Solitary in book 4 of *The Excursion*. The core of this passage, significantly, is a detailed explanation of what this "strange discipline" consists in:

>   . . . by contemplating these forms
> In the relations which they bear to man
> We shall discover what a power is theirs
> To stimulate our minds, and multiply
> The spiritual presences of absent things.
> Then weariness shall cease. We shall acquire
> The [   ] habit by which sense is made
> Subservient still to moral purposes
> A vital essence, and a saving power
> Nor shall we meet an object but may read
> Some sweet and tender lesson to our minds
> Of human suffering or of human joy.
> All things shall speak of man and we shall read
> Our duties in all forms and general laws
> And social accidents shall tend alike
> To quicken and to rouze and give the will
> And power which by a [   ] chain of good
> Shall link us to our kind. No naked hearts
> No naked minds shall then be left to mourn
> The burthen of existence. Science, then,
> Shall be a precious visitant; and then
> And only then be worthy of her name
> For then her heart shall kindle; her dull eye,
> Dull and inanimate no more shall hang
> Chained to its object in brute slavery
> But better taught and mindful of its use
> Legitimate and its peculiar power
> While with a patient interest it shall watch
> The processes of things and serve the cause
> Of order and distinctness, not for this
> Shall it forget that its most noble end

Its most illustrious province must be found
In ministering to the excursive power
Of intellect and thought. So build we up
The being that we are . . . .
. . . .
. . . . Thus disciplined
All things shall live in us and we shall live
In all things that surround us. This I deem
Our tendency . . .

[pp. 401–2]

Like the history of the Pedlar composed in the preceding weeks, this passage develops topics and tropes that afterward become part of the general currency of Wordsworth's poetry. The reason why the two passages are so seminal is that both seek to extend the same seminal line of thought. Both are concerned with moral formation; both focus on the transition from love of nature to love of man. Their common concerns are even marked by certain verbal resemblances. We note, for example, how the Pedlar is made to echo the line that sums up his own early education, "So was he framed," with his own summary comment, "So build we up / The being that we are." It is as if the Addendum used the speaker's reception of the tale the Pedlar now tells in order to offer a generalized and quasi-philosophical version of what had been recounted earlier, in particularized and biographical terms, with respect to the tales he once heard.[5]

What this generalized account tells us is that a tale like that of Margaret is an expression of the way one contemplates natural forms in relation to human beings. In this sense it embodies the power of natural objects to stimulate moral thought. Viewed from a different perspective, however, such power is simply the habit by which sense is made subservient to moral purpose. If we are to be fully human beings, not Rousseauist savages, then our naked hearts and minds must be clothed in this habit— this "glorious habit," as it is called in *The Excursion*, where the pun on clothing is more explicit: "That change shall clothe / The naked spirit" (1247, 1249–50). It is hard to resist concluding that Wordsworth's glorious habit of the moral imagination is in fact the functional counterpart to what Burke called "the moral wardrobe of the imagination."

Telling such a tale not only has causes in the character of the teller; it also has consequences in the character of the listener. It not only expresses the inclination to contemplate the natural forms of things in relation to man; it also inclines the listener to such contemplation, with all its attendant effects. The further burden of the Addendum, then, is to show how the dramatic framework of *The Ruined Cottage* serves to illustrate this sort of consequence. At the very start of the poem, when the speaker first approaches the ruined cottage, he has nothing but his own comfort in mind and can see nothing but what his pleasures permit. Here is the description of his initial encounter with the old man:

> With thirsty heat oppressed
> At length I hailed him, glad to see his hat
> Bedewed with water-drops, as if the brim
> Had newly scooped a running stream. He rose
> And, pointing to a sun-flower, bade me climb
> The [   ] wall where that same gaudy flower
> Looked out upon the road. It was a plot
> Of garden ground now wild, its matted weeds
> Marked with the steps of those whom as they pass'd
> The gooseberry trees that shot in long [lank skips]
> Or currants hanging from their leafless stems
> In scanty stings had tempted to o'erlap
> The broken wall. Within that cheerless spot
> Where two tall hedgerows of thick willow boughs
> Joined in a damp cold nook I found a well
> Half choaked
> I slaked my thirst and to the shady bench
> Returned, and . . . stood unbonneted
> To catch the current of the breezy air.
>
>   [306–24]

It would be wrong to say that the speaker's scrutiny of the scene around the cottage is *un*natural, exactly, but perhaps we can accurately call it *merely* natural. The speaker moves in the world of Rousseau's natural man, a world of sensations and inferences motivated alike only by animal appetite. Water drops on the old man's hat mean potable springwater in the vicinity. Footprints in the matted weeds of the garden mean edible fruit within reach. Human signs here signify insofar as they point to natural objects— objects, that is, of the speaker's "natural" desires.

The opening of the poem may therefore be said to establish the speaker's state of mind in the state of nature, a paradoxically unnatural state for a human being. Identifying this initial state enables us to mark the moral distance he has covered by the time the Pedlar has concluded his narrative. The completed Addendum brings the matter full circle with a detailed description not of the scene, but of the speaker's altered response to it:

> The old man ceased
> The words he uttered shall not pass away
> They had sunk into me, but not as sounds
> To be expressed by visible characters,
> For while he spake my spirit had obeyed
> The presence of his eye, my ear had drunk
> The meanings of his voice. He had discoursed
> Like one who in the slow and silent works,
> The manifold conclusions of this thought,
> Had brooded till Imagination's power
> Condensed them to a passion whence she drew
> Herself new energies, resistless force.
>   Yet still towards the cottage did I turn
> Fondly, and trace with nearer interest
> That secret spirit of humanity
> Which, 'mid the calm oblivious tendencies
> Of Nature, 'mid her plants, her weeds and flowers,
> And silent overgrowings, still survived.
>
>   [99–115]

The traveler's mind now moves in a reverse direction from the one it had taken earlier. He now views the scene in relation to another's feelings and so makes over the objects of nature into the spirit of humanity. No longer at the mercy of "the oblivious tendencies of Nature," he now follows what the Pedlar calls *"our* tendency": the "habit by which sense is made / Subservient to moral purposes / A vital essence, and a saving power." This tendency of our (human) nature is a saving power not only because it is theologically redemptive, but also because it is epistemologically conservative. It holds in view what Nature, taken in the narrow sense, would have us forget. This is probably Wordsworth's earliest thoroughgoing presentation of the dialectic of loss and recompense, the pattern deeply ingrained in his mature poetry. And it appears here unmistakably as a dialectic of second nature; for *our* tendency, the habit of conservation, proves to be an even more natural response to the world than what at first seemed a most objective and accurate scrutiny of nature's oblivious tendencies.[6]

The drafting of the Addendum completes the expansion of *The Ruined*

Cottage from a relatively simple story to an exercise in homespun anthropol-
ogy. No longer just a natural tale, the poem becomes an illustration of what
it means to tell a natural tale—how such a story is produced, how it is
received, and what difference its telling makes to speaker and listener. In
the development of this poem, in other words, Wordsworth has given sense
to the notion of a "lore which nature brings" without having to resort to
rational method. It was probably within days of writing the Addendum
that Wordsworth undertook those first experiments with ballad narrative
that would memorialize him in English literary history. Working *The
Ruined Cottage* into the poem it became by March 1798, however, was his
most important experiment of all.[7]

III

We can understand just how pivotal is the place of *The Ruined Cottage* in
Wordsworth's intellectual development if we view it as a transformation of
the poem Wordsworth produced during his most fervently radical period,
Salisbury Plain (1793–94).[8] The political allegiances of this earlier poem are
signaled in its opening stanzas, where, echoing Rousseau, Wordsworth
argues against the Hobbesian position that any state of civil society is
preferable to the state of savage nature:

> Hard is the life when naked and unhouzed
> And wasted by the long day's fruitless pains,
> The hungry savage, 'mid deep forests, rouzed
> By storms, lies down at night on unknown plains
> And lifts his head in fear, while famished trains
> Of boars along the crashing forests prowl,
> And heard in darkness, as the rushing rains
> Put out his watch-fire, bears contending growl
> And round his fenceless bed gaunt wolves in armies howl.
>
> Yet he is strong to suffer, and his mind
> Encounters all his evils unsubdued;
> For happier days since at the breast he pined
> He never knew, and when by foes pursued
> With life he scarce has reached the fortress rude,
> While with the war-song's peal the valleys shake,
> What in those wild assemblies has he viewed
> But men who all of his hard lot partake,
> Reposed in the same fear, to the same toil awake?

The thoughts which bow the kindly spirits down
And break the springs of joy, their deadly weight
Derive from memory of pleasures flown
Which haunts us in some sad reverse of fate,
Or from reflection on the state
Of those who on the couch of Affluence rest
By laughing Fortune's sparking cup elate,
While we of comfort reft, by pain depressed,
No other pillow know than Penury's iron breast.

[1–27]

This is so clear a paraphrase of the early parts of the Second Discourse as to constitute virtual proof of Wordsworth's knowledge of that important work.[9] The poem's contention is that, although life in the state of nature is no picnic, the "hungry savage" has a decisive advantage over his counterpart in an unjust civil society: the savage has never known otherwise, either from his own experience or from observation of his fellow human beings. Looking about him, the savage finds only men "who of his hard lot partake," and this makes him strong to suffer his pains. In civil society the case is quite otherwise:

When men in various vessels roam the deep
Of social life, and turns of chance prevail
Various and sad, how many thousands weep
Beset with foes more fierce than e'er assail
The savage without home in winter's keenest gale.

[32–36]

The narrative that these lines introduce will show just how fierce the pains of contemporary society can be.

There is ample warrant, I think, for regarding *The Ruined Cottage* as a transformation of this narrative. In both poems, an unnamed traveler crosses a deserted stretch of land in search of physical comfort, finds a solitary human figure at a ruin, hears a tale, and is deeply moved by it. The interpolated tale in *Salisbury Plain*, like the Pedlar's tale of Margaret, concerns a woman whose husband enters military service and eventually deserts her because of circumstances for which the poem does not hold him responsible. Further, *Salisbury Plain* closes with a passage which anticipates *The Ruined Cottage*'s Reconciling Addendum in that it seeks to encourage a particular response to the preceding narrative. When *Salisbury Plain* was

reworked into *Adventures on Salisbury Plain* (late 1795–early 1796), the
revised poem approached the shape of *The Ruined Cottage* even more closely
in at least one important respect: for Wordsworth divided the poem into
two "parts," with a central break falling, just as it does in *The Ruined
Cottage*, at an emotional pause in the narration of the interpolated tale.[10]

One can also point to dissimilarities, of course. In *Salisbury Plain*, the
woman tells her own story, whereas the tale of Margaret in the later poem is
related by the Pedlar. The earlier poem takes place in a specific and
allegorical setting, one with both historical and symbolic associations,
whereas the later poem is set in an unidentified countryside. Where the
earlier poem indulges Gothic pity and fear, the later poem restrains itself to
the more ordinary sorrows of human life. Yet the structural and thematic
similarities are sufficiently marked to suggest that the later poem is indeed a
reworking of the earlier and that at least some of the differences are to be
explained by a change in attitude toward a set of social and literary problems
that remained basically unchanged. Two of the most crucial differences
between the poems, one pertaining to the plot of the interpolated tale and
the other to the response encouraged by the dramatic framework, provide
the best clues to what motivates the changes.

Though both interpolated tales recount the suffering of a soldier's
widow, they differ in the way they represent the causes of her suffering. In
Salisbury Plain, the ordeal of the soldier's widow begins when her and her
father's substance falls into decay "by cruel chance and wilful wrong." All
we learn at this stage about the willful wrong is what is given in the
succeeding lines:

> Oppression trampled on his tresses grey:
> His little range of water was denied;
> Even to the bed where his old body lay
> His all was seized; and weeping side by side
> Turned out on the cold winds, alone we wandered wide.
>
> [257–61]

"Oppression" is an instance of abstract personification taken from the
eighteenth-century brand of poetic diction that Wordsworth later rejected.
Much of the rest of this poem does, however, give meaning to the abstrac-
tion by identifying the causes of oppression as they bear on this case and by
prescribing a general remedy.

The faint oxymoron in lines 260–61, "side by side . . . alone we
wandered," is reminiscent of Adam and Eve's wandering "hand in hand" on

"their solitary way." And initially *Salisbury Plain* invites us to see this piece of misfortune, like the one that befalls the couple in *Paradise Lost*, as a *felix culpa*. The dislocation of the father leads the daughter to seek out the extraordinary youth who was her former sweetheart. The two are married and spend four happy years together, blessed by "daily bread" and "three lovely infants" (289–91). The reprieve turns out to be short-lived, however, for a second calamity befalls them when "War the nations to the fields defied" (295). Without the woman's now-deceased father, the family crosses the ocean to face the American colonists, and in a short time the "pains and plagues" of wartime life leave the woman the lone survivor: "All perished, all in one remorseless year, / Husband and children one by one, by sword / And scourge of fiery fever" (320–22). For this second calamity there is no relief, as the woman discovers after surviving an arduous return crossing to England:

> . . . homeless near a thousand homes I stood,
> And near a thousand tables pined and wanted food.
>
> Three years a wanderer round my native coast
> My eyes have watched yon sun declining tend
> Down to the land where hope to me was lost;
> And now across this waste my steps I bend:
> Oh! tell me whither, for no earthly friend
> Have I, no house in prospect but the tomb.
>
> [384–93]

"Oppression" leads to the loss of her home and "war" to the destruction of her family; her continued suffering likewise has a social origin, the neglect of her plight by fellow citizens sufficiently well off to make her feel her pain the more keenly. The kind of care required, however, will involve more than immediate sympathy and personal charity.

The old Pedlar's account of how Margaret's misery is initially brought on suggests a very different way of locating responsibility for human suffering:

> —You may remember, now some ten years gone,
> Two blighting seasons, when the fields were left
> With half a harvest; it pleased heaven to add
> A worse affliction in the plague of war.
> A happy land was stricken to the heart.
> 'Twas a sad time of sorrow and distress.

> A wanderer among the cottages
> I with my pack of winter raiment saw
> The hardships of that season; many rich
> Sank down as in a dream among the poor
> And of the poor did many cease to be,
> And their place knew them not.

[381–92]

In the earlier poem, one chief cause of the woman's troubles is identified as "Oppression," and in the version revised for *Adventures on Salisbury Plain*, the oppression is clearly that of one class over another, as emblematized by the synecdoche of the mansion's hegemony over the cottage: "Then rose a mansion proud our woods among, / And cottage after cottage owned its sway" (300–301). In *The Ruined Cottage*, by contrast, oppression is not mentioned as a cause, and *all* classes in the happy land suffer, the rich along with the poor. The difference is one of degree. It is true that the poor "cease to be" whereas the rich, for now, only sink down to the level of the poor. But it is also true that the once-rich are now candidates for disappearance themselves.

In the later poem, then, suffering occurs not at the hands of other human beings, but at the hands of heaven: it is presumably heaven that sends the famine and explicitly heaven that adds the war. This is corroborated by the pedlar's description of how economic troubles multiply in a time of hardship:

> . . . shoals of artizans
> Were from their daily labor turned away
> To hang for bread on parish charity
> They and their wives and children, happier far
> Could they have lived as do the little birds
> That peck along the hedges, or the kite
> That makes his dwelling in the mountain rocks.

[402–8]

No further explanation of the course of these problems is forthcoming. We are left to conclude that heaven sent them all. Similarly, where in *Salisbury Plain* it is the war that brings on the poverty that drives the husband to join the armed services, the final straw in *The Ruined Cottage* is another blow from heaven:

> . . . Margaret
> Went struggling on through those calamitous years
> With chearful hope, but ere the second spring
> A fever seized her husband. In disease
> He lingered long, and when his strength returned
> He found the little he had stored to meet
> The hour of accident or crippling age
> Was all consumed.
>
> [394–401]

The rest of the story follows the pattern thus established. The husband never returns, and Margaret is eventually overcome, like the ruined cottage itself, by the calm oblivious tendencies of nature. The interpolated tale leaves us with no sense whatever of human complicity in the causes of her suffering and death.

Differences between the responses urged in the two poems' epilogues correspond to these differences between the tales themselves. When the woman finishes her narrative in *Salisbury Plain*, the narrator reports that "human sufferings and that tale of woe / Had dimmed the traveller's eye with Pity's tear" (399–400). This sort of passage can lead to the mistaken conclusion that the moral of this story is compatible with that of a later work like *The Ruined Cottage*. But *Salisbury Plain* goes on to insist that pity is not by itself an adequate response to such a story.[11] The narrator's ensuing reflection on the woman's case makes it clear that we are to see the real cause as a form of barbarism, the failure of the nation to achieve any real progress over the savagery of the Druids or the treachery of medieval lords and clerics:

> Though from huge wickers paled with circling fire
> No longer horrid shrieks and dying cries
> To ears of Daemon Gods in peals aspire,
> To Daemon Gods a human sacrifice;
> Though Treachery her sword no longer dyes
> In the cold blood of Truce, still, reason's ray,
> What does it more than while tempests rise,
> With starless glooms and sounds of loud dismay
> Reveal with still-born glimpse the terrors of our way?
>
> [424–32]

The passage of centuries has led England to find no greater role for reason's ray than that of an intermittent flashing on the storm-beaten plain. The landscape here is allegorical, like its prototypes in Spenser and Milton, and should be understood as an analogue for, among other things, society as a whole, the barren terrain of social life across which Wordsworth's more unfortunate contemporaries, like modern Adams and Eves, have to pursue their way. The purport of Wordsworth's figure, roughly, is that the state of affairs in which human society makes sacrificial victims of some of its members, though briefly illuminated from time to time, has remained essentially unchanged. In this poem, compassion alone is not enough because it generates too ephemeral a perception of existing evils to insure that abiding reforms are made.

For the young Wordsworth compassion may well issue in individual expressions of generosity, what he later calls little nameless acts of kindness and of love, but it is one of the clearest indications of the difference between Wordsworth's moral positions in 1793 and 1798 that these, too, are also ultimately inadequate. In *Salisbury Plain*, the narrator's farewell address to the "friendless hope-forsaken pair" shows where the young Wordsworth stands:

> Enter that lowly cot and ye shall share
> Comforts by pounder mansions unbestowed.
> For you the milkmaid bears her brimming load,
> For you the board is piled with homely bread,
> And think that life is like this desart broad
> Where all the happiest find is but a shed
> And a green spot 'mid wastes interminably spread.
>
> [417–23]

In "The Old Cumberland Beggar," the private charity of lowly cottage dwellers can both sustain the needy and redeem the rest. But in *Salisbury Plain*, such charity constitutes a tiny oasis that serves to damn rather than to save the barbarous region around it. The hypothesis of the redemptive "eye of Nature" in the "Beggar" and *The Ruined Cottage* is far too meager for this poem's vision of what is possible under the aegis of "reason's ray," too much like an acceptance of the social landscape, with all its terrors, as it is.

The poem's conclusion delivers an outline of the positive program that is implied in this critique of things as they are. Many of the stanzas Wordsworth composed for the conclusion have been lost, but the final stanza, which does survive, provides a clear idea of the poet's aspiration:

> Heroes of Truth pursue your march, uptear
> Th'Oppressor's dungeon from its deepest base;
> High o'er the towers of Pride undaunted rear
> Resistless in your might the herculean mace
> Of Reason; let foul Error's monstrous race
> Dragged from their dens start at the light with pain
> And die; pursue your toils, till not a trace
> Be left on earth of Superstition's reign,
> Save that eternal pile which frowns on Sarum's plain.
>
> [540–49]

The real enemy emerges here not as "Oppression" but as "Superstition," and it appears in a guise appropriate to the poem's stanza form: the figure of Error from book 1 of *The Faerie Queen*.[12] It is by defeating superstitious error that the hero of truth defeats oppression. Superstition *is* the deepest base of the oppressor's dungeon.

The concept of Error in this stanza, as in Spenser, is a Platonizing one, its ultimate source being the simile of the cave in book 7 of *The Republic*. We might recall here what Wordsworth had argued just months before in the Letter to Llandaff about the proper function of "sorrow" in the face of mendicancy: it must become a motive for the work of developing a "science of civil government." Feeling by itself is no match for superstitious error. Reasoned inquiry alone is capable of exposing error to the light it cannot bear, and *Salisbury Plain* asks that we read its central tale of suffering in this very same light.

Since the Pedlar's tale, by contrast, holds no human institutions responsible for Margaret's suffering, there is no need in *The Ruined Cottage* for those final stages in which sorrow issues in enlightenment and enlightenment produces reform. We see the traveler respond to the tale of woe with a feeling that proves to be its own reward. Lest the point be missed, the Pedlar is given a final speech in which to spell it out:

> My Friend, enough to sorrow have you given
> The purposes of Wisdom ask no more,
> Be wise and chearful, and no longer read
> The forms of things with an unworthy eye.
> She sleeps in the calm earth and peace is here.
> I well remember that those very plumes,
> Those weeds and the high spear-grass on that wall,
> By mist and silent rain-drops silvered o'er,

As once I passed, did to my mind convey
So still an image of tranquillity,
So calm and still, and looked so beautiful,
Amid the uneasy thoughts which filled my mind,
That what we feel of sorrow and despair
From ruin and from change, and all the grief
The passing shews of being leave behind
Appeared an idle dream that could not live
Where meditation was. I turned away
And walked along my road in happiness.

[118–35]

These lines describe a passage from "sorrow" to "happiness" that occurs in "meditation." The change of state takes place in the absence of any change in material circumstance. Indeed, "meditation" proves to be a region where natural and human history alike are debarred from entry. It is a realm in which the fortunate misfortune is a paradigm of human fate, in which grief itself becomes the occasion of a feeling happier far than what might result from the effort to discover and eliminate the cause of grief.

There is perhaps in this conclusion, as in that written for *Salisbury Plain*, a Platonizing impulse at work, but it serves an antithetical purpose. Social evils that in the earlier poem had been symbolized as "foul Error's monstrous race," an enemy to be attacked with the herculean mace of reason, can now be simply dismissed as part of "the passing shows of being." They cannot live in the ideal realm where meditation is. If anything is to be understood as following from this meditation as enlightened action follows from the encounter with the tale in *Salisbury Plain*, it must only be another story—just as the story the Pedlar tells issues from his own tale-stamped meditation at the beginning of *The Ruined Cottage*. The speaker's own tale, the narrative of his noontime encounter with the Pedlar, is perhaps to be understood as just such a consequence.

Pedagogically, then, the Pedlar and his pupil have fulfilled the "purposes of Wisdom" without having to traffic in the methods and procedures of enlightenment. That this occasion has indeed been a *lesson* for the speaker is emphasized in the pedlar's imperative that the younger man "no longer read / The forms of things with an unworthy eye," a comment that establishes yet another link between the education described in the Addendum and the one recounted in the Pedlar's biography. We have already been told that the pedlar had early on "learned . . . / To look on nature with an humble heart / Self-questioned where it did not understand, / And with a superstitious eye of love" (162–66). If it is fair, as I think it is, to infer that this is the kind of vision that the Pedlar seeks to reproduce in the speaker, and the speaker in the reader, then we have a further, very powerful indication of how diametrically opposed is the tendency of *The Ruined Cottage* to that of *Salisbury Plain*. For in the earlier poem the purposes of Wisdom plainly require that the superstitious eye be cured of its presumed debility.

The coda to the Salisbury Plain story, I should add, is Wordsworth's recasting of the experience as an episode in book 12 of *The Prelude* (312–53). Here he represents himself "raised" as never before to the superstitious vision of second nature and to the feeling that a work of his, "Proceeding from the depth of untaught things, / . . . might become / A power like one of Nature's" (310–12). The hypothetical Rousseauist savages from *Salisbury Plain* become figures in a sublime dream of Burke's immemorial British past:

> I have a reverie and saw the past,
> Saw multitudes of men, and here and there
> A single Briton in his wolf-skin vest,
> With shield and stone-ax, stride across the wold;
> The voice of spears was heard, the rattling spear
> Shaken by arms of mighty bone, in strength
> Long mouldered, of barbaric majesty.
>
> [320–26]

As for the Druidic markings—"Lines, circles, mounts, a mystery of shapes" (340)—their mystery is now an occasion of the poet's enchantment:

> I was gently charmed,
> Albeit with an antiquarian's dream,
> And saw the bearded teachers, with white wands
> Uplifted, pointing to the starry sky,
> Alternately, and plain below, while breath
> Of music seemed to guide them, and the waste
> Was cheared with stillness and a pleasant sound.
>
> [347–53]

Such terrible beauty is born out of things, as Yeats says, transformed utterly.

IV

In *The Ruined Cottage* as it stood in March 1798, Wordsworth had produced a work that would provide the agenda for his emerging literary program, the scheme for what he would later call his great "gothic church" of poetry. The poem offers a picture not only of natural education but also, as I have begun to suggest, of natural culture as well—that is, of culture as a second nature. Further, the poem could serve as a guideline for a literary program because it implies a view of how literature functions within a culture. This view turns out to be rather like the one offered in the 1800 Preface to *Lyrical Ballads*. But the derivation of this view in *The Ruined Cottage* must be indirect, for the poem conveys its view of the social function of literature by way of a representation of the social function of discourse. Indeed, to understand why the former is couched in terms of the latter is to make an important discovery about what, for Wordsworth, makes natural lore natural.

The clearest evidence that literature is treated at one remove in *The Ruined Cottage* can be found in the pointed phrasing of that seminal passage in the Pedlar's biography: "Small need had he of books; for many a tale / Traditionary . . . / Nourished Imagination in her growth." The counterpart passage in "Michael," we recall, includes a similar contrast: "this Tale, while I was yet . . . / Careless of books . . . / . . . led me on to feel / for passions that were not my own." The speakers of both poems take pains to indicate that decisive moral development occurs in the absence of book learning. Other poems reinforce this suggestion. Oral and written language are invidiously compared in "The Brothers" (1800), a poem composed in the period between *The Ruined Cottage* and "Michael." A country priest responds to the charge that the absence of written records from his graveyard shows him to be "heedless of the past":

> We have no need of names and epitaphs,
> We talk about the dead by our fire-sides.
> And then for our immortal part, *we* want
> No symbols, Sir, to tell us that plain tale:
> The thought of death sits easy on the man
> Who has been born and dies among the mountains.
>
> [178–84]

And this deprecation of writing in favor of speech is echoed in another "Churchyard Among the Mountains" when the speaker of *The Excursion* pays a similar compliment to the unlettered people of his neighborhood:

> These Dalesmen trust
> The lingering gleam of their departed lives
> To oral record, and the silent heart;
> Depositories faithful and more kind
> Than fondest epitaph.
>
> [6:610–14]

In asserting the natural alliance of oral record and the silent heart, and in praising both for their faithful conservation of the human spirit, these lines only spell out what was already suggested in the earlier poems. But are we, then, to conclude that literacy has no place in Wordsworth's natural scheme of things?

Even if we did not have the argument in book 5 of *The Prelude* about the value of "Books," we would still have to recognize that the Pedlar grew up literate and is described as having been an avid reader of books from the shelves of his vicar and schoolmaster. We must also face the inescapable fact that Wordsworth himself is a poet who both hopes his words will teach as nature teaches and intends that they will be read in books. Natural teaching is evidently not, for Wordsworth, exclusively oral. It does, however, prove to be paradigmatically so, which is to say that books teach as nature teaches only insofar as they teach as speech does. Part of the proof is to be found in what might be called the rhetorical structure of *The Ruined Cottage*, in the way that poem seeks to promote a specific approach to its own interpretation.

Every careful student of this poem has noticed that the "I" of the poem, the character normally called the speaker, is a representative of the reader. Though this speaker has certain universalized instincts and appetites, as we have seen, he is finally a man without qualities. He has, as Jonathan Wordsworth says, "almost no characteristics. His views are never asked, never offered."[13] His chief purpose in the poem is to provide a place for the reader to stand.[14] The second feature to take note of is the way the poem initially seems to foster the assumption that, to quote Jonathan Wordsworth again, "this is to be a first-person narrative."[15] What else could one be expecting after reading the poem's opening lines?

> 'Twas Summer, and the sun was mounted high,
> Along the south the uplands feebly glared
> Through a pale steam, and all the northern downs
> In clearer air ascending shewed far off
> Their surfaces on which the shadows lay

Of many clouds far as the sight could reach
Along the horizon's edge, that lay in spots
Of clear and pleasant sunshine interposed.
. . . .
Across a bare wide Common I had toiled
With languid feet which by the slippery ground
Were baffled still; and when I stretched myself
On the brown earth, my limbs from very heat
Could find no rest, nor my weak arm disperse
The insect host which gathered round my face
And joined their murmurs to the tedious noise
Of seeds and bursting gorse which crackled round.

                                                     [1–9, 19–26]

This is an invitation to settle into the familiar mode of eighteenth-century
nature poetry: the mode of Thomson, Goldsmith, and Cowper. The reader
assumes his position as the subjective center of the action, steps into the
poem's "I," confident that he is embarking on a sensory adventure in the
summer landscape.

In this mode of poetry, the "I" is often indistinguishable from its
"eye," a point that can be illustrated by the passage from which Words-
worth seems to have been cribbing when he composed those opening lines
of *The Ruined Cottage.* It is from Thomson's "Summer":

            'Tis raging noon; and, vertical, the sun
Darts on the head direct his forceful rays.
O'er heaven and earth, far as the ranging eye
Can sweep, a dazzling deluge reigns; and all,
From pole to pole is undistinguished blaze.
In vain the sight dejected to the ground
Stoops for relief; thence hot ascending steams
And keen reflection pain. Deep to the root
Of vegetation parch'd, the cleaving fields
And slippery lawn, an arid hue disclose,
Blast fancy's blooms and wither even the soul.
. . . .
                        Distressful Nature pants;
The very streams look languid from afar;
Or, through the unshelter'd glade, impatient seem
To hurl into the covert of the grove.

                                                     [432–50][16]

With the speaker himself in such poetry, we watch the eye rove, scan, or wander, be checked, baffled, or dazzled. And the range of the eye typically defines the area of the poem's concern. Wordsworth's "far as the sight / Could reach" parallels Thomson's way of indicating the horizon's extent— "far as the ranging eye / Can sweep"—and (in MS. D) mimics the line-break that emphasizes the *eyesight's (/) power*. This is the "bodily eye" that Wordsworth calls the most despotic of all the senses, and its work is what we find recorded at the start of *The Ruined Cottage*. Even before the speaker reaches the grove with its cottage and well, the details of the landscape are enumerated with a vividness that is unsurpassed in Wordsworth's mature poetry. We are ultimately meant to understand that the speaker's experience at this stage, like Wordsworth's in the jaded years he recalls in book 11 of *The Prelude*, is "vivid but not profound" (188).[17]

If the experience of the "I" in this landscape is mere sensation, then the experience of the reader who is invited to identify with this "I" is analogously striking but shallow. The thoughtless "I" and the thoughtless reader who steps so readily into his place will be disciplined in similar ways. Their parallel experiences are simultaneously brought to a surprising halt with the ironic first words of the Pedlar: "I see around me [here] / Things which you cannot see" (67–68). Both the speaker's sensory adventure and the reader's vicarious participation in it are now to be replaced by a second-order experience—that of listening to a voice, heeding its words, following its tale. We have already seen how the speaker finds his barbarous faculties humanized by this second-order experience; a similar therapy is intended for the reader. Encouraged to think of himself as the poem's "subject," the reader finds that he must give way to the Pedlar as the Pedlar gives way to Margaret. In the end, both speaker and reader are being taught to read—the speaker (as the Pedlar tells him) the landscape, and the reader the text—by being made to listen.[18]

The effort to subject barbarous reading to the discipline of oral performance is central to Wordsworth's literary program. Although his own work is carried out in writing, it can only succeed by aspiring to the condition of speech. This aspiration finds expression in the critical prose we now associate with Wordsworth's programmatic ambitions. For example, in his first public announcement after the emergence of his plan in early 1798, the Advertisement he wrote that summer for the first edition of *Lyrical Ballads*, Wordsworth opens with the now-famous suggestion that "the majority of the following poems are to be considered as experiments." He then explains that they are experimental in that "they were written chiefly with a view to ascertain how far the language of conversation in the middle and lower classes of society is adapted to the purposes of poetic pleasure" (*PrW* 1:116). Critical interpretation of this passage has tended to emphasize the ancillary comment about the class of the speakers being imitated over the actual claim about the attempt to *write* in the language of *conversation*. But Wordsworth's point may be summarized in the terms of the Preface to the second edition: while engaged immediately in "the act of *writing* in verse" the poet must remain ultimately true to his role as "a man *speaking* to men" (pp. 122, 138; italics mine). The comment about the class of the speakers should be seen as ancillary because Wordsworth assumes that the language of conversation exists in a more pristine state among classes less affected by the practices and value of literacy-as-such. The middle and lower classes preserve the ethos of speech from an encroaching ethos of letters.

I would like to expand upon this notion of an "ethos of letters," partly because it requires clarification and partly because the easiest way to show the ideological purport of writing that aspires to the condition of speech is to consider the view of writers who wanted things the other way around.[19]

V

The ethos of letters must first be understood as a condition of "enlightenment." Recent historians such as Peter Gay and Elizabeth Eisenstein have suggested that we could most accurately think of the philosophes not as philosophers but as "men of letters," and presumably the Enlightenment itself might best be understood as an Age of Letters rather than an age of philosophy, or science, or criticism.[20] The suggestion is meant to be revisionist. Such a view actually goes back at least as far as Hazlitt, however, who included an account of the Enlightenment in his last book, *The Life of Napoleon* (1828, 1830). Because Hazlitt's account is a powerful one, and because his ideas on this subject have special relevance to the case of Wordsworth, we need to consider what he says in some detail.

On the assumption that Napoleon's fate became at some point "bound up with" that of the French Revolution, Hazlitt devotes an early chapter of his massive biography to the Revolution's "origin and progress." Part of his aim is to show—contrary to the view of observers who think it "burst out like a volcano, without any previous warning, only to alarm and destroy"— that the Revolution was in the making for "near a century" during which time enlightened writers "were unanimous in their wish to remove or reform [the old regime's] abuses, and the most dispassionate and well-informed part of the community joined in the sentiment" (*CWWH* 13:42–

43). Hazlitt's more central claim, the one he argues at length, is that these writers could only do what they did by virtue of the general spread of writing and reading made possible by the use of the press. The thesis, perhaps derived from Condorcet's *Sketch of a Tableau of Human Progress* (1795), is stated boldly in the opening sentences of Hazlitt's analysis:[21]

> The French Revolution might be described as a remote but inevitable result of the invention of the art of printing. The gift of speech, or the communication of thought by words, is that which distinguishes man from other animals. But this faculty is limited and imperfect without the intervention of books, which render the knowledge possessed by every one in the community accessible to all. There is no doubt, then, that the press (as it has existed in modern times) is the great organ of intellectual improvement and civilisation. It was impossible in this point of view, that those institutions, which were founded in a state of society and manners long anterior to this second breathing of understanding into the life of man, should remain on the same proud footing after it, with all their disproportions and defects. [*CWWH* 13:38]

Hazlitt suggests that there have been two epochal "breathings of understanding" in human history. The first is the divine invention of the word; the second is the human invention of the letter. The first is the gift of intelligence and marks our distinction as human beings. Yet the second development, culminating in the art of printing, seems for Hazlitt to establish as much of an advance over the circumstances of oral culture as oral culture does over the purely animal state.

Hazlitt's notion that printing represents a change equivalent in magnitude to that represented by language is perhaps best understood if we think of his oral stage of human history as an epoch of political order and his literate stage as an epoch of political justice. The characteristic social system of the oral stage is feudalism—"the feudal system was in full vigor almost up to the period of the discovery of printing" (p. 38)—and its political regimes were for the most part "the growth of brute force or of barbarous superstition" (p. 39). In this phase, says Hazlitt, ("power was in the hands of a few, who used it only to gratify their own pride, cruelty, or avarice, and who took every means to extend and cement it by fear and favour" (p. 39). Such a state of things could not improve "while knowledge and power were confined within merely local and personal limits." The reason is simply this:

> As long as any unjust claim or transaction was confined to the knowledge of the parties concerned, the tyrant and the slave, which is the case in all unlettered states of society, *might* must prevail over *right*; for the strongest would bully, and the weakest must submit, even in his own defence, and persuade himself that he was in the wrong, even in his own despite. [p. 40]

Without letters, order is purchased with might; right is powerless to interfere.

Justice emerges in lettered states of society by a dialectical process in which the means of appeal to the community at large produces in that community a consciousness of a "common standard" or "impartial judge"—it is "only to be found in public opinion, the offspring of books"—and in which this consciousness in turn generates more powerful and far-reaching appeals. The tyrant and the slave, says Hazlitt, "had to settle their pretensions by themselves, and in the night of ignorance." The conditions are mutually reinforcing: the slave is isolated because he is ignorant and ignorant because he is isolated. He lives in the "dark cave of despotism and superstition" (p. 41). Literacy's "diffusion of knowledge and inquiry" leads him out of it, however, for as soon as "the world (that dread jury) are impannelled, and called to look on and be umpires in the scene, so that nothing is done by connivance or in a corner, then reason mounts the judgment-seat in lieu of passion or interest, and [public] opinion becomes law, instead of arbitrary will; and farewell feudal lord and sovereign king!" (pp. 41, 40).[22] Hazlitt's figure of reason mounting the judgment seat over passion or interest recalls that part of *The Prelude* where, as we saw, Wordsworth describes his moral crisis in just such terms. And when Hazlitt describes the birth of justice out of letters as a function of abstract thinking, we will recognize another set of familiar terms:

> Books alone teach us to judge of truth and good in the abstract: without a knowledge of things at a distance from us, we judge like savages or animals from our senses and appetites only; but by the aid of books and of an intercourse with the world of ideas, we are purified, raised, ennobled from savages into intellectual and rational beings. Our impressions of what is near to us are false, of what is distant feeble; but the last gaining strength from being united in public opinion, and expressed by the public voice, are like the congregated roar of many waters, and quail the hearts of princes. [p. 40][23]

This distillation of what I have called the ethos of letters sums up the position Wordsworth seeks to overturn in *The Ruined Cottage* and in the program it spawned. Because Hazlitt believes that books alone teach us to be fully human, they constitute his paradigm for education and culture. Speech, the "public voice," only realizes its potential insofar as it conforms to this paradigm. What is at issue between these two perspectives can be stated in logical terms as follows: for Hazlitt, exposure to books is both a necessary and a sufficient condition of the transformation from savage into moral being; for Wordsworth, it is neither. But can we accept an account dating to the 1820s as representative of a position that Wordsworth is supposed to be countering a quarter of a century earlier? There is good reason to think that we can, for much of what Hazlitt writes in the *Life of Napoleon* simply explicates what was implicit in the controversy over the freedom of the press in the 1790s. Those English radicals assembled in London to celebrate Bastille Day in 1791 could toast Burke for the part he played in generating the Great Debate of the day because this kind of combat—public, published, and presumably not dependent upon power—necessarily resulted in gains for truth and justice. This attitude found its most striking form of expression in the work of the quintessential printer's poet, William Blake, whose passionate care for the graphic presentation of his materials stemmed from more than just artistic fastidiousness. Blake's ideological commitment to the art of printing is represented in his sublime allegory by the recurring symbol of the press. In *Milton*, for example, the "Wine-press of Los" (27:1) is another name for "the Printing-Press / Of Los" (27:7–8), and both are called "War on Earth" (27:7).[24] The key to this wondrous equation lies in the poem's famous verse preface, where Blake announces his enlistment in the service of "Mental Fight" (1:13), a battle that will be played out on the open field of the press. The connection is made more explicit in *Jerusalem*, where the wine-press becomes "the great Wine-press of Love" (72:52) and where, in "wars of life" opposing friends mutually inflict "wounds of love / With intellectual spears & long winged arrows of thought" (34:14–15). Once the "water clear" has been stained by the pen, there is no returning to the world of innocent song.[25] Only through the press will Blake the gladiator and the Reader/ Friend he opposes build Jerusalem in England's green and pleasant land.[26]

There is also the case of the young, still radical Coleridge. His moving lyric of 1795, "Reflections on Having Left a Place of Retirement," belongs to his most intensely millenarian phase. At the time he wrote the poem he was at work on "Religious Musings," where he imagines that "The massy gates of Paradise are thrown / Wide open" and "the Thousand years / Lead up their mystic dance" while "the Desert shouts!" and "Old Ocean clasps his hands!" (345-46, 359–61)[27] The "reflections" of the former poem concern Coleridge's departure from his cottage at Clevedon for Bristol in early 1796. Though he has known personal comfort there, he is "constrained" to leave his "Valley of Seclusion" by the thought of the "unnumbered brethren" who toil and bleed, and for whose sake the kingdom must be purchased:

> I therefore go, and join head, heart, and hand,
> Active and firm, to fight the bloodless fight
> Of science, Freedom, and the Truth in Christ.
>
> [60–62]

Like the verse preface to Blake's *Milton*, this passage announces a poet's enlistment to fight in the millennial wars. And like Blake, Coleridge is off to battle with pen and press: what awaits him in Bristol is *The Watchman*, his forthcoming periodical.[28]

In *The Spirit of the Age* (1825), a work roughly contemporary with the biography of Napoleon, Hazlitt observed that the great philosopher of England's mental fight was William Godwin: "no one was more talked of, more looked up to, more sought after, and wherever liberty, truth, justice was the theme, his name was not far off" (*CWWH* 11:16). Godwin's *Enquiry Concerning Political Justice*, as Hazlitt succinctly describes it, "took abstract reason for the rule of conduct and abstract good for its end" (p. 18). And what Godwin's abstract reason stood opposed to, according to Hazlitt, were "the gross and narrow ties of sense, custom, authority, private and local attachment" and "the force of habit" (pp. 18–19, 23). The extent to which Godwin typifies the kind of spirit Hazlitt discusses in *The Life of Napoleon* may be judged from the words of Godwin himself. Two of the "principles" which Godwin prefixed to his discussion in *Political Justice* present the matter plainly:

> Soundness of understanding is inconsistent with prejudice: consequently, as few falsehoods as possible, either speculative or practical, should be fostered among mankind.

> Soundness of understanding is connected with freedom of enquiry: consequently, opinion should, as far as public security will admit, be exempted from restraint.[29]

In *Political Justice* Godwin moves back and forth at will between the public and the private spheres in illustrating and applying his principles. While in the above statements he seems to have public understanding and public prejudice in mind, he takes up the matter in the body of the text as a problem of individual epistemology. Here we can see just *why* "freedom of enquiry," either in the public or private sphere, is necessary to understanding and preventive of prejudice, habit, or custom (he tends to use these terms interchangeably):

> In proportion as our experience enlarges, the subjects of voluntary action become more numerous. In this state of the human being, he soon comes to perceive a considerable similarity between situation and situation. In consequence he feels inclined to abridge the process of deliberation, and to act today conformably to the determination of yesterday. Thus the understanding fixes for itself resting places, is no longer a novice, and is not at the trouble continually to go back and revise the original reasons which determined it to a course of action. Thus the man acquires habits, from which it is very difficult to wean him, and which he obeys without being able to assign either to himself or others, any explicit reason for his proceeding. This is the history of prepossession and prejudice. [pp. 65–66]

As with the individual, so with society. What Godwin calls the "trouble" of constant revision is his prosaic version of the poets' mental fight. Similarly, Godwin's "resting-places" of the understanding seem to be fairly precise analogues for Blake's allegorical "Beulah" and Coleridge's symbolic "Valley of Seclusion."[30] They are worlds of custom and habit, second natures.

As for Wordsworth's involvement in the intellectual warfare of the 1790s, we have seen that it is not a matter of speculation. He not only took part in battle, with his attack on Bishop Watson; we know from his June 1794 letter to Mathews that he also sought a position of active leadership at the head of his own periodical. This same letter shows, moreover, both that he was aware of his ideological commitment and that he saw it much as the other radicals did. "Freedom of inquiry," he told Mathews in that same letter, "is all that I wish for; let nothing be deemed too sacred for investigation; rather than restrain the liberty of the press I would suffer the most atrocious doctrines to be recommended: let the field be open and unencumbered, and truth must be victorious" (*EY*:125). The doctrine elaborated by Hazlitt in 1828 and subverted by Wordsworth in 1798 had once, five summers earlier, been Wordsworth's own.[31]

VI

There is however another, more speculative reason for considering Hazlitt's account of the enlightened ethos of letters as an accurate representation of Wordsworth's cultural target in 1798. For this same writer, just turned twenty, first met Wordsworth in the late spring of that year and evidently engaged the poet in a heated discussion on just this subject, the importance of books. Hazlitt's account of the occasion can be found in "My First Acquaintance with Poets": "I got in a metaphysical argument with Wordsworth while Coleridge was explaining the difficult notes of the nightingale to his sister, in which we neither of us succeeded in making ourselves perfectly clear and intelligible" (*CWWH* 17:119). It was probably in the following days that Wordsworth wrote the two poems for which he included the special note at the end of his Advertisement to the first edition of *Lyrical Ballads*: "The lines entitled Expostulation and Reply, and those which follow ["The Tables Turned"], arose out of conversation with a friend who was somewhat unreasonably attached to modern books of moral philosophy" (*PrW* 1:117). That the "friend" is Hazlitt, and the "conversation" the metaphysical argument later reported by him, we have no reason to doubt.[32] And after looking over the terms of this "conversation" as recorded in Wordsworth's poems we may be inclined to agree with Herschel Baker that Hazlitt's opinions on such matters—the contrast with Wordsworth's case is striking—remained essentially unchanged from early adulthood on.[33]

The title of the first of these poems, "Expostulation and Reply," invites us to read it as a debate in itself—that is, even before we see "the tables turned"—and most critics have accepted this invitation at face value. Like the poem itself, however, this invitation is not as ingenuous as it seems. The poem falls into two parts divided by a middle stanza that sets the scene and, true to the account in "First Acquaintance with Poets," identifies "Matthew" (the Hazlitt character) as the expostulator. "William," his interlocutor, is of course the poem's speaker. Matthew expostulates as follows:

"Why William on that old grey stone,
Thus for the length of half a day,
Why William, sit you thus alone,
And dream your time away?

"Where are your books? that light bequeath'd
To beings else forlorn and blind!

Up! Up! and drink the spirit breath'd
From dead men to their kind.

"You look around on your mother earth,
As if she for no purpose bore you;
As if you were her first-born birth,
And none had lived before you!"

[1–12]

Although one might wonder about the relation of the third stanza to the two that precede it, no important questions can be raised about these stanzas, which seem so utterly jejune, until we consider William's reply. It begins as follows:

"The eye it cannot chuse but see,
We cannot bid the ear be still;
Our bodies feel where'er they be,
Against, or with our will.

"Nor less I deem that there are powers,
Which of themselves our minds impress,
That we can feed this mind of ours,
In a wise passiveness."

[17–24]

Whatever interest this poem has must derive, chiefly from the evidently oblique angle of William's approach. We might well wonder how these remarks even qualify as a "reply." Matthew urges William to read books. William responds with some cryptic comments about involuntary feeling. He is certainly not answering his "good friend Matthew" on Matthew's own terms (15).

Yet it is possible to make some sense of this exchange by extrapolating the chain of assumptions implicit in Matthew's questions and juxtapositions: we are born for a purpose; that purpose is realized in action rather than in contemplation; action requires will guided by understanding; understanding operates best in the accumulated light of knowledge; such enlightenment is to be found in books; therefore one should read books. Matthew urges a course of action and supplies a reason for following it. When we understand Matthew's expostulation this way, the response it calls forth from William is explicable within the general frame of reference we have been using. For the mental faculty that sees by the light of books is what the poet of *The Prelude* disparagingly calls "the open eye of Reason," or what the author of the Letter to Llandaff exalted as "the eyes of the human race." The mental faculty William describes to Matthew, on the other hand, is that "eye of Nature" in which the Cumberland Beggar lives and dies, an eye that "cannot chuse but see" because it is compelled by the mild necessity of use. Just as sensation occurs without the intervention of the will, in William's analogy, so is our mental activity likewise involuntary.[34]

But this kind of summary does not do full justice to the subversiveness of William's response. The analogy between the operations of the senses and the intellect is supposed to be established in the crucial transition between the two stanzas. "Nor less" indicates the parallel between "our bodies" and "our minds." Yet when we stop to consider the precise terms of the analogy we are baffled. Where do those "powers, / Which of themselves our minds impress" come from? Do "eye" and "ear" constitute the antecedent of "powers"? If so, then we must consider whether we are willing to accept that the eye and the ear impress the body "of themselves." And if not, what *is* the antecedent? Just what are the powers that impress the body "of themselves," and in what sense is it true that they are like the powers that impress the mind "of *them*selves"? The apparently simple collocation of apparently self-evident assertions becomes a maze of mirrors upon closer inspection.

The succeeding stanza continues William's line of "argument," but offers complication rather than clarification:

> "Think you, mid all this mighty sum
> of things for ever speaking,
> That nothing of itself will come,
> But we must still be seeking?"

[25–28]

In the earlier stanza, the problem was to find grounds for the assertion that "there are powers / Which of themselves our minds impress." Here, in effect, this dubious assertion is transformed into its converse: it is false to say "that nothing of itself will come." Once again, apparent sense proves elusive to an inquiring eye. In a play obsessed with problems of causality, Lear says "nothing will come of nothing." Is William's question an endorsement or a contradiction of Lear's claim? If we translate the stanza "something of itself will come," do we have a meaningful assertion? Like Shakespeare's play, William's response defies the dissections of the meddling intellect.

William claims that he cannot choose but to see, hear, and think as he does. Insofar as an expostulation attempts to persuade by enlightening the understanding to alter the will, therefore, expostulation itself must be rejected—not just Matthew's specific comments but his very mode of argument. This is clear in the next and final stanza of the poem, in which William draws his "conclusion":

> "—Then ask not wherefore, here, alone,
> Conversing as I may,
> I sit upon this old grey stone,
> And dream my time away."

[29–32]

What William seems to think he has refuted, if that is the term, is not so much Matthew's point as his attempt to make one. Matthew seeks to engage William in the kind of mental fight that his books have taught him to value, but William will have none of it. Like Callicles in Plato's *Gorgias*, William rejects the very premises of the kind of debate his philosophical opponent wants to have.

It is for this reason that we must regard the poem's title as disingenuous. From William's point of view, this exchange has been not so much a debate as the successful evasion of one. And while even as reliable a reader as Paul Sheats describes the poem as balancing its points of view, I can see no reason to doubt the triumph of the point of view bearing the author's name.[35] William has the last word in the poem, and he is awarded the decisive extra stanza beyond the three allotted to Matthew. The sequel poem, furthermore, whose title proves to be similarly but more conspicuously disingenuous, confirms one's sense of the success of William's evasion.

"The Tables Turned" offers not even the slightest gesture toward realizing the promise of symmetry implied in the title phrase. Only William speaks in this poem. His comments seem to silence Matthew entirely, and the reason may simply be that they do not call for an answer. "Quit your books," William tells Matthew at the start of the poem. But in the ensuing stanzas, which are doubly pertinent since they form the context of the line I quoted earlier about natural lore, we see that William does not really expostulate with Matthew:

> Books! 'tis a dull and endless strife,
> Come, hear the woodland linnet,
> How sweet his music; on my life
> There's more of wisdom in it.

And hark! how blithe the throstle sings!
And he is no mean preacher;
Come forth into the light of things,
Let Nature be your teacher.

She has a world of ready wealth,
Our minds and hearts to bless—
Spontaneous wisdom breathed by health,
Truth breathed by chearfulness.

One impulse from a vernal wood
May teach you more of man;
Of moral evil and of good,
Than all the sages can.

Sweet is the lore which nature brings;
Our meddling intellect
Misshapes the beauteous forms of things;
—We murder to dissect.

Enough of science and of art;
Close up those barren leaves;
Come forth, and bring with you a heart
That watches and receives.

[9–32]

William does not suggest that Matthew leave the light of bookish lore for the light of natural lore *because* life is sweeter that way. He simply presents that sweetness and counts on nature to do the rest. He assumes that the power of sweetness will impress the mind "of itself," against or with the will of the listener. Where William uses the vocabulary of pedagogy in this context, we sense that he does so simply for its appeal to Matthew. Always the pleasure of the scene is mentioned first, its "educational value" added afterward, and then only perfunctorily.

Does it make sense at all, then, to say that these poems present a literary debate? It does, but only if we take the subject at issue to be the value of literary debate itself, and only if we see that the side arguing "pro" is the distinct loser. This is properly termed a question about *literary* debate because in this poem, as in the decade generally and in Hazlitt's retrospective account of thirty years later, philosophic debate, the strife of the meddling intellect, is identified with the medium of books. Indeed, the curious grammar of the line in question—"Books! 'tis a dull and endless strife"—suggests an even more intimate connection, as if books were to be *equated* with "endless strife." And the very phrase "endless strife" resonates with the radical notion of Blake, Godwin, and others that literate inquiry had to be contentious to become truly productive and had to be perpetual to remain truly free.

It is important to see that William is not rejecting conversation as such. Quite the contrary: he insists on his prerogative to go on "conversing as [he] may." What he rejects is the bookishness of Matthew's conversation, the way he speaks for books, from books.[36] Matthew puts sweet habitual speech in the service of contentious writing. William would have things the other way around. William the poet does, of course, have things the other way around—as the author not only of these two poems but also of the celebrated collection of ballad imitations in which they first appeared.[37]

Seven

Traditionalism

O reader! had you in your mind
Such stores as silent thought can bring,
O gentle reader! you would find
A tale in every thing.

"Simon Lee," *Lyrical Ballads*

*O*ne ulterior aim of my discussion of "natural lore" in Wordsworth's major work has been to prepare the ground for the suggestion that, even in his poetry of "low and rustic life," Wordsworth's conception of culture, despite the proclaimed differences in class affiliation, is quite compatible with the one we find in Burke. In fact Burke has never been far from view in this discussion. His specter seems to hover behind Hazlitt's chapter on the Revolution in the *Life of Napoleon*, for example, where he is tacitly invoked in those passages quoted earlier about feudalism and abstraction, as well as in this one about "prescription" (a word Burke brought into public currency in the 1790s):

> Public opinion must become active, and break the moulds of prescription in which [the privileged individual's] right derived from his ancestors is cast, and this will be a Revolution. Is that a state of things to regret or bring back, the bare mention of which makes one shudder? [*CWWH* 13:42]

Hazlitt's rhetorical shudder surely alludes to Burke's celebrated lamentation of the passing of the age of chivalry. By the end of Hazlitt's chapter, moreover, Burke figures explicitly in the account, and his remarks there on Burke are more extended than those on anyone else. Hazlitt's claim for Burke's role in opposing the progress of the Revolution, indeed, is nothing short of spectacular: ". . . it was Mr. Burke who, at this giddy, maddening period, stood at the prow of the vessel of the state, and with his glittering, pointed spear *harpooned* the Leviathan of the French Revolution, which darted into its wild career, tinging its onward track with purple gore" (pp. 51–52). In this remarkable conceit, which looks backward to Hobbes, Hazlitt implies that Burke drew first blood against the Revolution and that the Terror was itself somehow a consequence of this initial act of aggression. But Hazlitt's overall argument suggests that there is a further implication in this denouement—for the Revolution Burke opposed was a "result of the invention of the art of printing" and embodied the spirit of letters.

Although Hazlitt does not himself draw out this implication of his history, he could have found good evidence for doing so. Burke showed his resistance to the free exchange of written and printed materials as early as the *Reflections*, which opens with an expression of outrage against the work of the correspondence clubs.[1] He grew only more adamant as he perceived the situation in England to worsen. At least one of Burke's opponents, Robert Hall, apparently thought this issue central enough to publish criticisms of Burke under the title *An Apology for the Freedom of the Press* (1793).[2] And that same year Burke addressed the issue of press freedom head on in his *Observations on the Conduct of the Minority*. Chastising Fox for his role in the formation of a society called "The Friends of the Liberty of the Press," Burke claims that "the mischievous writings circulated with much industry and success" by such groups were "the means used in England to cöoperate with the Jacobin army in politics" (*BW* 5:18). Burke opposed the open press for a reason very like the one the radicals urged in its defense. Hazlitt, we remember, advocated freedom of the press because "the press (as it has existed in modern times) is the great organ of intellectual improvement and civilisation." Burke advocated restriction, analogously, because the present was in his view "a time in which the press has been the grand instrument of the subversion of order, of morals, of religion, and, I may say, of human society itself" (p. 19).

Taken together with his related comments about the poverty of philosophy and the virtue of principles immanent in the medium of social life, Burke's comments about the press show how deliberately he opposed the emerging ethos of letters. Perhaps it was in recognition of this stand that Wordsworth, who certainly learned his Burke chiefly from books, eulogized the "genius of Burke" as an orator, impressive in his eloquence, and depicted him not so much in a posture of debate as in that of a man handing down truths to those younger men who have ears for his wisdom. By general reputation, however, Burke has seldom been associated with a critique of the values of print culture and even more seldom with a positive claim for the values of oral culture. And in this last point lies an irony that suggests an important truth about Wordsworth's reputation.

I

In our own century, at least, the Burkean position I have summarized under such headings as "second nature" and "the doctrine of experience" has in fact more commonly been discussed under the rubric of "tradition." It is a rare modern discussion of Burke, whether in a history of political theory or in a more specialized commentary, that does not call Burke a "traditionalist" or make some reference to his "traditionalism."[3] To call Burke a "traditionalist" is to focus attention on what he said about the preservation of social practices and values, to take these comments as central to his thought. A good example of such a comment occurs in the *Reflections*, where he states that "it has been the uniform policy of our Constitution to claim and assert our liberties as an *entailed inheritance* derived to us from our forefathers, and to be transmitted to our posterity,—as an estate specially belonging to the people of this kingdom, without any reference whatever to any other more general or prior right" (3:274). One can easily enough see the relation of this sort of comment to second-nature thinking as soon as Burke goes on to add that "this policy appears to me to be the result of profound reflection,—or rather the happy effect of following Nature, which is wisdom without reflection, and above it." But it would be quibbling to insist on the one rubric over the other. Insofar as Burkean "tradition" is understood to refer to his central notion of inheritance, then modern commentators are on solid ground with it, as Burke's ensuing summary makes clear:

> The idea of inheritance furnishes a sure principle of conservation, and a sure principle of transmission, without at all excluding a principle of improvement. It leaves acquisition free; but it secures what it acquires. Whatever advantages are obtained by a state proceeding on these maxims are locked fast as in a sort of family settlement, grasped as in a kind of mortmain forever. By a constitutional policy working after the pattern of Nature, we receive, we hold, we transmit our government and our privileges, in the same manner in which we enjoy and transmit our property and our lives. [274–75]

These are obviously propositions that underlie much of the Burkean creed as it would have appeared—did appear—to Wordsworth.

The irony I mentioned is that in Burke's own time the term "tradition" usually conveyed the sense of an activity carried out in oral circumstances. Virtually all the relevant entries under "tradition" in the *Oxford English Dictionary* include some such qualification: e.g., "The action of transmitting, or 'handing down,' or fact of being handed down, from one to another, or from generation to generation; transmission of statements, beliefs, rules, customs, or the like, esp. by word of mouth or by practice without writing." A passage from *Gulliver's Travels*, not included among the *OED*'s examples, illustrates the point nicely. In his account of "the Learning of the Houyhnhnms," Gulliver explains: "the Houyhnhnms have no Letters, and consequently, their knowledge is all Traditional."[4] Just as in the nineteenth century "traditionalist" is typically opposed to such terms as "rationalist," so in the eighteenth century one is likely to find "traditional" opposed to such terms as "written."

One recent commentator, J. G. A. Pocock, who writes incisively both about Burke and about the concept of tradition, has illuminated Burke's link with the values of oral culture by approaching Burke through English legal history. In his essay on "Traditions and Their Understanding," Pocock describes tradition "in the pure state" as "an indefinite series of repetitions of an action, which on each occasion is performed on the assumption that it has been performed before; its performance is authorized . . . by the knowledge, or the assumption of previous performance."[5] And the nature of this kind of tradition, says Pocock, "was pointed but by Burke, who was an acute analyst as well as an eloquent expositor, of the traditional society and its mind."[6] Later in his discussion, Pocock proceeds to the crucial qualification that "a literate tradition is never a pure tradition." His explanation is worth citing at length:

> The authority of written words is not dependent on usage and presumption only. As durable material objects they cut across the processes of transmission and create new patterns of social time; they speak direct to remote generations, whose interpretation of them may differ from that of intervening transmitters of the tradition they express. If the position can be firmly maintained that documents are no more than occasional expressions of an essentially unwritten tradition, the doctrine that equates authority with simple transmission may survive; the concept of English politics we find in Burke is directly connected with the fact that common-law records were assumed

to be declarations of an immemorial *jus non scriptum.*
[pp. 254–55]

In showing the ramifications of Burke's commitment to a common-law
political order backed by an unwritten constitution—a commitment
openly challenged by adversaries like Paine, who pointedly insisted that
wherever a constitution "cannot be produced in a visible form, there is
none"[7]—Pocock reaches a conclusion about Burke very much like the one I
have been arguing for in the case of Wordsworth. Both writers represent
social welfare as crucially dependent upon the continuity of literate culture
with oral culture and upon writing's subservience to the cause of speech.
Both see documentation as a threat to usage.

The last few years have seen an increased interest in the topic of
Wordsworth and tradition.[8] "Tradition," in this context, is usually under-
stood either in the sense of literary tradition, or else of Judeo-Christian
religious tradition, and Wordsworth is usually found to be balancing the
claims of "revolution" or "experiment," on the one hand, with those of
"tradition," on the other. But when we consider Wordsworth's relation to
tradition in this broadly cultural sense of the term as it is employed in
discussions of Burke, we discover that he is in most ways as much a
"traditionalist" as Burke, the acknowledged avatar of traditionalism.
Further, Wordsworth proves to be an even more thoroughgoing tradi-
tionalist than Burke in some ways, since, unlike Burke, he embraces
"tradition" with an explicit awareness of its roots in illiterate forms of
cultural life. We saw this clearly enough in the virtue attributed to
"traditionary tales" in shaping the Pedlar's character.

Wordsworth's sense of "tradition" can be established from any num-
ber of instances, but a passage from book 7 of *The Excursion* glosses the term
straightforwardly. The Pastor, who throughout the poem treats the post-
Enlightenment malaise of the Solitary by recounting local tales and legends
for him, notices that the Solitary is scrutinizing a monument for some clue
to its meaning. The Pastor informs the Solitary that such a "task would foil"
the "sagest Antiquarian's eye," and, by way of supplying the desired
explanation, reports to him what "Tradition tells" about the spot. Pausing,
mid-narrative, the Pastor observes that the acceptance of what he says
depends upon whether "belief may rest / Upon unwritten story fondly
traced / From sire to son" (921–22, 941–43). Clearly, the Pastor hopes that
belief *may* be secured in this way and that the Solitary will accept the tale, as
we say, on faith. For the Solitary's recovery will require that he quiet the
baffled eye of reason and place his trust in the voice he hears repeating tales

that have been taken on faith by so many others before him, as the very survival of the tales well proves.

When the Pastor speaks of "unwritten *story* fondly traced / From sire to son" he includes another important feature of Wordsworth's sense of tradition. What "tradition tells" (the phrase recurs frequently in Wordsworth's writing) typically takes the form of a tale, and when Wordsworth uses the article form, "*a* tradition," the phrase is usually interchangeable with a phrase like "a traditionary tale" or even more simply "a tale." That the Pedlar's meditation on the ruins of Margaret's cottage should assume narrative form is therefore not a matter of coincidence, but rather an important part of what makes *The Ruined Cottage* so seminal for Wordsworth's subsequent work. The poem presents an oral tale told by an experienced father figure to an immature son figure for the purposes of passing on appropriate moral habits from the former to the latter. Seen in that light, *The Ruined Cottage* seems all that one could expect a traditionalist poem to be. Wordsworth's complex traditionalism does not emerge full-blown until "Michael," however, and two particular circumstances of its composition helped this meditative narrative to become a succinct expression of what the poet now stood for. The first is that it was written right after Wordsworth's effort to articulate his views about literature and society in the prose of the 1800 Preface. The second is that it was written in the final months of the eighteenth century: the last in a series of references to "Michael" in Dorothy's Grasmere Journal for 1800 occurs in the entry for 9 December—"Wm finished his poem today."[9]

What did William see from his vantage point at the end of this ambitious century? Before all else, of course, he saw a pile of stones; Dorothy's journal suggests that "the sheepfold" may have been the poem's early working title (pp. 67–72). What he saw in the stones, however, was a tale, the story of Michael—"a tradition" in the sense just described. But that tale suggests that the sheepfold displayed to Wordsworth another sense of tradition as well, the sense explained by Pocock in his account of preindustrial England's increasingly self-conscious image of itself:

> A society thinks of itself in purely traditional terms in proportion as it is aware of itself simply as a cluster of institutionalised modes of transmitting behaviour. We may, somewhat in the manner of Victorian anthropologists, envisage a simple kinship society, in which everything is learned from the fathers before the shrines of the ancestors; in such a society. . . . everything will be thought of as transmitted, continuous, immemorial and—since each father must speak on the authority of his

father—presumptive. . . . In pre-industrial England, for exam-
ple all social and national institutions could be conceived as
bound up with the common law, that law was conceived as
custom, and the activity of law-making was conceived as the
conversion into written precedents of unwritten usages whose
sole authority was that of immemorial antiquity. Consequent-
ly, to the end of the eighteenth century it could be argued that
the constitution was immemorial, its authority prescriptive and
our knowledge of it presumptive. The character of English
institutions, in short, was such as to favour the assumption that
the only form of action was transmission and the only form of
knowledge the inheritance of learning.[10]

The tale of Michael ultimately suggests that the pile of stones which stands
as the poem's central symbol stands for just the sort of "cluster of institu-
tional modes of transmitting behaviour" that Pocock describes as the purely
traditional society's self-image. "Michael" is a tradition that describes and
enacts a tradition, and what gives the poem its special character is the
relation it establishes between the various senses of tradition thus invoked.

<h1 style="text-align:center">II</h1>

Although we normally call the poem's interpolated narrative the story of
Michael, it actually concentrates attention on the relation between Michael
and his son. The first half of the poem is primarily concerned to show the
process by which the father, having "learn'd the meaning of all winds" (48),
passes on what he knows—the customs and usages of his life—to his son.
Michael's mind is said to be *"like* a book" in the way it preserves the past,
but Michael's education in fact depends on books themselves very little.[11]
Similarly in the teaching of his son, Michael's instruction is chiefly by his
own example. Constant companionship gives the power of imitation time
enough to work its ways, and Luke's character is formed by the assimilation
of his father's daily rituals:

> I may truly say,
> That they were as a proverb in the vale
> For endless industry. When day was gone,
> And from their occupations out of doors
> The Son and Father were come home, even then
> Their labor did not cease . . .
> . . . .
> . . . [For] when their meal
> Was ended, LUKE (for so the Son was nam'd)

And his old Father, both betook themselves
To such convenient work, as might employ
Their hands by the fire-side; perhaps to card
Wool for the House-wife's spindle, or repair
Some injury done to sickle, flail, or scythe,
Or other implement of house or field.

[95–111]

Michael and Luke are shown working together at these indoor chores, but there should be no question about who is teaching whom. Since Michael is a shepherd, to become a shepherd is the biggest part of what it means to be Michael's son, and one can more clearly see the subordination of the young apprentice in those passages which describe the outdoor labors with the flock. Shearing sheep under the clipping tree, for example,

. . . while they two were sitting in the shade,
With others round them, earnest all and blithe,
Would Michael exercise his heart with looks
Of fond correction and reproof bestow'd
Upon the child, if he disturb'd the sheep
By catching at their legs, or with his shouts
Scar'd them, while they lay still beneath the shears.

[180–86]

Though Luke's education in the trade, like his rearing generally, has nothing to do with "book learning," it cannot in its earliest stages be entirely entrusted to imitation either. "Ministry more palpable," to borrow a phrase from *The Prelude* (where it appears in a not dissimilar context), was required in cases where his actions risked danger to the flock: at such times, "nought was left undone which staff or voice, / Or looks, or threatening gestures could perform" (202–3).

The more inclusive and important gesture in the poem, though, is Michael's *passing* on of his shepherd's staff rather than his *laying* it on:

And when by Heaven's good grace the Boy grew up
A healthy Lad, and carried in his cheek
Two steady roses that were five years old,
Then Michael from a winter coppice cut
With his own hand a sapling, which he hoop'd
With iron, making it throughout in all
Due requisites a perfect Shepherd's Staff,
And gave it to the Boy.

[187–94]

This act of handing on to Luke the handmade staff, at once the tool and symbol of Michael's way of life, metaphorically sums up the poem's central action to this point. What the poem has presented, in effect, is a social analogue for one of Wordsworth's most famous epigrams about the individual, for the man this natural child is "father of" is to be a replica of the child's father. The remainder of the poem shows the circumstances, motives, and consequences of Michael's decision to send Luke off to work in the city.

Wordsworth wrote to Thomas Poole in April 1801 that he had attempted in "Michael" to "give a picture of a man, of strong mind and lively sensibility, agitated by two of the most powerful affections of the human heart; the parental affections, and the love of property, *landed* property, including the feelings of inheritance, home, and personal and family independence" (*EY*:322). These two feelings, though, operate as one in the poem, for the love of property emerges as a *filial* affection, and the parental and filial affections become two sides of the same coin. This is nowhere clearer than in the poem's portrayal of Michael's ill-starred decision. Earlier on, as we learn, Michael had bound himself in "surety for his Brother's Son"; the nephew being subsequently visited by "unforeseen misfortunes," Michael is called upon, just as his own son approaches manhood, to "discharge the forfeiture." Though Michael is aware of the dangers in sending Luke to the city to help earn the needed money, his only alternative is "to sell / a Portion of his patrimonial fields." The motive for his decision is presented as an attempt to avert this latter possibility.

We are asked, in other words, to view the decision as resulting from the enormous value Michael places on the land. Michael's decision may thus certainly be said to illustrate "the love of property," but the fact that the land is called his "patrimonial fields" is the clue that this affection, which Wordsworth likens to "feelings of inheritance," is rooted in Michael's association of the land with his father and his father's father. The property is "loved" not as wealth, but as a symbol of the ancestral experience to which Michael owes a pious son's allegiance. Obversely, this same emotion behind Michael's decision can also be viewed as parental in character. As regards this land, Michael has no illusion that he can take it with him. His concern is simply that, along with all the other accouterments of his life, it be passed on to his son. "If these fields of ours," he tells his wife Isabel, "Should pass into a Stranger's hand, I think / That I could not lie quiet in my grave" (240–42). This property, then, is the "ground" both of what the father hands on to the son and of what the son owes to the father. In either case, it is important not in itself, but rather for the parental-filial bond it represents.[12]

The building of the sheepfold (the same one on whose ruins the speaker of the poem gazes as he tells the story) is intended by Michael precisely as a way of insuring against Luke's forgetting his place on the family land and in the family line. This intention is made clear in the ceremony Michael devises on the eve of Luke's departure for the laying of the sheepfold's cornerstone. Michael opens the ritual by relating to Luke "some little part / Of [their] two histories," which of course center on the natural bond of love between them. He then goes on to show the place of this bond in a long line of interconnected parental-filial relations:

> —Even to the utmost I have been to thee
> A kind and good Father: and herein
> I but repay a gift which I myself
> Receiv'd at others hands, for, though now old
> Beyond the common life of man, I still
> Remember them who lov'd me in my youth.
> Both of them sleep together: here they liv'd
> As all their Forefathers had done, and when
> At length their time was come, they were not loth
> To give their bodies to the family mold.
> I wish'd that thou should'st live the life they liv'd.
>
> [371–81]

Though Michael insists that Luke has "been bound to [him] / Only by links of love" (411–12), the "great secret of morals" he reveals here (to use Shelley's phrase) is not love (as it was for Shelley) but repetition. Michael repeats the moral lives of his forefathers. Michael's wish is that the life of his own son should be a repetition of his own. "Family mold" captures this with rich Wordsworthian paronomasia. That Michael couches his wish in past tense—"I wish'd that thou should'st live the life they liv'd"—may show disappointment that Luke must at least temporarily leave shepherding behind him; it by no means indicates that Michael has ceased to wish for Luke's imitation of his fathers' moral lives. Indeed, we learn that the sheepfold ceremony itself expresses Michael's specific hope that Luke will continue to follow the family way in the city, that he will preserve contact with ancestral sources of moral power even while apart from their physical circumstances. Here is the final speech of Michael's commemorative ceremony:

> Lay now the corner-stone,
> As I requested, and hereafter, Luke,
> When thou art gone away, should evil men
> Be thy companions, let this Sheep-fold be
> Thy anchor and thy shield; amid all fear
> And all temptation, let it be to thee
> An emblem of the life thy Fathers liv'd,
> Who, being innocent, did for that cause
> Bestir them in good deeds. Now, fare thee well—
> When thou return'st, thou in this place wilt see
> A work which is not here, a covenant
> 'Twill be between us—but whatever fate
> Befall thee, I shall love thee to the last,
> And bear the memory with me to the grave.
>
> [414–27]

The lines could hardly be more explicit. The literal focal point of the poem, the stone sheepfold, is now explicitly identified as an "emblem" of the moral life of the ancestors and, what amounts to the same thing, as a symbol of the natural convenant between father and son.

In "the dissolute city," however, Luke is quick to break this covenant and to forget the usage of his ancestors. Removed from the habitual contact with his father's example, Luke goes the way of his baleful namesake:

> [he] gave himself
> To evil courses: ignominy and shame
> Fell on him, so that he was driven at last
> To seek a hiding-place beyond the seas.
>
> [453–56]

In the context of a poem where illiteracy plays so beneficial a role, we should probably have expected such an end as soon as we learned of Luke's letters home, especially since they are full of news:

> the Boy
> Wrote loving letters, full of wond'rous news,
> Which, as the House-wife phrased it, were throughout
> The prettiest letters that were ever seen.
>
> [441–44]

As the son grows in literacy and in knowledge of the world, the unwritten reminder of the life of his fathers is readily forgotten. And in terms of this tale, forgetting the meaning of the sheepfold *is* breaking the ancestral covenant.

We are now in a position to see the full purport of the tale's framing structure, for the poem as a whole attempts to redeem the covenant broken by Luke, by reversing the influence of the dissolute city on the rural community. Nature's oblivious tendencies are on the verge of annihilating the last vestiges not just of Michael's own life, but also of what it stood for: the inheritance of the ancestral line and the traditional means by which that inheritance is handed down. From the oral tales told by his own elders the poet of the poem has learned the meaning of the rocks, as Michael learned the meaning of the winds.[13] In his recovery of the sheepfold's meaning, the poet-speaker thus steps into Luke's place to restore the covenant and to become the loyal son of Michael that Luke failed to be. The poet's very recognition of the stones in the landscape is evidence of his filial piety.

The poem's act of redemption is not complete, however, until the son becomes the father in his turn. The poet assumes the same stance toward his audience as Michael assumes toward his son. As Michael hands on the inherited customs of his trade to Luke, so the poet hands on the inherited tale of Michael, for "the delight of a few natural hearts," he says:

And with yet fonder feeling, for the sake
Of youthful Poets, who among these Hills
Will be my second self when I am gone.

[37–39]

Had Luke escaped the effects of "the great national events which are daily taking place," of "the increasing accumulation of men in cities" and of the degraded taste of his age, he would have become Michael's second self. The reader who escapes these same influences, which loom so ominously over the coming century, and who submits to such natural lore as the tale of Michael, will have become this poet's second self among the hills of Westmoreland.[14] In both cases, we glimpse the ultimate extension of the principle of repetition, what Pocock calls the "timeless society" in which "each transmitting ancestor" would be "thought of as the reincarnation of his predecessor."[15]

E. P. Thompson has argued passionately that "Wordsworth fell back within the forms of paternalistic sensibility" only after he had written his major poetry.[16] And this claim supports an even more far-reaching argument "that capitulation by the Jacobin poets to the traditional, paternalistic culture was *in fact* inimical to the sources of their art" (p. 173). The best poetic evidence that Thompson can bring to bear on Wordsworth's case is the post-1805 revision of *The Ruined Cottage*, when it was being fitted out to serve as the opening book of *The Excursion*. "As he revised 'The Ruined Cottage,' " writes Thompson, "so the old paternalistic tag-words drop back in: 'rosy' children, 'homely' fare, 'the keen, the wholesome, aire of poverty" (p. 175). But by focusing on these relatively superficial matters of diction, Thompson seems to miss the entire paternalist-traditionalist design of *The Ruined Cottage*, a design reincarnated in "Michael," where the relationship between paternalism and traditionalism shows forth in the relationship between the covenant and story of the stones.

III

Thompson's comment about the late revisions of *The Ruined Cottage* does, however, point to an important fact: as we move forward from the "golden decade" we find that Wordsworth becomes more and more explicit and less and less provisional in his traditionalism. It is worth looking briefly at this extended phase of Wordsworth's career, both to note the peculiar tenacity of Wordsworth's traditionalism and to glimpse how it eventually begins to lead beyond itself. Apart from *The Excursion* (whose origin actually dates to 1798), by far the greatest part of the verse Wordsworth wrote after the publication of the 1807 *Poems* assumes the form of sonnets and sonnet sequences. Though any of a number of these might be used to illustrate the later Wordsworth's concern with tradition, a brief look at the *River Duddon* sequence (composed between 1806 and 1820, and published in 1820) will serve our present purposes.

The sequence is introduced by stanzas titled "To the Rev. Dr. Wordsworth," which dedicate the sequence to Wordsworth's brother Christopher, who, as we learn, has left his "native hills" to practice medicine in Lambeth, on "the proud margin of the Thames." The occasion of the poem is a caroling ceremony on Christmas Eve—"The Minstrels played their Christmas tune / Tonight beneath my cottage-eaves" (1–2)— which puts the poet in mind of the absent brother:

> . . . would that Thou, with me and mine,
> Hadst heard this never-failing rite;
> And seen on other faces shine
> A true revival of the light
> Which Nature and these rustic Powers,
> In simple childhood, spread through ours!

[25–30]

The light that shines in the faces of the carolers is the light of the past innocence as preserved by the caroling ritual itself. Thus the emotional climax of the poem comes with Wordsworth's salute to all such ritual functions:

> Hail, ancient Manners! sure defence,
> Where they survive, of wholesome laws;
> Remnants of love whose modest sense
> Thus into narrow room withdraws;
> Hail, Usages of pristine mould,
> And ye that guard them, Mountains old!
>
> [55–60]

The pristine usages which preserve past innocence are themselves preserved by the mountains, in that the mountains close off the rustic community from intercourse with the wider social world, turn it on itself, and therefore mold human lives into patterns of (as Wordsworth says in the 1800 Preface) "repeated experience." The caroling ceremony repeats itself year after year, but unlike the "imperial City's din" which "Beats frequent on [Christopher's] satiate ear," it is a repeated act on which "pleasure hath not ceased to wait" (pp. 31–34, 73–74). Because the rite is pleasurable, the rustic turns to it with alacrity, and because it is an unchanging repetition, it bears to him the innocent light of the past. This introductory poem concludes by urging Christopher to make such occasions for himself in the hustle-bustle of urban life:

> Yes, they can make, who fail to find,
> Short leisure even in busiest days;
> Moments, to cast a look behind,
> And profit by those kindly rays
> That through the clouds do sometimes steal,
> And all the far-off past reveal.
>
> Hence, while the imperial City's din
> Beats frequent on thy satiate ear,
> A pleased attention I may win
> To agitations less severe,
> That neither overwhelm nor cloy,
> But fill the hollow vale with joy!
>
> [67–78]

Wordsworth's mention of the "agitations" to which he hopes to win Christopher's attention is a reference to the sonnets which follow these prefatory stanzas. The poet's wish is that these sonnets will provide occasions of leisure for city dwellers similar to the occasions which the "ancient Manners" provide for those who have not left their native hills. Words-worth's poetry, then, becomes a clear analogue for the rustic ritual; like the ritual it specifically helps the participant (reader) to "look behind" and profit from a vision of the "far-off past."

The "far-off past" thus revealed, though it may be distinct, is not distinct from the present. As Wordsworth's sonnet sequence follows along the course of the River Duddon, we discover that sequence and river are analogues for one another and, together, emblems for time. We also come to see that they emblematize time from a point of view which is traditional-ist, in that it sees time as always passing on and never passing away. Wordsworth presents himself during his crisis in *The Prelude* as one who only sees the past as "passed away." In the final sonnet on the Duddon, "After-thought," he expressly denies this view and reaffirms its contrary:

> I thought of Thee, my partner and my guide,
> As being past away,—Vain sympathies!
> For, backward, Duddon! as I cast my eyes,
> I see what was, and is, and will abide;
> Still glides the Stream, and shall for ever glide;
> The Form remains, the Function never dies;
> While we, the brave, the mighty, and the wise,
> We Men, who in our morn of youth defied
> The elements, must vanish;—be it so!
> Enough, if something from our hands have power
> To live, and act, and serve the future hour;
> And if, as toward the silent tomb we go,
> Through love, through hope, and faith's transcendent dower,
> We feel that we are greater than we know.

It would be a terrible mistake to attempt to explain away these lines as the opinions of the fifty-year-old conservative Christian Tory. The "ideas" expressed in these lines are essentially unchanged from those expressed in the lines added to *The Ruined Cottage* between January and March of 1798. By 1820, Wordsworth has simply decided that he can make do with the sonnet sequence, where he earlier represents himself as "experimenting" with the rustic oral narrative. The "something from our hands" is the sequence itself, which is passed on to serve the future hour as it has been passed on to serve in the present. Like the caroling ritual, the poem itself is a surviving form and an undying function.

This "After-thought," no doubt calculated to help the city-dweller "to cast a look behind," is just the last of several such backward glances in the sequence. Other examples are Sonnets XXI and XXII. Sonnet XXI is untitled:

> Whence that low voice?—A whisper from the heart,
> That told of days long past, when here I roved
> With friends and kindred tenderly beloved;
> Some who had early mandates to depart,
> Yet are allowed to steal my path athwart
> By Duddon's side; once more do we unite,
> Once more beneath the kind Earth's tranquil light;
> And smothered joys into new being start.
> From her unworthy seat, the cloudy stall
> Of time, breaks forth triumphant Memory;
> Her glistening tresses bound, yet light and free
> As golden locks of birch, that rise and fall
> On gales that breathe too gently to recal
> Aught of the fading year's inclemency!

This sonnet illustrates the sequence's developing identification of its own course with the course of the river. The poet's two paths, one through the poem and one along the river, (more explicitly here even than in similar passages in *The Prelude*), are conflated. And "here" (l. 2), as happens at so many "places" in *The Prelude*, the poet's progress is blocked by a memorial spirit. The whisper here that tells of "days long past" brings more than just a vision of the poet's deceased friends; it brings him into *union* with them, in an earthly version of the Day of Judgment: "once more do we unite, / Once more beneath the kind Earth's tranquil light." The sestet recasts the return of "friends and kindred" as an act of Memory, which is personified as a Nature-spirit rather like Keats's spirit of the season in "To Autumn."

The next sonnet forms a companion piece to XXI:

XXII: TRADITION

> A love-lorn Maid, at some far-distant time,
> Came to this hidden pool, whose depths surpass
> In crystal clearness Dian's looking-glass;
> And, gazing, saw that Rose, which from the prime
> Derives its name, reflected as the chime
> Of echo doth reverberate some sweet sound:

> The starry treasure from the blue profound
> She longed to ravish;—shall she plunge, or climb
> The humid precipice, and seize the guest
> Of April, smiling high in upper air?
> Desperate alternative! what fiend could dare
> To prompt the thought?—Upon the steep rock's breast
> The lonely Primrose yet renews its bloom,
> Untouched memento of her hapless doom!

The female figure who is associated with Diana here stands in contrast to the female spirit of Memory in Sonnet XXI. Where the spirit of Memory is autumnal, the "love-lorn Maid" is vernal: she is the spirit of expectation. For her, the primrose is only a promise of coming pleasure, and because of the way she regards the flower, it leads her to the "desperate alternative." The path away from desperation in the poem is represented by the mind of the speaker himself, for whom the primrose becomes a "memento"; he sees the flower in the autumnal perspective, the "sunset" light of the end of the Intimations Ode. In the end, as we discover, the speaker reveals the same habit of mind in this sonnet as emerged in its predecessor: the one is prompted by a memento of "some far-distant time," the other by a voice that tells "of days long past."

Wordsworth's pairing of these two sonnets manifests his powerful sense of analogy not only between the general operations of personal and communal memory but also between "spots of time" and "spots of tradition," a relation we shall be considering more carefully in the following chapter. Sonnet XXI might be called a private tradition, Sonnet XXII a public memory, but both describe a mentality that stands opposed to the sense of the past as foreign to the present, and both show the persistence of form and function over time. A sonnet composed thirteen years later, which appeared in the *Yarrow Revisited* sequence of 1835, shows still another aspect of Wordsworth's interest in this analogy:

FANCY AND TRADITION

> The Lovers took within this ancient grove
> Their last embrace; beside those crystal springs
> The Hermit saw the Angel spread his wings
> For instant flight; the Sage in yon alcove
> Sate musing; on that hill the Bard would rove,
> Not mute, where now the linnet only sings:
> Thus everywhere to truth Tradition clings,
> Or Fancy localises Powers we love.

> Were only History licensed to take note
> Of things gone by, her meagre monuments
> Would ill suffice for persons and events:
> There is an ampler page for man to quote,
> A readier book of manifold contents,
> Studied alike in palace and in cot.

The key to the poem lies in the relation of the two statements in lines 7 and 8, which together comprise the conclusion ("Thus . . .") to the octave. Showing the same phenomenon from opposite points of view, these lines present a kind of dialectical equation. To say that tradition clings everywhere to truth is to describe from outside the individual mind what the clause "Fancy localises Powers we love" describes from inside the mind. Powers we love seem to cling to places; tradition is universal love localized by fancy. Lover, Hermit, Sage, and Bard are drawn to this ancient grove by virtue of their individual affections, and the poet/speaker is drawn to the grove because those before him were.

In juxtaposing "Fancy and Tradition," the octave points not to their opposition but to their apposition and their mutual correspondence: they both show the power of feeling the past in the present. The contrary to this view, which, as we have already seen, understands the past as passed away, is presented in the sestet. Wordsworth there identifies this other way of understanding the past as "History," and identifies it with the study of written documents. (The comparatives in the final three lines—"ampler page," "readier book"—make it clear that history's "meagre monuments" are literary sources.) The reason this view of the past cannot "suffice" is that it fails to take into account the crucial ways in which the past survives into the present, for these are unwritten, unwilled, and, most importantly, unconscious. The book whose ampler page does take account of what is handed down from the past cannot be referred to, argued over, or cited for evidence. It is the unwritten text which comprises the mind itself—"makes up" the mind, so to speak—and which one reads by second nature, whether one chooses to do so or not.[17]

IV

That Wordsworth shows signs of recognizing documentary history as a threat to his cultural ideal long before 1833 may (itself) be documented by a letter he wrote to Walter Scott in 1808. In the early part of that year, Scott heard that Wordsworth was at work on a poem about the Norton uprising (*The White Die of Rylstone*) and offered to pass along "some very curious letters from a spy, sent in to Scotland at the time of the great Northern

Rebellion, in which there is a good deal of mention made of the Nortons"
(*PW* 5:542). Wordsworth answered Scott's letter in May:

> Thank you for the interesting particulars about the Nortons; I
> shall like much to see them for their own sakes; but so far from
> being serviceable to my Poem they would stand in the way of it;
> as I have followed (as I was in duty bound to do) the traditionary
> and common historic records — —. Therefore I shall say in this
> case, a plague upon your industrious Antiquarianism that has
> put my fine story to confusion. [*MY*:237]

"History," as some modern historiographers define it, is the criticism of
tradition, and Wordsworth's understanding of the meaning of history
seems well expressed by this formulation.[18] Insofar as he feels himself
"duty-bound" to tell a fine story out of traditionary material, his chances for
success are jeopardized by the availability of a historical explanation of that
story's events. The power of such a story derives not from its factual
veracity, but simply from the assumption that it has been believed when
told before.

Just as interesting as the message of this remarkable letter is its tone,
for Wordsworth shows a sense of uneasiness about his baldly obscurantist
position. One detects a kind of nervous laughter in his effort to dismiss the
issue with a playful but self-conscious curse on Scott's "industrious Anti-
quarianism." Wordsworth's traditionalist position is in fact characterized
by a strange ambivalence almost from his first adopting it. The critical
confusion over the meaning of "The World Is Too Much With Us"[19]
composed *by* 1804) issues from a deep-rooted ambiguity analogous to the
one Empson sees at the center of "Tintern Abbey": "probably it was
necessary for Wordsworth to shuffle" in the key passages of that poem,
Empson writes, "if he was to maintain his peculiar poetical attitude."[20] The
sestet of the sonnet offers none of the grammatical difficulty of the sublime
passages of "Tintern Abbey," but its purport has proved equally elusive:

> It moves us not.—Great God! I'd rather be
> A Pagan suckled in a creed outworn;
> So might I, standing on this pleasant lea,
> Have glimpses that would make me less forlorn;
> Have sight of Proteus rising from the sea;
> Or hear old Triton blow his wreathèd horn.

What is the poem's attitude toward the notion entertained here by the
speaker? To see the relevance of this passage to our discussion of Words-

worth's traditionalism, we should set next to it the passage with which it is often compared, the Wanderer's speech in book 4 of *The Excursion*:

> "Life's autumn past, I stand on winter's verge;
> And daily lose what I desire to keep:
> Yet rather would I instantly decline
> To the traditionary sympathies
> Of a most rustic ignorance and take
> A fearful apprehension from the owl
> Or death-watch: and as readily rejoice,
> If two auspicious magpies crossed my way;—
> To this would rather bend than see and hear
> The repetitions wearisome of sense
> Where soul is dead, and feeling hath no place;
> Where knowledge, ill begun in cold remark
> On outward things, with formal inference ends.

[611–23]

Clearly, the "glimpses" that would console the speaker of the sonnet derive from what the Wanderer calls "traditionary sympathies," and in both cases such sympathies are presented as salutary alternatives to modern skepticism. On the other hand, these salutary alternatives are themselves portrayed as inadequate to the speaker's needs; in the one case, as "a creed outworn," in the other, as a "most rustic ignorance." The flirtation with a full-blown primitivism, though perhaps not endorsed in either poem, is certainly indulged in both. The difference of opinion over these passages in Wordsworth dates back to the varying responses of Keats and De Quincey; I make no effort here to resolve it, only to suggest what it owes to Wordsworth's inner conflict on the issue.

One of the most interesting expressions of this ambivalence is an 1835 sonnet from *Yarrow Revisited*:

IN THE SOUND OF MULL

Tradition, be thou mute! Oblivion, throw
Thy veil in mercy o'er the records, hung
Round strath and mountain, stamped by the ancient tongue
On rock and ruin darkening as we go,—
Spots where a word, ghost-like, survives to show
What crimes from hate, or desperate love, have sprung;
From honour misconceived, or fancied wrong,
What feuds, not quenched but fed by mutual woe.

> Yet, though a wild vindictive Race, untamed
> By civil arts and labours of the pen,
> Could gentleness be scorned by those fierce Men,
> Who, to spread wide the reverence they claimed
> For partriarchal occupations, named
> Yon towering Peaks, "Shepherds of Etive Glen?"

Unlike the early "poems on the naming of places" from which it is descended, this poem immediately places its subject matter in problematic perspective. The octave is, simultaneously, a silencing of Tradition and a condemnation of a traditionary race who were "untamed / By civil arts and labours of the pen." The "crimes" and "feuds" seem, in the first part of the poem, to have contaminated the "spots of tradition" topos. The sestet, however, abruptly reverses the direction of the poem—the sonnet pivots on "Yet" in line 9—and takes the sting out of its initial criticism. The traditionary name for the local mountains, "Shepherds of Etive Glen," shows to the speaker that this primitive race revered the patrimonial occupation, and, evidently, any race which pays such reverence cannot be all bad (cannot scorn gentleness) in this speaker's eyes. Even if Michael had been a feuding Hatfield or McCoy, we must conclude, Luke would have been morally bound to revere his patrimonial occupation. Thus, though the "civil arts and labours of the pen" are ostensibly supposed good by the poem, its movement works to undermine that supposition, even in the face of barbarity.

Though such murky ambivalence clouds Wordsworth's traditionalism almost from its inception, it is not until his last major work that he attempts to confront his misgivings head on and to clarify his ideas and assumptions—especially with reference to the crucial issue of his avoidance of the historical approach. *The Memorials of a Tour in Italy*, composed chiefly in 1841 and published in 1842, begins with a series of poems which address themselves specifically to the tension between the claims of tradition and history. The poems of special interest are Sonnets III through VI: "At Rome"; "At Rome.—Regrets.—In allusion to Niebuhr, and Other Modern Historians"; "Continued"; and, lastly "Plea for the Historian." Their common occasion is Wordsworth's first visit to the Capitoline Hill and the thoughts aroused by that visit. The man who dominates these thoughts, as the titles of the sonnets suggest, is Barthold Georg Niebuhr, whose monumental *History of Rome* first appeared in English a decade before Wordsworth and Henry Crabb Robinson undertook their Italian tour.

Niebuhr is now recognized as a pioneer in modern historical methods.

G. P. Gooch calls him "the first commanding figure in modern historiography, the scholar who raised history from a subordinate place to the dignity of an independent science."[21] Peter Gay, using Niebuhr's own metaphor (which is echoed by Wordsworth), writes that Niebuhr "wielded source criticism to penetrate the veil of legend behind which the history of the early Roman republic moved in barely recognizable form."[22] But Niebuhr was himself an acute commentator on what he had done and how he had done it. In his foreword he explains that his work does not account for the origins and development of Rome "by the dim light of late and dubious traditions," but undertakes its task through rational extrapolation from authentic documents:

> I shall endeavor to examine the history, especially during the first five centuries, not under the guidance of dim feelings, but of searching criticism. Nor shall I merely deliver the results, which could only give birth to blind opinions, but the researches themselves at full length. I shall strive to lay open the groundworks of the ancient Roman nation and state, which have been built over and masked, and about which the old writers preserved to us are often utterly mistaken.[23]

Niebuhr was aware of the irony of his applying such a method to the history of a city whose origins were, in the Burkean sense of the word, "immemorial." Noting that the story of Rome's foundation was scant and shadowy, Niebuhr wryly observed that "it well became the eternal city, that its roots should be lost in infinity" (p. 115). At the same time, however, he was determined to make historical sense of its *development*, for he felt that a better account could be made than the traditional "story told by the poets of the infancy and deification of Romulus": "while I allow the heart and the imagination their full claims; I at the same time assert the right of reason, to refuse to admit any thing as historical, which cannot possibly be so; and I purpose, without excluding that noble tradition from its place at the threshold of my history, to inquire whether there be any possibility of ascertaining to what people the first Romans belonged, and what were the changes attending the rise of that state, which, when the light of historical truth begins to dawn, is Rome" (116). The "light of historical truth" is the one that guides the critical eye of reason in its scrutiny of the past. Knowledge must build on *facts* and, writes Niebuhr, "history critically treated becomes much richer in facts; then the credulous repetition of traditional tales" (p. 113).

One of the legends which Niebuhr describes as still current in modern

Rome is the story of Tarpeia's betrayal of the city of Romulus to the attacking Sabines on Capitoline Hill:

> The rememberance of her guilt is still living in a popular legend. The whole Capitoline hill is pierced with quarries or passages cut in very remote times through the loose tufo. . . . Some girls from the neighboring houses were our guides, and told us as we went along, that in the heart of the hill the fair Tarpeia is sitting, covered with gold and jewels, and bound by a spell; none who tried to go to her could ever find out the way; once only had she been seen, by the brother of one of the girls. The inhabitants of this quarter are smiths and common victuallers, without the slightest touch of that seemingly living knowledge of antiquity, which other classes of the Romans have drawn from books. So that genuine oral tradition has kept the story of Tarpeia for five-and-twenty hundred years in the mouth of the common people, who for many centuries have been total strangers to the names of Cleolia and Cornelia. [p. 125]

The context of Niebuhr's recounting of the legend of Tarpeia makes clear his opinion of the story's historical veracity. This legend is an example of the "credulous repetition of traditional tales" that his own narrative aims to terminate by insisting on what Gay calls "the unique, privileged status of the contemporary document."[24]

Though Wordsworth does not explicitly say so, Niebuhr's account of the Tarpeia legend stands behind Sonnet III in the "Tour in Italy" sequence, just as Niebuhr's general observations about history and tradition stand behind the succeeding sonnets which are occasioned by the encounter with the Capitoline Hill. The four sonnets must be read as a group.

AT ROME

Is this, ye Gods, the Capitolian Hill?
Yon petty Steep in truth the fearful Rock,
Tarpeian named of yore, and keeping still
That name, a local Phantom proud to mock
The Traveller's expectation?—Could our Will
Destroy the ideal Power within, 'twere done
Thro' what men see and touch,—slaves wandering on,
Impelled by thirst of all but Heaven-taught skill.
Full oft, our wish obtained, deeply we sigh;
Yet not unrecompensed are they who learn,

From that depression raised, to mount on high
With stronger wing, more clearly to discern
Eternal things; and, if need be, defy
Change, with a brow not insolent, though stern.

AT ROME.—REGRETS.—IN ALLUSION TO NIEBUHR,
AND OTHER MODERN HISTORIANS

Those old credulities, to nature dear,
Shall they no longer bloom upon the stock
Of History, stript naked as a rock
'Mid a dry desert? What is it we hear?
The glory of Infant Rome must disappear,
Her morning splendors vanish, and their place
Know them no more. If Truth, who veiled her face
With those bright beams yet hid it most, must steer
Henceforth a humbler course perplexed and slow;
One solace yet remains for us who came
Into this world in days when story lacked
Severe research, that in our hearts we know
How, for exciting youth's heroic flame,
Assent is power, belief the soul of fact.

CONTINUED

Complacent Fictions were they, yet the same
Involved a history of no doubtful sense,
History that proves by inward evidence
From what a precious source of truth it came.
Ne'er could the boldest Eulogist have dared
Such deeds to paint, such characters to frame,
But for coeval sympathy prepared
To greet with instant faith their loftiest claim.
None but a noble people could have loved
Flattery in Ancient Rome's pure-minded style:
Not in like sort the Runic Scald was moved;
He, nursed 'mid savage passions that defile
Humanity, sang feats that well might call
For the blood-thirsty mead of Odin's riotous Hall.

PLEA FOR THE HISTORIAN

Forbear to deem the Chronicler unwise,
Ungentle, or untouched by seemly ruth,
Who, gathering up all that Time's envious tooth
Has spared of sound and grave realities,
Firmly rejects those dazzling flatteries,
Dear as they are to unsuspecting Youth,
That might have drawn down Clio from the skies
To vindicate the majesty of truth.
Such was her office while she walked with men,
A Muse, who, not unmindful of her Sire
All-ruling Jove, whate'er the theme might be
Revered her Mother, sage Mnemosyne,
And taught her faithful servants how the lyre
Should animate, but not mislead, the pen.

                                        [PW 3:213–15]

Wordsworth builds this sequence around one of the recurrent patterns of his major poetry: discovery after defeated expectation. Like many of those earlier poems, too, the sequence enacts the process of which it is also the culmination. The old metaphors are here as well. The poet fears that the stock of History will be "stript naked" and that Truth will no longer decently "veil" her face. Yet this sequence works toward ends very different from those of the major poetry. Indeed, it is best construed as a revision of what that earlier work had promoted.

The septuagenarian author of these lines can no longer ignore, though he would still like to do so, the competition between the claims of traditional power and historical accuracy. The simple kinship society that was upheld as an ideal in *The Ruined Cottage* and in "Michael" is itself now plainly understood as a thing of the past, and the "coeval sympathy" that once prepared a world to accept flattering fictions as historical fact is likewise seen as passed away. Wordsworth is clearly not of the opinion, however, that this ancient sympathy has been dead for long. Even when *he* came into the world, it was still alive; even *those* were "days when story lacked / Severe research." But the Age of History is now arrived, and Niebuhr's compelling rational attack on the traditionary relation of present to past demands its due. At his back, the aged poet feels the stare of Clio, an even more threatening muse than the author of the Prospectus had imagined, a muse always ready to vindicate the majesty of truth. In deference to Clio's truth, the poet must "steer / Henceforth a humbler course perplexed and slow," for his pen, no longer confident in speechlike spontaneity, must respect the demands of historical knowledge (Mnemosyne) and not be misled by the demands of power (Jove). He has learned that the written records left spared by Time's envious tooth represent "sound and grave realities."

The emergent historicism of the Rome sonnets suggests how thoroughly Wordsworth's intellectual development epitomizes the more general plot of modern intellectual history as schematized by Hans-Georg Gadamer. Building on the work of Friedrich Meinecke, Gadamer recounts the history of historical consciousness as a dialectical succession of four phases—tradition, enlightenment, traditionalism, and historicism—the same four phases through which we have followed Wordsworth in his long career. Part of Gadamer's aim is to show how inevitable is the development of historicism out of enlightenment, despite the intervening phase of traditionalism, which he calls the "romantic critique of enlightenment" and which he associates with Burke.[25] Gadamer defines traditionalism straightforwardly as "the critical attitude that again addresses itself to the truth of tradition and seeks to renew it" (p. 250): "In contrast to the enlightenment's belief in perfection, which thinks in terms of the freedom from 'superstition' and the prejudices of the past, we now find that olden times, the world of myth, unreflective life, not yet analysed away by consciousness . . . acquire . . . a priority of truth" (p. 242). Romantic traditionalism remains only a wrinkle in Gadamer's story, however, because its critique adopts the opposition's mental schema—the Enlightenment view of history as the "conquest of mythos by logos" (p. 242). Hence, traditionalism's own accomplishments were doomed to precipitate its undoing.

> The great achievements of romanticism—the revival of the past, the discovery of the voices of the peoples in their songs, . . . the cultivation of ancient customs, . . . —have all motivated the historical research that has slowly, step by step, transformed the intuitive revival into historical knowledge proper. [p. 244]

Gadamer must thus draw his (for him) sad conclusion: "the romantic critique of enlightenment ends itself in enlightenment, in that it evolves as historical science and draws everything into the orbit of historicism" (p. 244).

What finally surfaces as historicism in the late sonnets on Niebuhr was, as Gadamer's account would lead us to expect, an undercurrent in

Wordsworth's poetry from the beginning of his major work. It was there in the uneasiness of the letter rejecting Scott's historical documents; it was there in the ambivalence toward the primitives in "The World Is Too Much With Us." But Wordsworth's early misgivings manifest themselves in other ways as well, such as in the curious personae that he evidently thought it necessary to assume. In "Michael," for instance, poetic logic requires that we understand the speaker to be "Wordsworth" himself, yet, as Parrish has shown, the poem was initially conceived as a "Pastoral ballad" with a semicomic, country-bumpkin speaker.[26] The poem's genesis reveals a deep ambivalence in the mind of its maker.

The poet figure in *The Ruined Cottage*, the Pedlar, is similarly problematic, as Coleridge was quick to point out when this character emerged as the Wanderer of *The Excursion*. "Is there one word," asks Coleridge in the *Biographia Literaria*, "attributed to the pedlar in the "EXCURSION," characteristic of a *pedlar?*" (*BL* 2:107–8). What motivates Coleridge's question is his conviction that the Pedlar damages this poem in particular and typifies a defect of Wordsworth's poetry in general, his practice in "THE CHOICE OF HIS CHARACTERS" (2:103). With specific regard to the elaborate biography that Wordsworth constructs to make the Pedlar's remarks appear "probable," Coleridge quotes Sir William Davenant's criticism of certain modern writers who would "take away the liberty of a poet, and fetter his feet in the shackles of an historian" (2:101). Why does Wordsworth encumber himself with these contrivances? Coleridge sees them as desperate efforts to force the issue with the reader, "attempts of the author to *make* him {the reader} believe" (2:107; Coleridge's italics). Coleridge does not go so far as to try to account for the sense of urgency itself. My suggestion here has been that it derives from Wordsworth's inescapable awareness of the difficulty of his intellectual position. A paradox inheres in the very idea of a traditionalist program, as I think Wordsworth recognized: the sense of having to "go back" to recover the past is itself proof that the desired past is not fully recoverable.[27]

This digression on the later fate of Wordsworth's traditionalism must not distract us from the central subject here, the major and programmatic poetry of the golden decade. Returning to that subject in chapter 8 I will be broadening the literary scope of the argument I have so far made about it. One further point, however, is in order here. In one of the several passages from *The Prelude* in which Wordsworth speaks from a point of view that is difficult to assign exclusively to either his younger mind or his maturer mind, we read:

> Enough, no doubt, the advocates themselves
> Of ancient institutions had performed
> To bring disgrace upon their very names;
> Disgrace of which custom and written law,
> And sundry moral sentiments, as props
> And emanations of those institutes,
> Too justly bore a part. A veil had been
> Uplifted. Why deceive ourselves?—'twas so,
> 'Twas even so—and sorrow for the man
> Who either had not eyes wherewith to see,
> Or seeing hath forgotten. Let this pass,
> Suffice it that a shock had then been given
> To old opinions, and that the minds of all men
> Had felt it—that my mind was both let loose,
> Let loose and goaded.
>
> [10:849–63][28]

Though Wordsworth campaigns incessantly to restore the veil of habit, he can never entirely escape the traumatic recollection of its brief uplifting. The shock of this sight is never completely forgotten, the mind let loose never entirely re-bound. These lines bear witness to that memory and its mysterious persistence. Who speaks the words "why deceive ourselves? 'Twas so, / 'Twas even so . . . "? It is hard to say for certain, but the voice seems to come as a reminder *from* the young republican to the author of *The Prelude*. The voice of 1793 says, "Sorrow for the man who hath forgotten he hath seen." "Let this pass," answers the aging poet, carrying on with his tale.

Eight

The Discipline of an English Poet's Mind

> Such minds are truly from the Deity
> For they are powers; and hence the highest bliss
> That can be known is theirs—the consciousness
> Of whom they are, habitually infused
> Through every image, and through every thought,
> And all impressions.
>
> *The Prelude*, book 13

*I*n the now-celebrated Prospectus for his epic program—lines published in 1814 but initially drafted perhaps as early as the seminal period of February to March 1798—Wordsworth announced that his task calls for us to "look / Into our Minds, into the Mind of Man— / My haunt, and the main region of my song" (39–41). For many readers, perhaps for most, the primary interest of Wordsworth's poetry owes to his skill in surveying this haunt and reporting precisely and candidly what he finds there. Prizing as they do the "psychological Wordsworth," such readers not only give pride of place in his canon to *The Prelude* but also, within *The Prelude*, concentrate attention on the powerful lyric passages where Wordsworthian self-scrutiny most intensifies. Jonathan Bishop speaks for these readers in the opening words of the well-known essay that first established the "spot of time" as a distinctive subgenre in the poetry: "*The Prelude* is at the center of our experience of Wordsworth; at the center of our experience of *The Prelude* are those 'spots of time' where Wordsworth is endeavoring to express key moments in the history of his imagination."[1] Bishop's strong claim about the centrality of the spots in "our experience" of Wordsworth has been

184

dramatically borne out in the last decade by the popularity of the 1799 text of *The Prelude*, which its editors recommend to the public precisely on the grounds that it offers a relatively uninterrupted sequence of these special passages.

In light of such evidence, it would seem that a discussion of the political dimension of Wordsworth's major poetry runs the risk of remaining peripheral if it cannot take some account of the spots of time and the meditative Wordsworthian mode they epitomize. To be more specific: in commenting on the politics of *The Prelude*, the important case in point, one must do more than determine the ideology of the France books, even if one extends these findings to the poem's educational polemic. One must also be able to say what is ideologically significant about those arresting childhood memories recounted in book 1.

Much recent commentary on the spots of time would lead us to believe that these passages do not have an important ideological dimension, that they are properly understood in more privately psychological terms. Setting the tone for this kind of commentary, Bishop modeled his inquiry on psychoanalytic research into "earliest memories" which are said to "reveal, probably more clearly than any other single psychological datum, the central core of [the subject's] psychodynamics, his chief motivations, form of neurosis, and emotional problem." Bishop's approach is thus to "isolate the genuine element in Wordsworth by collating these passages" (p. 45) and thereby to show that the *The Prelude* constitutes a record, "half-concealed in a commonplace autobiographical structure, of a process which, in these days, we would call a self-analysis; the precipitate of an interior battle, a sequence of manuevers against the incomprehensible, fought out in the public domain of verse" (p. 60). For Bishop, the spots of time provide a direct index, as the chemical metaphor of the precipitate makes clear, of the poet's authentic and private self. It is from this point of view that commentators are prompted to speak of Wordsworth's "private vision," his "private myth," his "personal myth of memory," or his "consciousness of consciousness."[2] Reading *The Prelude* this way, one is likely to praise the poem for its modernism, perhaps even to claim that it is the first modern poem, as its enthusiasts are sometimes heard to do.

There is no denying that those early spots of time are susceptible of a psychologizing interpretation. Summer, fall, winter, and spring, Wordsworth's recollections of early experience show the operation of strong personal emotion (whether of guilt, as in the raid on the raven's nest, or joy, as in the sunset skating episode) in what seem to be the most nonsocial circumstances, occasions on which he seems to be simply alone with nature.

Nonetheless, the truth of an account like Bishop's is a dangerously partial one, and its limitations are largely attributable to his isolation of the spots from their context in the poem.[3] Quite apart from what they may or may not reveal about the authentic interior self of their author, the passages that record the spots of time in fact serve a number of specific purposes in *The Prelude*. To understand them properly, we must therefore attend to their role in what Bishop curiously dismisses as the poem's "commonplace autobiographical structure." We must look both at the immediate context of the spots of time in book 1 and then at how book 1 is in turn contextualized by the larger patterns of the thirteen-book poem. We will then be in a position to see how the larger structural exigencies affect the interpretation of the spots of time themselves.

In undertaking such an analysis, one does well to keep in mind Earl Wasserman's well-known account, in the central chapter of *The Subtler Language*, of the great break that "separates the last century and a half from all that had gone before." For Wasserman explains this change primarily in terms of what he calls "the eighteenth-century tendency to translate all ontologies into psychologies" (p. 172). What had formerly made sense of the world, he says, was the presence in the public domain of a "set of organizing patterns of the order of myth":

> These systems transformed man and his world into a lexicon of symbols and integrated the symbols by meaningful cross-references. But by the end of the eighteenth-century these communally accepted patterns had almost completed dis-appeared—each man now rode his own hobby-horse. [p. 170]

The correspondences formerly "accepted as true in the divine scheme of things" are now "neither true nor felt as truth; they are the result of associative procedures of mind"—movements of a hobby-horse (p. 182).

The ironic twist in Wasserman's story is that the hobby-horse even-tually emerges as the means of the Romantic poet's deliverance. For even after the "cosmological groundwork" for analogy had dissolved, the hobby-horse offered evidence of the mind's fundamental impulse to analogize. Possessed of such an impulse and faced with a world of potential chaos, the poet's one chance for ordering his own life and the lives of his readers was to develop a legitimate bent of mind. The poet had to learn, as Wasserman neatly sums it up, "to put his private hobby-horse through its paces" (p. 182). Though Wasserman is not speaking specifically of Wordsworth, his way of linking Romantic psychologizing with the problem of mental discipline—what Wordsworth late in *The Prelude* calls "the discipline . . .

of the poet's mind" (13:270–71)—is a valuable insight. My contention here will be that the spots of time serve *The Prelude* by proving the power of his discipline. It is Wasserman's emphasis on the "privacy" of this discipline which needs revision, I will be arguing, in that the discipline represented by the spots is ultimately a psychological manifestation of a national character and a native tradition.

I

To understand the place in *The Prelude* of the initial spots of time, those which appear in the second half of book 1, is to recognize that their emergence coincides with what Wordsworth represents as the true starting point for his poem. This is one reason why Bishop's suggestion that the autobiographical structure of the poem is "commonplace," a suggestion directly tied to his eagerness to disregard that structure, is so curious. For surely one of the great marvels of *The Prelude* is the intricacy with which it interweaves the autobiographical account of Wordsworth's life with the autobiographical account of his telling of that life. And (just as surely) one of the great marvels of book 1 is the way the poem tries to contain the immediate circumstances of its own inception, to contextualize itself. From its very outset, that is, the poem admonishes its reader *not* to focus on the spots of time to the exclusion of the temporal field behind them.

The Prelude represents its immediate context as a problem to which the poem itself, whose true beginning is marked by the advent of the spots of time, provides a kind of solution. The problem is specifically depicted as a crisis of mental discipline, and therefore both the poem in general and the spots in particular must be understood specifically as a triumph of discipline. This immediate context as well as its implication are most explicitly conveyed in the first full-length version of book 1 in the thirteen-book *Prelude* of 1805. Context and implication are both discernible, however, in the manuscript evidence that shows the unusual manner in which Wordsworth first opened the poem. From the two-book manuscript of 1798–99 until perhaps as late as early 1804, the poem's first lines were these:

> Was it for this
> That one, the fairest of all rivers, loved
> To blend his murmurs with my Nurse's song,
> And from his alder shades, and rocky falls,
> And from his fords and shallows, sent a voice
> That flowed along my dreams? For this didst thou
> O Derwent, travelling over the green plains

Near my 'sweet birth-place,' didst thou beauteous Stream
Make ceaseless music through the night and day,
Which with its steady cadence tempering
Our human waywardness, composed my thoughts
To more than infant softness, giving me,
Among the fretful dwellings of mankind,
A knowledge, a dim earnest of the calm
Which Nature breathes among the fields and groves?

[1799 *Prel.* 1–15]

Not only does this draft of the poem begin at the half-line, but its opening sentence contains a pronoun, "this" (repeated in both this verse paragraph and the one to follow), for which no antecedent is provided. Such an opening calls attention to itself in the same way as does the opening of Pound's *Cantos*: "And then went down to the ship . . ."[5] In both cases we are made to ask what comes before the beginning. In the Wordsworthian case, specifically, we are made to ask "what is *this?*"

The question looms over the early text of *The Prelude* as a conspicuous mystery; the inferences we might draw serve rather to heighten its importance than to solve it. We may surmise that "this" refers to the poet's present condition, the (presumably) untoward state of affairs out of which these very lines have issued. Since the poet speaks of an untempered "human waywardness" that lacks the steady cadence of a remembered strain of music, we may even guess that "this" refers to a problem of mental discipline. What makes it hard to say more, or even to be sure about this much, is that the condition to which "this" refers is allowed to dissolve into the developing cadence of the passage itself. The matter is left behind without further clarification. One may be tempted to speculate that, in a more general way, "this" is precisely the situation over which poetry triumphs to come into being. Precisely what that situation is, however, would then necessarily remain unexpressed.[6]

And yet book 1 of the completed *Prelude* shows that Wordsworth eventually did try to express the inexpressible. To the early draft that begins "Was it for this . . ." he prefixed a 270–line "Introduction" (to use the label from the heading for book 1). The final lines of the Introduction, those immediately preceding the question "Was it for this . . . ?," describe in detail the circumstances out of which the poem is supposed to have emerged:

                    Thus from day to day
I live a mockery of the brotherhood
Of vice and virtue, with no skill to part
Vague longing that is bred by want of power,
From paramount impulse not to be withstood;
A timorous capacity, from prudence;
From circumspection, infinite delay.
Humility and modest awe themselves
Betray me, serving often for a cloak
To a more subtle selfishness, that now
Doth lock my functions up in blank reserve,
Now dupes me by an over-anxious eye
That with a false activity beats off
Simplicity and self-presented truth.
Ah, better far than this to stray about
Voluptuously through fields and rural walks
And ask no record of the hours given up
To vacant musing, unreproved neglect
Of all things, and deliberate holiday.
Far better never to have heard the name
Of zeal and just ambition than to live
Thus baffled by a mind that every hour
Turns recreant to her task, takes heart again,
Then feels immediately some hollow thought
Hang like an interdict upon her hopes.
This is my lot. . . .

                                        [1:238–63]

The "this" of the poem's original opening is no longer problematic, for now
it is preceded by other instances of the same pronoun (explicitly at 252 and
263; implicitly at 238 and 258 with "thus," i.e., "in *this* manner") and in
these instances the deictic reference is supplied by the poet's dramatization
of his condition. "This," as is now clear, is the lot of a poet who, trying to
get his poem under way, has suffered what Hartman calls "an experience of
aphasia," a paralysis of the faculties of composition.[7] In effect, then,
Wordsworth has solved the problem of his initial opening only at the
expense of creating another: book 1 as we know it employs the paradoxical
fiction that a poem can go on at length about its failure to get going at all.

This paradox, no doubt recognized by most careful readers of *The Prelude*, is part of what makes book 1 so rich a subject for meditation and analysis. It is indeed a bold and complex gambit: the poem not only dramatizes the development of a crisis that threatens to end the poem before it begins, but goes on to suggest that this same crisis eventually enables the poem to find its authentic or natural course. But again, what has not been widely recognized, certainly not widely discussed, is that this crisis is represented as a crisis in the discipline of the poet's mind. This point, which as we saw is only suggested in the ur-beginning of 1799, is left unmistakable in lines 239–71. The poet has lost his ability to judge vice from virtue, impotent longing from potent impulse, justified confidence from subtle selfishness. He feels caught between equally unpromising alternatives: vacant musing and bootless effort, listlessness and vain perplexity. His vacillation between these states in *both* directions, however, shows a mind turning "recreant to her task." One could hardly ask for a better illustration of what Wasserman has called the Romantic poet's struggle to put his psychological steed through its paces.

It is true that the passage also seems to dramatize the poet's sense of his mind's isolation and autonomy and that there is little in these lines to suggest that the problem is anything but the poet's own private affair. The very attitude responsible for this impression, however, is ultimately to be understood as part of the problem. As in those passages from the France books discussed earlier, in other words, Wordsworth employs shifting and doubling perspectives to reveal what he has come to understand about views he himself once held. To reconstruct the underlying argument we must look carefully at how the Introduction represents the poet's arrival at the difficult straits described in lines 238–71. And since the Introduction begins with the joyful mood of the "glad preamble" (1–54), we must inevitably confront the question of where the poet goes wrong.

Working backward from lines 238–71, one can safely say that the immediate occasion of Wordsworth's crisis of discipline is his effort to decide on a subject for his poem; the passage that precedes the description of the crisis is a catalog of some nine or ten possible topics. These are of various kinds—romantic, chivalric, historical, personal, and philosophical—and all of them, as we are told beforehand, have been found unacceptable:

> Time, place, and manners, these I seek, and these
> I find in plenteous store, but nowhere such
> As may be singled out with steady choice—
> No little band of yet remembered names

Whom I, in perfect confidence, might hope
To summon back from lonesome banishment
And make them inmates in the hearts of men
Now living, or to live in times to come.

[169–76]

These lines supply some hint as to why the poet finds himself unable to choose any of the items he goes on to mention. He fears that the kind of stories ambitious poets once told, stories that lent coherence to their poems, are no longer credited in "the hearts of men." Earlier in the Introduction, Wordsworth reports that on one occasion his soul "made trial of the strength" required for poetic composition but found that despite "Eolian visitations," the "harp / Was soon defrauded, and the banded host / Of harmony dispersed in straggling sounds" (104–6). It is thus that he has turned to the search for fabled names that survive already "banded," already part of a story, and thus that he becomes apprehensive about whether these names can be recalled from literary exile and made to live again for his readers.

To stop here, however, would be to accept an incomplete explanation of why the poet initially comes up empty-handed in his quest. His apprehensiveness about the credibility of his candidate narratives, or about the likelihood of his success in dealing with them, must be understood in relation to the perspective the poet adopts in the "glad preamble" itself. After his cheerful announcement that he comes "from a house / Of bondage," having been "set free" from "yon city's walls . . . / . . . where he hath been long immured," the poet expands on his newly awakened sense of liberation:

Now I am free, enfranchised and at large,
May fix my habitation where I will.
What dwelling shall receive me, in what vale
Shall be my harbour, underneath what grove
Shall I take up my home, and what sweet stream
Shall with its murmurs lull me to my rest?
The earth is all before me—with a heart
Joyous, nor scared at its own liberty,
I look about, and should the guide I chuse
Be nothing better than a wandering cloud
I cannot miss my way.

[9–19]

These thoughts seem all to the good: spontaneous, authentic, hopeful, natural. And they do emphasize the privacy, isolation, and autonomy of the poet's outlook. Yet they spring from the very attitude that, by the middle of book 1, leads the poet into his terrible self-doubt.

Elizabeth Sewall has written about this opening that the poet confronts "a prospect of wide landscape and open sky" on a walk that is "the great over-all poetic figure or trope of a journey which he is about to undertake."[8] Other commentators have helped to expose the rich network of correspondences between literal and figurative traveling in the poem.[9] Implicit in many of these commentaries and virtually explicit in Sewall's is the sound observation that, in the poem's metaphorical scheme of things, the prospect the poet confronts in the preamble is the prospect of the unwritten poem. Understood within such a scheme, the poet's free decision about where to take up residence must be understood as a metaphorical adumbration of his decision about what subject he will freely choose ("single out" with "steady choice") for his poem.

This particular connection is reinforced by certain key repetitions. In the preamble the poet says that with his new freedom he can "fix [his] habitation where he will[s]." Later, speaking of his ambition to gather his thoughts together into a great poem he says that he had hopes

> that with a frame of outward life
> I might endue, might fix in a visible home,
> Some portion of those phantoms of conceit,
> That had been floating loose about so long. . . .

> [128–31]

Or again, in the 1850 version of the preamble, the passage corresponding to lines 8 ff. (quoted above from the 1805 version) begins: "now free / Free as a bird to settle where I will" (8–9). Later, beginning his catalog of subjects, the poet echoes himself: "Sometimes," he writes, "I settle on some British theme, some old / Romantic tale by Milton left unsung" (179–180). Working throughout the Introduction, in other words, is a submerged pun on "place," a pun that perhaps comes closest to the surface in the very next lines from the catalog:

> More often resting at some gentle place
> Within the groves of chivalry I pipe
> Among the shepherds, with reposing knights
> Sit by a fountain-side and hear their tales.

> [181–83]

Confronting the prospect of his unwritten poem, the poet must settle on the proper "topic" on which to compose.

Let us draw out the implication of this metaphorical scheme of things a little further. If the landscape the poet initially faces is to be understood as a literary prospect, the uncomposed poem, then the freedom he asserts must be similarly understood as literary freedom. He claims the opportunity to exercise what is later called "the ambitious Power of choice" (*Prel.* 1850, 1:166) unencumbered by what has been done before. Behind him lies literary history, cultural tradition, the great stretch of places upon which men and women have already composed. The poet attempts to exercise his freedom by turning his back on all that and facing the unwritten page with single-mindedness of purpose; he will generate the poem out of his own choices. In Burke's economic metaphor, he wants to live and trade on his private stock instead of availing himself of the general bank and capital of ages.

The flaw in this conception of the poet's freedom does not begin to show conspicuously until the poet finds that he must turn to topics from the cultural past even as he continues to regard them in this exclusively prospective manner. In his desire to see these topics in the vista of a future to be determined solely by his own decisions, the poet would deny their role in a history that has formed his own very character. One can, however, find hints about the incoherence of this position as early as the preamble. Many commentators have remarked on the way the preamble echoes the concluding lines of *Paradise Lost*:

> The World was all before them, where to choose
> Thir place of rest, and Providence thir guide:
> They hand in hand with wand'ring steps and slow,
> Through *Eden* took thir solitarie way.[10]

> [12:646–49]

The Wordsworthian poet uses these lines to represent the condition of his being released from bondage. His changes of person, number, and tense from those of Milton's lines suggests that in this new poem the poet is by himself assuming the point of view of Adam at the moment of his entrance into the world. The poet wants to be seen confronting a prospect as fresh as the one Adam faced at the east gate of Paradise. But insofar as this is a literary prospect and insofar as the point is to dramatize a sense of literary freedom, the very fact of the allusion, like the similar allusion to Exodus in lines 6–7, betrays the limits of his poetic independence. The poet who requires the Miltonic and biblical contexts to make his point is to that extent not free to settle where he will(s). The time, place, and manners of his poem cannot be singled out with steady choice. They will always be to some extent a function of who he is—and that means of who he has been. He cannot, for example, *choose* to "settle on some British theme" or to carry on with Milton's work; his theme will inevitably be in some sense British, just as his verse, in some measure, will be Miltonic. The poet's mistake is to think that he can write a poem as Thoreau says we must live our lives— deliberately—that he can determine its course by weighing alternatives at every step. To so proceed, the poet must set himself up as arbiter of both the worth of the topic and the extent of his ability to treat it. His private stock of reason spends itself all too quickly under so taxing a responsibility.

II

Since some of these remarks about the implicit social and historical dimension of the Introduction may seem oversubtle, I want to support them with an argument that depends on a premise about *The Prelude*'s general structure. The premise is that the crisis we see enacted in book 1 with respect to the psychology of poetic composition is congruent or homologous with the crisis we see narrated in book 11 with respect to the psychology of political morality. The argument that follows from this premise is that the Introduction in book 1 can be glossed with terms from books 9–11 and that the sentiments of the glad preamble correspond to those that characterize the poet's mind as he comes under the influence of French rationalism.

Just before reaching the crisis of his strong disease in book 10, we recall, Wordsworth describes in detail the false delight he had indulged when he thought of himself as psychologically autonomous. Like the poet of the preamble, the young radical just returned from France labors under a mistaken conception of "the freedom of the individual mind." In his assumption that the free mind need adopt only "one guide," the "light of circumstances flashed / Upon the independent intellect" (10:828–29), the radical is on common ground with the poet whose freedom of choice is such that any wandering cloud can serve to guide him. Though the errors that lead to the crisis of book 10 are made more explicit than those that lead to the crisis of book 1, the parallels between the two developments run deep. In book 10, the error that stands as corollary to the thought that intellect needs only the guide of circumstances is the assumption that one can "look through all the frailties of the world" and succeed in "shaking off / The accidents of nature, time, and place / That make up the weak being of the past" (820–23). Set in the perspective of these more obviously self-critical lines, the apparent declaration of health in the preamble begins to look suspicious:

> I breathe again—
> Trances of thought and mountings of the mind
> Come fast upon me. It is shaken off,
> As by miraculous gift 'tis shaken off,
> That burthen of my own unnatural self,
> The heavy weight of many a weary day
> Not mine, and such as were not made for me.
> Long months of peace—if such bold word accord
> With any promises of human life—
> Long months of ease and undisturbed delight
> Are mine in prospect. Whither shall I turn,
> By road or pathway, or through open field,
> Or shall a twig or any floating thing
> Upon the river point me out my course?
>
> [19–33]

Perhaps the very repetition of "shaken off" in lines 21–22 should be taken as a clue that the being of the past cannot be left behind just because one wishes to turn to one's prospects. The echo of the same phrase in book 10 leaves the matter relatively unambiguous. The radical poet clearly believes that the way to discover the natural course of action is to divest oneself of the influence of second nature, to shed the habits and customs acquired in our social experience of particular times and places. And the poem just as clearly judges the poet wrong in this belief.

Such evidence would count for less if these apparently parallel errors did not lead to crises that are themselves deeply similar. The psychological breakdowns described in books 1 and 10 are both characterized as states of turmoil induced by self-inquiry. In each case the poet loses nerve, confidence, and stability because he has appointed himself devil's advocate against his own most strongly held convictions. In each case he turns his intellect against his feeling instead of preserving their native alignment. Book 1 even employs the kind of legalist metaphors that we saw at work in book 10. Whenever the aspiring poet "takes heart" in some idea for his poem, some "hollow thought" of its shadowiness and insubstantiality arrives to "stand like an interdict upon her hopes." In both cases the mind challenges itself with the impossible task of establishing the ground of its own most fundamental sentiments.

That this compulsion for metaphysical grounding is what threatens the poet's enterprise in book 1 is nowhere clearer than in his description of the penultimate item of his catalog of topics, the idea for an autobiographical poem:

> Sometimes it suits me better to shape out
> Some tale from my own heart, more near akin
> To my own passions and habitual thoughts,
> Some variegated story, in the main
> Lofty, with interchange of gentler things.
>
> [220–24]

The oddity here, as at least one critic has noted, is that this project sounds rather like the one that Wordsworth goes on to undertake.[11] The explanation of why it is rejected therefore calls attention to itself in a special way:

> But deadening admonitions will succeed,
> And the whole beauteous fabric seems to lack
> Foundation, and withal appears throughout
> Shadowy and unsubstantial.
>
> [225–28]

The topic seems unacceptable to the poet at this point because he thinks he needs a "foundation"—or in the words of book 10, a "ground" or "rule" or "sanction" or "proof"—for his choice. And he thinks so precisely because he has arrogated all evaluative responsibility to himself.

Once we begin to follow the pattern of correspondences that link the France books to the Introduction, we discover that the one crisis illuminates the other in more and more particular ways. Especially relevant to the opening lines of the poem, for example, is the detailed account in the later books of how Wordsworth's Gallic rationalism affected his sense of the cultural past. Reviewing the crisis experience in book 11, he writes that in the ardor of his revolutionary perfectibilianism, he had formed so strong a "hope to see . . . / The Man to come parted as by a gulph / From him who had been" that he could "no more / Trust the elevation which had made [him] one / With the great family that here and there / Is scattered through the abyss of ages past" (57–63). The radical who sees things as they are and desires to see things as they might be creates a gulf between present and future human beings. The more closely he identifies himself with the being of the future, however, the more he locates the gap behind him, between himself and the past. He thinks himself no longer one with the great human family of the past by virtue of a separation which is the mirror image of the one he initially imagines between himself and the human future.

The very noblest representatives of the human past—"Sage, patriot, lover, hero"—seemed to be tainted by "something false and weak, which could not stand / The open eye of reason" (64–67). Even "the poets," he says, who speak "More perfectly of purer creatures," failed to satisfy his rigorously rational and exclusively private criteria:

> If reason be nobility in man,
> Can aught be more ignoble than the man
> Whom they describe, would fasten if they may
> Upon our love by sympathies of truth?
>
> [69–74]

Applied with sufficient rigor, the utopian standards of Gallic rationalism make even the idealized heroes of the poets unacceptable as cultural models. Under the new dispensation, indeed, the cultural inheritance ceases to have any relevance whatsoever to the prospects of society:

> . . . hence an emptiness
> Fell on the historian's page, and even on that
> Of poets, pregnant with more absolute truth.
> The works of both withered in my esteem.
> The sentence was, I thought, pronounced—their rights
> Seemed mortal, and their empire passed away.
>
> [90–95]

The cultural inheritance is here seen as an empire from whose sway the young radical believes himself liberated in much the same way that the young poet of the preamble thinks himself free of what he presumes to put behind him. The major difference between this part of book 11 and the preamble is that in book 11 the identification of the past as cultural is made more explicit and the judgment of the attitude as delusory is made more obvious.

Also more explicit in book 11 is the link between the traditionalist perspective and the so-called premise of feeling. [12] The cultural past survives in moral sentiments, or what in book 11 Wordsworth calls:

> Those mysteries of passion which have made,
> And shall continue evermore to make—
> In spite of all that reason hath performed,
> And shall perform, to exalt and to refine—
> One brotherhood of all the human race,
> Through all the habitations of past years,
> And those to come.
>
> [84-90]

The role of inner feeling, so understood, has important implications for the "psychological" view of Wordsworth. For it suggests that what this Romantic poet finds when he looks into the disciplined mind of man is not a substitute for tradition, as an account like Wasserman's would lead us to expect, but rather tradition itself, in its psychological recapitulation.

Indeed, if what Friedrich Meinecke writes about Burke is true, then we may even be forced to conclude that traditionalism actually depends upon a strongly psychologized view of the world. On this account, the psychological mode is an aid to showing that tradition has survived despite suspicions to the contrary. The "chief evidence" that Burke's thought represents high traditionalism, according to Meinecke, lies precisely "in its concern with the inner psychological life of man, and not merely with the faithful preservations of the institutions, customs, rights and so on that had been handed down the centuries":[13]

> This psychological life circulates through a people like a blood-stream, builds up something interconnected and organic in the body of the State and society as a whole. And this psychological life no longer seemed to Burke, as it had to all others up till then, including Hume, a juxtaposition of rational and irrational mechanisms, but a unity in which feeling and thought, the conscious and the unconscious, the inherited factor and the individual will, blend with one another. He saw the danger that "the hair-splitting subtleties of reason" would fail to recognize the wisdom hidden in the natural voice of sentiment. "Wisdom without reflection and above it" was the quintessence of his teaching on the creative forces in history and in the life of the State. [p. 228]

Something very close to this, I am arguing, is the conception of psychological life that we find in Wordsworth: the second nature of which he tries to "unsoul" himself when, in the grip of French rationalism, he sought to expose its mysteries of passion as so many groundless prejudices of the weak being of the past. That Wordsworth could not destroy his second nature, not even in the name of nature itself, is "proved" in *The Prelude* by the eventual emergence of the spots of time.

III

We are now in a position to see that the structure of *The Prelude* requires that these passages stand for "psychological life" in a much broader sense than is to be inferred from taking them as isolated lyric moments. The spots of time must be understood as representing the triumph not only of mental discipline, but also of discipline-as-tradition, a discipline grounded on what Burke calls prejudice. In Burke's description, as we have seen, this conception of discipline is specifically English. The French aspired, he said, to "a discipline which has for its basis the destruction of all prejudices" (*BW* 4:205). And the superiority of English discipline, which preserves prejudice and even measures the value of a particular prejudice by the duration of its survival, lies precisely in the advantage it offered in making critical choices: "Prejudice is of ready application in the emergency; it previously engages the mind in a steady course of wisdom and virtue, and does not leave the man hesitating in the moment of decision, skeptical, puzzled, unresolved" (3:347). A similar claim for the discipline of the poet's mind in *The Prelude* is implicit in the crises recounted in book 11 and dramatized in book 1.

But should we regard the discipline of this poet's mind as a specifically *English* phenomenon? We have already considered some of the evidence for doing so. There is the general mapping of Wordsworth's moral crisis with respect to his experience on either side of the English Channel, and there are the implied judgments about the differences between and relative merits of the two national characters. When Wordsworth says that the name of Englishman appeared (to the French) to license some unruliness of mind, for example, he is pointing out a discrepancy between the mutual perceptions of French and English minds—and of course suggesting that the error lies on the side of the French. But still more powerful evidence linking the spots of time to English nationalism can be found in Wordsworth's claim that being turned against his country was the very heart of his moral crisis. His unwitting expatriation was, he says in retrospect, the only "lapse" or "turn of sentiment" that "might be named / A revolution" (10:235-37). Wordsworth's extended metaphor spells out his point.

> I, who with the breeze
> Had played, a green leaf on the blessed tree
> Of my beloved country—nor had wished
> For happier fortune than to wither there—
> Now from my pleasant station was cut off,
> And tossed about in whirlwinds.
>
> [253-58]

One could hardly ask for a plainer conceit for the Burkean "psychological life" that, as Meinecke says, circulates organically through a people. Wordsworth seemed to himself to have been for a time severed from the national organism. The healing spots of time mark his reunion. It is a reunion not only with the English countryside but also with the English mind and character, with a way of thinking and feeling.

What makes this issue of *The Prelude*'s Englishness especially important is that it suggests specific lines of connection with a controversy of some moment in the late 1790s. We unfortunately know very little of Wordsworth's reading in the crucial months leading up to the Alfoxden period when he began to articulate his great poetic ambitions. What evidence we do have, however, proves to be most valuable. On 20 March 1797, Wordsworth received from James Losh a parcel of reading material, whose contents Mary Moorman describes as follows: "the *Monthly Magazine* from March to December 1796: Coleridge's *Conciones ad Populum* in which he protested against the Government's 'gagging Bills'; Burke's *Letters on a Regicide Peace* and *Letter to the Duke of Portland*; Coleridge's *Ode on the Departing Year*, a political poem which had been published in pamphlet form; some sermons against atheism by Estlin, the well-known Bristol Unitarian who was a friend of Coleridge; and Thomas Erskine's *View of the Causes and Consequences of the Present War*" (Moorman *EY*:309). "These details are of interest," Moorman writes, "because such a parcel must have been sent at Wordsworth's own request."

What do these details tell us? The choice of Coleridge's work requires no explanation: the two poets had long been corresponding and reading one another's work by this time; as early as May 1796, Coleridge had referred to Wordsworth as a "very dear friend" (Reed *EY*:181). As for Estlin's sermons, they may very well have been the recommendation of the mutual friend Coleridge; Wordsworth would find himself delivering a letter from Coleridge to Estlin in the following year (Reed *EY*:237). Apart from the magazines, which I shall be discussing in the next chapter, the selections of genuinely *political* importance are those publications of Burke and Thomas Erskine, especially since both Burke's *Regicide Peace* letters and Erskine's *View* concern England's war with France, the event which, according to the account in *The Prelude*, marked the great turning point in Wordsworth's moral and intellectual life. Not until "the strength of Britain was put forth / In league with the confederated Host" (10:229–30) against France did Wordsworth begin to experience the internal warfare which nearly led to his total undoing. It makes sense, therefore, that the first question Wordsworth would want to clear up for himself in rethinking his position on public affairs should be that of the "causes and consequences" of the Anglo-French War. And if this was the case, then certainly Burke and

Erskine would have made an ideally matched pair of adversaries for considering the pros and cons of the issue.

Erskine's recent biographer probably goes too far in calling him "the most enlightened liberal of his times." [14] Erskine was, nonetheless, the advocate who, in the notorious treason trials of 1794, successfully defended John Horne Tooke, Thomas Hardy, and, of course, Tom Paine, who was being tried for the book he wrote in answer to Burke's *Reflections*. And in defending these men, Erskine had gained a wide reputation as a defender of freedom of the press and of the cause of government reform. On Erskine's account, Burke had played into Pitt's hands by fomenting xenophobic alarm in England about the influx of "French principles." [15] For Erskine, the war was a mistake from the start—chiefly England's mistake—and needed to be ended as quickly as possible by negotiated settlement with France. The aim of his *View* was to show the English their mistake and to persuade them to urge an immediate acceptance of peace terms. Burke, on the other hand, saw Erskine as a part of that growing number of deluded Englishmen who had lost sight of what it means to be English and who, spellbound by French metaphysicians, had been unknowingly turned against their own country's best interests. For Burke, the threat posed by France—both in books and in arms—was genuine and would demand all the national strength England could muster. Like the anonymous author of a direct reply to Erskine's *View* (probably influenced by Burke himself), Burke believed Erskine's way of thinking fostered "national despondency." [16] The *Letters on a Regicide Peace* are thus offered as a kind of national pep talk; they are Burke's exhortation to the English to remember their heritage, their moral superiority, and their military tradition, and thereby to find the strength to resist the temptation of accepting France's unacceptable peace terms.

Typical of Burke's aim in *Letters* is his inspirational anecdote about an earlier crisis of national morale in England:

> I remember, in the beginning of what has lately been called the Seven Years' War, that an eloquent writer and ingenious speculator, Dr. Brown, upon some reverses which happened in the beginning of that war, published an elaborate philosophical discourse to prove that the distinguishing features of the people of England had been totally changed, and that a frivolous effeminacy was become the national character. Nothing could be more popular than that work. It was thought a great consolation to us . . . that we had found the causes of our misfortunes in

our vices. Pythagoras could not be more pleased with his
leading discovery. But whilst, in that splenetic mood, we
amused ourselves in a sour, critical speculation, of which we
were ourselves the objects, and in which every man lost his
particular sense of public disgrace in the epidemic nature of the
distemper, . . . whilst we were thus abandoning ourselves to a
direct confession of our inferiority to France, and whilst many,
very many, were ready to act upon a sense of that inferiority,
—a few months effected a total change in our variable minds.
We emerged from the gulf of that speculative despondency,
and were buoyed up to the highest point of practical vigor.
[5:239–40]

Burke was obviously writing in the hope of effecting in England's "variable
minds" the change that would bring the country out of the "speculative
despondency" of 1797.[17]

The problem of locating Wordsworth's response to the positions of
Erskine and Burke is complicated by the fact of Wordsworth's emotional
ties to France. In light of the presence there of Annette Vallon and their
daughter Caroline, it is impossible to imagine that Wordsworth could have
wanted anything but peace with that country. On the ideological issues,
though, the Wordsworth of 1798 and after seems to be aligned fairly
consistently with Burke and against Erskine. And this is nowhere clearer
than in respect to their stands on the question of the "psychological life" of
the nation. Indeed, Burke opens discussion in the first of the *Regicide Peace*
letters by playing on the word "revolution" very much as Wordsworth does
in the passage quoted above from *The Prelude* ("neither lapse / Nor turn of
sentiment that might be nam'd / A revolution, save at this one time").
Burke writes: "To a people who have once been proud and great, and great
because they were proud, a change in the national spirit is the most terrible
of all revolutions" (*BW* 5:253). The significance of Wordsworth's echo of
Burke's play on words is reinforced by its immediate context, which
suggests that he and Burke are speaking to very similar points:

> Not in my single self I found,
> But in the minds of all ingenuous youth,
> Change and subversion from this hour.
>
> [*Prel*. 10:231–33]

Wordsworth's idea of "subversion," like Burke's, is at once interior and
exterior, psychological and political. He means the term to describe an
undermining of the feelings, but they are feelings for the nation. He sees

the process, moreover, as taking place simultaneously across an entire generation of England's citizenry, which means that this "revolution," like the one Burke fears, is properly described as a "change in the national spirit" in both senses: that is, both a nationwide change in English spirit and a change in the spirit of English nationalism. We might say that if the personal dimension of Wordsworth's "personal epic" invites us to read the poem as a "crisis-autobiography," then its epic dimension invites us to see its crisis as national in scope. [18]

IV

To insist, as *The Prelude* does, that this "critical" revolution failed in Wordsworth's exemplary case is to insist that the poet's English discipline never completely gave way and that the cultural past continued to affect the young radical deeply in spite of his most rigorous efforts to renounce it. In the overall narrative, full recognition of this truth is not forthcoming until the poet reaches the nadir described in book 11. As always, however, Wordsworth provides early intimations of the eventual outcome. In this case the promises of better things date right from the time when his mind begins to take its turn for the worse. The earliest and most important of these intimations supplies one further contextual clue as to how we are to understand the spots of time proper when they do arrive.

Toward the end of the long passage in book 9 that recounts Wordsworth's initiatory conversation with Beaupuy, he describes an unexpected encounter with the mysteries of passion that link him to his race. Walking and talking with the young French officer along the Loire Valley, Wordsworth wants to consider only the future of society but finds his imagination inexorably drawn to things past. The high woods, inwoven roots, and smooth forest moss remind him of old romantic tales about Ariosto's Angelica, Tasso's Ermenia, and Spenser's Una. The recently sacked convents recall the age of monastic faith when the matin bell, the evening taper, and the cross were all still powerful symbols. And finally there is Wordsworth's curious response to the celebrated *châteaux de la Loire*:

> And when my friend
> Pointed upon occasion to the site
> Of Romarentin, home of ancient kings,
> To the imperial edifice of Blois,
> Or to that rural castle, name now slipped
> From my remembrance, where a lady lodged
> By the first Francis wooed, and bound to him

In chains of mutual passion—from the tower,
As a tradition of the country tells,
Practised to commune with her royal knight
By cressets and love-beacons, intercourse
'Twixt her high-seated residence and his
Far off at Chambord on the plain beneath—
Even here, though less than with the peaceful house
Religious, 'mid these frequent monuments
Of kings, their vices and their better deeds,
Imagination, potent to enflame
At times with virtuous wrath and noble scorn,
Did also often mitigate the force
Of civic prejudice, the bigotry,
So call it, of a youthful patriot's mind,
And on these spots with many gleams I looked
Of chivalrous delight.

[481–503]

These three responses acknowledge the persistence of the past under three aspects: the literary, the religious, and the social-political. More specifically, they acknowledge under each of these aspects the power of what Burke called the age of chivalry. They do not offer an unqualified endorsement of the medieval system of manners—Burke's own endorsement of it is not unqualified[19]—but they do offer the beginnings of a critique of the Enlightenment position that attempts or pretends to leave this era's cultural legacy, with all of its power, behind. Wordsworth records these recollections as a challenge to the idea that one can simply take from the past what one chooses.

In her essay on "Wordsworth's Historical Imagination" in *The Prelude*, Barbara Gates, one of the few commentators to deal with the Loire Valley reminiscences, has argued that these lines are meant to represent the poet's naïveté, his inability to measure up to the more mature brand of history advanced by the enlightened Beaupuy. "When Beaupuis tried to nurture Wordsworth in history as well as statecraft, partly teaching by examples from the past, Beaupuis's impact was more personal than pedagogical," writes Gates: "Despite their weighty discussions, the poet still fell into reveries inspired by fancy's fair forms rather than history's."[20] Gates is right to link the Loire Valley reminiscences with book 9's earlier passage about history, but I think she has mistaken the purport of both passages.

The earlier passage shows us, in effect, the attitude toward history that follows from Wordsworth and Beaupuy's peripatetic social planning:

We summoned up the honorable deeds
Of ancient story, thought of each bright spot
That could be found in all recorded time,
Of truth preserved and error passed away,
Of single spirits that catch the flame from heaven,
And how the multitude of men will feed
And fan each other—thought of sects, how keen
They are to put the appropriate nature on,
Triumphant over every obstacle
Of custom, language, country, love and hate,
And what they do and suffer for their creed,
How far they travel, and how long endure—
How quickly mighty nations have been formed
From least beginnings, how, together locked
By new opinions, scattered tribes have made
One body, spreading wide as clouds in heaven.

[372–87]

The two young philosophers are depicted scrutinizing the past in search of honorable deeds that will corroborate their hopes for the future. They are working, furthermore, on legendary materials—stories themselves generated out of human hopes and fears—without recognizing that they are legendary. In the name of social revolution, Wordsworth and Beaupuy make claims upon the past. Their error, so we are to understand, lies in their failure to take account of the claims the past may be making upon them. This error emerges only gradually in *The Prelude*, but the first inkling of it comes in those ensuing reminiscences on the banks of the Loire.

To see that these reminiscences are indeed meant to disclose the error of the enlightened position—and that this position is not meant to offer a valuable intellectual standard too high for the young Wordsworth to attain—we need to recognize in them that recurring Wordsworthian topos, the psychological *felix culpa*. The Loire Valley reminiscences are explicitly triggered by a mental lapse: from his "earnest dialogues" about the future of man, Wordsworth has, he says, "*slipped* in thought, / And let remembrance steal to other times" (446–47; italics mine). Nor can there be any question that the lapse is fortunate, for these recollections mitigate the force, to use Wordsworth's Burkean phrase, of Enlightenment prejudice and bigotry. Moreover, these short-lived stirrings of the imagination pointedly adumbrate its final deliverance in book 11: "on these *spots* with many gleams I looked / Of chivalrous delight." Like the spots of time in both books 1 and 11, these spots of the chivalric age come to the poet unwilled. Both the

Loire Valley reminiscences and the spots of time thus stand in sharp contrast
to the earnest dialogues in which Wordsworth and Beaupuy call up the
past:

> . . . [we] thought of each bright *spot*
> That could be found in all recorded *time*.

This deliberate summoning up is the very sort of earnest activity from
which the later recollections offer a happy relaxation.

Further evidence of how we are meant to connect the two book 9
passages can be seen in Wordsworth's rhetorical handling of the metaphor
of light. Talking with Beaupuy, Wordsworth initially seeks out "each
bright spot" in recorded time; he understands the spots to be illuminated
by "single spirits that catch the flame from heaven." The gleams of
chivalrous delight that attend the later passage, on the other hand, have
their origin in the flickering love-beacons by which Francis's lady "prac-
ticed to commune with her royal knight." The brightness of the first spots
is explained metaphysically, that of the second spots naturalistically. The
chivalric gleams are generated by human passions; the metaphysical gleams
purport to be generated irrespective of human passions. Both young
Wordsworth's and Beaupuy's passions, we are to understand, are at work in
producing these gleams. The point is that when the radicals converse these
passions never get to hear the sound of their own names.

Like the spots of time, the Loire Valley reminiscences are traditional-
ist in that they represent a post-enlightenment return to tradition. What
makes them doubly interesting in this respect is that they link the quasi-
involuntary pattern of "spot syndrome" to something Wordsworth is
willing to call "tradition." What "Tradition tells" of Francis I is im-
mediately responsible for Wordsworth's response to that chateau, much as
what "Tradition tells" (the phrase is the same) about Sir Alfred's stone in
book 1 of *The Excursion* is responsible for the Pastor's response to it. Here
again the contrast of the reminiscences with the earlier summoning up of
bright spots is instructive. Whereas Wordsworth and Beaupuy comb
through the annals of "*recorded* time," Francis's story is evidently, like Sir
Alfred's, an "*unwritten* story fondly traced / From sire to son." To call the
poet's moments of chivalrous delight "spots of tradition" is not to misrepre-
sent their purport, and the epithet applies by extension to the spots of time
as well.

V

When we consider the spots of time in reference to the structure in which
they are embedded, then, we discover that an implicit traditionalism is

implied even in what seem to be Wordsworth's most intensely lyric and "psychological" moments. The spots of time are obviously not themselves traditions in the way that this is true of the stories of Francis and Alfred, or even of the stories of Michael and Margaret. Wordsworth seems to want to preserve the discrepancy between the sense of psychological privacy conveyed in the spots themselves and the more public function they are made to serve, as if to suggest that the way in which one records one's most personal experiences already presupposes a great deal about one's relation to the larger social world. Nonetheless, when we return to read the spots-of-time passages themselves, we discover that, *mutatis mutandis*, they do share certain important features with the oral tales that Wordsworth more explicitly presents as traditionary.

For heuristic purposes, we can set the spots of time against their traditionary counterparts in *The Excursion*: the tales the Pastor tells about various "spots" (his term) in the surrounding countryside. The comparison is easy to make for a number of reasons. Both the Pastor's tales and the spots of time tend to be narrative in form, a point which goes without saying for the Pastor's tales but which is too often forgotten in discussions of the spots of time, despite their self-consciously storylike openings. Further, both of these groups of tales are clusters of discrete units "scattered" through their respective poems. Both are represented as coming without calculation; they are products of second nature that sometimes seem to take even their tellers by surprise. Perhaps this sense is what Wordsworth means to capture in calling them, once in each poem, "those passages of life" (*Prel.* 11:269 and *Exc.* 7:294)—the only two instances of this phrase in the poetry. Finally, both are to be understood as embodying a discipline that gives them, to use Arnold's phrase, their "healing power." At least in these ways, then, we can say that what the spots of time are to the action of *The Prelude*, the Pastor's tales are to the action of *The Excursion*.

Of course, the actions of the two poems do differ in important ways, the most fundamental difference being that *The Excursion* is an action between characters and *The Prelude* is an action of a single character. It is the difference, roughly, between a Platonic dialogue and a philosophical monologue like Descartes's *Meditations*. There is dialectical interchange in the latter, to be sure, but instead of representing dialectical interchange as occurring between dramatis personae, it represents all points of view as held by the author himself. This difference has some important consequences in how we see the component narratives as supplying the emotional power for each poem: for example, the therapy in *The Prelude* is ostensibly self-directed, whereas the Pastor's therapy is intended for the despondent

Solitary.[21] Still, the similarities of their function are substantial enough to invite comparison of their internal structure.

The task of comparison is best approached by considering what is understood as a "spot" in each use. The spots to which the Pastor's narratives are attached are all, in his words, "spots of earth" or "spots of ground." They are to be understood as physical places that can be indicated by ostensive reference. Like the "spot" where the ruined sheepfold's stones are piled in "Michael," those in *The Excursion* might not be noticed by the uninitiated but they can be seen by anyone. And like the spot in "Michael," too, the Pastor's spots are made meaningful by the memorializing tale. The spots to which the poet's narratives are attached in *The Prelude* are also made meaningful by memorializing tales, but these spots appear to the poet in imagination and can be made visible to his audience (Coleridge, let us say) only likewise in imagination. Given this great difference, however, the relationship of spot to narrative is strikingly similar in each case.

Each of the Pastor's spots is associated with an emotion about some person whose life made some significant contact with that spot, another respect in which these spots resemble Michael's sheepfold or Margaret's cottage: in each case the spot is distinct, but the emotion is not. The explanation for the indistinctness comes in the first *Essay upon Epitaphs*, which Wordsworth appended as a note to the Pastor's tales. "The character of a deceased friend or beloved kinsman is not seen, no—nor ought to be seen, otherwise than as a tree through a tender haze or a luminous mist" (1:58). In telling the story of this character, the story that gives meaning to the spot, a narrator is therefore not a strictly accurate historian. His account is "the joint offspring of the worth of the dead and the affections of the living" (p. 58). Consider, then, the strange fate of the Pastor (the fate Wordsworth would insist is everyman's): his present perception of the world—what he notices, what has meaning for him in the present—is conditioned by past events of which he can give no accurate account.

The closest counterpart in *The Prelude* to the explication provided in the *Essay upon Epitaphs* is a passage that occurs near the close of book 1:

> Thus often in those fits of vulgar joy
> Which through all seasons on a child's pursuits
> Are prompt attendants, 'mid that giddy bliss
> Which like a tempest works along the blood
> And is forgotten, even then I felt
> Gleams like the flashing of a shield. The earth
> And common face of Nature spake to me
> Rememberable things; sometimes, 'tis true,

By chance collisions and quaint accidents—
Like those ill-sorted unions, work supposed
Of evil-minded fairies—yet not in vain
Nor profitless, if haply they impressed
Collateral objects and appearances,
Albeit lifeless then, and doomed to sleep
Until maturer seasons called them forth
To impregnate and to elevate the mind.
And if the vulgar joy by its own weight
Wearied itself out of the memory,
The scenes which were a witness of that joy
Remained, in their substantial lineaments
Depicted on the brain, and to the eye
Were visible, a daily sight. And thus
By the impressive discipline of fear,
By pleasure and repeated happiness—
So frequently repeated—and by force
Of obscure feelings representative
Of joys that were forgotten, these same scenes,
So beauteous and majestic in themselves,
Though yet the day was distant, did at length
Become habitually dear, and all
Their hues and forms were by invisible links
Allied to the affection.

[609–40]

The epistemology here is hard to paraphrase, but with the help of the nearly contemporary discussion of similar matters in the 1800 Preface one can piece together a coherent summary. Childhood sensory experience, by virtue of the giddy emotion that characterizes it, impresses the images of certain objects on the mind. These images survive the expiration of the emotion itself and remain, as Wordsworth says, "depicted on the brain." The images are thus present to the mind in its continuing perception and indeed modify current sensory experience. The vulgar emotions that were responsible for impressing the image in the first instance also continue to have a life in the mind even after they have wearied themselves out of memory. They are "re-presented" there by (or as) what in this passage are called "obscure feelings" associated with the mind's surviving images.

What we are supposed to be witnessing in the spots-of-time passages are moments when, as Wordsworth says in "Tintern Abbey," "we are laid asleep / In body, and become a living soul" (46–47). The realm of immedi-

ate sensation drops away, and the poet is left in the presence only of the
images depicted on his brain and the obscure feelings that represent the
emotions that were initially responsible for those images. If we regard the
images as the spots and the obscure feelings as the means of temporalizing
the spots, we can then say that the narrative passages as they appear in the
poem are the result of the poet's efforts to imagine what the obscure feelings
of the present *re*-present. Thus understood, the spot narratives in *both*
poems give us a present fact (the spot) in association with present feelings
that are obscurely representative of some past fact—an experience of the joy
of nature in the first case and of the worth of another person in the second.
The narratives are in both cases genetic accounts of the power of the spots in
question, but are in neither case properly "historical." They are rather to be
understood as a joint production of past fact and present feeling. In both
poems, that is, the narratives embody the oral-traditional structure of time
that we examined in the last chapter. One's present sense of the world is
necessarily affected by a past that cannot itself be grasped apart from one's
position in the present.[22]

To see how this temporal structure inheres in a particular spot of time,
we might consider the example of the boat-stealing episode from book 1.
This narrative is quite explicitly identified as a genetic account of how
"huge and mighty forms" still visible to his mind's eye first began to move
through Wordsworth's mind and trouble his dreams. The story itself is well
known: young Wordsworth steals a rowboat, rows to the middle of Ullswa-
ter with a "steady view" fixed on the top of a ridge, and, as he rows, sees a
"huge Cliff" rise up to dominate over his point of bearing. The more he
rows, the larger grows the cliff. Forced to turn back toward shore, he
returns the boat to its mooring place and leaves the lake a changed boy. Not
only does he carry with him the image of those huge and mighty forms, he
carries obscure feelings as well:

> . . . for many days my brain
> Worked with a dim and undetermined sense
> Of unknown modes of being. In my thoughts
> There was a darkness. . . .
>
> [418–21]

The point that commentators on this passage sometimes miss—and it is a
crucial one—is that these obscure feelings are responsible for the recon-
struction of the experience that impressed Wordsworth's mind with the
image of huge and mighty forms. The passage is thus simultaneously a
narrative of a past experience and an enactment of a present experience, the

present experience of recalling and recounting the earlier one through the medium of these surviving feelings.

Although the lines make no reference to the physical scene of composition (such as we find, say, in "Tintern Abbey"), the mature poet's present circumstances have left their mark on the narrative in at least two apparent ways. The first is that the events are being recalled under the influence of verse. The motion of the boat through the water is described as a movement "in cadence," a cadence enacted in the line's striking iambs: "I push'd, and struck the oars and struck again" (385–86). The cliff itself is said to have pursued the boy "With measur'd motion" (411). And surely it is because the poet writes specifically in Miltonic blank verse that he envisions the progress of the boat through the water in the same way that Milton describes Michael's narrative manner in *Paradise Lost*. (Compare Wordsworth's "my little boat moved on / Even like a man who moves with stately step / Though bent on speed" [386–88] with Milton's "As one who in his journey bates at Noon, / Though bent on speed" [12:1–2].

The second way in which the poet's present circumstances have left their mark on the narrative is less obvious but more important. It has to do with the fact that the entire psychological drama of the Introduction is recapitulated in this episode. Like the older poet setting out at the start of *The Prelude*, the boy tries to fix his will on a steady point only to find his great enterprise mysteriously obstructed:

> . . . lustily
> I dipped my oars into the silent lake,
> And as I rose upon the stroke my boat
> Went heaving through the water like a swan—
> When from behind that craggy steep, till then
> The bound of the horizon, a huge cliff,
> As if with voluntary power instinct,
> Upreared its head. I struck, and struck again,
> And growing still in stature, the huge cliff
> Rose up between me and the stars, and still
> With measured motion, like a living thing
> Strode after me.
>
> [401–12]

The "voluntary power" which the cliff appears to have—such is the genius of Wordsworth's contrivance—is a reflection of the boy's own misguided will. The more desperately this will is asserted, the greater the force of the adversary. This way lies madness, for the boy as for the poet of the

Introduction, a parallel that is supported by Wordsworth's invocation of the ancient association of the striking of the oar with metrical composition. Only the will's retreat can defeat this kind of adversary. As the boy pivots his boat in mid-lake, so the poet pivots midway through book 1; prospect becomes retrospect and the sweet stream that will guide him, the Derwent, suddenly turns up behind him, the last place he expected to find it.[23]

The temporal status of such a narrative is evidently problematic. A past experience is interpreted in terms of a present experience which is itself informed by what has preceded it. What Wordsworth writes here is the lyric forerunner of the kind of history Thomas Carlyle would later write in *Past and Present*. In both, the distinction between the past and the present dissolves into a relationship of thoroughgoing reciprocity, an epistemological circle. *The Prelude*'s interiorized place traditions are by no means the only "passages" he traveled on his circle, however, for this same structure inheres in the great lyrics of 1802–4. Like the spots of time, these lyrics seek to represent memory's temporal conundrum, and their complex tense shifts mark some of his most ingenious efforts to come to terms with it.

The simplest and most celebrated of these lyrics illustrates the point most economically:

> I wandered lonely as a cloud
> That floats on high o'er vales and hills,
> When all at once I saw a crowd,
> A host, of golden daffodils;
> Beside the lake, beneath the trees,
> Fluttering and dancing in the breeze.
>
> Continuous as the stars that shine
> And twinkle on the milky way,
> They stretched in never-ending line
> Along the margin of a bay;
> Ten thousand saw I at a glance,
> Tossing their heads in sprightly dance.
>
> The waves beside them danced; but they
> Out-did the sparkling waves in glee:
> A poet could not but be gay,
> In such a jocund company:
> I gazed—and gazed—but little thought
> What wealth the show to me had brought:

> For oft, when on my couch I lie
> In vacant or in pensive mood,
> They flash upon that inward eye
> Which is the bliss of solitude;
> And then my heart with pleasure fills,
> And dances with the daffodils.

The shift in tense between stanzas three and four encourages us to find two distinct phases in the poem. The first three stanzas relate the encounter with the flowers and comprise the past-tense narrative which ends with the speaker's gazing on "the show," unaware of its benefits. The last stanza comes as an apparent explanation ("*For* oft . . .") of these benefits: it describes the effects of the encounter on the habitual workings of the speaker's mind. But this distinction is encouraged only to baffle the kind of reader who would insist on preserving it. If the past experience has important consequences for the speaker's mind, then we cannot take the speaker's account of that experience at face value. Hence the importance of the speaker's reference to himself as "a poet." It demands we recognize that the mind providing the narrative is the very one that has been shaped by the events related.

Only after reading the description of the "later" benefits (in stanza four) can we account for the peculiar features of the initial narrative. A vacant mind musing in solitude ("I wandered lonely as a cloud . . ."), the flashing of the daffodils on the inward eye (". . . all at once I saw . . . Ten thousand . . . at a glance"), and then the pleasure and dancing of the poet's heart. These components of the habitual vision make the past-tense narrative what it is—poetry. The show the poet says he *once* saw *without* thought proves to be the show he *still* sees *in* thought, as he lies on his couch. Such is the treachery of Wordsworth's tenses: a past-tense narrative becomes the spontaneous expression of what crossed the poet's mind in the moment of composition; the present-tense declaration becomes an account of the mental event which has just occurred.[24]

Wordsworth's consummate lyric achievement in this mode is probably "Resolution and Independence." The notorious shifts of tense in this poem's introductory stanzas are so baffling that by the time we reach the beginning of the narrative proper we have no idea when or where the narrated action is supposed to be taking place:

> Now, whether it were by peculiar grace,
> A leading from above, a something given,

Yet it befell that, in this lonely place,
When up and down my fancy thus was driven,
And I with these untoward thoughts had striven,
I saw a Man before me unawares:
The oldest Man he seem'd that ever wore grey hairs.

[50–56; text of 1807 *Poems*]

Is this a narrative of Wordsworth's physical encounter with the Leech-Gatherer or a reenactment of it as a mental encounter with his image? Are "these untoward thoughts" being reported from a past occasion or dramatized on the occasion of this poem's composition? In the case of both questions it is finally impossible to decide.

This temporal doubling produces another crux in the stanza that concludes the narrative of the encounter, the final lines of the poem:

And soon with this he other matter blended,
Cheerfully uttered, with demeanour kind,
But stately in the main; and, when he ended,
I could have laugh'd myself to scorn, to find
In that decrepit Man so firm a mind.
"God," said I, "be my help and stay secure;
I'll think of the Leech-gatherer on the lonely moor."

The future-tense declaration, I *will* think of the Leech-gatherer, anticipates when the poet *does* think of the Leech-gatherer, and how in so doing he achieves firmness of mind, resolution and independence, discipline. Such a moment is responsible for this poem just as the thought of the daffodils is responsible for "I wandered lonely as a cloud." Thinking only of Chatterton and insanity, Wordsworth is visited by the flashing of the Leech-gatherer on his inward eye: "I saw a Man before me unawares." Even the syntax of the counterpart moment in the simpler poem is similar: "I saw a crowd, / A host, of golden daffodils." If Wordsworth had written for "Resolution and Independence" the sort of coda that he wrote for "I wandered . . . ," it might have gone like this: For oft when on my couch I lie, struggling with untoward thoughts of despondency and madness, I think back to when I said I would think of the Leech-gatherer and his firmness of mind; then I am again returned to discipline and gladness.

The discipline of the poet's mind is thus a double-sided concept whose two sides correspond to the two primary senses of the word: firmness of mind, on the one hand, and the process by which this condition is achieved, on the other. This is the pun at work in all of Wordsworth's writings about discipline. In the great moralizing poetry of Wordsworth's major period—especially in *The Prelude* and in the great lyrics of 1802–4 that derive from it—one's present discipline resides in the habitual contemplation of how one supposes oneself to have been disciplined in the past. Future virtue is entirely dependent upon the presumption of past virtue in this scheme of things. Schemes of radical human improvement are out of the question. Feeling will come in aid of feeling only insofar as we can lay claim to having once been strong.[25]

Nine

An Ideology against "Ideology"

> I therefore much prefer [after considering other possible names for this new course of study] that we adopt the name *ideology*, or science of ideas. This is most prudent, for the word supposes nothing which is doubtful or unknown. . . . Its meaning is very clear to everyone.
>
> Destutt de Tracy, *Mémoire de l'Institut national*

I have discussed the three chief stages of *The Prelude* in reverse order: first the thirteen-book stage of 1805, then the five-book stage of 1804, and finally the two-book stage of 1799. This procedure can be taken as paradigmatic for my argument as a whole in that it follows a course from later texts and relatively explicit positions to earlier texts and relatively more implicit positions. But the discussion of *The Prelude* also seeks to associate those three stages, in that reverse order, with increasingly latent points of historical reference. In chapter 3 we examined the France books of the thirteen-book *Prelude* to discern Burkean views of the Great Debate in Wordsworth's portrayal of both the French Revolution and its effect on him as an Englishman. Chapter 5 looked to *The Prelude*'s education books for an index to the early five-book design of the poem. We saw how the poem then comprised a polemic against the programs for systematic education that were perceived in the 1790s, both by Burke in England and by leading legislators in France, to stem from the writings of Rousseau. Discussion in chapter 8 concentrated on the introductory book of *The Prelude*, with special attention to those "spots of time" in which the poem is presumed to have its

216

origin. The effort there was to derive the psychologized epistemology by which Wordsworth justifies his ideas about both education and politics. What remains, therefore, is to establish the corresponding historical context for that epistemology. The pursuit of this task will also make it possible to bring together a number of the points so far argued about the ideology of Wordsworth's major work.

I

I have from the start been using this term "ideology" in its now ordinary sense: roughly, a body of thought or manner of thinking (especially about society) that is characteristic of some person or group.[1] One can speak of the ideology, understood this way, of any person or group one happens to choose, but one could not speak of ideology as coming to an end—not so long as one could count on a continuing human community. There is, however, a more historically particularized sense in which ideology might be understood as ending before human community does. This is the sense Daniel Bell intends when he speaks of an "end of ideology": "a way of translating ideas into action" or "a conversion of ideas into social levers."[2] It is also close to what Michael Oakeshott means by "the ideological style of politics," the belief that the arrangements of society should (or even that they could) be made to conform to a "premeditated set of ideas."[3]

While few observers would agree with Bell that ideology in this sense came to an end in the 1950s, many would agree with his suggestion that it has its beginning in the age that produced the French Revolution. This latter suggestion, after all, carries the authority of Napoleon, the man who first used the term ideology as Bell does:

> C'est à l'idéologie, à cette ténébreuse métaphysique qui, en recherchant avec subtilité les causes premiers, veut sur ces bases fonder la législation des peuples, au lieu d'approprier les lois à la connaissance du coeur humain et aux leçons de l'histoire, qu'il faut attribuer tous les malheurs qu'a éprouvés notre belle France. Ces erreurs devaient et ont effectivement amené le régime des hommes de sang. En effet, qui a proclamé le principe d'insurrection comme un devoir? qui a adulé le peuple en le proclamant à une souveraineté qu'il était incapable d'exercer? qui a détruit le respect et la sainteté des lois, en les faisant dépendre, non des principes sacrés de la justice, de la nature des choses et de la justice civile, mais seulement de la volonté d'une assemblée composée d'hommes étranger à la connaissance des

lois civiles, criminelles, administratives, politiques et militaires?

Lorsqu'on est appelé à régénérer un État, ce cont des principes constamment opposés qu'il faut suivre. L'histoire peint le coeur humain; c'est dans l'histoire qu'il faut chercher les avantages et les inconvenients des différentes législations.[4]

I have quoted this passage in French from Napoleon's 1812 response to the State Consul because parts of it are frequently mistranslated, and I have quoted it at length to show how much of it sounds like a plagiarism of Burke's *Reflections*. If Napoleon did crib from Burke, he was no doubt borrowing from a writer who would have opposed him as vigorously as he opposed the revolution that was their common nemesis. Nonetheless, the parallels between the two positions are striking: the rejection of an aprioristic political metaphysics that seeks to establish human laws on subtly researched first principles; the claim for a causal connection between such metaphysics and widespread wanton bloodshed; the recommendation that political affairs be guided by the knowledge of the human heart and the lessons of history; the claim of a causal connection between what we see when we look into the heart and what we see when we look into the past. The very phrasing often sounds Burkean: "History paints the human heart; it is to history that we must look for the advantages and disadvantages of various legislations."

Like Burke, Napoleon takes a stand against the intellectual tradition of the French Enlightenment, and his ultimate targets are much the same as Burke's. One obvious case in point is Rousseau, whom Napoleon is supposed to have derided as an "eloquent ideologue" as early as 1803, and at whose tomb he is supposed to have said: "It would have been better had this man never lived [for] it was he who prepared the French Revolution."[5] If we understand this historically particularized sense of ideology as, broadly, the politics of the French Enlightenment, then the Burkean ideology that informs Wordsworth's poetry—"traditionalism" or "the doctrine of second nature" or whatever we shall call it—must be understood as an ideology against "Ideology." Oakeshott's sense of "Ideology" as "an abridgement of tradition" is germane to this point. For in his terms "tradition" informs practice invisibly or insensibly—as it were "naturally"—until the ideologue or rationalist (Oakeshott would, like Napoleon, use these terms interchangeably) precipitates or condenses it into a series of principles that become steps in a recipe.[6] The work of the traditionalist or anti-ideologue, would then be to make these principles invisible again by redissolving them back into the continuity of practice. The traditionalist, in other words, must return ideology to a state of second nature.[7]

The effort to particularize the meaning of ideology historically can, however, be carried somewhat further. For while Napoleon's attack on ideology ultimately extends to the entire Enlightenment, his more immediate targets were the very last generation of philosophes, a circle of philosophical educators who gained fame only after the publication of the *Reflections*—though their role was clearly adumbrated in Burke's *Letter to a Member of the National Assembly*. This is the group whom succeeding generations have followed Napoleon in calling the Ideologues: Destutt de Tracy, Cabanis, Daunou, Garat, Laromiguière, and others. They are linked in several ways. Most were active in the political events of 1789 and most attended regular sessions of the salon of Mme Helvétius. They subscribed almost uniformly to the philosophic method of Condillac and followed the intellectual leadership of Condorcet. Basically Girondist in party affiliation, like the young Wordsworth, their common political aim was to keep the Revolution in the service of enlightened goals and values. Although a few of them enjoyed some power before the ascendancy of the Montagnards in 1792, their collective historical moment arrived only after the fall of Robespierre in 1794. It was the Ideologues who, under the aegis of Rousseau, successively promoted the great education programs of 1794–95. Indeed, nothing better epitomizes the spirit of Ideology than the outlook of the Committee on Public Instruction, whose aims and accomplishments were surveyed above in chapter 5.[8]

There is no need to repeat here what we observed earlier about the importance of the Committee's educational system in the history of the Revolution or in the development of Wordsworth's mature thought. Earlier, for reasons having to do with his role in the five-book *Prelude* and with his having been the object of Burke's 1791 attack, we considered these issues in relation to Rousseau. Now, on the other hand, I want to stress that what I then called "the Rousseau of the 1790s" was in fact the Ideologues' Rousseau, and that the Ideologues' praise for Rousseau's methodical critique of society was in part a projection of their own commitment to the epistemological method they learned from Condillac and the "social science" they learned from Condorcet. These two developments—the notion of a "new metaphysics" of the mind, as it was called, and the notion of a social science implemented through educational programs—go hand in hand in the Ideological movement of the 1790s. And in the relationship between these developments lies the movement's special relevance to Wordsworth's major work.

II

The views of the French Ideologues are probably best approached through the work of Destutt de Tracy. He not only coined the word "ideology" but he also did the most to show the role of what it named in grounding the projected edifice of the social sciences. His early pronouncements about ideology, moreover, were already being publicized in England as early as 1796–97. The forum for these pronouncements, as for the research of most of his colleagues in the movement, was the Institut National des Sciences et des Arts. Founded in 1795 at the urging of the Ideologues themselves, the Institute fulfilled Condorcet's vision of a unified national academy at the center of a vast educational network that was to stretch to the ends of the (ever-expanding) empire. The Institute was divided into four "classes," each of which was to convene quarterly for the reading of summaries or *mémoires* of work in progress, documents later to appear in the official publication of the Institute's proceedings. Tracy was associated with the second of these classes, Sciences Morales et Politiques, which was itself divided into sections listed as follows: Analyse des Sensations et des Idées, Morale, Science Sociale, et Legislation, Economie Politique, and so on. Within the Second Class, Tracy's affiliation was with the first of these sections. The importance of the class with which Tracy was associated may be measured by the fact that Napoleon, who had curried the favor of the Ideologues as a rising military leader, and actually been named a Member of the Institute in 1797, shut this class down in 1803 for the political threat it posed to his newly acquired power. The importance of Tracy's section on the analysis of ideas within the Class may be measured by the fact that it became the center of "ideology," which was for the Ideologues the center of everything else. Tracy, in short, epitomizes the prevailing outlook of the intellectual leadership of the Directory. It was a time, as Emmet Kennedy sums it up in his recent study of Tracy, when "philosophy and education were to remedy the 'barbaric anarchy' of the Terror," and therefore when what was "at stake was not a vague *philosophie* of the Enlightenment, but a rigorous discipline in need of a name."[9]

Tracy gave his "rigorous discipline" its name, explained its operation, and outlined its grand social mission all in a series of *mémoires* he read to the Institute at various meetings during 1796–97. These reports were not published until February 1798, when they were collected under a single title, *Mémoire sur la Faculté de penser*, but each had been widely publicized after the meeting to which it was delivered.[10] In what was probably his second appearance before them, in 1796, Tracy told his assembled colleagues that although "it was no doubt for the advancement of this science that the first section of this Class was consecrated," this same science "is so new that it still has no name."[11] Dismissing "metaphysics" and "psychology" for carrying unwanted connotations, Tracy decided in favor of the neologism: "I much prefer that we adopt the name ideology."[12] Tracy would later credit Condillac with having "actually created ideology,"[13] but in naming what Condillac had made he followed a principle recently advanced by Lavoisier, whose work he praised, who said that a new science required a new and unambiguous nomenclature.[14]

In light of the subsequent history of this word it is ironic that Tracy specifically chose it because he thought it could have only one meaning: "science of ideas."[15] On the other hand, to suggest, as some have done, that Napoleon permanently twisted the politically neutral meaning that Tracy had assigned to the term is to overlook the Ideologues' own responsibility for what happened to the term subsequently. For whatever the narrowly technical definition of the term in the movement, it was apparent to all involved that ideology was conceived to serve the ends of radical political and social change.

When Joanna Kitchin makes this argument in her study of the Ideologues, she supports it with the testimony of Maine de Biran who, after his first meeting with Cabanis and Tracy in 1802, reported: "L'idéologie, m'ont-ils dit, doit changer la face du monde."[16] But we needn't rely on secondhand testimony, for the point is made plainly enough in the very opening sentences of Tracy's first published *mémoire*:

> I am deeply persuaded that the speculative sciences are to be recommended chiefly by their applications; for, in the final analysis, what is the end of all research if not utility? Also I fervently want this assembly to occupy itself with some of the great works that have an immediate influence on the prosperity of society. Nothing is more capable of honoring, in the eyes of the nation, the second class of the Institute, and to make palpable to the most ignorant the advantages they can receive from the vigil of sages: but I think that in delivering a practical utility from these works to you it is above all worthy of you to create the theory of moral and political science, which has languished until now in a deadly uncertainty. For you are not ignorant of the fact that the success of all that remains practical is necessarily subordinated to the degree of current perfection of

the theory on which it depends. It is thus principally in ground-
ing the moral sciences on a stable and certain base that you
respond to the hopes that an enlightened Europe envisions from
the first body of sages that addresses itself to these questions
with some freedom. This is the motive that engages me to direct
your attention to the knowledge of the formation of our ideas.[17]

The practical improvement of society depends on the current state of
theory, and the current state of theory depends on one's "ideological"
sophistication. Ideology is not only the first of the sciences "in genealogical
order," as Tracy goes on to explain, but is "properly the only science; all
others, without exception, are only applications of this one to various
objects of our curiosity." The Ideologue movement would thus seem to be a
powerful historical embodiment of the notion, vividly portrayed but vehe-
mently renounced in book 10 of *The Prelude*, that if the Revolution could
only get its theory straight, sufficiently develop its analysis of human
experience, then all other stages of progress toward utopia would be realized
in their turn.

Tracy's explanation of how ideology works is too complicated to
admit of brief summary, but a later *mémoire* does provide a rough epitome of
its operation in an admiring account of what Condillac did in bringing the
new science to the state of perfection Tracy now supposes it to enjoy:

> This celebrated metaphysician had so few rivals in the course he
> followed that the history of his thought is in effect the history of
> science during this long stretch of time. For this alone it would
> be most interesting to follow him step by step. But it is,
> moreover, most useful to observe how an excellent mind grad-
> ually perfects its ideas and makes them more precise, how its
> analyses become successively more rigorous and more detailed,
> and how, to the extent that it penetrates further into its subject,
> stripping itself of its prejudices and habits, the questions clarify
> themselves, but multiply in subdividing, and present them-
> selves as new subjects of discussion.[18]

Here again, the thematic connections with the France books of *The Prelude*
call out to be noticed. Tracy's honorific portrayal of Condillac as prototypi-
cal ideologist highlights the very same qualities that become part of
Wordsworth's ironic self-portrait in books 10 and 11 where, in reference to
this same Thermidorean reaction, he describes the experience of a mind in
the grip of French philosophism. What Tracy represents as the means of
ideology's great triumph—the progressive rigor of the analysis and the

proliferation of questions through repeated subdivision of issues—are what Wordsworth represents as the means of his near self-destruction. The task in both cases is understood as an effort to penetrate to the nature of the mind. And the obstacle in both cases, for Wordsworth a providential obstacle, is the second nature that resides in those "prejudices and habits" which ideology would strip away.

That second nature—or *l'habitude*, as Tracy calls it—is indeed the great nemesis of ideology is a point that becomes explicit by the end of Tracy's first *mémoire*. It is nothing less, he says, than "the source of all the trouble we have in sorting out what happens inside us and by itself alone constitutes almost all the difficulties of the science called ideology."[19] Part of the problem habit poses for ideology is that it blurs the boundaries between things that, if the nature of the mind is to be finally determined, must be kept distinct. As Tracy says in summarizing his later work, *Elements of Ideology* (1801), "our sole and only means of preserving ourselves from error, is to assure ourselves well that we comprehend the idea of which we judge, and if it be doubtful, to make the most complete enumeration possible of the elements which compose it."[20] Habit inhibits this sort of enumeration. It leads us to conflate past experience with present, memory with sensation, so that the two can seem altogether inextricable. The confusion of past and present elements in our ideas reaches its most intense levels when we are under the spell of what Tracy calls *imagination*: "when our memory is very lively, when it is carried to that point of exaltation that we call imagination, we believe ourselves really and actually to feel the affections that we are making ourselves recall."[21]

In the plot of *The Prelude*, as we have seen, the spots of time come to save Wordsworth from a self-destructive mental activity that bears strong resemblance to Condillac's new metaphysics. They provide poetic answers to the philosophical problems this activity poses for him. Epistemologically, they are supposed to ground the conservative social and political position of *The Prelude* just as ideology is supposed to ground the social and political views of the neo-Enlightenment Directorate. As moments of high "imagination," in both the Wordsworthian and Tracean senses of the word, the spots represent the final triumph of habit, the mysterious and impenetrable fusion of sensation once experienced with sensation now experienced. The images presented in those passages and in the famous lyrics modeled on them—images of uprearing mountains, admonishing winds, dancing daffodils, and grave-living leech-gatherers—belong neither to the past nor the present, but to an epistemological no-man's land in between. This is the temporal realm where an old man can seem like a stone that seems like a seabeast, as Wordsworth explains in the 1815 Preface, drawing his paradigm of the imagination at work from "Resolution and Independence" (*PrW* 3:33). There is no reducing the poetic "ideas" presented in the spots to their component elements; they are themselves the most fundamental facts of the mind as Wordsworth understands it. Unlike the facts of ideology, however, these are not so much validly known as they are deeply felt. They are the essence of what Wordsworth meant when, appropriating the idiom of ideology to his own purposes, he defined poetry as "the history of science of feelings" (*PW* 2:513).

III

For readers who might grant the plausibility of the thematic connections that link Wordsworth's high lyric mode with French ideology but who might at the same time wish to see more historical evidence for the case, I can add a few brief points. The first is the chronology of the events recorded in the France books of *The Prelude*. The first half of book 10 of the 1805 poem ends with Thermidor and the death of Robespierre. The second half, which would become a separate book in the 1850 version of the poem, takes up from the beginning of the Directory: "From this time forth in France, as is well-known, / Authority in France put on a milder face." The Thermidorean reaction is the period of the Revolution when the Ideologues come to power in France, and the second half of book 10 is the section of *The Prelude* which recounts the phase that Wordsworth presents as an obsessive involvement with theory. "This was the time," he says in introducing this phase, when "the philosophy / That promised to abstract the hopes of man / Out of his feelings, to be fixed thenceforth / In a purer element / Found ready welcome" (805–10). It is true that the second half of book 10 contains some retrograde motion of the narrative back through earlier stages, but the earliest possible date of "this . . . time" is determined more specifically by the topical allusion that introduces the immediately preceding verse paragraph: "And now, become oppressors in their turn, / Frenchmen had changed a war of self-defense / For one of conquest" (791–93). The reference, accurately glossed by the editors of the Norton *Prelude*, is to the military campaign of May–July 1794.

The second point pertains to Wordsworth's interest in and access to information about "ideology." There is of course very little documentation of Wordsworth's interests between the fall of Robespierre and the summer of 1797 when he becomes Coleridge's neighbor at Alfoxden—the period that marks the emergence of France's National Institute and the promulgation of Ideology. What evidence we do have, however, suggests that he was watching French affairs keenly. I have already discussed the letter to William Mathews (June 1794) that records Wordsworth's intention to keep up with the *Moniteur*, national gazette of the French republic. Seven months later, in the only one of his letters from the period from autumn 1794 to autumn 1795 to survive, Wordsworth tells Mathews of his idea about "translating from the French or Italian Gazettes" (*EY*:137). This suggests not only continuing interest on Wordsworth's part, but also the presumption that gazettes like the French *Moniteur* were accessible to him—a point about which he had expressed some doubt in June.

And then there is that package of books Wordsworth received, presumably upon request, from James Losh in 1797. Among the items sent by Losh, as we noted earlier, were copies of the *Monthly Magazine* from February to December 1796—its first eleven numbers. One of the distinctive features of the *Magazine*, as Wordsworth no doubt knew, was its coverage of intellectual developments on the Continent. "In addition to the usual magazine features," writes John O. Hayden, "the *Monthly Magazine* contained 'proceedings of Learned Societies' and showed a special interest in foreign attitudes and philosophy."[22] If Wordsworth had seen the number for February 1797, however, he would have known something more specific about the journal. For under the heading of its report on the fourth quarterly sitting of the Institut National, this issue informs its readers that they can find "Accounts of the Three former Sittings, and of the Plan, and of the Names of the Members, of this Establishment" in numbers 2, 8, and 10 of the *Magazine*: that is, March, September, and November of 1796.[23]

The *Magazine*'s reports on the new Institute convey much of the air of enthusiasm that surrounded it in Paris. The founding of the Institute was covered in the March issue. This article, to which the *Magazine*'s later reports about the Institute repeatedly refer, outlined the structures of the Institute by class and section and listed the philosophers and scientists affiliated with each section. But all this is prefaced by an expression of hope in the face of rising French militarism, a hope that sounds much like the one mocked as delusory in book 10 of *The Prelude*:

> The great exertions of France in military preparations have excited apprehensions, that, as, according to Mr. Burke, the country *"had been blotted out of the map of Europe,"* it had also no longer any place in the republic of letters. But the cruelties of the reign of terror are over: all the men of science and genius are not destroyed; and those who have survived the wreck, seem to be inspired with tenfold ardour, to supply the losses their country has sustained. The executive government co-operates

with them, and from the united effort of genius and power, whatever may be the political results of the present state of Europe, literature and science seem likely to be more fostered in France, in this, than in any former period.

On the 7th of last December, THE NEW ACADEMY OF ARTS AND SCIENCES, founded on a decree of the new constitution, was opened with proper ceremonies.[24]

In June 1794, Wordsworth told Mathews that despite the untoward developments of the Terror they must both keep their attention adverted to France so that they might not fail to notice "such of their regulations and decrees as are dictated by the spirit of Philosophy" (*EY*:128). Such is this decree, like the one that founded the educational program of which the Institute was to be the centerpiece. Indeed, the *Magazine*'s claims for the Institute can hardly be exaggerated. In the September number it is called "the most splendid and important establishment for the promotion of knowledge that perhaps ever existed"![25]

I can find no conclusive proof that Wordsworth saw any issues of the *Monthly Magazine* beyond those first eleven numbers. But in view of his known interest in the subject matter and the relative accessibility of the *Magazine* chances seem generally good that he did. We do know that in mid-April Losh sent Wordsworth "another large parcel of pamphlets," but this time the contents were unspecified (*EY*:186). Wordsworth also visited with Losh twice in late March (Reed *EY*:195). These facts are of interest because at the time Wordsworth received his back run from Losh, the *Magazine* was in the midst of a three-part report on the proceedings of the fourth sitting of the Institute. The third part, which appeared in the April number, opens up a discussion, the first to appear in English, of Tracy's plan to replace the ancient metaphysics with the new and improved science of ideology. It begins:

> Tracy, an associated member, communicated two memoirs on the analysis of thought, or rather on the faculty of thinking; which he also calls the faculty of perceiving.—He proposes, that the science which results from this analysis, be named ideology, or the science of ideas, in order to distinguish it from the ancient metaphysics. According to him, this science is almost entirely new, and possesses few evident and generally acknowledged truths, notwithstanding the labours of many celebrated men; and although, by proceeding upon facts, it is as susceptible of certitude as any of the sciences which are termed *exact*. He proceeds to observe, that this science has not been

hitherto investigated with method and freedom; and that, to this day, it has never been the direct object of the researches of any learned body.[26]

The emphasis on novelty and discovery, the demand for method and freedom, the presumption to certainty and exactitude, these all form crucial parts of *The Prelude*'s picture of the Revolution's late hypertheoretical phase. And the display of confidence in human learning and reason is for Wordsworth ample ground for the charge of vain presumption.

Students of Wordsworth's development have long known that some of the material in this portrait of destructive Theory had already been used in connection with *The Borderers*, especially in connection with the character of Rivers, the poem's moral anarchist. Because of lost manuscripts, the genesis of *The Borderers* is difficult to chronicle with precision. We can surmise, however, that Wordsworth was at work on some stage of the poem in April 1797, for on 28 May Dorothy writes Richard Wordsworth that the play is "nearly finished" (*EY*:186). It is in this connection that the second paragraph of the *Magazine*'s report on "ideology" is especially interesting:

> Tracy, with a view to execute this plan himself, exhibits, in these two memoirs, a summary table of such ideological truths, as he conceives to be evident. He maintains, that the faculty of thinking, as it exists within us, may be decomposed into five distinct and essential faculties: that of apprehending or perceiving, of remembering, of judging, of willing, and finally that of moving, which appears to him to be an integral part of the faculty of thinking, and necessary to its action. . . . He then proceeds to examine the relations of four of these sensations, with that of volition or willing; and concludes, that they are all partly dependent on, and partly independent of the latter. He next investigates the formation of our ideas, considered as knowledge or things known, and of our ideas considered as sentiments and passions. He remarks, that liberty is the faculty of acting agreeably to our own will, and thence infers, that liberty and happiness is but one and the same idea, considered with relation to the means, and with relation to the end.[27]

Both in its general tenor and in its particular terms this passage bears curiously striking resemblance to certain speeches Wordsworth added to his early drafts of *The Borderers*, probably sometime after February 1797. These passages seem to have been composed in order to give the play those political overtones that, although absent from the early drafts, allowed him to describe the play to Isabella Fenwick as being about the French Revolution (*PW* 1:343).

One such speech, for example, is the soliloquy by Rivers that opens act 1 in MS. B:

> Methinks
> It were a pleasant pastime to construct
> A scale and table of belief—as—thus—
> Two columns, one for passion, one for proof;
> Each rising as the other falls: and first,
> Passion a unit and *against* us—proof—
> Nay, we must travel in another path,
> Or we're stuck fast for ever; passion, then,
> Shall be a unit *for* us; proof—oh no
> We'll not insult thy majesty by time,
> And place—the where, the when, the how, and all
> The Dull particulars whose intrusion mars
> The dignity of demonstration.[28]

These speeches are often taken to refer more or less exclusively to Godwinism, even over the objections of scholars who have argued for the implausibility of this reading.[29] But there is nothing I know in Godwin's work that seems as close to this passage as Tracy's Baconian "summary table" and his division of his subject into "things Known," on the one hand, and "ideas considered as sentiments and passions," on the other.[30] When Rivers goes on in the same speech to ask the rhetorical question—"We dissect / The senseless body, and why not the mind?" (MS. B)—he shows a deeper affinity with the analytic method of "ideology," a method Tracy himself allies with the new medical work of his colleague Cabanis.[31]

Among the other of the politically loaded speeches added to the play after February 1797, the one most closely linked to *The Prelude* and the one most often cited as referring to Godwin is Rivers's speech to Mortimer later in act 3 in reference to Mortimer's presumed execution of old Herbert:

> . . . you have shown, and by a signal instance,
> How they who would be just must seek the rule
> By diving for it into their own bosoms.
> To-day you have thrown off a tyranny
> That lives but in the torpid acquiescence
> Of our emasculated souls, the tyranny
> Of moralists and saints and lawgivers
> By which they uphold their craft from age to age:

To have obeyed the only law that wisdom
Can ever recognize; the immediate law,
Flashed from the light of circumstances
Upon an independent Intellect.
Henceforth new prospects open on your path;
Your faculties should grow with the demand.

[MS. B]

There may be something of Godwinism echoed here, but surely the epitome of this doctrine lies in the work of the *French* theorists of the period. Not only do the tenets of Rivers's creed correspond closely with those of Ideology, but leaders like Lakanal were, as Godwin was not, directly involved in the task of justifying a regicide.[32]

Neither in *The Borderers* nor in any of the major poetry of the decade that follows it does Wordsworth ever identify his target as "ideology" in the more specific sense we have been considering here. Again, I do not claim to have *proven* that the Ideologue movement was his target or even, for that matter, that he knew of its existence. I do contend, however, that Wordsworth's real fears centered on developments in France, where Ideology had become, as one commentator puts it, "the approved doctrine of the government."[33] The Ideologue movement was, in effect, the apotheosis of the position Wordsworth came to fear most, and doctrines such as Godwinism would have been worrisome to him chiefly as symptoms of France's increasing influence in England. And while there is no mention of Ideology or the Ideologues by name in the major poetry, we must remember that Wordsworth is explicit about few such matters in this period.[34] Moreover, he may well be presuming on a better knowledge of the course of the Revolution than most readers now bring to his work. Writing book 10 of *The Prelude* in 1804, for example, he can refer to French affairs under the Directory as "well-known" (567).

Soon after the major period, when Wordsworth begins to express with greater openness his Burkean distrust of France and French "metaphysical politics," he does make a fairly pointed reference to the Ideologue movement. It occurs in that Burkish paragraph from the *Convention of Cintra* about the "pestilential philosophism of France" and the "infidel harpies" who propound it: "A Spanish understanding is a hold too strong to give way . . . to the pellets of logic which Condillac has cast in the foundry of national vanity, and tosses about at hap-hazard—self-persuaded that he is proceeding according to art. The Spaniards are a people with imagination" (*PrW* 1:333). The charge is couched just as we might have expected. Condillac's name is linked with the notion of delusory method and with the vice, familiar from Burke's *Letter to a Member of the National Assembly* and from book 5 of *The Prelude*, of French national vanity. Opposed to this pestilence, again as we might have expected, is "imagination," the power so-called because human language is incapable of giving it a better name. Indeed, for Wordsworth, imagination is the constant reminder that human language is incompetent to all the tasks that infidel harpies like Rousseau, Condillac, and Tracy would assign it. Imagination constantly admonishes us to put our faith in the divine word of which the human word can never be more than an imperfect echo.

IV

Since these suggestions about Wordsworth and Ideology lean heavily on the case for Wordsworth's deep concern about the spread of Continental schemes of systematic education, it may be appropriate to close this discussion with some additional remarks on that subject. One question that needs to be addressed, for example, is why, if they are so central, Wordsworth's aims have been so infrequently attended to. The answer, or part of it, is that Wordsworth must keep these aims half-hidden from the reader's eye. That Wordsworth did in fact attempt such an act of camouflage is suggested by the documents pertinent to the genesis of the five-book *Prelude*.

We have seen that the topic of education begins to occupy Wordsworth in earnest with his work on the Pedlar's biography in the period of the birth of his great plan (January to March 1798) and that evidence of a polemic against systematic education appears in MS. 18a, part of the very earliest work on *The Prelude*. This is the material later reworked for the discursive section that was probably intended to sum up the purport of the five-book *Prelude*. But how different is our sense of Wordsworth's purposes if we take at face value his way of introducing the discussion of contemporary education in the completed version of book 5:

> Rarely and with reluctance would I stoop
> To transitory themes, yet I rejoice,
> And, by these thoughts admonished, must speak out
> Thanksgivings from my heart that I was reared
> Safe from an evil which these days have laid
> Upon the children of the land—a pest
> That might have dried me up body and soul.
>
> [223–29]

This is a moment rather like the recognition of Burke's genius, later added to book 7, when the poet is surprised by his own conscience's admonishment that he must not play the ingrate's part. It is also, we are to believe, like the originary moment that gets the poem under way midway through book 1. In all these cases, the verse is supposed to be unpremeditated, wrung from the heart by sentiments of thanks and praise. We are to think it a product of second nature.

Matter and manner are perhaps even more intimately linked in book 5 than in the other cases, however, for it is especially crucial that Wordsworth not allow himself to appear too calculated in his attack on modern educators when his specific criticism of them is that they themselves rely too heavily upon calculation. These are, we recall, the sages "who in their prescience would control / All accidents." If Wordsworth the teacher were to make too clear or too coherent his polemic against modern educators, he might be suspected of falling prey to the evil he denounces. The reluctance that makes his "drift" scarcely obvious (291–92) is his defense against the charge of carrying out a programmatic assault on programs.[35]

Carrying out such an assault is of course roughly what Wordsworth *is* doing, a point which returns us to the paradox of traditionalism. The irony of Wordsworth's great plan of early 1798, what has been called his program for poetry, is that it bears within itself the seed of the evil it would stamp out. If he had been more like Blake, Wordsworth might have dealt with this paradox by insisting that he must create a system or be enslaved by a Frenchman's. Instead, he chooses to deny that what he offers is a system at all, or, alternatively to suggest that if it is a system it is not one of his own creation but of God's—a part of the providential design of human history. These "sages," Wordsworth asks in book 5, who would confine us down like engines to the roads they have made themselves,

> . . . when will they be taught
> That in the unreasoning progress of the world
> A wiser Spirit is at work for us,
> A better eye than theirs . . . ?

[383–86]

Wordsworth's drift evades ready detection all through *The Prelude*, as many of the poem's bewildered readers have attested. That this is especially so in book 5 is also a commonplace of the criticism. The explanation for the heightened sense of confusion in book 5 may simply be that straightforward or "reasoning" progress is more explictly represented as a negative value there than elsewhere in the poem. Indeed, Wordsworth's very idiom is meant to display the easy movement of a wanderer in second nature in contrast to the verbal action of system's child, whose cultivation has only succeeded in turning his linguistic world into a monstrous jungle: "Rank growth of propositions overruns / The stripling's brain; the path in which he treads / Is choked with grammars" (323–25).

To allow his pupil to wander—to "err" salutarily—the teacher himself must be something of a wanderer, never certain of his purpose or destination and always willing to heed the impulse for excursion. Both as agent and narrator, the figure of the wanderer dominates Wordsworth's self-representation in *The Prelude*. And in retrospect it seems inevitable that after developing a whole series of meandering narrators in the wake of *The Ruined Cottage* Wordsworth should return to his Pedlar, rechristen him the Wanderer, and make him chief spokesman in the poem that comes closest to realizing his project of early 1798. It seems equally inevitable that at the end of what Byron called the Wanderer's "rather long 'Excursion,'" through both the places of his countryside and the topics of his discourse, he wanders into a vision of his country's destiny that instantly turns into a dream of education:

> O for the coming of that glorious time
> When prizing knowledge as her noblest wealth
> And best protection, this imperial Realm,
> While she exacts allegiance, shall admit
> An obligation, on her part, to teach
> Them who are born to serve her and obey . . .
>   [Exc. 9:293–98]

Like Lakanal, the Wanderer envisions a future in which all citizens will be educated by the state, but the Wanderer's dream resembles the philosopher's dream only far enough to be perceived as its antithesis. For the Wanderer's dream is a national education in the service of hereditary monarchy, not of republican government, and its aim is not to teach citizens their rights but to teach duties to those "born to serve and obey." Similarly, the kind of knowledge that will be prized as the "noblest wealth / And best protection" of England's imperial realm is the antithesis of the knowledge whose dissemination was advocated under the aegis of Rousseau by the Committee on Public Instruction, as well as by Wordsworth himself, in the 1790s. Enlightenment knowledge is Promethean knowledge. It is a means of criticizing and regulating those social institutions such as authority, prejudice, and example that might be summed up under the name of tradition. The Wanderer's knowledge, on the other hand, is tradition itself. In his account, the Promethean figure is a "rude boy" who "mutinously knits his angry brow" and "lifts his wilful hand on mischief bent" and "turns the godlike faculty of speech / To impious use" (315–19). Contrary to the terms of the myth, in other words, the Wanderer makes the Promethean rebel the epitome of what happens when one does *not* possess knowledge, a point rather like the one made in that 1835 sonnet we considered back in chapter 1. When the curse of the young rebel "mounts to reach the State's parental ear" (326), the state must recognize it as a demand not so much for enlightenment or liberty as for discipline. The child's curse is not to be met with the "discipline of slavery." That, according to the Wanderer, is "unknown / Among us" in England (315–52). It is rather to be met with "the discipline of virtue":

> order else
> Cannot subsist, nor confidence, nor peace.
> Thus, duties rising out of good possessed,
> And prudent caution needful to avert
> Impending evil, equally require
> That whole people should be taught and trained.
> So shall licentiousness and black resolve
> Be rooted out, and virtuous habits take
> Their place; and genuine piety descend,
> Like an inheritance, from age to age.
>
> [353–62]

This kind of education is built not on the systematic promulgation of method and information, but on a principle of piety, the child's imitation of parental virtues—on authority, prejudice, example, and routine.

The contrast with the enlightened views of the French revolutionists is not left to inference. We recall that Lakanal had prophesied an educated Continental republic, stretching "to the Pyrenees and to the Alps," over the entire expanse of which "the art of teaching will be the same as in Paris."[36] The Wanderer surveys this same expanse for the purposes of invidious comparison with the glorious realm in which his kind of education takes place:

> Look! and behold, from Calpe's sunburnt cliffs
> To the flat margin of the Baltic sea
> Long-reverenced titles cast away as weeds;
> Laws overturned; and territory split,

Like fields of ice rent by the polar wind,
And forced to join in less obnoxious shapes
Which, ere they gain consistence, by a gust
Of the same breath are shattered and destroyed.
Meantime the sovereignty of these fair Isles
Remains entire and indivisible:
And, if that ignorance were removed, which breeds
Dark discontent, or loud commotion, each
Might still preserve the beautiful repose
Of heavenly bodies shining in their spheres.

[336–50]

The "genuine piety" that lies at the essence of English knowledge is supposed to descend from age to age "like an inheritance." It is to be preserved, therefore, in roughly the same way that England's "Long-reverenced titles" are to be preserved. The Wanderer's aspersions against a French-dominated continent shows that Wordsworth has joined "the admirers of the British Constitution," that he now sees "hereditary distinctions" as advancing rather than counteracting "the progress of human improvement." The Burkean overtones of the Wanderer's speech are unmistakable. Burke had praised England's pious traditionalism, lamented the loss of age-old titles, and criticized France's effort to divide its land into "less obnoxious shapes" (the newly drawn *départements*) than custom had determined. Wordsworth could not have written such a passage fifteen or even ten years before he published *The Excursion*. Yet the disorder the Wanderer points to across the Channel is fully implicit in Wordsworth's early attack on modern educators. It is the chaos he believes not bridged over, but brought on, by the mighty workmen of the age of Enlightenment.

Ten

The Role of Coleridge

> For the meanest of men has a Theory: and to think
> at all is to theorize.
>
> Coleridge, *The Friend*

ith these last remarks, we come to the end of the argument proper, having followed it through both Wordsworth's autobiographical epic and the literary career it purports to narrate. Much more might be said to fill out, support, and qualify this argument. More could be said, for example, about the conclusion that the one really pivotal point in Wordsworth's thinking about politics and culture occurs in early 1797. I have suggested that this crucial change is to be understood in relation to ongoing events in France, and I have tried to establish some of the diametrical differences that mark off the ideology of *The Ruined Cottage* and the great literary program it spawned from the positions Wordsworth had maintained from 1793 to 1795. One problem with this claim is that the notion of an ideological "pivot" may be charged with oversimplification. In defense of its use here I would simply say not only that it explains evidence otherwise unaccounted for but also that peripety is a structure that looms very large in the poetry Wordsworth writes after 1797. *The Prelude* is haunted throughout by that early eerie image of a child's rowboat abruptly reversing its course on a moonlit lake. After 1797, Wordsworth's mind seems ever to be seeing itself "turned round / As with the might of waters" (*Prel.* 1850 7:643–44).

I am less troubled by the hypothesis of an ur-turnabout, in other words, than by not offering a full discussion of how it might have occurred. Precious little documentation exists for the period of Wordsworth's residence at Racedown Lodge (September 1795–July 1797). The most useful documents we have for this period are surely the manuscripts for the successive early stages of his tragedy, *The Borderers*. Careful study of this play's genesis will, I think, corroborate what I have argued here. It will show that as Wordsworth reworks the Othello-Iago scenes he borrowed for the early core of his play, he makes them progressively more political and topical, less a pastiche of Shakespearean psychology.[1] Wordsworth seems to have composed the outcome of his tragic action first, a scene depicting a man isolated and anguished by the sense of having been perverted into the commission of a great sin—perhaps a projection of the poet's own emotional situation at Racedown. In the early manuscripts there is little to suggest either that this protagonist (the later Mortimer) is a regicide or that his perverter (the later Rivers) is a revolutionary theorist. It is not clear that Mortimer was initially intended to be the leader of a band of rebels. It is not even certain that Wordsworth initially meant to give the play the ideologically loaded title it came to bear. The earliest instance of its being called by this name is Dorothy's reference to its completion in a letter of June 1797 (*EY*: 189); in letters prior to this date the play is referred to simply as "a tragedy" (pp. 172, 177, 189). What seems to have happened sometime before June 1797 (it is hard to say just when) is a process rather like the one Frank Kermode describes for the development of Judas Iscariot out of the function of Betrayal in the Passion narratives: Wordsworth fleshes out the character of Perversion with material drawn from affairs in France, and in ways that bespeak a thoroughgoing disavowal of the convictions he announced to Watson and Mathews (and incorporated into *Salisbury Plain*) a few years earlier.[2]

I alluded briefly to these things in the last chapter. But it is not possible to do full justice to *The Borderers'* genesis in the present context. Since the manuscripts are so fragmentary and so difficult to date, every claim about them must be carefully prepared and circumscribed. The question of Godwin's influence has to be addressed and set in proper perspective. Many more literary sources than *Othello* need to be considered: not only other Shakespearean plays like *King Lear* and *Macbeth*, but also Schiller's *The Robbers*, English translations of Kotzebue's dramatic works, and fashionable gothic novels of the time. Indeed, a proper genetic analysis of *The Borderers* would have to trace Wordsworth's changing attitude toward the ideology of the entire literary context of the 1790s—toward those "frantic novels, sickly and stupid German Tragedies, and deluges of idle and extravagant stories in verse" that he denounced in the 1800 Preface (*PrW* 1:128).[3] I suspect that my argument would be improved by rigorous pursuit of these and related matters. Rather than trying to refine the argument I have made, however, I intend to use the remaining pages to consider what I take to be one of its major implications. Many studies of Wordsworth's poetry and thought begin with the role of Coleridge in the shaping of both. Since this study has begun elsewhere, and thereby drawn some other conclusions, it ought to confront the question of what these conclusions imply for that most celebrated of literary friendships.

It must be initially understood that Coleridge's Burke is much like Wordsworth's and that, like Wordsworth, Coleridge came to admire Burke immensely. No reader of Coleridge's later political writings in *The Friend* (1809–10), the *Lay Sermons* (1816-17) or *On the Constitution of the Church and State* (1830) could fail to recognize the debt. But for all his admiration of Burke's genius and for all his assimilation of Burkean opinions on politics and culture, Coleridge harbored a profound distrust of Burke. It had to do with what in *The Friend* he called "a certain inconsistency in his fundamental Principles."[4] Eager to avoid having his own charge of inconsistency confused with the one Paine brought against Burke (and young Wordsworth against Watson), Coleridge immediately explains that he does "not mean, that this great Man supported different Principles at different æras of his political Life. On the contrary, no Man was ever more like himself! From his first published Speech on the American Colonies to his last posthumous Tracts, we see the same Man, the same Doctrines, the same uniform Wisdom of *practical* Councils, the same Reasoning and the same Prejudices against all abstract grounds, against all deduction of Practice from Theory" (pp. 123–24). This is perhaps the first full attempt, after Burke's own, to save him from Paine's charges, and modern commentators tend to agree with Coleridge's line of defense. But we must proceed to what Coleridge does mean:

> The inconsistency to which I allude, is of a different kind: it is the want of congruity in the Principles appealed to in different parts of the same Work, it is an apparent versatility of the Principle with the Occasion. If his Opponents are Theorists, *then* every thing is to be founded on PRUDENCE, on mere calculations of EXPEDIENCY: and every Man is represented as acting according to the state of his own immediate self interest. Are his Opponents Calculators? *Then* Calculation itself is represented as a sort of crime. God has given us FEELINGS, and we are

to obey them! and the most absurd Prejudices become vener-
able, to which these FEELINGS have given Consecration.
. . . Burke himself defended these half contradictions, on the
pretext of balancing the too much on the one side by a too much
on the other. . . . He acted, therefore, under a perpetual System
of Compromise. . . .

    THE FRIEND, however, acts and will continue to act under
the belief, that the whole Truth is the best antidote to False-
hoods which are dangerous chiefly because they are half-truths:
and that an erroneous System is best confuted, not by an abuse
of Theory in general, nor by an absurd opposition of Theory to
Practice, but by a detection of the Errors in the particular
Theory. [p. 124]

Comparing this penetrating analysis of Burke with Wordsworth's later
praise of him for "Exploding upstart Theory," we discover an invaluable
key to understanding the intellectual relationship of the two poets. For
what Coleridge finds so unacceptable in Burke is just the sort of second-
nature dialectic that Wordsworth so much took to heart.

Until recently, Coleridge's influence on Wordsworth was generally
thought to be powerful—by some, decisive. In the last few years, Words-
worth's agreement with Coleridge on some fundamental issues, even at the
early stage of their friendship, has been called into question.[5] The many
studies of Wordsworth that have begun with Coleridge tend to see the
major poetry as deeply committed to metaphysical speculation and philo-
sophical system. Having discovered the problems in this characterization,
we are in a position to recognize that much of the responsibility for it can be
traced right back to Coleridge, who aspired to the condition of poet-
philosopher himself and, after deciding that he could not measure up,
urged his friend to accept the challenge. Coleridge frequently showed a
proprietary interest in Wordsworth's success with this challenge, as is well
known, and he tended to characterize that success to his friends and his
public very much on his own terms. Whether Coleridge's terms suit
Wordsworth's words remains to be seen. Their divergent responses to
Burke certainly give us reason to suspect some strong discrepancies over
philosophical questions. As we strengthen our sense of Burke's unacknowl-
edged role in forming Wordsworth's mature mind, we may have to make
corresponding adjustments in our sense of the acknowledged role of
Coleridge.

I

For an index to the role Coleridge plays in Wordsworth's life, we might examine the role he plays in the poem about that life. As speaker of *The Prelude*, we have seen, Wordsworth exemplifies something close to Burke's idea of the English mind disciplined, healthy, and triumphant.[6] But as addressee of the poem, conversely, Coleridge is made to represent the English mind in disarray, in illness, and in need of rescue. If Coleridge's role in the poem has not usually been so viewed by its readers, the reasons are not far to seek. After all, Wordsworth appeals to Coleridge more than once in the poem as a *partner* in his program to reform contemporary taste and to heal the impaired imagination of English readers. Coleridge is even thanked (in 10.905–41) for *his* role in healing Wordsworth. More typically, however, Wordsworth offers his words to Coleridge as a balm for the afflictions of an inquiring spirit. And this is especially true of those passages which occur at the major crossroads of the progress of composition: the passages which correspond to the beginning and end of the early two-book manuscript of *The Prelude* and the address to Coleridge on the occasion of his departure for Malta (in book 6), written at about the time Wordsworth decided to expand his poem to include the account of his excursion into Continental rationalism. To avoid confusion here, I want to emphasize that my argument concerns Coleridge's public role as a character in the poem. He was, we must remember, a writer of some reputation even as early as 1798–99. By 1804, the reviewer of the third edition of Coleridge's *Poems* could begin with this assertion: "The character of Mr. Coleridge, as a poet, is so well known, and his merit so fully acknowledged, that nothing more can be expected of us on announcing the third edition of his poems, than a few remarks suggested by comparison with the last."[7] In book 6, Wordsworth himself calls Coleridge's career a "march of glory" (328). And Wordsworth had every reason to expect that Coleridge's fame could only spread more widely in the coming years.

The question about Coleridge's mental health is first raised explicitly in the closing lines of book 2, the farewell to Coleridge which concluded the 1799 MS of *The Prelude*:

> Fare Thee well!
> Health, and the quiet of a healthful mind
> Attend Thee! seeking oft the haunt of men,
> And yet more often living with Thyself,

And for Thyself, so haply shall thy days
Be many, and a blessing to mankind.
                    [2: 479–84; cf. 1799, 2:509–14]

Though Wordsworth has tactfully emphasized that he and Coleridge "by different roads, at length have gained / The self-same bourne" (468–69), and though he insists that he writes to Coleridge in order to have a sympathetic ear for his own self-exploration, it is nonetheless true that Coleridge is addressed here as a man in trouble by a poet who thinks he can help. The "Coleridge" of *The Prelude* turns out to be one of those many Englishmen who have been traumatized by the "vast city" and by the failure of those revolutionary expectations which the "encreasing accumulation of men in cities" (*PrW* 1:128) helped to create.

That this intention governs the poem from the start is suggested by Wordsworth's bracketing of the entire 1799 manuscript of *The Prelude* within allusions to "Frost at Midnight." The first allusion occurs in the original poem's second sentence:

For this didst thou,
O Derwent, travelling over the green plains
Near my "sweet birth-place" didst thou beauteous Stream
Make ceaseless music through the night and day . . . ?
                    [1799, 1:5–8; cf. 1805, 1:276–79]

The second allusion introduces the concluding address to Coleridge from which I have just quoted:

Thou, my Friend, wast reared
In the great city 'mid far other scenes. . . .
                    [1799, 2:496–97; cf. 1805, 2:466–67]

To understand how these allusions function in *The Prelude*, we must recall their original context. "Frost at Midnight," the prototype for "Tintern Abbey," is a dramatization of the poet's reverie as he sits before his cottage fire, his babe in his arms, on a February night. The reverie is controlled by the lore which Coleridge knows about the "film" or "stranger" fluttering on the grate: it is supposed, as his note informs us, "to portend the arrival of some absent friend." Because the firm is "unquiet" on the grate, the speaker sees it as an image of himself,

a companionable form,
Whose puny flaps and freaks the idling Spirit
By its own moods interprets, every where

Echo or mirror seeking of itself,
And makes a toy of Thought.

[19–23]

To the complex spatial mirroring of this situation is then added a kind of temporal mirroring, as the speaker, still under the spell of the superstition of the "stranger," now calls to mind moments from his days at school in London when, "with most believing mind," he would similarly gaze "upon the bars / To watch the fluttering *stranger*." In such moments, moreover he would be carried back to still earlier times:

> . . . and as oft
> With unclosed lids, already had I dreamt
> Of my sweet birth-place, and the old church-tower,
> Whose bells, the poor man's only music, rang
> From morn to evening, all the hot Fair-day,
> So sweetly, that they stirred and haunted me
> With a wild pleasure, falling on mine ear
> Most like articulate sounds of things to come!

[26–33]

The reason why Wordsworth's allusion to this passage cannot be taken innocently is that Coleridge does not represent this reverie-within-a-reverie as a pleasant experience. It is rather an exercise in frustration, a case of unrelieved anxiety:

> So gazed I, till the soothing things, I dreamt,
> Lulled me to sleep, and sleep prolonged my dreams!
> Awed by the stern preceptor's face, mine eye
> Fixed with mock study on my swimming book:
> Save if the door half opened, and I snatched
> A hasty glance, and still my heart leaped up,
> For still I hoped to see the *stranger's* face,
> Townsman, or aunt, or sister more beloved,
> My play-mate when we both were clothed alike!

[34–43]

The movement of Coleridge's mind in this poem is meant to betray the profound self-*in*sufficiency that is acknowledged in the closing address to the infant Hartley, i.e., in the passage to which Wordsworth alludes at the conclusion of the 1799 MS of *The Prelude* (book 2 of the 1805 and 1850 versions):

My babe so beautiful! it thrills my heart
With tender gladness, thus to look at thee
And think that thou shalt learn far other lore,
And in far other scenes! For I was reared
In the great city, pent 'mid cloisters dim,
And saw nought lovely but the sky and stars.
But *thou*, my babe! shalt wander like a breeze
By lakes and sandy shores, beneath the crags
Of ancient mountain, and beneath the clouds,
Which image in their bulk both lakes and shores
And mountain crags: so shalt thou see and hear
The lovely shapes and sounds intelligible
Of that eternal language, which thy God
Utters, who from eternity doth teach
Himself in all, and all things in himself.

[48–64]

Wordsworth alludes to Coleridge's poignant confession of city-caused anxiety and emotional instability in order to offer himself to Coleridge as a man who already has wandered like a breeze by lakes and sandy shores, beneath mountains and clouds. He also offers himself as a poet who has learned "far other lore" than that which informs the mind of Coleridge, and he will go on in *The Prelude* to show how the power of this natural lore saved him from psychic harm in a time of trouble. If *The Prelude* can become "A power like one of Nature's," as Wordsworth hoped, it could then be a source of natural lore for debilitated urbanites who suffer what Coleridge suffers.

"Frost at Midnight" was written in February 1798, in the midst of the two-month period during which Wordsworth conceived his great program for poetry. *The Prelude* was begun later in that year. During the latter part of the winter of 1803–4, when Coleridge's health suffered its sharpest decline, Wordsworth worked hard on the poem to expand it to its planned five-book form. During his stay with the Wordsworths in December and January, Coleridge was, in W. J. Bate's words, "very ill, probably from an overdose of narcotics" and "suffering with repressed guilt" over his decision to leave the country.[8] At some point between 6 March and 29 March, just before Coleridge did leave the country, Wordsworth decided to expand the poem to include his own debilitating experiences in London and in France. Not long after this decision was taken, probably in late March (Reed *MY*:13, 257, 647), Wordsworth composed for *The Prelude* a second farewell to his

friend and auditor, the longest address of its kind in the entire poem. The
opening blessing recalls the conclusion of book 2:

> Speed thee well! divide
> Thy pleasure with us; thy returning strength
> Receive it daily as a joy of ours;
> Share with us thy fresh spirits, whether gift
> Of gales Etesian, or of loving thoughts.
>
> [6:256–60]

Following this reference to Coleridge's ill-health, Wordsworth's reminder
that *The Prelude* is written *for* Coleridge, like the earlier allusions to "Frost
at Midnight," cannot be taken naïvely:

> Throughout this narrative,
> Else sooner ended, I have known full well
> For whom I thus record the birth and growth
> Of gentleness, simplicity, and truth,
> And joyous loves that hallow innocent days
> Of peace and self-command.
>
> [265–74]

Such remarks as Wordsworth's parenthetical comment, "Else sooner
ended," are usually understood as expressions of the poet's modesty: he
would not go on at such length if he could not count on a friendly ear. But
this presumes that while Wordsworth may write *to* Coleridge, he writes *for*
himself. The wording of this passage, and the general rhetorical design of
the poem as a whole, would seem to contradict such an interpretation.
Coming where it does, the parenthetical remark may also imply, I think,
that he would not go on at such length if his friend's welfare—and by
extension the national welfare—did not require it.

In broaching this subject, here as in the earlier passage, Wordsworth
is diplomatic. He describes himself and Coleridge as "Twins almost in
genius and in mind." He suggests that they were "framed / To bend at last
to the same discipline." He even says that the two poets are "Predestin'd, if
two Beings ever were, / To seek the same delights, and have one health, /
One happiness" (6:265–69). But the tone of these comparisons ("if two
Beings ever were") is compensatory, and is so because the days of peace and
self-command recorded for Coleridge in *The Prelude* are Wordsworth's days.
If the discipline, health, and happiness of the two poets must in the end be
the same, they are nonetheless such as will be prescribed by Wordsworth—

or, to adopt his own fiction, such as will be prescribed by Nature and passed on through Wordsworth's agency.

The suspicion that Wordsworth's assertion of identity with Coleridge is compensatory can be borne out by a look at the way this passage develops. For Wordsworth immediately returns to a discussion of the differences between their lives, and again these differences are described along lines which make Coleridge look very like a representative of those "men in cities" where the human heart is sick:

> Of Rivers, Fields,
> And Groves, I speak to Thee, my Friend; to Thee,
> Who, yet a liveried School-Boy, in the depths
> Of the huge City, on the leaded Roof
> Of that wide Edifice, thy Home and School,
> Wast used to lie and gaze upon the clouds
> Moving in Heaven; or haply, tired of this,
> To shut thine eyes, and by internal light
> See trees, and meadows, and thy native Stream
> Far distant, thus beheld from year to year
> Of thy long exile.
>
> [274–84]

Clearly, these lines take us back to Christ's Church, and to Coleridge's self-criticism in "Frost at Midnight." It would be wrong to accuse Wordsworth of playing on Coleridge's sense of his own inadequacies in these lines. They seem too well intentioned to admit of such a reading. Yet Wordsworth does seem to be suggesting that he is more qualified to deal with Coleridge's situation than is Coleridge himself.

As we read on through the crucial passage, the resemblance of these "Twins almost" diminishes, and Wordsworth's condescension to Coleridge becomes less disguised. The next phase of Coleridge's career brings him to Cambridge, which Wordsworth, at this point in his narrative, is about to leave forever:

> From the heart
> Of London, and from Cloisters there Thou cam'st,
> And didst sit down in temperance and peace,
> A rigorous Student. What a stormy course
> Then follow'd. Oh! it is a pang that calls
> For utterance, to think how small a change
> Of circumstances might to thee have spared

A world of pain, ripen'd ten thousand hopes
For ever wither'd.

[289–96]

We do not yet know what small change of circumstances might have saved Coleridge from this world of pain and host of withered hopes. At this point we are told instead of Coleridge's characteristic mental activity during these years:

> I have thought
> Of Thee, thy learning, gorgeous eloquence,
> And all the strength and plumage of thy youth,
> Thy subtle speculations, toils abstruse
> Among the Schoolmen, and Platonic forms
> Of wild ideal pageantry, shap'd out
> From things well-match'd, or ill, and words for things,
> The self-created sustenance of a mind
> Debarr'd from Nature's living images,
> Compell'd to be a life unto itself,
> And unrelentingly possess'd by thirst
> Of greatness, love, and beauty.

[305–16]

In the *Essay on Morals* fragment of 1798, Wordsworth's elaborated his assertion that the error of moral philosophers "is the consequence of an undue value set upon that faculty which we call reason," by explaining that the "whole secret of this juggler's trick[?s] lies (not in fitting words to things (which would be a noble employment) but) in fitting things to words" (*PrW* 1:103). The description of Coleridge at Cambridge shows that Wordsworth thought his partner in *Lyrical Ballads* the victim of a similar error. And since these lines mimic the abstruse thought process they describe, the danger of Coleridge's undue value of "reason" is enacted before the reader's eyes. The crucial phrase "words for things" itself happens to mark the point where the passage's frame of reference breaks down. For while the main clause ("I have thought / Of . . .") controls the catalog of substantives up to and including "Platonic forms," the phrase "words for things" escapes such clear control because of the intervening participial phrase "shap'd out / From." The effect of this construction is that "words for things" is left unclaimed in the midst of this passage, where it illustrates the broken continuity of thought that occurs when words gain dominion over things.

What is that small change of circumstances that might have saved
Coleridge from such confusion and from its attendant emotional pain?
Simply Coleridge's coming to Cambridge a year earlier or Wordsworth's
leaving a year later, as we learn from the curious conclusion of this personal
address:

> Not alone,
> Ah! surely not in singleness of heart
> Should I have seen the light of evening fade
> Upon the silent Cam, if we had met,
> Even at that early time: I needs must hope,
> Must feel, must trust, that my maturer age,
> And temperature less willing to be mov'd,
> My calmer habits and more steady voice
> Would with an influence benign have sooth'd
> Or chas'd away the airy wretchedness
> That batten'd on thy youth. But thou hast trod,
> In watchful meditation thou has trod
> A march of glory, which doth put to shame
> These vain regrets; health suffers in thee; else
> Such grief for Thee would be the weakest thought
> That ever harbour'd in the breast of Man.
>
> [316–31]

Though these remarks strive for tact and delicacy, we cannot fail to
recognize their purport. Wordsworth first suggests that meeting Coleridge
at Cambridge would have meant a boon to himself, a friend with whom to
share the pleasures of the place. And he concludes with an expression of
shame for having spoken of Coleridge's life as if it needed apology or
redirection. Yet read in context, these words seem, again, compensatory.
Clearly, Coleridge's life as it is represented here does need redirection, and
in the crucial middle of this passage Wordsworth appears as a figure capable
of effecting it, a man of mature age, stolid temper, calm habits, and a steady
voice. It is the same voice, the same man, who addresses Coleridge now.
Although Wordsworth constructs a hypothetical meeting fourteen years
earlier, and although he couches his advice in the past conditional, no one
who keeps in mind the occasion of this address can miss the immediate
relevance of these remarks. Indeed, one sure clue to the present practical
aims of this passage lies in the urgency with which Wordsworth expresses
his conviction about his healing powers. He must hope, must feel, must
trust that he would have helped Coleridge, because he must believe that

such aid is still possible in the form of the present poem. And he must hope that such aid is also possible for his many English contemporaries whom he takes to be ailing in similar ways.

We should not fail to observe that the description of Coleridge's entanglement in rationalist philosophy closely resembles the description in book 9 of Wordsworth's own "subtle speculations" and "toils abstruse." Nor should we lose sight, however, of the crucial difference in situation: although Wordsworth eventually left off his sophomoric (as he came to regard it) quest for "the ground / Of moral obligation" and for its "rule . . . and sanction," Coleridge did not. The fact is that between 1798, when work on *The Prelude* was begun, and 1804, when this passage was composed, Coleridge became only more of a critical philosopher—and less of a poet—than ever. In December 1800, when Wordsworth had just completed "Michael," written to take the place of the poem ("Christabel") that Coleridge could not finish, Coleridge wrote to John Thelwall: "As to Poetry, I have altogether abandoned it, being convinced that I never had the essentials of poetic Genius, & that I mistook a strong desire for original power."[9] The true poet who has shown up the inadequacy of Coleridge's own talent is, of course, Wordsworth. Coleridge draws the comparison explicitly two days later in a letter to Francis Wrangham:

> Wordsworth & I have never resided together—he lives at Gras-
> mere, a place worthy of him, & of which he is worthy—and
> neither to Man nor Place can higher praise be given. . . . As to
> our literary occupations they are still more distant than our
> residences—He is a great, a true Poet—I am only a kind of
> Metaphysician.—He has even now sent off the last sheet of a
> second Volume of his Lyrical Ballads—. [p. 658]

The enterprise which had begun as a collaboration is now *"his* Lyrical Ballads." No longer partners, the two men are now, Coleridge suggests, miles apart—as far apart as Poet and Metaphysician. In the years to follow, Metaphysician is what Coleridge would remain, with another metaphysician, Kant, as his new spiritual partner. The extended version of *The Prelude* represents both the private fact and public gesture of Wordsworth's effort to woo Coleridge away from this dangerous influence, one which we have seen to be especially strong during the terrible winter (1803–4) of Coleridge's discontent.

As with so many other issues central to Wordsworth's thought, what he expresses by indirection in the major poetry of the great decade he puts more straightforwardly in remarks made later. On the question of

Coleridge's failure of discipline, Wordsworth begins to speak more openly
in letters of 1809. In late May of that year he wrote to Daniel Stuart:

> Of the Friend and Coleridge, I hear nothing, and am sorry to say
> I hope nothing. It is I think too clear that Coleridge is not
> sufficiently master of his own efforts to execute anything which
> requires a regular course of application to one object. I fear
> so—indeed I am assured that it is so—to my great sorrow.
> [*MY*:350]

In a letter written two days later to Thomas Poole, Wordsworth spoke more
frankly and "in the most sacred confidence" of his onetime collaborator:

> I give it to you as my deliberate opinion, formed upon proofs
> which have been strengthening for years, that he neither will
> nor can execute any thing of important benefit either to himself
> his family or mankind. Neither his talents nor his genius
> mighty as they are nor his vast information will avail him
> anything; they are all frustrated by a derangement in his intel-
> lectual and moral constitution—In fact he has no voluntary
> power of mind whatsoever, nor is he capable of acting under any
> *constraint* of duty or moral obligation. [p. 352]

The remarks to Poole are especially useful in their suggestion that Words-
worth had been gathering evidence of Coleridge's presumed debility of
character "for years." Wordsworth makes explicit the other important
feature of *The Prelude*'s implicit portrait of Coleridge in an obiter dictum
recorded by Graves in 1831:

> Wordsworth, as a poet, regretted that German metaphysics had
> so much captivated the taste of Coleridge, for he was frequently
> not intelligible on the subject; whereas, if his energy and his
> originality had been more exerted in the channel of poetry, an
> instrument of which he had so perfect a mastery, Wordsworth
> thought he might have done more permanently to enrich the
> literature, and to influence the thought of the nation, than any
> man of the age.[10]

Coleridge's moral and intellectual derangement, on the one hand, and his
taste for German metaphysics, on the other, would appear to be mutually
linked—each is named as the cause of Coleridge's failure to serve his fellows
in a way commensurate with his talents.[11]

When we compare Wordsworth's attitude toward Coleridge in 1804
and in 1809, the most concrete difference to emerge is that at the earlier

date, not yet having despaired of Coleridge's condition, Wordsworth was still writing poetry that tried to do something about the problem—and by extension the problem of others like him. One poem from the major period that straightforwardly addresses the issue of discipline and that obliquely relates it to "German metaphysics" is the "Ode to Duty," a lyric whose composition seems to have been intimately involved with Coleridge and his troubles. In order to consider how this poem takes its moral stand, we must clear up certain misconceptions that have cropped up around it in recent years. Harold Bloom, for example, proceeding from a mistaken assumption about the poem's date, argues that the "Ode" represents a betrayal of Wordsworth's "myth of Nature."[12] "The Nature of *Tintern Abbey* and *The Prelude*," according to Bloom, "is an unrestrained effluence from a fountain beyond the relevance of traditional morality." And this is the nature with which Bloom sees the poet of the "Ode" severing relations: "The youth who moved with the wind's freedom, whose heart was an impulse to itself and reciprocated Nature's promptings, now supplicates for the control of 'a rod to check the erring, and reprove'" (pp. 198–99).

Bloom's contrast of the poet's youth and maturity derives from the thumbnail autobiography which the speaker of the "Ode" provides midway along:

> I, loving freedom, and untried;
> No sport of every random gust,
> Yet being to myself a guide,
> Too blindly have reposed my trust:
> And oft, when in my heart was heard
> Thy timely mandate, I deferred
> The task, in smoother walks to stray;
> But thee I now would serve more strictly, if I may.

These lines do bear an important relation to "Tintern Abbey" and *The Prelude*, but not the one that Bloom describes. For what is recorded here is not the renunciation of the mind responsible for those poems. It is the very same sort of renunciation that is made *in* those poems, the renunciation of that earlier mind for which Nature was "all in all" and Nature's colors and forms an "appetite." Like "Tintern Abbey" and *The Prelude*, in other words, the "Ode to Duty" rededicates the poet to a life of disciplined mental conduct; far from renouncing what these poems stand for, the "Ode" may thus be Wordsworth's most concise articulation of it.

Further, what we know of the chronology of composition corroborates such a reading, at least with respect to the "Ode's" relation to *The Prelude*.

The work of Moorman and Reed indicates that the "Ode" was probably composed not in 1805, as Bloom states, but sometime from January to March of 1804 (Moorman *LY*:4–5; Reed *MY*: 36). Thus, if Moorman's and Reed's surmises are right, then the composition of the Ode actually predates most of *The Prelude*. Just as important, though, is the probability that the "Ode" was composed in the same months during which Wordsworth wrote the Introduction (1–270) of book 1, for the poet represented in the "Ode" would thus appear to be a character very similar to the poet whose triumph of discipline is recorded in the second half of book 1 (and in the opening of the two-book manuscript of 1799).

Geoffrey Hartman's discussion of this poem and its relation to the rest of Wordsworth's major work redresses some of what is wrong with Bloom's reading but falls into another, related error. Bloom had described the "Ode" as a retreat into "traditional morality." Hartman, anxious to show that the true subject of the "Ode" is the "humanization of the spirit," argues that the poet has internalized an external moral system. Hartman saves *his* Wordsworth, in other words, by explaining that everything in the "Ode" depends on the inner strength required by the poet's voluntary dedication of himself to the household chores of life: "Take away the idea of voluntary obedience, substitute for it a decision to rely on external authority, and you make nonsense of Wordsworth as you do of Milton." Stated succinctly, Hartman's point about the "Ode" is that "the emphasis remains on the inner man."[13] The problem with this attractive reading of the poem is that it seeks to retain precisely that dichotomy between the volition of the "inner man" and the moral constraints of external authority which the poem itself means to transcend. The speaker's hope in the poem is for a "second Will more wise" than the rational will which seeks "in the school of pride, / For 'precepts over dignified.'" Thus, when one reaches the goal at which the poem aims, acting according to one's volition means invariable conformity to moral law just as the activity of flowers and stars conforms to natural law:

> Flowers laugh before thee on their beds
> And fragrance in thy footing treads;
> Thou dost preserve the stars from wrong;
> And the most ancient heavens, through Thee, are fresh and
>   strong.
>
> To humbler functions, awful Power!
> I call thee: I myself commend
> Unto thy guidance from this hour;

Oh, let my weakness have an end!
Give unto me, made lowly wise,
The spirit of self-sacrifice;
The confidence of reason give;
And in the light of truth thy Bondman let me live![14]

To the extent that the condition described here is realized, the distinction between inner and outer ceases to be important. In terms of Kantian ethics, such action may be action according to duty (*pflichtmässig*) but is not action *from* duty (*aus Pflicht*) and therefore cannot properly be called morally good. To employ another of Kant's distinctions, insofar as this "second Will" becomes a matter of *inclination*, it ceases to be, strictly speaking, *rational* (Wordsworth wants only the *confidence* of reason in his judgments), and thus ceases to be a matter of Kantian will, ceases to be what Hartman calls "voluntary obedience." [15]

Why bring Kant's *Foundations of the Metaphysics of Morals* to bear on Wordsworth's modest Horatian ode? According to Reed, the "Ode" was probably composed in the weeks following Coleridge's departure from Dove Cottage on 14 January 1804; a draft of the poem was completed in time to be sent off to Coleridge in mid-March. Upon leaving Grasmere, Coleridge had asked Wordsworth for copies of all his unpublished poetry to take with him to Malta (he would leave London for Portsmouth on 27 March). Coleridge was thus very much on Wordsworth's mind in these hectic and productive weeks during which he revised and composed the verse that Dorothy and Mary copied into the manuscript (MS. M) to be sent to Coleridge in London. Time being so short in these weeks, a wholly new composition, such as the "Ode to Duty" seems to be, is likely to have been written *for* Coleridge. Secondly, the "Ode" was written after an extended period of intellectual intimacy *with* Coleridge, who had been visiting the Wordsworths for nearly a month when he left them on 14 January (he had arrived on 20 December). What would they have discussed in their long talks at this time? If Coleridge had had any say in the matter, and surely he would have, one of the central topics would have been ethics, for the *Notebooks* show how thoroughly Coleridge's thought was preoccupied with ethical questions during this winter. And the *Notebooks* show further that the particular text which most actively engaged him was Kant's *Foundations*.[16]

Coleridge wrestled long and hard with this difficult work, and he did not accept a number of Kant's conclusions. But one of the passages he singled out for special praise was Kant's early argument against thinkers such as Hutcheson and Hume who treated moral problems empirically:

Here then we see philosophy brought to a critical position, since it has to be firmly fixed, notwithstanding that it has nothing to support it either in heaven or earth. Here it must show its purity as absolute dictator of its own laws, not the herald of those which are whispered to it by an implanted sense or who knows what tutelary nature. Although these may be better than nothing yet they can never afford principles dictated by reason, which must have their source wholly *a priori* and thence their commanding authority, expecting everything from the supremacy of the law, and the due respect for it, nothing from inclination, or else condemning the man to self-contempt and inward abhorrence.

Thus every empirical element is not only quite incapable of being an aid to the principle of morality, but is even highly prejudicial to the purity of morals: for the proper and inestimable worth of an absolutely good will consists just in this, that the principle of action is free from all influence of contingent grounds, which alone experience can furnish. We cannot too much or too often repeat our warning against this lax and even mean habit of thought which seeks for its principle amongst empirical motives and laws; for human reason in its weariness is glad to rest on this pillow. . . . [17]

If Coleridge's endorsement of this passage is as wholehearted as it seems to be from the December entries in the *Notebooks*, then it is plausible—even likely—that he would have advanced such a position during his long talks with Wordsworth later in that month. And if the "Ode" is Wordsworth's answer to Coleridge, as again seems a reasonable assumption, then it surely argues against Kant's absolute rationalist distinction between will and inclination in favor of the concept of the "second Will" which coincides with inclination and derives from experience. This is the faculty whose work is responsible for *The Prelude*, a will become a part of one's nature. It is the ideal held up as exemplary both to Coleridge and to the readers for whom he stands. [18]

III

Just as Coleridge's plight in early 1804 is the occasion of the "Ode to Duty," so also is it the occasion of the decision to expand the five-book *Prelude* to include Wordsworth's experience in revolutionary France. In the thirteen-book poem, Wordsworth not only shows the discipline of his mind (the task of the five-book poem) but also recounts how urbanization and French theory almost doomed that mind. One might immediately object that, like Wordsworth himself, Coleridge had long since rejected French philosophy and politics. In a letter of 10 March 1798 to his brother George, for example, Coleridge had recorded his disenchantment with the Revolution in no uncertain terms. "A man's character," he explained, referring to his reputation as "a Democrat and a Seditionist," "follows him long after he has ceased to deserve it—but I have snapped my squeaking baby-trumpet of Sedition & the fragments lie scattered in the lumber-room of Penitence."[19] Anxious to distinguish himself from "those men in England and in France, who have modestly assumed to themselves the exclusive title of Philosophers & Friends of Freedom," Coleridge avers: "If I know my own opinions, they are utterly untainted with French Metaphysics, French Politics, French Ethics, & French Theology" (p. 395). The question to consider, then, might be put this way: would Wordsworth have interpreted Coleridge's later fascination with Kant as a sign that Coleridge simply did *not* know his own opinions at this time, and that the French influence on his mind survived in ways of which he was unaware.[20]

In the absence of direct statement by Wordsworth himself, the best historical evidence available would probably be from contemporary responses to Kant's work. The first two books on Kant in English (both written by pupils of the philosopher at Königsberg) were reviewed at some length in the *Monthly Review*. Both reviewers complain about Kant's language in terms which recall Wordsworth's criticism of Coleridge in book 6. Said the anonymous author of the first review: "this philosopher, like many of his predecessors, has bewildered himself in a labyrinth of words."[21] More to the point for us here is the reference in the second review to "the notorious Gallicanism of [Kant's] opinions, which must endear him to the patriotism of the philosophers of the Lyceum."[22]

Kant's writings of the 1790s, chiefly applications of his philosophical principles to history, politics, and theology, would in themselves have constituted sufficient justification for suggesting Kant's appeal to the young philosophers of the Lycée. *Religion within the Limits of Reason Alone* (1793), *The End of All Things* (1794), *Perpetual Peace* (1795), and *The Strife of the Faculties* (1798) all show the signs of Kant's sympathetic attention to affairs in France.[23] In *Religion within the Limits of Reason Alone*, for example, a book for which he was censured by Frederick William II, Kant wrote as follows:

> I grant that I cannot really reconcile myself to the following expressions made use of even by clever men: "A certain people (engaged in a struggle for civil freedom) is not yet ripe for freedom"; "The bondmen of a landed proprieter are not ready

for freedom"; and hence, likewise, "Mankind in general is not yet ripe for freedom of belief." For according to such a presupposition, freedom will never arrive, since we cannot *ripen* to this freedom if we are not first of all placed therein (we must be free in order to make purposive use of our power in freedom). The first attempts will indeed be crude and usually will be attended by a more painful and more dangerous state than that in which we are still under the orders and also the care of others; yet we never ripen with respect to reason except through *our own* efforts (which we can make only when we are free).[24]

Michelet no doubt had a passage much like this one in mind when, a half-century later, he composed his rapturous, metaphoric account of Kant's response to the Revolution:

> In a remote region of the northern seas, there then existed an extraordinary, powerful creature, a man, or rather a system, a living monument of scholastic science, callous and impenetrable. . . . For sixty years, this perfectly abstract being, devoid of all human connection, had gone out precisely the same hour, and, without speaking to anybody, had taken precisely the same walk for a stated number of minutes; just at we see in the old townclocks, a man of iron come forth, strike the hour and then withdraw. Wonderful to relate, the inhabitants of Koenigsberg (who considered this as an omen of the most extraordinary events) saw this planet swerve and depart from its long habitual course. . . . They followed him and saw his hastening towards the west, to the road by which they expected the courier from France.[25]

Michelet is here adapting an old legend about Kant to suggest that it was the events of 1789 which, by making Kant look to France, first turned Kant outward from his life of regimented introspection in Königsberg. But the fact is that Kant had been "looking to France" for quite a while by the time the Bastille fell, and Taylor intimates as much when he says that the "Notorious Gallicanism" of Kant's opinions will endear him to the patriots of the Lycée (i.e., that the Gallicanism *preceded* the Revolution). Indeed, the original legend on which Michelet draws is itself instructive in this respect. It is, as Ernst Cassirer tells it, "the story that he who was a model of punctuality, and accustomed to regulate his daily routine by the clock, departed only once from this regular routine. When Rousseau's *Emile* appeared, fascinated by the study of the work in which he had become absorbed, Kant gave up his daily walk."[26] *Emile*, we must bear in mind, appeared in 1762, and there is evidence that Kant attended carefully to Rousseau's earlier social and political writings as well.[27]

Like many historians before him and since, Michelet sees Kant as a genuine sympathizer with the revolutionary cause in France, but because Michelet draws a sharp distinction between metaphysics and politics, he presents this sympathy as an effect of the "New Religion" of the 1790s. For observers such as Wordsworth and Burke, on the other hand, who came to see the Revolution as issuing directly from Enlightenment rationalism, the career of Kant prior to the Revolution would have constituted sufficient grounds for considering even those philosophic works that were not *engagé* as potentially very dangerous. Right from the start of his major period in print, Kant wrote explicitly and approvingly of the enlightened mind of his times. In the Preface to the first edition of the *Critique of Pure Reason* (1781), for example, we read:

> Our age is, in especial degree, the age of criticism, and to criticism everything must submit. Religion through its sanctity, and law-giving through its majesty, may seek to exempt themselves from it. But they then awaken just suspicion, and cannot claim the sincere respect which reason accords only to that which has been able to sustain the test of free and open examination.[28]

Kant plainly sees the *Critique* itself as the product of "the age which refuses to be any longer put off with illusory knowledge": reason is now called upon "to undertake anew the most difficult of all its tasks, namely, that of self-knowledge, and to institute a tribunal which will assure to reason its lawful claims, and dismiss all groundless pretensions, not by despotic decrees, but in accordance with its own eternal and unalterable laws. This tribunal is no other than the *critique of pure reason*." (He here emphasizes that he means by this a critique of reason "in respect of all knowledge after which it may strive *independently of all experience*" [p. 9; Kant's italics].) The interior tribunal of reason to which he commends all judgments appears to be the same tribunal that lords over Wordsworth's interior reign of terror, the nadir and crisis of his soul: "Thus I fared, / Dragging all passions, notions, shapes of faith, like culprits to the bar, suspiciously / Calling the mind to establish in plain day / Her titles and her honours . . ." (10:889–93).

Perhaps George Herbert Mead goes too far in presenting Kant as *the* philosopher of the French Revolution.[29] Such a claim must at any rate be

qualified along lines suggested by Karl Mannheim, who, discussing gener-
ally the relation between philosophy and political life, uses Kant's relation
to the Revolution as his example:

> We do not mean that every philosopher is nothing but a
> political propagandist, or even that he himself is necessarily
> committed consciously to a certain political point of view. A
> philosopher, or even an isolated thinker, may be quite unaware
> of the political implications of his thought, the social genesis of
> which can be traced to a special type of political activity. Kant,
> for example, is the philosopher of the French Revolution, not
> primarily because he was in full sympathy with its political
> aims, but because the form of his thought (as reflected for
> example in his concept of the *ratio*, in his belief in gradual
> progress, in his general optimism, and so on), is of the same
> brand as that which was a dynamic force behind the activities of
> the French revolutionaries. It is the same form of active penetra-
> tion into the world. It is this which unconsciously produces the
> categories and ways of interpretation common to those who are
> bound by the mutual bond of a common style of thought.[30]

If Kant's Critical Philosophy is not what we normally call political prop-
aganda (and obviously it is not), then clearly Coleridge's admiration for this
philosophy does not make him a political propagandist. More clearly still,
Wordsworth does not represent him as such in *The Prelude*. The terms of
Mannheim's explanation, however, return us to Coleridge's letter to
George and to the phrasing of our initial question: that is, would Words-
worth have interpreted Coleridge's fascination with Kant as a sign Cole-
ridge did not know his own mind when he claimed to have overthrown the
influence of France? The answer, I think, is yes. From Wordsworth's point
of view, insofar as Coleridge remained Metaphysician and kept company
with Kant, he would remain the victim of an ideology—roughly, what we
have called "Ideology"—whose moral, political, and psychological con-
sequences he did not comprehend.

IV

Coleridge's answer to Wordsworth was a long time coming. I do not mean
the answer of Coleridge the Poet, for the poems Coleridge wrote in response
to Wordsworth's Intimations Ode ("Dejection: An Ode") and to *The Prelude*
itself ("To William Wordsworth") do not fully represent the position of
Coleridge the Metaphysician.[31] The Metaphysician's hour would come
much later, after the falling out of the two friends, in Coleridge's own great

autobiographical work, *Biographia Literaria*. That the *Biographia* is the autobiography of the Metaphysician is clear from Coleridge's choice of Kant as the greatest influence on the development of his thought: "The writings of the illustrious sage of Königsberg, the founder of the Critical Philosophy, more than any other work, at once invigorated and disciplined my understanding" (*BL* 2:99). In March of 1798, when the plans for *The Recluse* and for *Lyrical Ballads* were taking shape, Coleridge wrote to Cottle about "The Giant Wordsworth—God love him!" In the *Biographia*, a new figure towers over Coleridge's intellectual life:

> The originality, the depth, and the compression of the thoughts; the novelty and subtlety, yet solidity and importance of the distinctions; the adamantine chain of the logic; and I will venture to add (paradox as it will appear to those who have taken their notion of IMMANUEL KANT from Reviewers and Frenchmen) the *clearness* and *evidence* of the "CRITIQUE OF THE PURE REASON"; of the "JUDGMENT"; and of his "RELIGION WITHIN THE BOUNDS OF PURE REASON," took possession of me as with a giant's hand. [*BL* 1:88]

Interestingly, in his praise of the new Colossus, Coleridge is careful to dissociate the true Kant from what the French have made of him and to defend him against the charge of verbal mystification.

Coleridge is by no means without charges of his own to make against those who oppose the procedures and conclusions of the Critical Philosophy. Viewed in context, these charges begin to look like an answer to Wordsworth along the very lines of the criticisms implicit in *The Prelude*. Coleridge's controlling purpose through most of the *Biographia* is to explain what he describes as seventeen years of "persecution" at the hands of reviewers and critics. After showing why he "cannot attribute this persecution to personal dislike, or to envy, or to feelings of vindictive animosity" on the part of his critics, he proposes to consider the suggestion that the problem stems from his habits of intimacy with Southey and Wordsworth (*BL* 134–39). He deals with his association with Southey in chapter 3 and, having "wandered . . . from" but not forgotten his "object in view," turns to Wordsworth in chapter 4 (1:50). In the chapters that follow, Coleridge is not reluctant to mention points of concurrence between his thought and Wordsworth's, or slow to claim credit for his own influence on Wordsworth, but most of the rest of the *Biographia* represents his dissociation of himself from, and his criticism of, Wordsworth's poetry and its philosophical bases.

We need not be concerned so much with chapters 14 to 22, in which Coleridge deals explicitly with Wordsworth's poetry, as with chapters 5 to 13, which offer an extended critique of associationism and look forward to the (indefinitely postponed) *true* account of the imagination. For in these chapters, Coleridge attacks just the sort of theoretical position on which Wordsworth takes his stand in the 1800 Preface, the document Coleridge says is responsible for the hostile reception to Wordsworth's verse (beginning of chapter 4—1:50–51). The crucial passage in the Preface, we recall, details the process by which such habits of association are formed in the poet's mind that simply "by obeying blindly and mechanically the impulses of those habits," he is "necessarily" assured of writing poetry with a worthy and redeeming purpose. Wordsworth's term "necessarily" indicates that the Preface rests on what Coleridge called "the doctrine of Necessity," which Hazlitt, in *The Spirit of the Age*, also attributes to Wordsworth (*CWWH* 11:17). We know that Coleridge had rejected this doctrine as early as January 1796, and his letters suggest that, in those years immediately following *Lyrical Ballads*, it was under this rubric of "Necessitarianism" that he and Wordsworth carried on their philosophical dispute. In those middle chapters of the *Biographia*, Coleridge launches a public attack on this same doctrine, though he does not at this time call it Necessitarianism and does not explicitly attribute it to Wordsworth.[32]

Coleridge's chief concern in these chapters is to save the concepts of the will and the "sciential reason" from the philosophy of "blind mechanism" in which their place is merely incidental:

> If in *ourselves* there be no such faculties as those of the will, and the scientific reason, we must either have an *innate* idea of them, which would overthrow the whole system; or we can have no idea at all. The process, by which Hume degraded the notion of cause and effect into a blind product of delusion and habit, into the mere sensation of proceeding life (nisus vitalis) associated with the images of the memory; this same process must be repeated to the equal degradation of every fundamental idea in ethics or theology. [*BL* 1:83]

Take away the derogatory terms ("degraded," "delusion," and "degradation") and the second sentence in this passage becomes a reasonably fair synopsis of Wordsworthian epistemology as it is described in the 1800 Preface and illustrated in, say, "Tintern Abbey." What Coleridge sees at the center of this empirical psychology is "the assumption, that the will and, with the will, all acts of thought and attention are parts and products of this blind mechanism, instead of being distinct powers, whose function it is to controul, determine, and modify the phantasmal chaos of association" (*BL* 1:81). And what Coleridge sees as the problem with such an assumption is that it subordinates "final to efficient causes in the human being." If we turn back once more to the Preface, we will recall that Wordsworth contrived to represent his poetry's purpose as deriving blindly and mechanically from his habits of association precisely because he wanted to gain for himself a kind of poetic authority that would transcend the conscious intention of the rational will. Viewed in the terms of the *Biographia*, Wordsworth's account merely begs the question by subordinating final causes to efficient.

This point becomes clearer when Coleridge, too, turns his attention to the acts of writing and reading:

> According to this hypothesis the disquisition, to which I am at present soliciting the reader's attention, may be as truly said to be written by Saint Paul's church, as by *me*: for it is the mere motion of my muscles and nerves; and these again are set in motion from external causes equally passive, which external causes stand themselves in interdependent connection with every thing that exists or has existed. Thus the whole universe co-operates to produce the minutest stroke of every letter, save only that I myself, and I alone, have nothing to do with it, but merely the causeless and *effectless* beholding; for it, is neither an act nor an effect; but an impossible creation of a *something-nothing* out of its very contrary! It is the mere quick-silver plating behind a looking-glass; and in this alone consists the poor worthless I! The sum total of my moral and intellectual intercourse, dissolved into its elements, is reduced to *extension, motion, degrees of velocity*, and those diminished *copies* of configurative motion, which forms what we call notions, and notions of notions. . . .
>
> The inventor of the watch, if this doctrine be true, did not really invent it; he only looked on, while the blind causes, the only true artists, were unfolding themselves. [*BL* 1:82]

Since Coleridge means to expose the concealed error in the position he describes, his account is couched in loaded terms. Wordsworth certainly could not have subscribed to any position so represented. At no point, for example, could Wordsworth have accepted the idea that the "I" has "nothing to do with" literary composition, that it is mere quicksilver plating behind the looking glass. Wordsworth would, on the other hand, have assented wholeheartedly to what Coleridge says in the first part of this ironic sentence: that "the whole universe co-operates to produce the minutest stroke of every letter." Moreover, he would not have agreed with Coleridge that such a belief leads to the annihilation of the "I." Coleridge sees associationism as a reduction of human affairs to material affairs, or action to "mere motion"; Wordsworth, to go back to "Tintern Abbey," insists that the same force impels all thinking things *and* all objects of all thoughts, and that this force is at once a motion *and* a spirit. Wordsworth wants to have it both ways; Coleridge insists that, to have a mind at all, one must use it to reason and decide.

Coleridge presents as self-evidently absurd his account of the watch-maker who "looked on, while the blind causes, the only true artists, were unfolding themselves." Yet it captures something of the poet's characteristic posture in much of Wordsworth's most important poetry. The watch-maker's attitude is one of "wise passiveness," the attitude at work not only in the self-exploration of "Tintern Abbey," but also in "Resolution and Independence," where the "blind thoughts, I knew not, nor could name" unfold before the poet's inward eye to become the story of the encounter with the Leech-Gatherer, and in those moments of *The Prelude* where Wordsworth seems to stand aside and watch unconscious forces take over the poem. The symbolic apotheosis of the attitude occurs in the iconography of the Snowden passage in book 13, where the eye of the conscious mind looms over the blind rumblings of unconscious activity below. Its clearest discursive summary occurs perhaps in book 11, where Wordsworth writes that in his time of distress he was saved from total despair by "the laws of things which lie / Beyond the reach of human will or power" (97–98), the same laws, presumably, whose "blind restraint" he had mistakenly thought to rise above on the strength of "independent intellect" (10:827–30).

Even in 1815, Wordsworth's position was still, from Coleridge's point of view, in error. Indeed, Coleridge's discussion of associationism is bracketed by references to Wordsworth's 1815 Preface (even as the 1798–99 *Prelude* is bracketed by allusion to "Frost at Midnight"). The first reference comes at the end of chapter 4, where he actually *commends* Wordsworth for having shown that William Taylor's specification of "imagination" and "fancy" is "both insufficient and erroneous" (*BL* 1:64). True to his stated intention in this part of the *Biographia*, however, Coleridge quickly adds that Wordsworth's account differs from his own:

> The explanation which Mr. Wordsworth has himself given will
> be found to differ from mine chiefly, perhaps, as our objects are
> different. It could scarely indeed happen otherwise, from the

advantage I have enjoyed of frequent conversation with him on a subject to which a poem of his own first directed any attention, and my conclusions concerning which he had made more lucid to myself by many happy instances drawn from the operation of natural objects on the mind. But it was Mr. Wordsworth's purpose to consider the poetry, and from the different effects to conclude their diversity in kind; while it is my object to investigate the seminal principle, and then from the kind to deduce the degree. My friend has drawn a masterly sketch of the branches with their *poetic* fruitage. I wish to add the trunk and even the roots, as far as they left themselves about ground and are visible to the naked eye of our common consciousness. [p. 64]

Coleridge seems to be suggesting here that the two writers share an understanding of imagination, but are interested in two distinct aspects of its anatomy: Wordsworth the poetic and Coleridge the metaphysical, Wordsworth the fruit of the tree and Coleridge the roots. The differences in interest may imply differences in approach or method. Wordsworth works from the manifestations of imagination and fancy in poetry and proceeds inductively from the differences in effects to differences in kind; Coleridge's procedure, the reverse of Wordsworth's, is to investigate the "seminal principle" first, and "from the kind to deduce the degree." Yet these differences in approach or method seem nowise crucial here: as Coleridge moves forward into his investigation of this "seminal principle," we are left with the understanding that the two approaches are philosophically complementary.

At the end of this "investigation," however, when Coleridge pauses to return to Wordsworth's discussion in the 1815 Preface, we discover that the differences of approach to the thing (imagination) lead to different versions of the thing itself. I quote from the final paragraph of chapter 12:

I shall now proceed to the nature and genesis of the imagination; but I must first take leave to notice, that after a more accurate perusal of Mr. Wordsworth's remarks on the imagination, in his preface to the new edition of his poems, I find that my conclusions are not so consentient with his as, I confess, I had taken for granted. In an article contributed by me to Mr. Southey's Omniana, on the soul and its organs of sense, are the following sentences. "These (the human faculties) I would arrange under the different senses and powers: as the eye, the ear, the touch, &c; the imitative power, voluntary and automatic; the imagination, or shaping and modifying power; the

fancy, or the aggregative and associative power. . . ." To this, as
far as it relates to the subject in question, namely the words (*the
aggregative and associative power*) Mr. Wordsworth's "only objec-
tion is that to evoke and to combine, belong as well to the
imagination as to the fancy." I reply, that if, by the power of
evoking and combining, Mr. Wordsworth means the same as,
and no more than, I meant by the aggregative and associative, I
continue to deny, that it belongs at all to the imagination; and I
am disposed to conjecture, that he has mistaken the co-presence
of fancy with imagination for the operation of the latter singly.
A man may work with two very different tools at the same
moment; each has its share in the work, but the work effected by
each is distinct and different. But it will probably appear in the
next Chapter, that deeming it necessary to go back much
further than Mr. Wordsworth's subject required or permitted, I
have attached a meaning to both fancy and imagination, which
he had not in view, at least while he was writing that preface.
He will judge. Would be Heaven, I might meet with many
such readers. [1:194]

Wordsworth's inductive approach, his concern with poetic fruitage, has
now been placed in a new light, and we learn that it has led him to make the
same mistake that Coleridge has been attacking throughout the intervening
analysis: it has led him to see the mind's constitutive activity as merely
associative. Only "back much further," at the roots of the tree, can
imagination be seen plainly for what it is; and only through the eyes of
metaphysical speculation can this "seminal principle" be seen at all. Like
Wordsworth's criticism of this very sort of speculation in *The Prelude*,
Coleridge's rebuttal is handled with tactful indirection and all due respect;
at the same time, his polemical aims are no less clear than Wordsworth's.[33]

The criticism of Wordsworth's associative sense of imagination has an
immediate context which, in view of Wordsworth's philosophic national-
ism, lends special force to Coleridge's remarks. For Coleridge's topic in the
final pages of chapter 12 is the English mind's characteristic resistance to
speculative philosophy. "Great indeed," he laments, "are the obstacles
which an English metaphysician has to encounter" (1:191). English meta-
physicians who, for example, use "technical terms" in their philosophy,
find themselves faced with the "charge of pedantry and unintelligibility"
(*BL* 1:190)—the charge which, in effect, Wordsworth brings against
Coleridge in book 6 of *The Prelude*. Further: "Among his most respectable
and intelligent judges, there will be many who have devoted their attention

exclusively to the concerns and interests of human life, and who bring with them to the perusal of a philosophic system an habitual aversion to all speculations, the utility and application of which are not evident and immediate" (*BL* 1:191). Coleridge answers these critics with a quote from their beloved Bacon.[34] But the "obstacles" among British readers do not end here:

> There are others, whose prejudices are still more formidable, inasmuch as they are grounded in their moral feelings and religious principles, which had been alarmed and shocked by the impious and pernicious tenets defended by Hume, Priestley, and the French fatalists or necessitarians; some of whom have perverted metaphysical reasonings to the denial of the mysteries and indeed of all the peculiar doctrines of Christianity; and others even to the subversion of all distinction between right and wrong. [p. 191]

In describing this group, really a subgroup of the general British opposition to speculation, Coleridge refuses, contra Burke and Wordsworth, to define the Enlightenment movement along national lines. He is also careful to make "necessitarianism" a *French* movement, where Wordsworth had used necessitarian views to *oppose* French intellectual influence.[35] In the end, Coleridge's answer to this subgroup is his answer to his entire British audience, and to Wordsworth as well: "I would remind them . . . that false metaphysics can be effectually counteracted by true metaphysics alone; and that if the reasoning be clear, solid, and pertinent, the truth deduced can never be the less valuable on account of the depth from which it may have been drawn" (*BL* 1:191–92).[36] The echo of his 1809 comment on Burke is clear and telling.

One lingering question concerns Coleridge's sudden "discovery" at the close of chapter 12 that Wordsworth's account is unsatisfactory after all. Can such a maneuver be taken at face value from the author who, a few pages later, will evade the final step of his argument by accepting the advice of a mysterious correspondent who turns out to be himself? On second reading the "perhaps" back in chapter 4 looms much larger than on first reading (when, indeed, it is liable to go unnoticed): "The explanation which Mr. Wordsworth has himself given will be found to differ from mine chiefly, *perhaps*, as our objects are different." The future-tense construction "will be found" does not carry the sense of certainty that it conventionally does in expository prose; Coleridge does not seem entirely to have taken for granted the agreement he later repudiates. Moreover, at the very end of chapter 4, Coleridge offers this apology-in-advance for the rigor of his ensuing analysis: "I would gladly . . . spare both myself and others this labor, if I knew how without it to present an intelligible statement of my poetic creed; not as my *opinions*, which weigh for nothing, but as deductions from established premises conveyed in such a form, as is calculated either to effect a fundamental conviction, or to receive a fundamental confutation" (1:65; Coleridge's italics). In the Preface to *The Excursion*, a poem which Coleridge criticizes later in the *Biographia* and which appeared only a year before Coleridge wrote these words, Wordsworth had declared that *The Recluse* has "for its principal subject the sensations and opinions of a poet living in retirement" (*PW* 5:2). One could not say for sure that Coleridge intends the echo to suggest an individious comparison with Wordsworth's "Philosophical poem," or even that Wordsworth's announcement is the "source" of the remark at all. But in light of the other evidence we have considered, one hesitates to dismiss the matter as mere coincidence—especially since Wordsworth offers, in effect, no other authority than his own opinions for what he writes, and since he is on record in the 1800 Preface as describing the hope of "reasoning" a reader into assent as "fond and foolish" (*PrW* 1:120).[37]

The Poet of *The Prelude* can renounce the philosophical quest for the grounds of his beliefs only when he falls back to blind trust in his own habits of mind. The Metaphysician of the *Biographia*, for whom such a solution was untenable, must pursue his quest for these grounds. In chapter 12, Coleridge explains that "All truth is either mediate, that is, derived from some other truth or truths; or immediate and original. The latter is absolute, and its formula A.A.; the former is of dependent or conditional certainty, and represented in the formula B.A." (*BL* 1:178). It is the quest for the "A.A.," the truth which is "the ultimate ground of our knowledge," that impels Coleridge toward the theory of the esemplastic power in the chapter to follow. The project is both Cartesian and Kantian: "We are to seek therefore," he writes in thesis 3 of chapter 12, "for some absolute truth capable of communicating to other positions a certainty, which it has not itself borrowed; a truth self-grounded, unconditional and known by its own light" (p. 181). It is of a kind with the project that leads the Poet of *The Prelude* to the brink of insanity. Yet for Coleridge, evidently, not to have such a reasoned first principle is a fate worse than insanity, is perhaps insanity itself. In the "Scholium" to Thesis 2, Coleridge presents his conception of this fate in an ingeniously contrived metaphor:

A chain without a staple, from which all the links derived their stability, or a series without a first, has not been inaptly allegorized, as a string of blind men, each holding the skirt of the man before him, reaching far out of sight, but all moving without the least deviation in one straight line. It would naturally be taken for granted, that there was a guide at the head of the file: what if it were answered, No! Sir, the men are without number, and infinite blindness supplies the place of sight? [pp. 180–81]

No one can say whether Coleridge had Wordsworth in mind when he wrote these sentences, of course, but they stand as a marvelously fit epitome of the structure of Wordsworth's imaginative world, where indefinite repetition supplies the place of certainty and infinite blindness the place of sight. In the structure of this imaginative world, Wordsworth's model of mind and his model of society become one, the unity of these two models being the purest mark of his traditionalism. The society that thinks of itself in purely traditional terms is a "simply linear" one, as we have seen, where "everything is learned from the fathers before the shrines of the ancestors" and where "everything will be thought of as transmitted, continuous, immemorial and—since each father must speak on the authority of his father—presumptive." This sort of *social* organization is the ideal we saw plainly upheld in *The Ruined Cottage* and demonstrably implied in all the mature poetry into which Wordsworth admits the concerns of society. Yet this same infinite regression governs even the most exclusively personal or psychological moments of his poetry. In the most intense of such moments, the light of sense goes out, with a flash that reveals the invisible world. This is the poet's second nature. It is a world of associated thoughts, which stretch, like the daffodils, in never-ending line. The experience of this world overwhelms the poet, as his representation of it means to overwhelm us, with the recognition of how much one can feel and how little one can know.

Notes

Introduction

    1. Matthew Arnold, ed., *Poems of Wordsworth* (London: Macmillan, 1879), p. xi.

    2. One indication of Arnold's influence in the shaping of the present Wordsworthian corpus is that what he called "the English-speaking world" accepted no fewer than thirty-two editions of his volume by 1949.

    3. De Quincey's starkest exposition of the literature of power and the literature of knowledge occurs in *Letters to a Young Man* (1823), where he avows that he owes the invidious distinction to "many years' conversation with Mr. Wordsworth": "All that is literature seeks to communicate power; all that is not literature, to communicate knowledge." De Quincey than goes on to define communicating power as "the case in which I should be made to feel vividly, and with a vital consciousness, emotions which ordinary life rarely or never supplies occasions for exciting, and which had previously lain unawakened, and hardly within the dawn of consciousness" (*Collected Writings*, ed. David Masson, 14 vols. [London: A. & C. Black, 1897], 10:48). See De Quincey's related comments in his essay on Pope, 11:53–56. That De Quincey associates "knowledge" with what Arnold called "philosophy" is clear from his essay "On Wordsworth's Poetry," where, anticipating Arnold's own comments, De Quincey argued that the longer "direct philosophic poetry of Wordsworth" had been overvalued at the expense of "those earlier poems which are all short, but generally scintillating with gems of far profounder truth," 11:315.

4. *Poems of Wordsworth*, pp. xxii–xxiv.

5. Many of us would prefer to see in the major poetry what critics have often claimed to find there: strong evidence of Wordsworth's continuing alignment with the ideals, if not with the leaders, of the French Revolution. In disputing the accuracy of this claim, I have remained nonetheless mindful of E. P. Thompson's vivid account of the political setbacks and social pressures that established the conditions for the major poetry, "Disenchantment or Default? A Lay Sermon," in *Power and Consciousness*, ed. Conor Cruise O'Brien and William Dean Vanech (New York: New York University Press, 1969), pp. 149–81. I should add that Thompson makes a strong distinction between "apostasy, a relapse into received patterns of thought and feeling, often accompanied by self-mutilation and the immoderate reverse of attachments, and disenchantment." For him, apostasy is "at enmity with poetry," but disenchantment is not: "one might as well suppose that honesty is so" (p. 177). My account here calls for a severe narrowing of the gap between Wordsworth's disenchantment and his apostasy and concludes that the latter condition, however we name it, has powerfully set in by 1798.

6. The poetry of second nature in this sense, as many readers will recognize, is very close to what David Perkins calls "the poetry of sincerity." See *Wordsworth and the Poetry of Sincerity* (Cambridge, Mass.: Harvard University Press, 1964), esp. pp. 33–60.

7. "The Four Ages of Poetry," in *The Works of Thomas Love Peacock*, ed. H.F.B. Brett-Smith and C. E. Jones, 10 vols. (London: Constable & Co., 1924–34; repr. ed., New York: AMS Press, 1967), 8:19.

8. Marilyn Butler's terse and perspicuous overview of literature and politics in this age, *Romantics, Rebels and Reactionaries* (New York: Oxford University Press, 1982) unfortunately appeared too late to be adequately addressed in my text. Admiring the book in many ways, I also disagree with it on many points, especially in respect to Wordsworth; see, for example, pp. 57–68. It would be impossible to do justice to these disagreements in a note, particularly since Butler and I employ certain key terms such as "enlightenment" and "nature" in very different senses. Readers will simply have to judge for themselves when they compare our very different accounts of, for example, Wordsworth's intellectual commitments, his cultural manifestos, and his relation to Coleridge.

9. On *akedah*, see Hartman's *Wordsworth's Poetry 1787–1814* (New Haven: Yale University Press, 1964), p. 225. I should also make special mention here of the four thoroughgoing contextual studies of *Lyrical Ballads* that appeared in the mid-seventies: Stephen Parrish, *The Art of the Lyrical Ballads* (Cambridge, Mass.: Harvard University Press, 1973); Paul Sheats, *The Making of Wordsworth's Poetry, 1785–1798* (Cambridge, Mass.: Harvard University Press, 1973); Mary Jacobus, *Tradition and Experiment in Wordsworth's Lyrical Ballads (1798)* Oxford: Clarendon Press, 1976); and John E. Jordan, *Why the Lyrical Ballads?* (Berkeley and Los Angeles: University of California Press, 1976). Although these books are not much discussed below, they are the reason why I did not concern myself with extensive commentary upon individual ballads, though I do offer suggestions about the place of the ballads in the ideology of Wordsworth's larger plan.

10. Michael H. Friedman, *The Making of a Tory Humanist* (New York: Columbia University Press, 1979). The Freudianism and the Marxism are not well integrated in this recent study, and neither approach is carried as far as it needs to be. Despite its problems, however, the book offers some insights of real value: the discussion (on pp. 196–97) of the conservatively seminal contradictions implicit in *Lyrical Ballads* 1798, for example, or the analysis (on pp. 169–72) of the political economy implicit in "Stray Pleasures."

11. The concept of concentric horizons in ideological analysis has been developed by M. M. Bakhtin and P. N. Medvedev in *The Formal Method in Literary Scholarship*, trans. Albert J. Werhle (Baltimore: The Johns Hopkins University Press, 1978), pp. 16–37. For a different approach to differentiating the components of such analysis see Terry Eagleton, *Criticism and Ideology* (London: NLB, 1976), pp. 44–63.

Chapter 1: BEGINNING WITH WORDSWORTH

1. Geoffrey Little, ed., *Barron Field's Memoirs of Wordsworth* (Sydney: Sydney University Press, 1975), p. 55. Although this remark appears well along in the text of the *Memoirs*, Little surmises that "the original review would probably have started with [it]" (p. 15).

2. Given Field's *Memoirs* for review, Wordsworth scribbled his responses in the margins of the text. The account of his politics is one of the passages with which the poet took issue: "I am a lover of liberty, but know that liberty cannot exist apart from order & the opinions in favor of aristocracy found in my works the latter ones especially arise out of the consciousness I have, that in the present state of human knowledge, & its probable state for some ages—order cannot & therefore liberty cannot be maintained without degrees. It is pride & presumption & not a real love of liberty which has made the french & the Americans so enamoured of what they call equality" (p. 25). As I argue below, however, the author's disavowal does not in itself constitute grounds for rejecting the accuracy of the account.

3. Field, *Memoirs*, pp. 26–27.

4. One reason for thinking this strange is that in his little *London Magazine* piece of 1821, "On Consistency of Opinion," Hazlitt does discuss the matter of Wordsworth's political tergiversation, and here the discrepancies between, in Hazlitt's punning phrase, "poetical justice and political severity" are fully acknowledged:

> as far as I understand the Poems themselves or the Preface, his whole system turns upon this, that the thoughts, the feelings, the expressions of the common people in country places are the most refined of all others; at once the most pure, the most simple, and the most sublime:—yet, with one stroke of his prose pen, he disfranchises the whole rustic population of Westmoreland and Cumberland from voting at elections, and says there is not a man among them that is not a knave in grain. [*CWWH* 17:26]

Hazlitt's only recourse for resolving the matter is a universalized and cynical view of authorial psychology: "An author's political theories sit loose upon him, and may be changed like his clothes. His literary vanity, alas! sticks to him like his skin . . ." (p. 26).

5. See *Paradise Lost* 1:280, where the fallen angels are said to "lie / Groveling and prostrate on yon Lake of Fire." This and all subsequent references to Milton's poetry are cited from *Complete Poems and Major Prose*, ed. Merritt Y. Hughes (Indianapolis: Odyssey Press, 1957).

6. Besides the first volume of Mary Moorman's standard biography (Moorman *EY*) and Mark Reed's invaluable chronicle, the most useful biographical works on this period in Wordsworth's life are still Emile Legouis, *The Early Life of William Wordsworth* (London and Toronto: J. M. Dent & Sons, 1921), and the first volume of G. M. Harper, *William Wordsworth: His Life, Works, and Influence*, 2 vols. (London: John Murray, 1929; repr. ed., New York: Russell and Russell, 1960).

7. We have no reason to doubt Wordsworth's speculation in *The Prelude* that his

involvement in the Revolution was such that, if he had not been "compelled" to return to England in late 1792, he "doubtless should have made a common cause / With some who perished, haply perished too" (10:194–95).

8. For a fuller account of this pattern in "Tintern Abbey," see my "Romantic Allusiveness," *Critical Inquiry* 8 (Spring 1982): 470–72.

9. Richard Watson, *Anecdotes of the Life of Richard Watson* (London: T. Cadell & W. Davies, 1817), p. 57.

10. Ibid., pp. 59–60.

11. Richard Watson, *Principles of the Revolution Vindicated* (Cambridge: J. Archdeacon, 1776), pp. 21–22.

12. Richard Watson, *A Sermon Preached Before the Lord Spiritual and Temporal* (London: J. Nichols, 1784), esp. pp. 17–18.

13. Richard Watson, *A Charge Delivered to the Clergy of the Diocese of Llandaff*, June 1791 (London: T. Evans, 1792).

Chapter 2: BURKE BLAMED AND PRAISED

1. Edward Niles Hooker, "Wordsworth's Letter to the Bishop of Llandaff," *Studies in Philology* 38 (July 1931):522–31.

2. This scholarship is itemized by Owen and Smyser in *PrW* 1:23. A representative account of the Letter from this point of view can be found in F. M. Todd, *Politics and the Poet* (London: Methuen & Co., 1957), pp. 60–62. Todd claims that the "Letter to Llandaff contains little that is not in Godwin, and even Godwin's extensive borrowings from Paine and others were taken over into the work of his disciple" (p. 60).

3. Hooker, "Wordsworth's Letter," p. 522.

4. Among Burke scholars James T. Boulton stands out for his analysis of Burke's role in shaping radical rhetoric in the early 1790s in *The Language of Politics in the Age of Wilkes and Burke* (London: Routledge & Kegan Paul, 1963), pp. 75–133. Among literary scholars, Marilyn Butler should be mentioned for her comments about Burke's contribution not only to the radical pamphleteering but ultimately to the making of the Jacobin novel, *Jane Austen and the War of Ideas* (Oxford: Oxford University Press, 1975), pp. 37–42.

5. The resurgence of the radical movement in the wake of Burke's attack is noted briefly by Carl Woodring, *Politics in English Romantic Poetry* (Cambridge, Mass.: Harvard University Press, 1970), p. 13. For more extended discussion see S. Maccoby, *English Radicalism 1786–1832* (London: George Allen & Unwin, 1955), pp. 45–62; Carl B. Cone, *The English Jacobins* (New York: Charles Scribner's Sons, 1968), pp. 96–113; and especially Albert Goodwin's excellent new study, *The Friends of Liberty: The English Democratic Movement in the Age of the French Revolution* (Cambridge; Mass.: Harvard University Press, 1979), pp. 99–135. See also E. P. Thompson's valuable comments on the radical response to Burke in *The Making of the English Working Class* (New York: Random House, 1963), pp. 89–94.

6. Countess of Minto, ed., *Life and Letters of Sir Gilbert Elliot*, 3 vols. (London: Longmans, Green, & Co., 1874), 1:365–66. Burke goes on in this letter to defend himself from the charge, already brought against the work, that it betrays an inconsistency with his former views (p. 367).

7. James Prior, *Memoir of the Life and Character of the Right Hon. Edmund Burke*, rev. 2d ed., 2 vols. (London: Baldwin, Cradock, and Joy;, 1826), 2:121.

8. Boulton, *Language of Politics*, pp. 265–71.

9. See Richard Altick, *The English Common Reader* (Chicago: University of Chicago Press, 1957), p. 71.

10. Ibid., pp. 71–72; reactionary satirist T. J. Mathias complained in 1797 that "our peasantry now read the *Rights of Man* on mountains, and moors, and by the wayside" (quoted in Boulton, *Language of Politics*, p. 138)—a development that Wordsworth would also find alarming at that time.

11. Boulton makes a similar point when he says that "the response of Burke's contemporaries was not only to a body of ideas but rather to a complete literary achievement, a mode of writing effectively designed to convey a particular manner of thinking; when they attacked or praised the book it was that complete achievement they had in mind," *Language of Politics*, p. 97.

12. Italics mine; I have retranslated this passage from the French translation that appeared in the official organ of Revolutionary France, the *Gazette nationale ou Le Moniteur universel*, no. 202 (21 July 1791); reprinted in *Réimpression de L'Ancien Moniteur* (Paris: Henri Plon, 1863), 9:174. Paine made a similar point, with similar irony, in *The Rights of Man*: "Mr. Burke has done some service—not to his cause, but to his country—by bringing those clauses into public view"—*The Writings of Thomas Paine*, ed. Moncure Daniel Conway, 4 vols. (New York: G. P. Putnam's Sons, 1894), 2:279–80.

13. Paine, *Rights of Man*, pp. 270, 269. Generalizing this comment to embrace the responses of other radicals, including that of his wife, William Godwin wrote that "Burke had been warmly loved by the most liberal and enlightened friends of freedom, and they were proportionably inflamed and disgusted by the fury of his assault, upon what they deemed to be its sacred cause"—*Memoirs of the Author of a Vindication of the Rights of Women* (London: J. Johnson, 1798), p. 76.

14. Watson's own writing on America seems to have profited from Burke's famous published addresses on the subject. See *Principles of the Revolution Vindicated*, passim.

15. In his public answer to Burke De Pont wrote: "I had certainly no idea that my letter would lead to the publication of the work you have so kindly sent me. I will even confess that I should never have made the request, had I been able to foresee its effect; and that if I had at that time known your opinions, far from begging you to express them, I should have besought you not to make them public"—cited in Boulton, *Language of Politics*, p. 95. A further measure of Burke's fame abroad prior to the publication of the *Reflections* is Destutt de Tracy's published attack on Burke's remarks against the Revolution in Parliament (9 February 1790), *Translation of a Letter from Monsieur de Tracy, Member of the French National Assembly, to Mr. Burke* (London: J. Johnson, 1790); for more on Tracy, see below, chapter 9.

16. For more on the end of the Great Debate, see Goodwin, *Friends of Liberty*, p. 186.

17. Todd, *Politics and the Poet*, p. 48.

18. Wordsworth's "intoxicating bowl" may well be his answer to the metaphors of tavern carousing and intoxication with which Burke casts aspersions on working-class involvement in politics. For discussion of Burke's use of such terms, see Boulton, *Language of Politics*, p. 199.

19. Wordsworth has earlier resolved the "apparent contradiction" implicit in what he says about the Revolution's "principles of liberty," on the one hand, and the violence necessitated by the "state of war between the oppressors and the oppressed," on the other (p. 34).

20. Boulton, *Language of Politics*, p. 83.

21. Richard Watson, appendix to *A Sermon Preached before the Stewards of the Westminster Dispensary . . . , April 1785* (London: T. Cadell, 1793), p. 26.

22. Ibid., p. 26. Owen and Smyser also note the connection with Burke here, *PrW* 1:58.

23. Watson writes: "All that I contend for is this—that the foundations of our government ought not to be overturned, nor the edifice erected thereon tumbled into ruins, because an acute politician may pretend that he has discovered a flaw in the building, or that he could have laid the foundation after a better model" (Appendix, p. 28). Speaking of "the French builders" in the *Reflections*, Burke had used similar terms in a similar way:

> The means taught by experience may be better suited to political ends than those contrived in the original project. They again react upon the primitive constitution, and sometimes improve the design itself, from which they seem to have departed. . . . This is the case of old establishments; but in a new and merely theoretic system, it is expected that every contrivance shall appear, on the face of it, to answer its ends, especially where the projectors are no way embarrassed with an endeavor to accommodate the new building to an old one, either in the walls or on the foundations. [*BW* 3:461]

Burke himself may have derived the metaphor from the great proto-philosophe, Descartes, for whom it served a contrary purpose in the *Discourse on the Method*:

> One of the first things I thought it well to consider was that as a rule there is not such great perfection in works composed of several parts, and proceeding from the hands of various artists, as in those on which one man has worked alone, Thus we see that buildings undertaken and carried out by a single architect are generally more seemly and better arranged than those that several hands have sought to adapt, making use of old walls that were built for other purposes. Again, those ancient cities which were originally mere boroughs and have become larger towns in process of time, are as a rule badly laid out, as compared with those towns of regular pattern that are laid out by a designer on a open plain to suit his fancy; while the buildings severally considered are often equal or superior artistically to those in planned towns, yet, in view of their arrangement . . . one would say that it was chance that placed them so and not the will of men who had the use of reason. [In *Philosophical Writings*, ed. and trans. Elizabeth Ascombe and P. T. Geach (London: Thomas Nelson and Sons, 1954), p. 15.]

For Descartes, collective wisdom spells only spoiled broth.

24. The passage shows how the later Wordsworth is willing to extol Burke in largely the same terms he had earlier used to vilify him. One important exception to this rule is the word "philosophic," which does change in meaning. In the 1818 passage, the term clearly has little to do with the kind of metaphysical inquiry Wordsworth had in mind when he accused Watson of aiming an arrow at "liberty and philosophy," humanity's means of seeing its way to social reform. I believe "philosophic" is used in the 1818 passage in a way that is closer to what we find at the end of the "Intimations Ode," where the poet describes the "years that bring the philosophic mind" (p. 187). In both cases, the use of the word is polemically anti-rational, for the philosophic mind of the ode, as I argue below in chapter 4, is the mind that resigns itself to nature's "more habitual sway" (p. 192). This is philosophy as a means of consolation rather than of change.

25. Hartman, *Wordsworth's Poetry*, p. 46.

26. For a summary of this scholarship, both the older and the more recent, see my "Wordsworth and Burke," *ELH* 47 (Winter 1980):754–55 and notes 29–32 of that essay.

27. Quoted in Todd, *Politics and the Poet*, p. 11.

Chapter 3: A POET'S REFLECTIONS ON THE REVOLUTION IN FRANCE

1. David Cameron discusses Burke's role (along with that of Rousseau) in "the 'mythology' of European history," *Rousseau and Burke* (Toronto: University of Toronto Press, 1973), p. 165. No less a historian than Macaulay, after reading Burke's complete works, called him "the greatest man since Milton"—quoted in Thomas W. Copeland, "The Reputation of Edmund Burke," *Journal of British Studies* 1 (May 1962):82.

2. Alfred Cobban is one of the few scholars who have argued vigorously for Burke's influence in the writings of Wordsworth's major period. Cobban's commitment to the received notion that Wordsworth's conservatism is a late development, however, leads him to the peculiar conclusion that the early radical and later conservative periods straddle a middle phase, that of the major poetry, of a not-yet-conservative Burkean nationalism. See *Edmund Burke and the Revolt Against the Eighteenth Century* (New York: Barnes and Noble, 1929), pp. 140–52, esp. p. 151.

3. I follow M. H. Abrams in viewing Wordsworth's major work as a more or less coherent "program for poetry," *Natural Supernaturalism* (New York: W. W. Norton, 1970), p. 21. Explaining the genesis of this program in relation to the French Revolution, Abrams argues that it is best understood as a displacement of millenarian political expectations into an aesthetic principle that he calls "The Apocalypse of Imagination," a principle evolved out of Christian tradition. But Abrams's effort to show the continuity of theological perspectives in an age of rapid change leads him to disregard the clash of political perspectives in that age. Neither Burke's political writings nor the Great Debate they generated are anywhere mentioned in *Natural Supernaturalism*, and without them one cannot make an adequate account of Wordsworth's politics in any of his mature stages.

4. My discussion of "middleness" in Burke is indebted to an unpublished paper by Stuart M. Tave, "Burke Looks at a Revolution," English Department Colloquium, University of Chicago, 1977.

5. For Wordsworth's treatment of the dark side of Platonic metaphysical politics see *Prel.* 9:415–24 and David Erdman's commentary in "Wordsworth as Heartsworth; or, Was Regicide the Prophetic Ground of Those 'Moral Questions'?" in *The Evidence of the Imagination*, ed. Donald H. Reiman, Michael C. Jaye, and Betty T. Bennett (New York: New York University Press, 1978), p. 40, n. 27.

6. Burleigh Taylor Wilkins, *The Problem of Burke's Political Philosophy* (Oxford: Clarendon Press, 1967), p. 60.

7. Ibid., p. 61. On the Burke-Hume connection see George H. Sabine, *A History of Political Theory*, 3d ed. (London: George G. Harrap, 1963), pp. 597–619, and H. B. Acton, "Prejudice," *Revue internationale de philosophie* 6 (1952):328–36; see also Cobban, *Edmund Burke*, p. 78.

8. Wilkins, *Burke's Political Philosophy*, p. 61.

9. See Basil Willey's discussion of Hume's " 'Nature' as a Habit of the Mind," in *The Eighteenth Century Background* (London: Chatto and Windus, 1940), p. 110–19. Wordsworth's epistemological affinities with Hume, in some respects more striking than his heavily documented affinities with David Hartley, have never been adequately explored. One need only compare the opening pages of Hume's *Treatise of Human Nature* with the

epistemological discussion in the 1800 Preface to *Lyrical Ballads* (e.g., lines 115–132 in *PrW* 1:126) to see how much they share, especially in respect to the notion of a second nature.

10. For a discussion of Wordsworth's possession of this book and an account of its political context, see chapter 8 below.

11. James Boswell, *Life of Johnson*, ed. R. W. Chapman (Oxford: Oxford University Press, 1970), p. 615.

14. Burke likened himself to an old British oak, felled by the storm of Revolution, in his *Letter to a Noble Lord* (1796) (*BW* 5:208; cf. 3: 344).

12. See *Edmund Burke*, pp. 97ff.

13. J. G. A. Pocock, "Burke and the Ancient Constitutions: A Problem in the History of Ideas," in *Politics, Language and Time* (New York: Atheneum, 1973), pp. 202–3.

14. I refer to the famous portraits of Carruthers (1817), Pickersgill (1832), and Haydon (1842); see Francis Blanchard, *Portraits of Wordsworth* (London: George Allen and Unwin, 1959), plates 5, 14b, and 23.

15. Only Woodring, I believe, has remarked upon the propriety of the Burke tribute to *The Prelude* and what he calls its "defense of experience against the straightjacket of theory"—*Politics in English Romantic Poetry*, p. 105.

16. Cobban, *Edmund Burke*, p. 147.

17. An indication of the neglect of the matter is that Burke is nowhere mentioned in Owen and Smyser's extensive commentary on *Cintra* (*PrW* 1:374–415).

18. So far as I know, this echo has not been identified in any critical commentary on the tract, not even in Gordon Kent Thomas's book-length study of it, *Wordsworth's Dirge and Promise* (Lincoln: University of Nebraska Press, 1971).

19. Edith J. Morley, ed., *The Correspondence of Henry Crabb Robinson with the Wordsworth Circle* 2 vols. (Oxford: Clarendon Press, 1927), 1:59.

20. For example, neither the exhaustive commentary of R. D. Havens, *The Mind of a Poet* (Baltimore: The Johns Hopkins Press, 1941), nor that of Ernest de Selincourt, *The Prelude*, 2d ed. rev. by Helen Darbishire (Oxford: Clarendon Press, 1959), records any connection between Burke's political writings and the 1805 *Prelude*. Besides Woodring, another important exception to this trend is Herbert Lindenberger, who notes that the language of book 8 is "conservative," and suggests that its diction (*roots, ancient, birthright,* and *custom*) is "less directly related to any older conservatism than to the type we associate with Burke," *On Wordsworth's Prelude* (Princeton, N.J.: Princeton University Press, 1963), p. 250. Lindenberger goes on to make the valuable but tentative suggestion that the roots of this conservatism reach back to 1800 (p. 251).

21. Cobban, *Edmund Burke*, p. 147.

22. Willard L. Sperry, much of whose scholarship on Wordsworth is still valuable after a half-century, is the only critic I know who has connected the lines from *The Prelude* to the passage from *Cintra*, to the passage from Burke's *Reflections*, and to Wordsworth's commentary on the latter in the Letter to Llandaff—*Wordsworth's Anti-climax* (Cambridge, Mass.: Harvard University Press, 1935; repr. ed. New York: Russell and Russell, 1966), pp. 66–68.

23. The second part of the sentence from *Cintra*—"the good, the brave, and the wise, of all ages"—has strong affinities with, for example, the lines from book 11 of *The Prelude* where Wordsworth speaks of "the elevation which had made [him] one / With the

great family that here and there / Is scattered through the abyss of past, / Sage, patriot, lover, hero" (61–64).

24. I want to emphasize this point because of its importance to my argument thus far. My contention is that, coming to intellectual maturity in the political milieu I have described, young Wordsworth would have attached an overwhelming sense of opprobrium to the thought of turning his coat—this quite apart from the difficulty of admitting his own (ostensible) folly and Burke's (ostensible) acumen with respect to the great issue of the age. This sense of opprobrium is sufficiently powerful, I maintain, to account for an effort on Wordsworth's part to conceal his changed opinions (as much from himself as from the world), an effort which is itself obliquely exposed in that belated verse tribute to Burke's genius. To underestimate the power of this shame, furthermore, is to allow oneself to be misled by certain of Wordsworth's remarks. On 20 July 1804, for example, when he was probably well along in the composition of the French books (see Reed *MY*:14), Wordsworth wrote a letter to Beaumont in which a minor criticism of Reynolds became a major criticism of Burke: "The industry and love of truth which distinguish Sir Joshua's mind are most admirable, but he appears to me to have lived too much for the age in which he lived, and the people among whom he lived, though this in an infinitely less degree than his friend Burke, of whom Goldsmith said, with such truth, long ago

> 'that born for the universe, "he narrowed his mind"
> And to party gave up what was meant for mankind.'"
>
> [*EY*:491]

The comment has led Leslie Chard II, who considers the question of Wordsworth's conversion to Burke in *Dissenting Republican* (The Hague: Mouton, 1972), to what seems to me a mistaken conclusion: "While Wordsworth later changed his opinions of Burke, the fact remains that he was utterly opposed to everything Burke stood for in the 1790s (including the appeal to tradition as a means of maintaining the status quo); as late as 1804 his letters reveal hostility to Burke, and the lines of *The Prelude* that praise him were not added until 1820 or after" (p. 150). F. M. Todd reaches a similar conclusion in *Politics and the Poet*, although less depends on the matter for Todd since he underestimates Wordsworth's initial opposition to Burke, taking Wordsworth's later accounts at face value and dismissing the comments on Burke in the letter to Llandaff as a "backhanded reference" (pp. 169–70).

25. Abrams, *Natural Supernaturalism*, pp. 236–37.

26. Havens, *Mind of a Poet*, p. 535.

27. Isaac Kramnick quotes this passage as "the fairy wand of philosophy," which would make the resemblance to Wordsworth's line uncannily striking—*The Rage of Edmund Burke* (New York: Basic Books, 1977), p. 21. But this seems to be simply a mistaken transcription.

28. The following discussion of *The Prelude*'s Burkean plot by no means denies the role of other influences on Wordsworth's shaping of the action. *Paradise Lost* is an obvious case in point. We need only think of how books 9 and 10 of *The Prelude* follow books 9 and 10 of Milton's epic is showing man's fall into Satanic or Promethean forbidden knowledge.

29. Perhaps the fullest elaboration of Burke's notion of the homebred rusticity of English thought, a passage that shows his kinship with Wordsworth in an especially revealing way, occurs in a document that Wordsworth could not have seen, "Several Scattered Hints Concerning Philosophy and Learning," in *A Note-book of Edmund Burke*, ed. H. V. F. Somerset (Cambridge: Cambridge University Press), p. 90:

> A man who considers his nature rightly will be diffident of any reasonings that carry
> him out of the ordinary roads of Life; Custom is to be regarded with great deference
> especially if it is to be an universal Custom; even popular notions are not always to be
> laughed at. There is some general principle operating to produce Customs, that is a
> more sure guide than our Theories. They are followed indeed often on odd motives,
> but that does not make them less reasonable or useful. A man is never in greater
> danger of being wholly wrong than when he advances far in the road of refinement.

In this same essay, Burke also articulates the paradox that seems to lie at the heart of
Wordsworth's experiments in *Lyrical Ballads* and to have occasioned the latter criticisms of
Coleridge: "The more a man's mind is elevated above the vulgar the nearer he comes to them
in the simplicity of his appearance, speech, and even not a few of his Notions" (p. 90).

   30. On Burke's use of images and metaphors of "family," see Boulton, *Language of
Politics*, pp. 112–14.

   31. See below, chapter 8.

   32. See J. R. Jones, *The First Whigs* (London: Oxford University Press, 1966; first
pub. 1961, pp. 45; for a fuller discussion of anti-French sentiment in the 1670s see John
Miller, *Popery and Politics in England 1660–1688* (Cambridge: Cambridge University Press,
1973), pp. 108–53, esp. pp. 148–52, where Miller discusses Marvell's *Account of the Growth
of Popery and Arbitrary Government* (1678), an anti-French attack on the earl of Danby. This is,
of course, the period to which Burke alludes in the passage quoted immediately below.

   33. For a discussion of this address ("Speech on the Army Estimates") in its political
context, see F. O'Gorman, *The Whig Party and the French Revolution* (London: Macmillan,
1967), pp. 45–48.

   34. Wordsworth's Burkean claim to be upholding the Whig tradition sheds light, I
think, on the kind of distinction Michael Friedman wishes to make when he says that
Wordsworth became a "Tory Humanist" but never a "mean-spirited Tory." Friedman's
suggestion that this change may have occurred as early as 1800 moves in the right direction
but, since Wordsworth's program was conceived in 1798, does not go far enough. See *The
Making of a Tory Humanist*, p. 234.

   35. Quoted in Cobban, *Edmund Burke*, pp. 142–43.

Chapter 4: THE USES OF SECOND NATURE

   1. See, for example, Paine, *Rights of Man*, in *Writings*, 2:86–87; Mary Woll-
stonecraft, *Vindication of the Rights of Men* (London: J. Johnson, 1790), p. 66; and Brooke
Boothby, *Letter to . . . Burke* (London: J. Debrett, 1791), pp. 72–73. Some writers prefaced
their response to Burke with explicit attempts to disarm him of the rhetorical weaponry with
which his poetic imagination supplied him. James Mackintosh's introductory caveat is
representative: "It must be confessed, that in this miscellaneous and desultory warfare, the
superiority of a man of genius over common men is infinite. . . . He can sap the most
impregnable conviction by pathos, and put to flight a host of syllogisms with a sneer.
Absolved from the laws of vulgar method, he can advance a groupe of magnificent horrors to
make a breach in our hearts, through which the most undisciplined rabble of arguments may
enter in triumph"—*Vindiciae Gallicae* (London: J. Johnson, 1790), p. 66. On the "literature
of power" and its antithesis, see above, p. xvii and n. 2. How far Wordsworth's theory and
practice of the literature of power can be said to derive from the 1790s conception of Burke's
writing is hard to say, but sometimes Burke's opponents almost seem to be describing *The
Prelude* when they write about the *Reflections*: "In the field of reason the encounter would not

be difficult, but who can withstand the fascination and magic of his eloquence? The excursions of his genius are immense. . . . His imagination is, in truth, only too prolific: a world of itself, where he dwells in the midst of chimerical alarms, is the dupe of his own enchangments, and starts, like Prospero, at the spectres of his own creation"—Robert Hall, *Works*, ed. Olinthus Gregory, 3 vols. (New York: Harper, 1833), 2:69.

2. Wilkins points to this same implied distinction between feeling as such and "natural" feeling, *Burke's Political Philosophy*, p. 111.

3. Immanuel Kant, "What Is Enlightenment?" in *Critique of Practical Reason and Other Writings in Moral Philosophy*, trans. Lewis White Beck (Chicago: University of Chicago Press, 1949), pp. 286–92.

4. Wordsworth seems to echo this passage in *Cintra* where he says that he begins from his "invincible feelings, and the principles of justice which are involved in them," *PrW* 1:336.

5. For an example of Burke's use of "prejudice" in the pejorative sense see *BW* 4:468.

6. There is a large body of critical testimony about Burke's distinctively powerful way of wedding thought and expression. Among Burke's contemporaries, Hazlitt made this point in his "Character of Mr. Burke" (1807), *CWWH* 7:309–10. See also Boulton, *Language of Politics*, pp. 81–82, on the problems faced by the early French translator of the *Reflections*.

7. Raymond Williams, *Keywords* (New York: Oxford University Press, 1976), p. 184.

8. This controversy has generated too much argument to admit of brief summary here. Burke's relation to natural-law political theory is *the* problem in Burke studies, as Wilkins's title means to suggest. Wilkins's way of posing, and, insofar as this is possible, of resolving the problem is commendable. See especially pp. 160–62.

9. Laurence Lerner, "What Did Wordsworth Mean by 'Nature'?" *Critical Quarterly* 17 (Winter 1975):296.

10. This is not to claim, however, that the portrayal in *The Winter's Tale* of the country's redemption of the city was without its effect on Wordsworth's poetry. The connection has not been explored, so far as I know, but the place to start might be with the fourth act.

11. The intellectual affinities of these two enemies have been pointed out in both of the book-length comparative studies: Annie Marion Osborn, *Rousseau and Burke* (London: Oxford University Press, 1940), passim; and David Cameron, *Social Thought of Rousseau and Burke*, e.g., pp. 95–106. Modern readers might even question the absoluteness of the natural/civil distinction in Rousseau, though readers of the 1790s seems not to have done so.

12. Jean-Jacques Rousseau, *Discourse on the Origin and Foundations of Inequality among Men* in *The First and Second Discourses*, ed. Roger D. Masters, trans. Roger D. and Judith R. Masters (New York: St. Martin's Press, 1964), p. 102. Hereafter, where possible, cited by page number in the text.

13. I have found no history of the idea of second nature, but one can gain an idea of the potential value of such a work from the list of writers who, by virtue of their use of the notion, would figure prominently in that history: Simonides, Aristotle, Cicero, John Gower, Pascal, Rousseau, Kant, Reynolds, and of course Burke.

14. Cited in Gerald W. Chapman, *Edmund Burke: The Practical Imagination* (Cambridge, Mass.: Harvard University Press, 1967), p. 275.

15. Burke's *Appeal from the New to the Old Whigs* (1791) elaborates this paradox in a

way that reveals one of his central disagreements with the position of Rousseau: "For man is by nature reasonable; and he is never perfectly in his natural state, but when he is placed where reason may be best cultivated and most predominates. Art is man's nature. We are as much, at least, in a state of Nature in formed manhood as in immature and helpless infancy. . . . When great multitudes act together under that discipline of Nature, I recognize the PEOPLE" (*BW* 4:176).

16. As early as 1757, in the *Philosophical Enquiry into the Origin of Our Ideas of the Sublime and Beautiful*, ed. James T. Boulton (London: Routledge & Kegan Paul, 1958), Burke showed his aversion to strict definition and adumbrated his lifelong predilection for sliding terms: "I have no great opinion of a definition. . . . For when we define, we seem in danger of circumscribing nature within the bounds of our own notions, which we often take up by hazard, or embrace on trust, or form out of a limited and partial consideration of the object before us, instead of extending our ideas to take in all that nature comprehends, according to her manner of combining" (p. 12).

17. Boulton, *Language of Politics*, p. 132. Kramnick comments that the book reaches its "literary, emotional, and theoretical crescendo in the passages Burke devotes to the queen," *Rage of Edmund Burke*, p. 31.

18. Conway, ed., *Writings of Thomas Paine*, 2:297.

19. Abrams, *Natural Supernaturalism*, p. 379.

20. S. T. Coleridge, *Biographia Literaria*, ed. J. Shawcross, 2 vols. (London: Oxford University Press, 1907), 2: 6.

21. Mark Reed, "Wordsworth, Coleridge, and the 'Plan' of *Lyrical Ballads*," *UTQ* 34, (1965), 238–53.

22. *Enquiry*, ed. Boulton, p. 103.

23. Wilkins, *Burke's Political Philosophy*, pp. 119–51.

24. Boulton makes the point about "beauty" and "fear" in *The Prelude* in his survey of the *Enquiry*'s influence which forms part of his "Editor's Introduction," pp. xcix–cii. He also makes the noteworthy observation that the *Enquiry* saw no fewer than seventeen English and foreign language editions by 1798.

25. See David Erdman's persuasive decoding of the "Vaudracoeur" narrative, in conjunction with the plot of *The Borderers*, in "Wordsworth as Heartsworth," pp. 15–19.

26. Abrams, *Natural Supernaturalism*, p. 383.

27. On the dating of this essay, see Reed *EY*:34.

28. The reference for this and all subsequent citations from the *Essay on Morals* is *PrW* 1:103.

29. See Reed *EY*:32.

30. Wordsworth's announcement of a major work on "Nature, Man, and Society" at this time (*EY*:212) together with the manuscript evidence for this period have led Reed to surmise that the first work on the *Prospectus* lines ("On Man, on Nature, and on Human Life . . ."), published with *The Excursion* in 1814, may also date to these seminal weeks from late January to early March in 1798 (Reed *EY*:29).

31. Reed, who takes up the question of "The Old Cumberland Beggar" in an Appendix to his *Chronology*, shows that "the full conception of the OCB, as an overtly exhortatory poem much in its present form," can be dated to the period of 25 January to 5 March 1798 (p. 342). It is true that Wordsworth's work on earlier versions of the poem can be dated back as far as 1796, but these early lines adumbrate what Reed describes as "a poem

intended simply as the description of a beggar" and as "only a descriptive poem" (p. 342). Some of this work eventually found its way into "Old Man Travelling; Animal Tranquillity and Decay," which was completed much earlier than "Cumberland Beggar" and, interestingly, is neither framed as an address to statement nor informed by the kind of ideology that we find in the later poem.

32. M. H. Abrams, "Introduction: Two Roads to Wordsworth," in *Wordsworth: A Collective of Critical Essays*, ed. M. H. Abrams (Englewood Cliffs, N.J.: Prentice-Hall, 1972), p. 10.

33. Harold Bloom, *The Visionary Company* (New York: Doubleday, 1961), pp. 188–89.

34. Here again, some blame must be laid at the doorstep of Hazlitt, who wrote in his essay "On the Character of Rousseau": "The writer who most nearly resembles him in our own times is the author of the *Lyrical Ballads*. We see no other difference between them, than that the one wrote in prose and the other in poetry" (*CWWH* 4:92).

35. Bloom, *Visionary Company*, p. 191. Bloom claims that advocacy of such a doctrine would invoke Blake's "blistering reply": "Pity would be no more / If we did not make somebody Poor." This claim assumes agreement between Wordsworth and Blake on the issue and is intended to suggest that Wordsworth could not, on those grounds, have embraced such a doctrine. Part of my aim here is to call into question the all-too-common assumption of agreement between the two poets in 1798.

Chapter 5: ROUSSEAU AND THE POLITICS OF EDUCATION

1. One point of controversy in this chronology might be the suggestion that the five-book plan was close to the initial conception of 1798–99. The issue has to do with the status of the two books that survive from that early period, whether they were meant to stand alone as a "two-part *Prelude*" or to begin a multibook work. Reed's arguments against the former position seem to me compelling (Reed *MY*: 135, n. 3). And while the first two books of the five-book poem are not identical with the two books of 1798–99, they are similar. Further, there is the discursive material from MS. 18a., also dating to 1798–99, whose significance for the five-book poem I will be discussing below.

2. For a full exposition of the matter see Jonathan Wordsworth, "The Five-Book *Prelude* of Early Spring 1804," *JEGP* 76 (January 1977):1–25.

3. J. R. MacGillivray, "The Three Forms of *The Prelude*," in *Essays in English Literature from the Renaissance to the Victorian Age*, ed. Millar MacLure and F. W. Watt (Toronto: University of Toronto Press, 1964), p. 242; the description is cited with approval in Jonathan Wordsworth's later essay.

4. Hartman's assumption that book 5 is about "the presumptuous followers of Rousseau" is representative in this respect, *Wordsworth's Poetry*, p. 19.

5. De Selincourt and Darbishire gloss the lines that reappear in *The Prelude* in their text of the passage on the Pedlar's education, *PW* 5:381–88.

6. David V. Erdman, "Coleridge, Wordsworth, and the Wedgwood Fund," *Bulletin of the New York Public Library* 60 (September and October 1956):425–43, 486–507.

7. Joel Morkan, "Structure and Meaning in *The Prelude*, Book V." *PMLA* 87 (March 1972):251.

8. Erdman, "Wedgwood Fund," p. 429.

9. Morkan, "Structure and Meaning," p. 249.

10. See Northrop Frye, "Varieties of Literary Utopias," in *The Stubborn Structure* (Ithaca, N.Y.: Cornell University Press, 1970), p. 122; reprinted from *Daedalus* 99, no. 2 (1970).

11. For a discussion that clarifies the relationship of Rousseau's concerns in the *Second Discourse*, the *Social Contract*, and *Emile*, see William Boyd, *The Education Theory of Jean-Jacques Rousseau* (New York: Russell & Russell, 1963; first published 1911), pp. 126–27, and Roger D. Masters, *The Political Philosophy of Rousseau* (Princeton, N.J.: Princeton University Press, 1968), pp. 6–15.

12. The proposal was published in the *Gazette nationale ou Le Moniteur universel*, no. 356 (22 December 1790):88; reprinted in *Réimpression de L' Ancien Moniteur*, 6:697.

13. *BW* 4:3–55, see esp. pp. 25–35. Burke represented the commitment of the National Assembly to Rousseau as obsessive in its rigor:

> The assembly recommends to its youth a study of the bold experimenters of morality. Everyone knows that there is a great dispute among their leaders, which of them is the best resemblance of Rousseau. In truth, they all resemble him. Him they study; him they meditate; him they turn over in all the time they can spare from the laborious mischief of the day or the debauches of the night. Rousseau is their canon of holy writ; in his life he is their canon of Polycletus; he is their standard figure of perfection. To this man and this writer, as a pattern to authors and to Frenchmen, the foundries of Paris are now running for statues, with the kettles of their poor and the bells of their churches. (4:25)

14. Both the ceremony and its genesis have been carefully documented in Gordon Heath McNeil, *The Pantheonization of Rousseau during the French Revolution*, Master's thesis, University of Chicago, 1937.

15. Joseph Lakanal, *Rapport sur J. J. Rousseau, fait au nom de Comité d'instruction publique* (Paris: Imprimerie Nationale, n.d.). The passages cited below from this document are my translations and are cited by page number in the text. In view of Erdman's recent suggestions about Wordsworth and regicide, it may prove to be of interest that Lakanal the educational theorist had first made a name as one of the publicists for the cause that sought and gained the execution of Louis XVI. His *Opinion . . . sur la question de savoir: Si Louis XVI peut être jugé?* was printed by order of the National Convention in late 1792. See John Charles Dawson, *Lakanal the Regicide* (University, Ala.: University of Alabama Press, 1948).

16. Published in the *Moniteur*, 28 October 1794, cited below by page number in the Plon edition, my translations.

17. See Robert J. Vignery, *The French Revolution and the Schools* (Madison: The State Historical Society of Wisconsin, 1965), pp. 127–28. Vignery points out that Lakanal's address was actually drafted by another member of the Committee, Joseph Garat, a point which ultimately has little bearing on my argument here, though it may help to explain the differences between Lakanal's tactics then and two weeks earlier in the Pantheonization address. Garat was a central figure in the Ideologue circle discussed below in chapter 9.

18. As to the question of the *Moniteur*'s availability in England, I am told by Professor Jack Censor, the historian of Anglo-French press relations in the 1790s, that the circulation of the *Moniteur* would have been roughly 8,000 and that some copies would inevitably have circulated across the Channel, but that the number of such copies would be difficult to estimate. But for Wordsworth's own subsequent optimism about "procuring a perusal" of the gazette, see below, chapter 9.

19. Vignery, *French Revolution and the Schools*, pp. 128–29.

20. The earlier work of the Committee is usefully summarized in Charles Hunter van Duzer, *Contribution of the Ideologues to French Revolutionary Thought* (Baltimore: The Johns Hopkins Press, 1935), pp. 84–114, a chapter on "The Spirit of Ideology in Education." For a general review of the Revolution's educational projects through 1793, see also Albert Duruy, *L-instruction publique et la Revolution* (Paris: Hachette, 1882), pp. 67–99, and L. Pearce Williams, "The Politics of Science in the French Revolution," in *Critical Problems in the History of Science*, ed. Marshall Clagett (Madison: University of Wisconsin Press, 1959), pp. 291–308. The proceedings of the Committee are available for this period in one volume, *Procès-verbaux du Comité d'instruction publique*, ed. M. J. Guillaume (Paris: Imprimerie Nationale, 1889).

21. See Keith Baker, *Condorcet* (Chicago: University of Chicago Press, 1975), pp. 293–303. What Baker says about Condorcet's development of a "social art" on scientific principles shows how important a forerunner he was for the likes of Lakanal.

22. Unlike Lakanal's addresses of 1794, Condorcet's *Report on Public Instruction* has been translated and is available in a collection of such writings, *French Liberalism and Education in the Eighteenth Century*, trans. and ed. F. de la Fontainerie (New York and London: McGraw-Hill, 1932).

23. This text is included among the notes for *The Prelude*, ed. Ernest de Selincourt and Helen Darbishire, pp. 545–46.

24. In this case, however, the parallel is with the Pantheonization speech where Wordsworth's "smooth high-way" is anticipated by Lakanal's smooth "road to virtue."

25. *Collected Letters of Samuel Taylor Coleridge*, ed. Earl Leslie Griggs, 4 vols. (Oxford: Clarendon Press, 1956–59), 1:453.

26. Citations from *Emile* are to Allan Bloom's translation (New York: Basic Books, 1979) and will be noted by page number in the text wherever possible.

27. Though she does not mention the monster child of *The Prelude*, Sylvia W. Patterson does point to the "perceptible influence of Rousseau on the notion of the totally good child" in the literature of this period, *Rousseau's Emile and Early Children's Literature* (Metuchen, N.J.: The Scarecrow Press, 1971), p. 158.

28. For more on this distinction see Baker, *Condorcet*, pp. 285–93, and Vignery, *French Revolution and the Schools*, pp. 17, 125.

29. Owen and Symser have pointed out that in the letter to Llandaff Wordsworth's linking of the names Maury and Cazales may derive from a comment of Burke's in the *Letter to a Member of the National Assembly*, *PrW* 1:65.

30. "Le contenu de cinq ou six pages, repartie dans deux écrits de Burke, a déterminé pour un siècle la fortune de Rousseau dans l'opinion anglaise," Jacques Voisine, *J. J. Rousseau en Angleterre à l'epoque romantique* (Paris: Didier, 1956), p. 137. Voisine's discussion of the entire Burke-Rousseau controversy is comprehensive and astute; see pp. 127–54. On Rousseau's reputation in England as the "philosopher of vanity," see pp. 241–58. Voisine is less accurate, but still informative, in his treatment of Rousseau's reception by the first-generation English romantics, pp. 157–240. See also Henri Roddier, *J.-J. Rousseau en Angleterre au XVIIIᵉ siècle* (Paris: Boivin, 1947), pp. 307–80, and Edward Duffy's recent *Rousseau in England* (Berkeley and Los Angeles: University of California Press, 1979), pp. 54–85. For contemporary responses to Burke's attacks on Rousseau see Capel Lofft, *Remarks on the Letter of the Rt. Hon. Edmund Burke, concerning the Revolution in France*, 2d ed., with *Remarks on Mr. Burke's Letter to a Member of the National Assembly* (London: J. Johnson, 1791), pp. 180–86, and Boothby, *Letter to Burke*, pp. 71–73.

Chapter 6: NATURAL LORE

1. James Butler, in the introduction to his edition of *The Ruined Cottage and the Pedlar* (Ithaca, N.Y.: Cornell University Press, 1979), p. 17. Butler's general discussion of the genesis of *The Ruined Cottage* is a valuable addition to the work of Thomas Raysor, "Wordsworth's Early Drafts of *The Ruined Cottage* in 1797–98," *JEGP* 55 (1956):1–7, and to the Appendix on the subject in Reed *EY*:337–39.

2. I should emphasize that this is *not* the text that Butler prints as MS. B in his parallel reading text (where it faces MS. D of 1799. Butler's MS. B is the 525-line version to which Wordsworth made additions before March 1798. Perhaps Butler chose not to print the March text, so important for its temporal proximity to Wordsworth's announcement of his great plan, because it was already available in de Selincourt's edition.

3. After six decades, the best treatment of this question is still be to found in Authur Beatty's *William Wordsworth: His Doctrine and Art in their Historical Relations*, 3d ed. (Madison: University of Wisconsin Press, 1960; first printed in 1922 as no. 17 in the University of Wisconsin Studies in Language and Literature), pp. 97–127.

4. Jean-Jacques then goes on to list specific measures called for by the application of his maxims (pp. 223–26).

5. My claim about the relation of the tales that the Pedlar is said to have heard as a boy and the tale that he now tells the speaker may be no more than a specification of Reeve Parker's more general suggestion that "whatever the autobiographical relevance of the wanderer's history, the emphasis is on the basis it provides for his dramatic role in educating the narrator"—" 'Finer Distance': The Narrative Act of Wordsworth's 'The Wanderer'," *ELH* 39 (March 1972):98.

6. Both the *Ruined Cottage* and *Excursion* passages, moreover, echo what is said of the Pedlar's moral power in *The Ruined Cottage*'s educational biography: "He cloathed the nakedness of austere truth" (207).

7. As Butler suggests, it may only have been Cottle's decision to print the *Lyrical Ballads* instead that caused *The Ruined Cottage* to miss "the chance of being considered by literary historians as the public beginning of the English Romantic movement," Introduction to *The Ruined Cottage and The Pedlar*, p. 22.

8. My citation from this work and from *Adventures on Salisbury Plain* are to *The Salisbury Plain Poems of William Wordsworth*, ed. Stephen Gill (Ithaca, N.Y.: Cornell University Press, 1975). For a fuller discussion of the relationship between these poems than what I offer here, see Gill's Introduction to this edition as well as his " 'Adventures on Salisbury Plain' and Wordsworth's Poetry of Protest 1795–97," *Studies in Romanticism* 11 (Winter 1972):48–65.

9. For specific echoes, see Paul Kelley's half-page note, "Rousseau's 'Discourse on the Origins of Inequality' and Wordsworth's 'Salisbury Plain,' " *Notes and Queries* 24 (July-August 1977):323. The only conclusion Kelley draws from his observations, however, is that "it seems clear that Rousseau's work affected Wordsworth's vision of primitive man, and thus Wordsworth's conception of the relationship of man and nature." Gill makes no mention of Rousseau in his commentary on these stanzas.

For another important and equally neglected instance of Rousseau's influence on the early radical poetry see the passage in *Descriptive Sketches* (1793) that begins

Once Man entirely free, alone and wild,
Was bless'd as free—for he was Nature's child.

He, all superior but his God disdain'd,
Walk'd none restraining, and by none restrain'd,
Confess'd no law but what his reason taught,
Did all he wish'd, and wish'd but what he ought.

[520–25]

The passage echoed is of course the celebrated opening of *The Social Contract*.

10. In both *Adventures* (397) and *The Ruined Cottage* (439), we are told that the narrator "paused," overtaken by emotion. In both cases this is followed by a break between the first and second "parts" of the poem. In both cases the second part begins with the listener's request that the speaker continue and the speaker's subsequent compliance.

11. James Averill, for example, in *Wordsworth and the Poetry of Human Suffering* (Ithaca, N.Y.: Cornell University Press, 1980), pp. 76–82, makes *Salisbury Plain* out to be far more like *The Ruined Cottage* in these respects than seems to me justified. He fails to see, or at least to emphasize, the markedly enlightened outlook of *Salisbury Plain*—what I describe below as Wordsworth's insistence that the heroes of truth pursue their march if the world is to be saved. What Averill claims is true of both poems, that "the narration itself works the change" in the listener, and that this occurs by simple "catharsis," seems to me true only of *The Ruined Cottage* (p. 77).

12. For an extended elucidation of the allusion see T. J. Gillcrist, "Spenser and Reason in the Conclusion of 'Salisbury Plain,'" *English Language Notes* 7 (September 1969):11–18.

13. Jonathan Wordsworth, *The Music of Humanity* (New York: Harper & Row, 1969), p. 95.

14. On Wordsworth's way of "'identifying' his speaker with his reader" in the poem, see William Galperin, "Imperfect while Unshared: The Role of the Implied Reader in Wordsworth's *Excursion*," *Criticism* 22 (1980):196. See also Averill, *Poetry of Human Suffering*, who calls the speaker "a comfortable surrogate for the reader," p. 173; my argument here is that the speaker only *begins* as a comfortable surrogate, becoming less comfortable as the tale progresses.

15. Jonathan Wordsworth, *The Music of Humanity*, p. 95.

16. James Thomson, *The Seasons and the Castle of Indolence*, ed. James Sambrook (Oxford: Clarendon Press, 1972).

17. What strengthens the connection of these lines to the period of 1793 alluded to in "Tintern Abbey" is that the opening description of the landscape in *The Ruined Cottage*, as Parker has argued ("Finer Distance," pp. 91–92), appears to be a reworking of lines 53–76 from Wordsworth's own *An Evening Walk* (1793). Wordsworth is thus evidently using his own blind submission to Thomson as a model target for his 1798 rhetorical strategy.

18. Frances Ferguson, in *Wordsworth: Language as Counter-Spirit* (Baltimore: The Johns Hopkins University Press, 1977), argues contrariwise that the Pedlar reforms the speaker "through his own character *as reader*" (p. 205; italics mine). Because our usage does not mesh in respect to certain key terms, this may not imply the disagreement it seems to. I would only stress here that the Pedlar himself became the (figurative) Reader he is on the strength of his training in oral lore. See also Frank McConnell, *The Confessional Imagination* (Baltimore: The Johns Hopkins University Press, 1974), pp. 123–25, who suggests that Wordsworth's early failure to respond well to a widow's suffering (*Prel.* 8:368–91) must be understood along similar lines: "It is a reduction of the widow's history to the conditions prescribed by a bookish muse, a conversion of story into text; and Wordsworth, after the

manner of Luther, will insist that the story is of, but not in, the text" (p. 125). Or again: "for both Luther and Wordsworth, that rigidity [of the printed word] must at all costs be liberated into the fluid vitality, spoken and heard, of words and images as aural" (p. 120).

19.   What I have to say in this chapter about the challenge posed to oral culture by the "ethos of letters" and, in the next, about traditionalist reactions to this challenge owes much to the historical anthropology of Eric Havelock, *Preface to Plato* (Cambridge, Mass.: Harvard University Press, 1963), and Jack Goody and Ian Watt, "The Consequences of Literacy" in *Literacy in Traditional Societies*, ed. Jack Goody (Cambridge: Cambridge University Press, 1968), pp. 27–68. These writers are concerned with the advent of literacy in ancient Greece rather than with the modern Enlightenment. But their more generalized speculations about how literacy goes, and is perceived to go, hand in hand with the development of logical analysis, historicism, and democracy constitute a useful elaboration of the comments quoted below from Hazlitt's discussion of letters, thought, and politics. I should, however, enter a brief qualification about the relevance of this scholarship. With respect to Havelock's argument, one can accept the value of his speculations about the oral-poetic state of mind of the Greeks, and about how "literate bookish culture" affected that state of mind, without insisting on the accuracy of his interpretation of Plato's philosophy as aligned with (even determined by) the latter. Goody and Watt themselves seem to disagree with some of Havelock's specific claims about Plato while corroborating his account of the general cultural shift. For recent arguments against the notion that literacy must be politically liberating, see Martin Hoyles, "The History and Politics of Literacy," in *The Politics of Literacy*, ed. Martin Hoyles (London: Writers and Readers Publishing Cooperative, 1977), pp. 29–30.

20.   Eisenstein quotes from Gay's *The Party of Humanity* (New York: Alfred A. Knopf, 1964), p. 117: "The philosophes were men of letters. This is more than a phrase. It defines their vantage point and eliminates the stale debate over their status as philosophers." She approves of Gay's effort to relate the philosophes "to a distinctive occupational culture," but adds a salutary qualification: "Since their 'single career' entailed the harnessing of pens to the new powers of the press, their 'vantage point' is not adquately defined by referring to the pen alone"—*The Printing Press as an Agent of Change*, 2 vols. (Cambridge and New York: Cambridge University Press, 1979), 1:146–47.

21.   Condorcet describes the history of human progress in ten phases rather than in Hazlitt's three, but the general outlines of the two narratives are similar and Condorcet's book was well-known in its 1795 English translation. It is referred to, for example, by Godwin in an Appendix added to the 1798 edition of *Enquiry Concerning Political Justice*, ed. Isaac Kramnick (New York: Penguin Books: 1976), pp. 270–71. Condorcet discusses the indispensability of "the art of printing" to the Enlightenment and the Revolution in his chapter on the Ninth Stage of human progress, pp. 139–40.

22.   In "The Consequences of Literacy," Goody and Watt describe similar effects of literacy on the politics of conversation, but their argument takes a somewhat different course from Hazlitt's:

> In non-literate society . . . , the cultural tradition functions as a series of interlocking face-to-face conversations in which the very conditions of transmission operate to favour consistency between past and present, and to make criticism—the articulation of inconsistency—less likely to occur; and if it does, the inconsistency makes a less permanent impact, and is more easily adjusted or forgotten. While scepticism may be present in such societies, it takes a personal, non-cumulative form; it does not lead to

a deliberate rejection and reinterpretation of social dogma so much as to a semi-automatic readjustment of belief.

In literate society, these interlocking conversations go on; but they are no longer man's only dialogue; and in so far as writing provides an alternative source for the transmission of cultural orientations it favours awareness of inconsistency. One aspect of this is a sense of change and of cultural lag; another is the notion that the cultural inheritance as a whole is composed of two very different kinds of material; fiction, error and superstition on the one hand; and, on the other, elements of truth which can provide the basis for some more reliable and coherent explanation of the gods, the human past and the physical world. [pp. 48–49]

23. Hazlitt's notion here is captured quite neatly in Oswald Spengler's claim that "Writing is the grand symbol of the far"—*The Decline of the West*, trans. Charles Francis Atkinson, 2 vols. (New York: Alfred A. Knopf, 1926–28), 2:150. For more on literacy and the emergence of abstract thought see Havelock, *Preface to Plato*, pp. 229–30, and Goody and Watt, "The Consequences of Literacy," pp. 52–55.

24. This and subsequent references to Blake's poetry are by plate and line number in *The Poetry and Prose of William Blake*, ed. David B. Erdman (Garden City, N.Y.: Doubleday, 1965).

25. See the "Introduction" to the *Songs of Innocence*.

26. Blake's position is as complicated on this issue as it is on most. For though he takes over the Enlightenment of the free press as an instrument of liberation, he insists at the same time that he must use the press to "cast off Rational Demonstration" and to "cast off Bacon, Locke & Newton" in the process (*Milton*, 41:3–5).

27. Unless otherwise indicated, all quotations from Coleridge's poetry are to *The Complete Poetical Works*, ed. E. H. Coleridge, 2 vols. (Oxford: Clarendon Press, 1912).

28. See Walter Jackson Bate, *Coleridge* (New York: Collier Books, 1968), p. 24.

29. Godwin, *Political Justice*, 1:xxvii.

30. "The Lamb created Beulah," explains Blake's personal lexicographer S. Foster Damon, "as a refuge from the gigantic warfare of ideas in Eternity; here flock all those who are exhausted, the weak, the terrified Emanations to rest in Sleep"—*A Blake Dictionary* (New York: E. P. Dutton & Co., 1971), p. 43. To appreciate the purport of Coleridge's long description of the "Valley of Seclusion" we must bear in mind that the poem offers "Reflections *on having left* a Place of Retirement": Coleridge is already gone. The governing tense of the poem is past, right from the opening line: "Low was our pretty Cot. . . ." Coleridge's poem has anticipated the Beulah-like repose from Mental Fight it pretends in its conclusion only to be predicting:

> Yet oft when after honourable toil
> Rests the tir'd mind, and waking loves to dream,
> My spirit shall revisit thee, dear Cot!
> Thy Jasmin and thy window-peeping Rose,
> And Myrtles fearless of the mild sea-air.
> And I shall sigh fond wishes—sweet Abode!
> Ah!—had none greater! And that all had such
> It might not be so—but the time is not yet.
> Speed it, O Father! Let thy Kingdom come!

> [64–71]

These lines, which follow immediately on those quoted above about Coleridge's decision to "fight the bloodless fight," in effect naturalize Godwin's moral theory and Blake's sublime allegory into the elements of an autobiographical drama. Elements like these, with similar purport, are rearranged by Wordsworth to create the drama of *The Recluse*.

31. The value of mental fight in an open press can also be traced to the intellectual history of the English Reformation. See for example John Foxe's 1563 account of "The Invention and Benefit of Printing": "the power of the Lord began to work for his church; not with sword and target to subdue his exalted adversary, but with printing, writing, and reading: to convince darkness by light, error by truth, ignorance by learning" *Acts and Monuments*, vols. (London: Seeley, Burnside, and Seeley, 1844) 3:719. My thanks to Janel Mueller for this reference. Milton's *Areopagitica*, of course, speaks to the same point: "And though all the winds of doctrine were let loose to play upon the earth, so Truth be in the field, we do injuriously by licensing and prohibiting to misdoubt her strength. Let her and Falsehood grapple; who ever knew Truth put to the worse, in a free and open encounter"— *Complete Poems and Major Prose*, p. 746. For an argument linking the reputation of seventeenth-century English radicalism with the French Revolution, see Zera S. Fink, "Wordsworth and the English Republican Tradition," *JEGP* 47 (April 1948):107–11.

32. For an (I think unpersuasive) argument to the contrary, see Ernest Bernhardt-Kabisch, "Wordsworth's Expostulator: Taylor or Hazlitt," *English Language Notes* 2 (December 1964):102–5.

33. Herschel Baker, *William Hazlitt* (Cambridge, Mass.: Harvard University Press, Belknap Press, 1962), pp. 143–49.

34. Lest this seem to invest the little ballad with an unwarranted claim to involvement with these philosophical matters, I should mention some of the pertinent "extrinsic" evidence. At the time he visited Wordsworth and Coleridge at Nether Stowey, young Hazlitt was in fact hard at work on a philosophical treatise he published seven years later under the title *Essay on the Principles of Human Action*. And one of the central issues in the *Essay* is the relation of voluntary and involuntary actions, Hazlitt arguing that the mind is strictly "rational or voluntary" in its pursuit of the future objects in which it is interested (*CWWH* 1:1–2). We know, moreover, that Hazlitt spoke with Wordsworth about his philosophical essay at some point because he says so: "I once explained the argument of that Essay to Mr. Wordsworth" (*CWWH* 9:4). Since Hazlitt visited with Wordsworth again in 1803, the evidence is inconclusive. But given that Hazlitt did discuss "moral philosophy" with Wordsworth in 1798, as we infer from the 1798 Advertisement to *Lyrical Ballads*, it seems reasonable to conclude that young Hazlitt would have spoken about that aspect of moral philosophy on which he was then engaged in study. Wordsworth, for his part, never forgot his first acquaintance with Hazlitt either. Hazlitt's grandson records that his father (Hazlitt's son) received a letter (on 23 May 1831) after Hazlitt's death in which Wordsworth recalled Hazlitt's forensic performance of thirty-three springs earlier and specifically noted that Hazlitt "was then remarkable for analytic power, and for acuteness and originality of mind"—quoted in W. Carew Hazlitt, *Four Generations of a Literary Family*, 2 vols. (London: George Redway, 1897), 1:233.

35. Sheats, *The Making of Wordsworth's Poetry*, p. 188, cf. pp. 207–10. For other discussions of the tone and purport of these two poems see Geoffrey Durrant, *Wordsworth and the Great System* (Cambridge: Cambridge University Press, 1970), pp. 3–6, and Jacobus, *Tradition and Experiments in Lyrical Ballads*, pp. 98–101.

36. If William is not rejecting conversation as such, neither is he, I want to reemphasize, rejecting books, only a mistaken view of them. For Matthew, books set the standard for the work of tradition, the process of learning from those who "lived before." For

William, tradition sets the standard for the work of books. Indeed, the final irony of these poems is that William, in his retreat from "books" (as understood by Matthew) to habitual impulse is the character who remains in a position to "drink the spirit breath's / From dead men to their kind."

37. One study I have found particularly illuminating for considering Wordsworth's ballad experiments in regard to the "ethos of letters" is David Buchan's *The Ballad and the Folk* (London: Routledge and Kegan Paul, 1972), esp. pp. 51–61, 167–73, 219–22, and 271–77. Buchan applies the well-publicized findings of Parry and Lord to the cultural history of the folk ballad in the North of England. He argues that the crucial transitional phase between the oral and the modern stages should be dated 1750–1830, a period of accelerated literacy in the region, and offers a Wordsworth-like analysis of the cultural consequences of this transition. Some of Buchan's speculations have been called into question by Ruth Finnegan, *Oral Poetry* (Cambridge: Cambridge University Press, 1977), pp. 253–54. But even if Finnegan's objections are anthropologically or historically sound, they do not render Buchan's account useless for understanding Wordsworth, who may simply have erred in similar ways. For discussion of Wordsworth's early environment as an oral culture see T. W. Thompson, *Wordsworth's Hawkshead*, ed. with introd. by Robert Woof (London: Oxford University Press, 1970), esp. pp. xv–xvi.

Chapter 7: TRADITIONALISM

1. See *BW* 3:236–44.

2. Hall, *Works*, 2:51–56; cf. 68–76.

3. For a small sampling of commentaries on Burke's doctrine of "traditionalism" (or his idea of "tradition") see the following: Friedrich Meinecke, *Historicism*, trans. J. E. Anderson (New York: Herder & Herder, 1972), pp. 219–32; Sabine, *History of Political Theory*, p. 607–19; Action, "Prejudice," p. 335; Pocock, "Burke and the Ancient Constitution," 202–5; Michael Freeman, *Edmund Burke and the Critique of Political Radicalism* (Oxford: Basil Blackwell, 1980), pp. 29–34.

4. Jonathan Swift, *Gulliver's Travels* 2 vols. (London: Benjamin Motte, 1726), 2:138.

5. Pocock, "Time, Institutions and Action; An Essay on Traditions and Their Understanding," in *Politics, Language and Time*, p. 237. Two other recent works that I have found useful in thinking about tradition and traditions are S. N. Eisenstadt, *Tradition, Change, and Modernity* (New York: Wiley, 1973), and Edward Shils, *Tradition* (Chicago: University of Chicago Press, 1981).

6. Pocock, "Time, Institutions and Action," p. 237.

7. Paine, *Writings*, 2:309.

8. Besides Jacobus's *Tradition and Experiment in Lyrical Ballads* and Jared Curtis's *Wordsworth's Experiments with Tradition* (Ithaca, N. Y.: Cornell University Press, 1971), there is of course Abrams's *Natural Supernaturalism*, subtitled "Tradition and Revolution in Romantic Literature," which prompted *The Wordsworth Circle* to produce a special issue on the subject 3 (Autumn 1972):195–240.

9. Ernest de Selincourt, ed. *Journals of Dorothy Wordsworth*, 2 vols. (New York: The Macmillan Co., 1941), 1:76.

10. Pocock, "Time, Institutions, and Action," p. 240.

11. The phrase "book learning" is actually used by Dorothy in a letter to Mrs. John Marshall of 19 March 1797. Since the subject of her remarks is hers and William's rearing of

Basil Montagu, they are worth citing here: "You ask to be informed of our system respecting Basil; it is a very simple one, so simple that in this age of systems you will hardly be likely to follow it. We teach him nothing at present but what he learns from the evidence of his senses. He has an insatiable curiosity which we are always careful to satisfy to the best of our ability. It is directed to everything he sees, the sky, the fields, trees, shrubs, corn, the making of tools, carts, &c, &c, &c.; he knows his letters, but we have not attempted any further step in the path of *book learning*" (*EY*:180). Falling in the crucial transition year of her brother's development, the letter reflects a mixture of pre- and post-1797 attitudes.

12. Hartman errs, I think, when he insists that the poem is meant to illustrate "an immemorial covenant between man and the land"—"the covenant that holds the mind of man to the earth," *Wordsworth's Poetry*, p. 265. The covenant is between man and man, specifically between father and son. The land, like the sheepfold Michael begins to erect on it, is a monument to (reminder of) this social arrangement. Wordsworth does, as Hartman persuasively argues, bind himself to Nature, but what gets forgotten in this formula is the way Wordsworth uses terrestrial nature to forge the link with ancestral nature. Though the two natures operate dialectically, as we have seen, he corroborates the emphasis I place here on the bond of second nature in what he writes about men like Michael to Charles James Fox in 1800:

> Their little tract of land serves as a kind of permanent rallying point for their domestic feelings, as a tablet upon which they are written which makes them objects of memory in a thousand instances when they would otherwise be forgotten. It is a fountain fitted to the nature of social man from which the supplies of affection, as pure as his heart was intended for, are daily drawn. [p. 314–15]

Wordsworth's letter to Fox (as Chester Shaver explains), "one of some half-dozen sent, at S. T. C.'s suggestion, with complimentary copies of the second edition of *Lyrical Ballads* to 'persons of eminence'" (*EY*:312), has been interpreted by both his major biographers as evidence for his continuing liberalism in *Lyrical Ballads*. G. M. Harper claims that the ideas it expresses are "perfectly in harmony with his Revolutionary zeal of former years" (*William Wordsworth*, 2:233), and Moorman recommends comparison of the letter with the Llandaff document of 1793 so that we can see that, although "the revolutionary destructiveness is gone, . . . the glowing concern for human ills is still there, enriched by compassion and knowledge" (Moorman *EY*:503). But like the poem itself, Wordsworth's remarks about "Michael," to which (along with "The Brothers") Wordsworth directs Fox's attention, would seem to align him with Burke rather than with the young radical who attacked Burke in 1793. To see this we need only recall what Burke says about domestic affections in the *Reflections* (*BW* 3:494), quoted above on p. 39. To answer the question of why Wordsworth would choose so Whiggish a statesman as the target of his appeal, we need to recognize that Wordsworth *is* making an appeal. If Fox were already a champion of "domestic affections," then Wordsworth would have no need of so addressing him in the first place. Wordsworth does open his letter with high praise of Fox, but this flattery focuses on Fox's "sensibility of heart" rather than on his political opinions and seems aimed precisely to prepare the statesman to accept an idea to which he might not readily subscribe.

Fox's response is hospitable enough:

> The poems have given me the greatest pleasure; and if I were obliged to choose out of them, I do not know whether I should not say that "Harry Gill," "We are Seven," "The Mad Mother," and "The Idiot," are my favourites. I read with particular

attention the two you pointed out; but whether it be from early prepossessions, or whatever other cause, I am no great friend to blank verse for subjects which are to be treated of with simplicity. You will excuse my stating my opinion to you so freely, which I should not do if I did not really admire many of the poems in the collection, and many parts even of those in blank verse. [Moorman *EY*:505–6]

But whereas Wordsworth offers the volumes to Fox as social commentary, Fox seems to show interest in the poems only as poetry, and offers praise for some of the more innocuous of the ballads. Moreover, Fox's exclusively technical response to the two blank-verse poems Wordsworth singled out for special attention must, as Stephen Parrish has observed, "have been disheartening," especially since the blank verse is intended to show the weight of those poems' subject matter—*The Art of the Lyrical Ballads*, p. 183. The coda to this episode is Fox's remark on meeting Wordsworth, for the first and last time, six years later: "I am glad to see Mr. Wordsworth, though we differ as much in our views of politics as we do in our views of poetry," quoted in Harper, *William Wordsworth*, 2:113.

13. According to Dorothy Wordsworth, some of these tales were "half as long as an ancient romance," a report that corroborates William's feeling of having grown up in a powerfully oral culture—*Journals*, 1:309.

14. This reflexivity has also been noted in a recent essay by Sydney Lea, "Wordsworth and his 'Michael': The Pastor Passes," *ELH* 45 (Spring 1978):58; see also Peter J. Manning's psychological interpretation in " 'Michael,' Luke, and Wordsworth," *Criticism* 19 (Winter 1977):195–211.

15. We must note that the covenant at the center of "Michael" is transgenerational: it is the Burkean sort of covenant that, following Paine, Wordsworth had denounced in the Letter to Llandaff as barbaric, one which "yokes the living to the dead" (*PrW* 1:48); see Paine, *Writings*, 2:304–5.

16. Thompson, "Disenchantment or Default?," p. 175.

17. Havelock describes the oral-poetic psychology as "a state of total personal involvement and therefore of emotional identification with the substance of the poetised statement" (*Preface to Plato*, p. 44). It is a "way of reliving experience in memory instead of analysing and understanding it" (p. 45). But this sort of reenactment, Havelock adds, "does not insure that the past is accurately recorded and preserved. On the contrary, the confusion between past and present time guarantees that the past is slowly but continuously contaminated with the present as folkways slowly change" (p. 122). Goody and Watt speak to the same point when they assert that "the writing down of some of the main elements in the cultural tradition . . . brought about an awareness of two things: of the past as different from the present; and of the inherent inconsistencies in the picture of life as it was inherited by the individual from the cultural tradition in its recorded form" ("The Consequences of Literacy," p. 56).

18. This particular formulation is Pocock's in "Time, Institutions and Action," p. 253, but for related discussions see Goody and Watt, "The Consequences of Literacy," pp. 49–67, and Page Smith, *The Historian and History* (New York: Alfred A. Knopf, 1964), p. 55.

19. See Alex Zwerdling, "Wordsworth and Greek Myth," *University of Toronto Quarterly* 33 (July 1964):341–54; Zwerdling sets this sonnet next to the lines from *The Excursion* discussed below.

20. William Empson, *Seven Types of Ambiguity* (New York: New Directions, 1947; revised from British edition, 1930), pp. 151–54.

21. G. P. Gooch, *History and Historians in the Nineteenth Century* (Boston: Beacon Press, 1959; first pub. London: Longmans, Green, & Co., 1913), p. 14.

22. Peter Gay, *Style in History* (New York: Basic Books, 1974), p. 74.

23. Barthold Georg Niebuhr, *The History of Rome*, trans. Julius Charles Hare and Connop Thirlwall, 2 vols. (Philadelphia: Lea & Blanchard, 1844), 1:xi–xii.

24. Gay, *Style in History*, p. 74.

25. Hans-Georg Gadamer, *Truth and Method* (New York: Seabury Press, 1975), p. 242.

26. Parrish, *The Art of the Lyrical Ballads*, pp. 151–55.

27. For a related argument deployed to a somewhat different purpose, see Edward E. Bostetter, *The Romantic Ventriloquists*, rev. ed. (Seattle: University of Washington Press, 1973). Using "syntax" in the broadest sense, Bostetter describes the history of romantic poetry as "in part the history of a syntax that proved inadequate to the demands placed upon it" and describes Wordsworth's poetry as "a retreat back to a traditional and orthodox syntax . . . to protect fundamental illusions" (pp. 5–6).

28. This passage, with only minor revision, was retained through all the manuscripts of *The Prelude*, which means that Wordsworth wanted it to appear together with the "Genius of Burke" passage that he added to book 7, where he praises Burke as the vigorous old man who "the majesty proclaims / Of Institutes and Laws, hallowed by time" and "Declares the vital power of social ties / Endeared by Custom" /1850:525–28). We must conclude, therefore, either that the lines about the "advocates . . . Of ancient institutions" do not refer to Burke, or that they also (i.e., in addition to the lines following the mention of the "veil") are meant to reflect Wordsworth's attitude in 1793.

Chapter 8: The Discipline of an English Poet's Mind

1. Jonathan Bishop, "Wordsworth and the 'Spots of Time,'" *ELH* 26 (March 1959):45.

2. The first phase is Herbert Lindenberger's, *On Wordsworth's Prelude* (Princeton, N.J.: Princeton University Press, 1963), p. 3. The second two are Harold Bloom's, *The Visionary Company*, pp. 148, 149. The last, of course, is Geoffrey Hartman's, *Wordsworth's Poetry*, listed in his index.

3. See Lindenberger's similar criticism of Bishop in *On Wordsworth's Prelude*, p. 156.

4. Earl R. Wasserman, *The Subtler Language* (Baltimore, Md.: The Johns Hopkins University Press, 1959), p. 182.

5. See Hugh Kenner's excellent discussion of this strategy in canto 1: *The Pound Era* (Berkeley and Los Angeles: University of California Press, 1971), p. 349.

6. Stephen Parrish's extended discussion of the ambiguous question "Was it for this" goes awry, I think, where Parrish observes (partly on the basis of other manuscript evidence) that " 'This' seems here to have been the powerful disturbance of mind occasioned by a superabundant flow of inspiration—not incapacity, or guilt, or self-reproach of the type that later entered the 'post-preamble' [i.e., lines 55–271]"—Introduction to his edition of *The Prelude*, 1798–99, p. 6. Because the superabundance of "inspiration" betokens a problem in itself, it occasions the sense of incapacity, guilt, and self-reproach that is later spelled out in detail and prefixed to the 1799 *Prelude*. Viewed in the proper light, in other words, the conflict Parrish sees between the two accounts disappears.

7. Hartman, *Wordsworth's Poetry*, p. 38.

8. Elizabeth Sewall, *The Orphic Voice* (New Haven: Yale University Press, 1960), p. 342.

9. See, for example, Abrams, *Natural Supernaturalism*, pp. 284–92; Brian Wilkie, *Romantic Poets and Epic Tradition* (Madison and Milwaukee: University of Wisconsin Press, 1965), pp. 77–97; and Abbie Findlay Potts, *Wordsworth's Prelude* (Ithaca, N.Y.: Cornell University Press, 1953), pp. 218–43.

10. See especially Abrams, *Natural Supernaturalism*, pp. 115–16, and Sewall, *Orphic Voice*, p. 342. More recently, Edward Said, *Beginnings* (New York: Basic Books, 1975), pp. 44–45, has pointed out another Miltonic allusion in the Preamble, one which highlights the impropriety of the poet's initial sense of escape. Said recommends that we "compare Wordsworth's image of how he

> escaped
> From the vast city, where I long had pined
> A discontented sojourner: now free,
> Free as a bird to settle where I will,

in book 1 of *The Prelude* with Milton's Satan:

> Here at least
> We shall be free: th'Almighty hath not built
> Here for his envy, will not drive us hence:
> Here we may reign secure, and in my choyce
> To reign is worth ambition though in Hell:
> Better to reign in Hell, then serve in Heav'n."

Said sees the problem of the poet's "unrestrained sentiments" here in essentially formal terms: "As a poem of beginning, *The Prelude* shed its unconditional early liberty for the purpose of forging the beginning—as distinguished from a narrator's mere initial enthusiasm." The claim is right as far as it goes, but it needs to be extended to embrace the moral and historical issues at stake in the poem.

11. For a somewhat different account of the relation of Wordsworth's last two (apparently) discarded plans to the rest of his poem, see Frances Ferguson, *Language as Counter-Spirit* (New Haven: Yale University Press, 1977), pp. 128–29. Ferguson emphasizes the persistence of Wordsworth's indecision throughout the poem and suggests that it centers on the question of the relation between the individual mind and nature.

12. The phrase is Walter Jackson Bate's. See his *From Classic to Romantic* (New York: Harper & Row, 1961; first pub., Cambridge, Mass.: Harvard University Press, 1946), pp. 129–59.

13. Meinecke, *Historicism*, p. 228.

14. Lloyd Paul Stryker, *For the Defense* (Garden City, N.Y.: Doubleday & Company, 1947). The description of Erskine occurs in the book's subtitle. On the subject of Erskine's *View of the Causes and Consequences*, Stryker writes that "it deserves to live as the true foil for [the *Letters on a Regicide Peace*] which Edmund Burke was writing on the same subject" (p. 352).

15. Thomas Erskine, *View of the Causes and Consequences of the Present War with France* (London: printed for J. Debrett, 1797), p. 30.

16. *Reasons Against National Despondency: In Refutation of Mr. Erskine's View of the*

Causes and Consequences of the Present War (London: printed for T. Cadell and W. Davies, 1797). At the outset of the pamphlet, the unknown author gives the following account of his motives: "Thinking, as I do from my soul, that Mr. Erskine's View of the Causes and Consequences of the present war with France, is not calculated to inspire this country with such sentiments as accord with her present situation—that it tends to advise measures derogatory to her pristine glory, unworthy of her present power, and inconsistent with her future safety; I do not need an apology for the attempt to refute his options" (p. 5).

17. "Despondency" is of course the very same term Wordsworth uses to name the condition, also induced by Gallic speculation, of the Solitary in *The Excursion*—see books 3 and 4.

18. "Personal epic" is Karl Kroeber's way of characterizing *The Prelude* in *Romantic Narrative Art* (Madison: University of Wisconsin Press, 1960), pp. 84–85; "crisis-autobiography" is Abrams's term for the poem in *Natural Supernaturalism*, pp. 71–140.

19. See, for example, the qualifications Burke enters in his discussion of feudal political economy in the *Reflections* (3:528–32). See also Kramnick's discussion of Burke as a bourgeois critic of vestigial feudal practices, *The Rage of Edmund Burke*, pp. 161–62.

20. Barbara T. Gates, "Wordsworth's Historical Imagination," *Etudes anglaises* 30 (1977):175.

21. I say "ostensibly" because the moral rhetoric of *The Prelude* is complicated by the role of Coleridge, discussed below in chapter 10.

22. In a brief but illuminating comment linking Wordsworth's rationalist phase with Rousseau and his recovery with Burke, Margery Sabin points toward the political differences implied in the contrast between Rousseauist recollection in *The Confessions* and Wordsworthian recollection in *The Prelude*—*English Romanticism and the French Tradition* (Cambridge, Mass.: Harvard University Press, 1976), pp. 82–83.

23. For a related discussion of the temporal duality of the boat-stealing episode see McConnell, *The Confessional Imagination*, pp. 94–98. McConnell later makes a more general distinction between Wordsworth's "two movements of thought, one narrat*ed*, one narrat*ive*" (p. 127). See also Gene Ruoff's insightful account of Wordsworthian narrative in "The Sense of a Beginning: *Mansfield Park* and Romantic Narrative," *The Wordsworth Circle* 10 (Spring 1979):174–86.

24. The temporal structure of "The Solitary Reaper" is, roughly, that of "I wandered . . ." turned inside out. There the habitual imaginative vision (what flashes on the poet's eye) is presented first and is elaborated in three present-tense stanzas. The narrative of the past encounter, marked by the tense shift, occupies the fourth and final stanza. That the "twofold shout" of the bird in "To the Cuckoo" should be interpreted along similarly dual temporal lines is also suggested by a tense shift: "I have heard, / I hear thee" (1–2). And here again we find the same emphasis on temporal conflation:

> And I can listen to thee yet;
> Can lie upon the plain
> And listen, till I do beget
> That golden time again.
>
> [25–28]

25. As Wordsworth said, rather ungenerously, of a reader who professed no appreciation of *The Excursion*: "a Soul that has been dwarfed by a course of bad culture cannot, after a certain age, be expanded into one of even ordinary proportion" (*MY* 2:188).

Chapter 9: AN IDEOLOGY AGAINST "IDEOLOGY"

1. The definition I offer is in keeping with what John Plamenatz, for example, says about the "family of concepts" associated with the word; see *Ideology* (New York: Praeger Publishers, 1970), pp. 15–31. See also Raymond Williams, *Marxism and Literature* (Oxford: Oxford University Press, 1978), pp. 55–71.

2. Daniel Bell, *The End of Ideology* (Glencoe, Ill.: Free Press, 1960), p. 370.

3. Michael Oakeshott, "Political Education," in *Rationalism in Politics*, p. 122.

4. *Correspondance de Napoléon Ier*, publiée par ordre de l'Empereur Napoléon III, 32 vols. (Paris: Plon & Dumaine, 1858–70), 24:343.

5. Quoted in *The Mind of Napoleon* (New York: Columbia University Press, 1955), pp. 70, 67.

6. Oakeshott, "Political Education," pp. 119–23.

7. I should comment briefly on Roger Sharrock's *"The Prelude*: The Poet's Journey to the Interior," *English* 19 (Spring 1970):1–6. Whether or not one accepts Sharrock's claim that the France books constitute a "masterly analysis of the modern discursive intelligence," his observation about Wordsworth's implied political views in those books is worth taking seriously: "perhaps the only contemporary English political philosopher he might have sympathized with is Professor Michael Oakeshott, with his way of looking at political attitudes as a matter of man's habitual arrangements, and not either of theory or of scientific scrutiny" (pp. 2–3). Sharrock does not himself elaborate the remark, but he might have done so almost at random from Oakeshott's essay on "Political Education." He might, for example, have cited Oakeshott's attack on those who suppose "that a political ideology is the product of intellectual premeditation and that, because it is a body of principles not itself in debt to the activity of attending to the arrangements of a society, it is able to determine and guide the direction of that activity"; or he might have cited Oakeshott's corrected view of the matter: "Instead of an independently premeditated scheme of ends to be pursued, it is a system of ideas abstracted from the manner in which people have been accustomed to go about the business of attending to the arrangements of their societies" (pp. 118–19). Or he might have cited Oakeshott's account of what the French Revolution's *Rights of Man* owed to the common-law rights of Englishmen, the product not of the night of 4 August 1789, but of "centuries of the day-to-day attending to the arrangements of a historic society" (p. 120). Oddly, however, having seen the compatibility of Wordsworth's and Oakeshott's views, Sharrock seems not to see the immense debt each owes to a common source: Burke.

8. The most comprehensive study of the Ideologue movement is still François Picavet, *Les Idéologues* (Paris: Bailliere, 1894). Picavet surveys the Ideologues' involvement in educational schemes on pp. 32–85; he discusses the roles of Lakanal and Garat specifically on pp. 124–27 and 157–69. The best general studies in English are George Boas, *French Philosophies of the Romantic Period* (Baltimore: The Johns Hopkins University Press, 1925), pp. 1–69, and Van Duzer, *Contribution of the Ideologues to French Revolutionary Thought*, passim.

9. Emmet Kennedy, *A Philosophe in the Age of Revolution: Destutt de Tracy and the Origins of "Ideology"* (Philadelphia: American Philosophical Society, 1978), p. 40. Although Kennedy's study goes back over some of the same ground covered by Picavet's chapters on Tracy (*Les Ideologues*, pp. 293–398), it is an invaluable resource for those interested in Tracy or in the early use of the term he coined.

10. Antoine-Louis-Claude Destutt de Tracy, *Mémoire sur la Faculté de Penser*, in

Mémoires de l'Institut national des sciences et arts. Classes des Sciences morales et politiques, an IV–an XI, 5 vols. (Paris: an VI–1804), 1:283–450.

11. Ibid., p. 322; all translations from the *Mémoires* are mine. Relating the various parts of the *Mémoire sur la Faculté de penser* to specific addresses at earlier meetings must remain a matter of probable reasoning. I have relied on published reports of the contents of the earlier meetings and on Kennedy, *Philosophe in the Age of Revolution*, pp. 52–68.

12. Tracy, *Mémoire sur la Faculte de penser*, p. 324.

13. Tracy, *Elémens d'Idéologie*, 3 vols. (Paris: Madame Levi, 1827; first edition printed in 1801), 1:xxi, my translation.

14. Tracy, *Mémoire sur la Faculté de penser*, p. 287; see Kennedy, *Philosophe in the Age of Revolution*, p. 45.

15. Tracy, *Mémoire sur la Faculté de penser*, p. 324. The two articles that follow Tracy's in this first volume of the *Mémoires* are Laromiguière's attempts (in the same spirit of ideology) to specify precisely the meaning of the elements in Tracy's precise definition: *Sur la détermination de ces mots, "analyse des sensation" and extrait d'un mémoire sur la détermination du mot "idée," par le même* (pp. 451–74).

16. Joanna Kitchin, *Un journal "philosophique": La decade (1794–1807)* (Paris: J. Minard, 1965), p. 118, n. 7.

17. Tracy, *Mémoire sur la Faculté de penser*, pp. 285–86. For a full discussion of the Ideologues' philosophical reductionism, see Emmet Kennedy, "Destutt de Tracy and the Unity of the Sciences," *Studies on Voltaire and the Eighteenth Century*, ed. Haydn Mason (Oxford: Voltaire Foundation, 1977), 171:223–39.

18. Tracy, *Dissertations sur quelques questions d'idéologie, Mémoires de l'Institut*, pp. 492–93.

19. Tracy, *Mémoire sur la Faculté de penser*, pp. 443–44.

20. Tracy, *A Treatise on Political Economy: To Which Is Prefixed a Supplement to a Preceding Work on the Understanding, or Elements of Ideology*, trans. Thomas Jefferson (Georgetown, D.C.: Joseph Milligan, 1817), p. 3.

21. Tracy, *Mémoire sur la Faculté de penser*, p. 335.

22. John O. Hayden, *The Romantics Reviewed* (Chicago: University of Chicago Press, 1968), p. 58.

23. *Monthly Magazine* 3 (February 1797):125.

24. *Monthly Magazine* 1 (March 1796):119.

25. *Monthly Magazine* 2 (September 1796):632.

26. *Monthly Magazine* 3 (April 1797):285–86.

27. Ibid., p. 286.

28. The text for MS. B is my own transcription, with the aid of de Selincourt's apparatus, of the photocopy housed in the Cornell Wordsworth Collection, reproduced here by permission of Jonathan Wordsworth and the Trustees of Dove Cottage. (Cf. *Prel.* 10:805–29, 878–900.)

29. The controversy over how Godwin figures in *The Borderers* is reviewed by Alan Grob, "Wordsworth and Godwin: A Reassessment," *Studies in Romanticism* 6 (Winter 1967):98–119. Grob rightly observes that the "relationship of *The Borderers* to Godwinism still remains one of the most exasperating matters in Wordsworthian scholarship and has probably generated more conflicting and irreconcilable commentary than any other single issue" (p. 118 n). For a subsequent review of the positions, including Grob's, see Donald G.

Priestman, "The Borderers: Wordsworth's Addenda to Godwin," *University of Toronto Quarterly* 44 (Fall 1974):56–65.

30. On the Ideologues' debt to Bacon and use of the Baconian table, see Kennedy, *Philosophe in the Age of Revolution*, pp. 47–49.

31. For more on "methodical medicine" and the Ideologues see Martin S. Staum, *Cabanis* (Princeton, N.J.: Princeton University Press, 1980). A related comment occurs later in the act where Rivers flatters Mortimer: "You have taught mankind to seek the measure of justice / By diving for it into their own bosoms" (MS. B). The irony here, of course, is that, in following Rivers's advice, Mortimer has, like Rivers himself, ceased to consult his own bosom. The resemblance of Rivers's attitude to "Ideology," in this respect, is suggested by Kennedy's observation that "the unconscious is a phenomenon which the 'ideologist' sees into and explains, rather than something which influences him"—*Philosophe in the Age of Revolution*, p. 67.

32. See Dawson, *Lakanal the Regicide*, pp. 8–11.

33. Van Duzer, *Contribution of the Ideologues to French Revolutionary Thought*, p. 7.

34. See John E. Jordan's discussion of the absence of topical allusions from *Lyrical Ballads* in *Why the Lyrical Ballads?*, pp. 132-33. To the extent that one accepts George Watson's claim that Wordsworth's mind was "politically specific," the nonspecificity of the early major poetry seems that much more curious—"The Revolutionary Youth of Wordsworth and Coleridge," *Critical Quarterly* 18 (Autumn 1976):55.

35. What I am offering here, in effect, is not just a way of showing the subtle coherence of book 5, but also a way of explaining why that coherence has been so nettling an issue for the poem's critics. See Havens, *The Mind of a Poet*, p. 376; W. G. Stobie, "A Reading of *The Prelude*, Book V." *MLQ* 4 (December 1963):365–73; Morkan, "Structure and Meaning in *The Prelude*, Book V"; and David Wiener, "Wordsworth, Books and the Growth of a Poet's Mind," *JEGP* 74 (April 1975):209–20.

36. *Moniteur*, 28 October 1794, p. 349.

Chapter 10: THE ROLE OF COLERIDGE

1. One of the scenes on which Wordsworth drew heavily is act 3, scene 3. An example of the process I describe here can be seen in the way the Shakespearean language of proving and rationality from *Othello* (Othello's famous "give me the ocular proof," "a living reason") seems ideologically neutral in Wordsworth's earliest written scenes and only later takes on the Enlightenment and revolutionary connotations it has in the mouth of the fully developed character of Rivers.

2. Frank Kermode, *The Genesis of Secrecy* (Cambridge, Mass.: Harvard University Press, 1979), pp. 83–99.

3. There is, of course, a long history of criticism for *The Borderers*, much too long to summarize here. Though much of this criticism is contextual, and very good, Robert Osborn's "Meaningful Obscurity: The Antecedents and Character of Rivers," in *Bicentenary Wordsworth Studies*, ed. Jonathan Wordsworth, is the first essay to combine source studies with serious study of the play's manuscript history. Osborn effectively argues that Rivers's obscurity "is the result of a complex evolution from the various sources on which Wordsworth drew, and of the need to create a character who would fulfill a complex function in relation to Mortimer" (p. 395). But the usefulness of Osborn's analysis for present purposes is limited by his formalist premises, for in offering one kind of genetic explanation he means

to be refuting another: "Rivers's 'metaphysical obscurity' is neither a consequence of Wordsworth's private mental and emotional confusion, nor the product of a distinct Romantic purpose 'formally conceived' but poorly executed for lack of a suitable established artistic medium" (p. 395). This approach leads to Osborn's neglect of the play's evolving *ideological* patterns and explains why the fullest existing account of the play, perhaps the only truly genetic account of it, has comparatively little to say about the play's politics. Osborn's expected edition of the play in the Cornell Wordsworth will undoubtedly open up important new possibilities for such study.

4. *The Friend*, ed. Barbara E. Rooke 2 vols (London: Routledge & Kegan Paul; Princeton, N.J.: Princeton University Press, 1969), 2:123; this is vol. 4 in *The Collected Works of Samuel Taylor Coleridge*, ed. Kathleeen Coburn, Bolligen Series LXXV.

5. Recent discussions of the early divergence between Wordsworth and Coleridge include the following: George Whalley, "Preface to *Lyrical Ballads*: A Portent," *University of Toronto Quarterly* 25 (1956):467–83; A. M. Buchan, "The Influence of Wordsworth on Coleridge (1795–1800)," *University of Toronto Quarterly* 32 (July 1963):346–65; Parrish, *The Art of the Lyrical Ballads*, passim; Don Bialostosky, "Coleridge's Interpretation of Wordsworth's Preface to *Lyrical Ballads*," *PMLA* 93 (October 1978):912–24. William Heath touches on these matters in *Wordsworth and Coleridge* (Oxford: Clarendon Press, 1970), esp. pp. 68–107. For an interesting attempt to reassert the importance of Coleridge's influence while at the same time acknowledging critical divergences (including some I discuss here), see Thomas McFarland's very recent discussion, "The Symbiosis of Coleridge and Wordsworth" in *Romanticism and the Forms of Ruin* (Princeton, N.J.: Princeton University Press, 1981), pp. 56–103.

6. Woodring comments incisively on the role of the speaker as "archetype," though not on the similar function of the addressee, in *Politics in English Romantic Poetry*, pp. 102–3.

7. Review of *Poems* (3d ed.) in *Annual Review* 2 (1804):554; *Romantics Reviewed*, ed. Reiman, part A, 1:12.

8. Bate, *Coleridge*, p. 117.

9. *Collected Letters*, ed. Griggs, 1:656.

10. "Reminiscences of the Rev. R. P. Graves," in *The Prose Works of William Wordsworth*, ed. Alexander B. Grosart, 3 vols. (London: Edward Moxon, 1876), 3:469. As early as 1798, John Thelwall had remarked upon what he called Coleridge's "repugnance to all regular routine & application"—cited in Thompson, "Disenchantment or Default," p. 162.

11. That Wordsworth linked Coleridge's problems with those of the age generally—i.e., with his readers' problems—is strongly suggested by the remark recorded in Henry Crabb Robinson's Diary for 1812, as quoted in F. M. Todd, *Politics and the Poet*, p. 168: "mention of Coleridge's facile emotionalism 'led Wordsworth to observe on the false sensibility and tendency to tears in the present age.'" Like Burke, Wordsworth seems consistently to align the penchant for metaphysical speculation with the tendency to emotional self-indulgence. Like Burke, too, he argues that the way to avoid both of these problems is by trusting to those feelings that have been so disciplined as to make one's duty a part of one's nature—these alone constitute the "philosophic mind." It is probably worth adding in this connection that the celebrated estrangement between Wordsworth and Coleridge in 1812 occurred precisely over remarks Wordsworth is alleged to have made to Basil Montagu about Coleridge's "habits"—see *The Diary of Henry Crabb Robinson*, abridged and ed. Derik Hudson (London: Oxford University Press, 1967), p. 17.

12. Bloom, *The Visionary Company*, p. 199.

13. Hartman, *Wordsworth's Poetry*, p. 281.

14. De Selincourt and Darbishire's text for these stanzas is not substantially different from that of MS. M (DC MS. 44), which dates from the crucial month of March 1804.

15. Kant makes these distinctions in the first section of his *Foundations of the Metaphysics of Morals*, collected in *Critique of Practical Reason and Other Writings*, ed. Beck, pp. 58–61.

16. *The Notebooks of Samuel Taylor Coleridge*, ed. Kathleen Coburn, 3 vols. (New York: Pantheon Books, Bolligne Series L, 1957–73), vol. 1: Entries #1705 and n, 1710 and n, 1711 and n, 1717 and n, 1722, 1723 and n (all dating from December 1804). But notice the possible concession to empirical morality in #1722.

17. Ibid., vol. 1: Entry #1723 and n.

18. Leslie Brisman approaches the "Ode" through Milton rather than through the moral philosophy of Coleridge and Kant, but some of his points are quite compatible with my conclusions here—*Milton's Poetry of Choice and its Romantic Heirs* (Ithaca, N.Y.: Cornell University Press, 1973), pp. 234–46.

19. *Collected Letters*, ed. Griggs, 1:397.

20. Putting the question this way means that, for purposes of this discussion, not even the anti-French political journalism he undertook after snapping his seditious trumpet will decide the matter. Wordsworth might, for example, have taken Coleridge's enthusiastic involvement with the London press as stronger evidence of his frame of mind than the specific content of his articles. Coleridge's own view of his journalistic work, a view he may have shared with Wordsworth, certainly invites this interpretation:

> The dedication of much hope & fear to subjects which are perhaps disproportionate to our faculties & powers, is a disease. But I have had this disease so long . . . that I know not how to get rid of it; or even wish to get rid of it. Life were so flat a thing without Enthusiasm—that if for a moment it leave me, I have a sort of a stomach-sensation . . . like those which succeed to the pleasurable operation of a dose of Opium.

(Cited by David Erdman in "Coleridge as Editorial Writer," in *Power and Consciousness*, ed. O'Brien and Vanech, p. 187.) Moreover, Coleridge's journalism was not consistently anti-Gallic after 1798, a fact which prompts Erdman to speak of Coleridge's "oscillation" rather than his "recantation" (p. 188).

Putting the question this way also means, of course, that the fact that Coleridge also came round to praise the genius of Burke will likewise not decide the question. In 1833, for example, Coleridge spoke of Burke's "transcendent greatness," though he qualified his praise by noting that one finds "many half-truths in his speeches and writings"—*Table Talk*, 2 vols. (New York: Harper & Brothers, 1835), 2:77. Coleridge's debt to Burke in the important late political writings, such as *On the Constitution of Church and State* (1829), has been remarked upon by virtually every major commentator.

21. "Nitsch's *View of Kant's Principles*," *Monthly Review* 22 (January–April 1797):15.

22. William Taylor, "Willich's *Elements of Kant's Philosophy*," *Monthly Review* 28 (January–April 1799):65. According to René Wellek, Taylor's review was widely read in its day, *Immanuel Kant in England* (Princeton, N.J.: Princeton University Press, 1931), p. 268 n. 40. For a detailed discussion of "Kant's Introduction into England," see pp. 3–21. On the subject of Kant and France, Wellek mentions that the Abbé Barruel "had included Kant as a Jacobin and atheist" in his "Mémoires pour servir à l'Histoire du Jacobinism," a tract published in London in 1797 and translated into English in the same year (p. 14).

23. The most detailed discussions of Kant's response to the French Revolution are Paul Schrecker, "Kant et la Revolution Française," in *La Revolution de 1789 et la pensée moderne* (Paris: Alcan, 1940), pp. 266–97, and Jacques Droz, *L'Allemagne et la Revolution Française* (Paris: Press Universitaire de France, 1949), pp. 155–71.

24. Immanuel Kant, *Religion within the Limits of Reason Alone*, trans. Theodore M. Greene and Hoyt H. Hudson (Chicago: The Open Court Publishing Company, 1934), p. 176.

25. Michelet, *History of the French Revolution*, p. 455.

26. Ernst Cassirer, *Rousseau, Kant, Goethe*, trans. James Gutmann, Paul Oskar Kristeller, and John Herman Randall, Jr. (Hamden, Conn.: Archon Books, 1961; first printed 1945), p. 1.

27. Ibid., pp. 1–18.

28. Immanuel Kant, *Critique of Pure Reason*, trans. Normal Kemp Smith (New York: St. Martin's Press, 1965), p. 9.

29. George Herbert Mead, *Movements of Thought in the Nineteenth Century* ed. Merritt H. Moore (Chicago: University of Chicago Press, 1936), pp. 25–50.

30. Karl Mannheim, *Essays on Sociology and Social Psychology* (London: Routledge & Kegan Paul, 1953), p. 84.

31. But see Arthur O. Lovejoy, "Coleridge's and Kant's Two Worlds." *ELH* 7 (December 1940):349, where, discussing the original version of the Dejection Ode, Lovejoy points to "a delicate, perhaps a scarcely intended, hint of a criticism of Wordsworth, in the guise of a compliment—the suggestion that that 'simple spirit,' more serene and equable in temperament than Coleridge, and more fortunate in the circumstances of his life, 'rais'd from anxious dread and busy care,' was not wholly aware that he gave *to* nature the 'life' and 'joy' that he found in it, and that his power to do so was due to his temperament and circumstances." This criticism-in-the-guise-of-compliment is just the mode I have tried to describe in Wordsworth's addresses to Coleridge in *The Prelude*. Another of Lovejoy's observations is also apposite to the present discussion: "Coleridge's metaphysical speculations were, on the whole, the most characteristic manifestation of his mind, his persistently recurrent preoccupation, and often the tacit premises in what he says when he is not apparently talking metaphysics" (p. 341).

32. Coleridge's first recorded dissatisfaction with this doctrine shows up in Entry #174 of the *Notebooks* (which Coburn dates to December 1795 or January 1796) where Coleridge describes his plan to write a series of hymns: "In one of them to introduce a dissection of Atheism—particularly the Godwinian system of Pride. Proud of what? An outcast of blind Nature ruled by a fatal Necessity—Slave of an ideot Nature!"

The next important milestone in Coleridge's thinking about Necessitarianism can be dated to about the time when the 1800 Preface first appeared in print. On 16 March 1801, Coleridge wrote to Thomas Poole: "The interval since my last Letter has been filled up by me in the most intense Study. If I do not greatly delude myself, I have not only completely extricated the notions of Time, and Space; but have overthrown the doctrine of Association, as taught by Hartley, and with it all the irreligious metaphysics of modern Infidels— especially, the doctrine of necessity" (*Collected Letters*, ed. Griggs 1:706). Coleridge's letter to Poole three years later, which shows how closely Coleridge associated Necessitarianism with the name of Wordsworth, suggests that Coleridge's "study" of the problem was aimed in part at demonstrating its errors to Wordsworth: "I have convinced Southey—& Words- worth / & W. you know, was even to Extravagance a Necessitarian—Southey never believed,

& abhorred the Doctrine, yet thought the arguments for it unanswerable by human Reason. I have convinced both of them of the sophistry of the arguments, & wherein the Sophism consists—viz. that all have hitherto, both the Necessitarians & their Antagonists, confounded two essentially different things under one name—& in consequence of *this* Mistake the Victory has been always hollow in favor of the Necessitarians" (1:1036). The letter ends here without further explanation; the earlier letter of 1801, however, with its reference to the extrication of time and space, suggests that it is Kant's first *Critique* that enables Coleridge to "overthrow" the doctrines of association and Necessity. The influence of Kant is noted by Melvin Rader, *Wordsworth: A Philosophical Approach* (Oxford: Clarendon Press, 1967), p. 20, in his discussion of Coleridge's view of necessity. As regards Wordsworth's development, my discussion here differs from Rader's in that, where Rader accepts Coleridge's 1804 claim as conclusive, I try to show that Wordsworth, despite Coleridge's efforts, continues to hold to the doctrines that have been so conducive—and the contrast with Coleridge's situation looms large here—to his mental well-being and poetic creativity.

33. Clarence D. Thorpe discusses this passage in an essay that takes a position very similar to mine on the general question of Coleridge's relation to Wordsworth: "The Imagination: Coleridge Versus Wordsworth," *Philological Quarterly* 18 (January 1939):1–18. Thorpe writes: "Mistakenly or not, Coleridge appears to be saying that Wordsworth's expressed theory of the imagination lacks the solidity to be had in an explanation of the causes and first principles, lacks, in other words, scientific and philosophic support" (p. 2). Mary Warnock, in her more recent discussion of Coleridge and Wordsworth's review on this issue, *Imagination* (Berkeley and Los Angeles: University of California Press, 1976), pp. 72–130, notes that, unlike Wordsworth, Coleridge "had a very strong urge to establish a metaphysical foundation for his beliefs about imagination," but she does not suggest that this difference involved mutual criticism (p. 73).

34. "To these I would in the first instance merely oppose an authority, which they themselves hold venerable, that of Lord Bacon: non inutiles scientiae existimandae sunt, quarum in se nullus est usus, si ingenia acuant et ordinant" (*BL* 1:191).

35. Commenting on Coleridge's effort to make Wordsworth out to be a Godwinian Necessitarian, Helen Darbishire raises the following objection: "But the doctrine had very different meanings for Wordsworth and for Godwin. To Godwin Reason was the power which could deliver man from bondage and set him on the path of inevitable progress. Wordsworth believed this only in his darkest mood of disillusion; his saner thought drove down to the roots of life, and his faith in the human heart with its vital passions and affections become one with his reverence for the human mind"—in "Wordsworth's Belief in the Doctrine of Necessity," *Review of English Studies* 24 (April 1948):122.

36. I have used terms like "reason" and "experience," "rationalism" and "empiricism," or "metaphysical speculation" and "disciplined association" to describe national differences perceived from both the Coleridgean and the Burkean-Wordsworthian points of view. Such terms do, I am aware, cut in more ways than this sort of shorthand notation can suggest: one might plausibly describe the French Ideologues as, say, "empiricists." It may therefore be helpful to mention other commentators who elaborate these national distinctions along analogous lines and in similar terms. In discussing eighteenth-century premises of taste, for example, Bate speaks of "the British confidence in the teaching of experience," opposing this "strong empirical bent of English criticism" to the French concern with reason and rule; he argues further that one reason why the British considered "experience . . . necessary" was that it "feeds and disciplines the associations by which 'feelings of relation'

arise" (*From Classic to Romantic*, pp. 172–73). George Lefebvre, *The French Revolution from 1793 to 1799*, trans. John Hall Stewart and James Frigugliette (New York: Columbia University Press, 1964), glances across the Channel at how "English empiricism, which (as has been said) had long since become conservative with Hume, and even more so with Bentham, contested the claim of the French philosophes to recognize man's control over his destiny. It strove to restore authority and moral standards, not by metaphysical considerations, but through historical observation and political experience" (p. 332). See also Leslie Stephen, *History of English Thought in the Eighteenth Century*, 2 vols. (London: Smith, Elder & Co., 1881), pp. 194–95. "In England," writes Stephen, "sheer stupidity, unreasoning prejudice, a vigorous grasp of realities, and a contempt, healthy within certain limits, for fluent theories, opposed a powerful barrier to the inroad of the new creed, even when its fallacies were not detected. The societal order in England was not ripe for a revolution; but even had it been so, it is probable that the gospel according to Rousseau would have required some modification to fit it to English tastes."

37. I should add a word about the kind of remark in which Coleridge *praises* Wordsworth as a philosophic Poet—even as "the first & greatest philosophical Poet"—or prophesies that *The Recluse* will be "the first & finest philosophical Poem" (*Collected Letters* ed. Griggs, 2:1034). Such statements are no doubt largely responsible for the assumptions I have been calling into question about the extent of the critical agreement between the two men. I will not try to explain them away. I suggest, instead, that Coleridge was of two minds about Wordsworth in this respect, just as he was of two minds about the very possibility of uniting metaphysics and poetry—and just as, when doubting the possibility of such a union, he was of two minds about which was the higher calling. (Thomas McFarland discusses Coleridge's vacillation over this dilemma in *Coleridge and the Pantheist Tradition* [Oxford: Clarendon Press, 1969], pp. 112–16). Wordsworth's poetry deliberately sought to assimilate the function of metaphysics. At those times (such as January 1804 when he offered the praise quoted above) when he was especially susceptible to the power of "the Giant Wordsworth," Coleridge regarded Wordsworth's poetry as a true synthesis of the two functions. At other times, more confident in himself and in the "giant's hand" of Kant, he seems to have regarded Wordsworth's poetry as an irresponsible swallowing up of the proper function of philosophy.

General Index

Index of Wordsworth's Writings